KU-403-214

Advanced Programming for the Java™ 2 Platform

Calvin Austin

Monica Pawlan

WITHDRAWN

UNIVERSITY OF WOLVERHAMPTON
LEARNING RESOURCES

Acc No. 2231355   CLASS 523

CONTROL
0201715015

DATE   SITE
1. FEB 2001   W

OOS.
133
JAV/
AUS

ADDISON-WESLEY

Boston • San Francisco • New York • Toronto • Montreal
London • Munich • Paris • Madrid
Capetown • Sydney • Tokyo • Singapore • Mexico City

Copyright © 2000 Sun Microsystems, Inc., 901 San Antonio Road, Palo Alto, CA 94303, USA. All rights reserved.

Duke™ designed by Joe Palrang.

Sun Microsystems, Inc. has intellectual property rights relating to implementations of the technology described in this publication. In particular, and without limitation, these intellectual property rights may include one or more U.S. patents, foreign patents, or pending applications. Sun, Sun Microsystems, the Sun logo, and all Sun, Java, Jini, and Solaris-based trademarks and logos are trademarks or registered trademarks in the United States and other countries, exclusively licensed through X/Open Company, Ltd.

THIS PUBLICATION IS PROVIDED "AS IS" WITHOUT WARRANTY OF ANY KIND, EITHER EXPRESS OR IMPLIED, INCLUDING, BUT NOT LIMITED TO, THE IMPLIED WARRANTIES OF MERCHANTABILITY, FITNESS FOR A PARTICULAR PURPOSE, OR NON-INFRINGEMENT.

THIS PUBLICATION COULD INCLUDE TECHNICAL INACCURACIES OR TYPOGRAPHICAL ERRORS. CHANGES ARE PERIODICALLY ADDED TO THE INFORMATION HEREIN; THESE CHANGES WILL BE INCORPORATED IN NEW EDITIONS OF THE PUBLICATION. SUN MICROSYSTEMS, INC., MAY MAKE IMPROVEMENTS AND/OR CHANGES IN ANY TECHNOLOGY, PRODUCT, OR PROGRAM DESCRIBED IN THIS PUBLICATION AT ANY TIME.

The publisher offers discounts on this book when ordered in quantity for special sales. For more information, please contact:

Pearson Education Corporate Sales Division
One Lake Street
Upper Saddle River, NJ 07458
(800) 382-3419
corpsales@pearsontechgroup.com

Library of Congress Cataloging-in-Publication Data
Austin, Calvin.
    Advanced programming for the Java™ 2 platform / by Calvin Austin and Monica Pawlan.
      p. cm.
    ISBN 0-201-71501-5 (alk. paper)
    1. Application software—Development. 2. Java (Computer program language) I. Pawlan, Monica, 1949- II. Title.

QA76.76.A65 A95 2000
005.2'762—dc21
                                                  00-057618

Text printed on recycled and acid-free paper.
ISBN 0201715015
2 3 4 5 6 7   MA   03 02 01 00
2nd Printing   October 2000

To Nicci, Penny, and Elliot
— Calvin

To Jeffrey, Helen, John, and Joseph
— Monica

Contents

Chapter 3
Data and Transaction Management 37

Preface

As an experienced developer on the Java™ platform, you undoubtedly know how fast moving and comprehensive the platform is. Its many application programming interfaces (APIs) provide a wealth of functionality for all aspects of application and system-level programming. Although there are many good books and online documents that detail all the parameters of an API, finding a book that brings these APIs together and uses them to solve an advanced business problem has always been a challenge.

This book fills that void by presenting the design, development, test, deployment, and debugging phases for an enterprise-worthy auction application. It is not purely a reference for the Java APIs, but a practical, hands-on guide to building successful projects with the Java platform. Like any good handbook about your car or house, it includes an entire section on what to do if things do not go so well. You will find sections that detail everything from what steps to take when troubleshooting bugs to tips on performance.

The example application does not cover every possible programming scenario, but it explores many common situations and leaves you with a solid base of knowledge so that you can go on and use the Java platform to design, build, debug, and deploy your own solutions. The use of one application throughout the book provides a tool to help you fast-track learning new features. For example, you gain a working knowledge of RMI in one section, and the following section on CORBA explains the similarities and differences between the two.

You can download the example application source code and explore more information on any topic presented here by visiting the Java Developer Connection^{SM} (JDC) Web site at `http://developer.java.sun.com/developer`, or the main Java Web site at `http://java.sun.com`.

The example for this book is an auction application, chosen because of the growing popularity of and interest in Web-based electronic commerce. The example runs on a real application server using Enterprise JavaBeans™ technology, which is particularly well-suited to electronic commerce applications. Later chapters expand upon the core example by adding advanced functionality, improvements, and alternative solutions to do some of the things you get for free when you use the Enterprise JavaBeans platform. Additional topics important to applications development, such as security, transaction management, and performance tuning, are also presented.

This book is for developers with more than a beginning-level understanding of writing programs in the Java programming language. The example application is written with the Java 2 platform APIs and explained in terms of functional hows and whys. So if you need help installing the Java platform, setting up your environment, or getting your first application to work, you should first read a more introductory book, such as *Essentials of the Java Programming Language: A Hands-On Guide* [Paw00] or *The Java Tutorial, Second Edition* [Cam98].

Acknowledgments

We would like to thank Tony Squier for writing the code for the Thread Pooling section and the Web session code for the Servlets section. Tony also helped on the initial design and content, and with Joe Sam Shirah came up with the idea for a book like this. We also would like to thank Margaret Ong for her encouragement in getting this book to publication and the staff at Addison-Wesley for their support, especially Julie DiNicola. In addition, special thanks go out to the following Addison-Wesley reviewers: Joshua Engel, Howard Harkness, Susanne Hupfer, Paul Brinkley, Murali Murugan, Bob Bell, Eric Vought, and Armin Begtrup.

Special thanks to Isaac Elias, Daniel Liu, Mark Horwath, Satya Dodda, and Mary Dageforde for their contributions to the advanced examples and to all the Java Developer Connection members who sent in suggestions and corrections. And thanks also go to Mary Aline who copyedited some of the examples used in this book when they first appeared in the JDC. Also, the Printing Graphics in Project Swing and Writing a Security Manager sections used code adapted from *The Java Tutorial* (by Mary Campione and Kathy Walrath) and *The Java Tutorial Continued* (by Mary Campione, Kathy Walrath, Alison Huml, and the Tutorial Team).

We would also like to thank the following people who also reviewed and checked the book for accuracy: Rama Roberts, Erik Larsen, Phil Race, and Merwyn Welcome.

Finally, thanks to our families for their patience and encouragement: Nicci Austin and Jeffrey Pawlan.

1

Matching Project Requirements with Technology

One challenge in writing a book on advanced application development for the Java™ platform is to find a project small enough to write about, while at the same time, complex enough to warrant advanced programming techniques. The project presented in this book is a Web-based auction house. The application is initially written for the Enterprise JavaBeans™ platform. Later chapters expand the core example by adding advanced functionality, improvements, and alternative solutions to do some of the things you get for free when you use the Enterprise JavaBeans platform.

To keep the discussion simple, the example application has only a basic set of transactions for posting and bidding on auction items. However, the application scales to handle multiple users, provides a three-tiered transaction-based environment, controls security, and integrates legacy-based systems.

This chapter covers how to determine project requirements and model the important steps that should always come before coding begins.

Covered in This Chapter

Project Requirements

The first step in determining project requirements is to interview the user base to find out what is wanted in an online auction. This is an important step, and one that cannot be overrated, because a solid base of user-oriented information helps you define your key application capabilities.

Chapter 2, Auction House Application, (page 11) walks through the application code, explains how the Enterprise JavaBeans platform works, and tells you how to run a live demonstration. If you have never seen or used an online auction, Duke's Auction Demonstration (page 7) shows mock-ups of the example auction application HTML pages.

Interview User Base

For the sake of discussion and to keep things simple, this section assumes interviews with the user base found the following auction house and user requirements.

Auction House Requirements

- Obtain buyer and seller information
- Bill sellers for posting item
- Record and report the day's transactions

User Requirements

- Bid on or sell an item
- Search or view items for sale
- Notify buyer and seller of sale

Model the Project

After analyzing the requirements, you can build a use case diagram to gain a better understanding of the elements needed in the application and how they interact. A *use case diagram* shows the relationships among actors and use cases within the system. A *use case* is a unique function in a system, and an *actor* is the person or software that performs the action or use case. For example, a buyer is the actor that performs the function (use case) of bidding on an auction item, and the seller is the actor that performs the use case of posting an item for auction. Not all actors are people, though. For example, the software is the actor that determines when an item has closed, finds the highest bidder, and notifies the buyer and seller of a sale.

The Unified Modeling Language (UML) (`http://www.rational.com/uml/ resources/documentation/notation/notation52.jtmpl`) is the tool of choice for creating use case diagrams. The use case diagram in Figure 1.1 uses UML to describe the buyer and seller use cases for the online auction application. In UML, squares group the systems, stick figures represent actors, ovals denote use cases, and lines show how actors use the system.

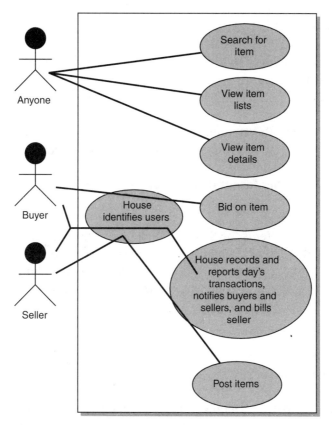

Figure 1.1 Use case diagram for an auction house

The following descriptions further define the project. These descriptions are not part of UML, but are a helpful tool in project definition.

House Identifies Buyers and Sellers. An auction application is used by buyers and sellers. A buyer needs to know who the seller is to pay him or her, and the seller needs to know who the buyers are to answer product questions and to finalize the sale. So, to post or bid on an auction item, buyers and sellers are required to register. *Registration* needs to get the following information from buyers and sellers:

- User ID and password for buying and selling
- E-mail address, so highest bidder and seller can communicate when item closes
- Credit card information, so auction can charge sellers for listing their items

Once registered, a user can post or bid on an item for sale.

House Determines Highest Bidder.   Nightly, the auction application queries the database to record and report the day's transactions. The application finds items that have closed and then determines the highest bidder.

House Notifies Buyers and Sellers.   The auction application uses e-mail to notify the highest bidder and seller of the sale and to debit the seller's account.

Anyone Searches for an Item.   Sellers and buyers enter a search string to locate all auction items in the database.

Anyone Views Items for Sale.   To popularize the auction and encourage new buyers and sellers, the application allows anyone to view auction items without requiring user ID and password identification. To keep things simple, the auction allows anyone to view summarized lists of items in the following three ways:

- All items up for auction
- New items listed today
- Items due to close today

Anyone Views Item Details.   The summarized lists of auction items should link each item to the following detailed information. Detail information on auction items is available to anyone without identification.

- Item summary
- Auction item number
- Current price
- Number of bids
- Date posted for auction
- Date item closes
- Seller ID

- Highest bid
- Item description

Seller Posts Items for Sale. To post an item for sale, a seller needs to identify himself or herself and describe the item for sale, as follows:

- User ID and password for seller identification
- Summary description of item
- Starting price for bidding
- Detailed description of item
- Number of days item is available for bidding

Buyer Bids on Items. The detailed summary page for each item lets registered users identify themselves and bid on the item by providing the following information:

- User ID
- Password
- Bid amount

Activity Diagram

The activity diagram in Figure 1.2 outlines the flow of tasks within the auction house as a whole. The solid black circle on the left shows the beginning of activities, and the white circles with black dots in the center denote where activities end.

Choosing the Software

With the application modeled and project requirements defined, it is time to think about which Java APIs to use. The application is clearly client-and-server-based because you will want to accommodate 1 to n buyers, sellers, and viewers at any given time. Because registration and auction item data must be stored and retrieved from somewhere, you will need an API for database access.

The core application can be created in a number of ways by using any of the following APIs (to name a few):

- Servlets and HTTP
- Sockets, multithreading, and JDBC™ APIs
- Remote Method Invocation (RMI) and JDBC APIs
- RMI over IIOP
- Enterprise JavaBeans platform.

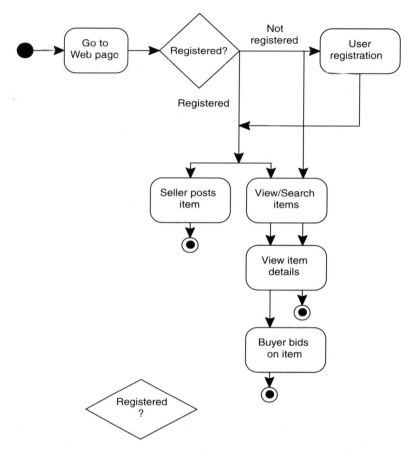

Figure 1.2 Activity diagram

- Java Transaction Architecture (JTA)
- Common Object Request Broker Architecture (CORBA)
- Java Native Interface (JNI)

Instead of using all of these APIs as individual APIs in one application, you can use Enterprise JavaBeans. The Enterprise JavaBeans platform handles transaction and state management, multithreading, resource pooling, search functionality to handle common situations, and other complex, low-level details so you can focus on creating the best business solution. You get a distributed database application without writing any socket, thread, JDBC, or RMI code. For example, simple database transactions are rolled back (not written to the database) in the event of an error, database connections are cached so there is always a connection available when the application needs one, and items in the database are retrieved and displayed to the requestor using a simple search string.

Chapter 2, Auction House Application, (page 11) explains the core Enterprise JavaBeans application code and how to set up and run the example. Later chapters explain how you can implement such things as your own transaction management for more complex transactions, database caching to improve performance, or a more complex or comprehensive search algorithm.

Duke's Auction Demonstration

This section shows you how the auction house application Web pages look.

Home Page

The home page (Figure 1.3) introduces the auction and makes auction house features available to buyers and sellers.

Figure 1.3 Duke's Auction home page

Registration Page

The Registration page (Figure 1.4) gets information from new buyers and sellers so that all individuals initiating transactions at the auction house can be identified.

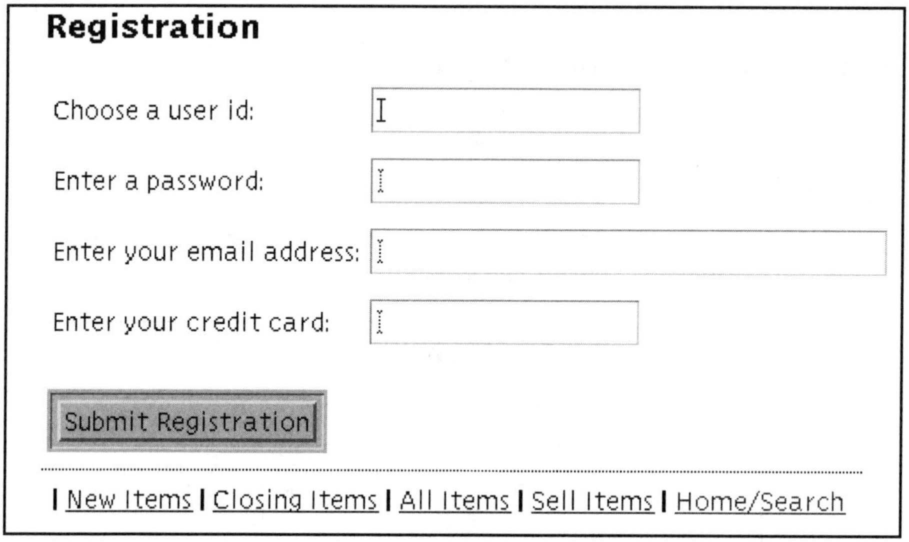

Registration

Choose a user id:

Enter a password:

Enter your email address:

Enter your credit card:

Submit Registration

| New Items | Closing Items | All Items | Sell Items | Home/Search

Figure 1.4 Duke's Auction buyer and seller registration

New Auction Items Today

The New Auction Items page (Figure 1.5) lets anyone view new items for sale.

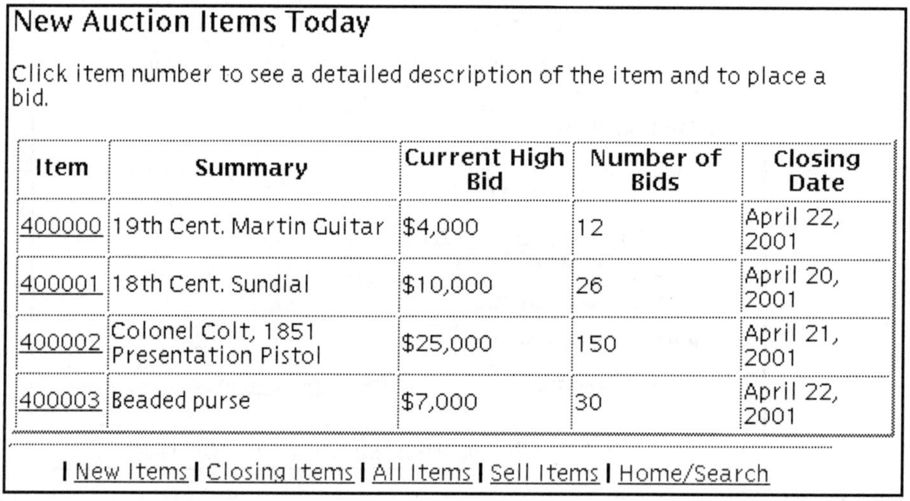

New Auction Items Today

Click item number to see a detailed description of the item and to place a bid.

Item	Summary	Current High Bid	Number of Bids	Closing Date
400000	19th Cent. Martin Guitar	$4,000	12	April 22, 2001
400001	18th Cent. Sundial	$10,000	26	April 20, 2001
400002	Colonel Colt, 1851 Presentation Pistol	$25,000	150	April 21, 2001
400003	Beaded purse	$7,000	30	April 22, 2001

| New Items | Closing Items | All Items | Sell Items | Home/Search

Figure 1.5 New items at Duke's Auction today

Items Closing Today

The Items Closing page (Figure 1.6) lets anyone view auction items about to be sold to the highest bidder.

Items Closing Today

Click item number to see a detailed description of the item and to place a bid.

Item	Summary	Current High Bid	Number of Bids	Closing Date
400000	19th Cent. Martin Guitar	$4,000	12	April 22, 2001
400001	18th Cent. Sundial	$10,000	26	April 20, 2001

| New Items | Closing Items | All Items | Sell Items | Home/Search

Figure 1.6 Items closing today at Duke's Auction

All Items

The All Items page (Figure 1.7) lets anyone view all items available for sale.

All Items (Current and Closed)

Click item number to see a detailed description of the item and to place a bid.

Item	Summary	Current High Bid	Number of Bids	Closing Date
400000	19th Cent. Martin Guitar	$4,000	12	April 22, 2001
400001	18th Cent. Sundial	$10,000	26	April 20, 2001
400002	Colonel Colt, 1851 Presentation Pistol	$25,000	150	April 21, 2001
400003	Beaded purse	$7,000	30	April 22, 2001

| New Items | Closing Items | All Items | Sell Items | Home/Search

Figure 1.7 All items available at Duke's Auction

Search for Items

The Search Items page (Figure 1.8) lets anyone search for auction items for sale.

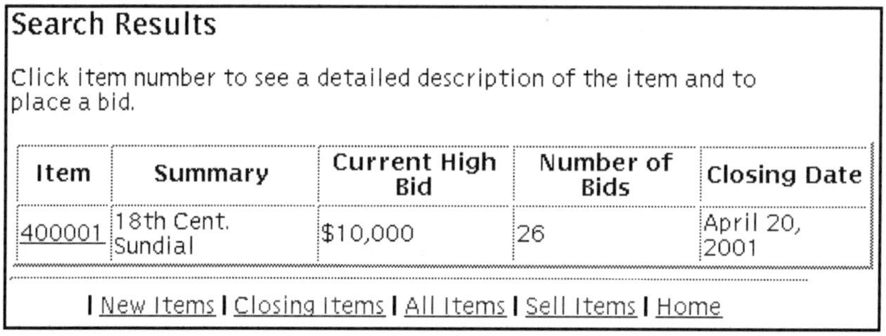

Item	Summary	Current High Bid	Number of Bids	Closing Date
400001	18th Cent. Sundial	$10,000	26	April 20, 2001

Search Results

Click item number to see a detailed description of the item and to place a bid.

| New Items | Closing Items | All Items | Sell Items | Home

Figure 1.8 Search for items in Duke's Auction

Sell Item

The Sell Item page (Figure 1.9) lets registered sellers post an item for sale.

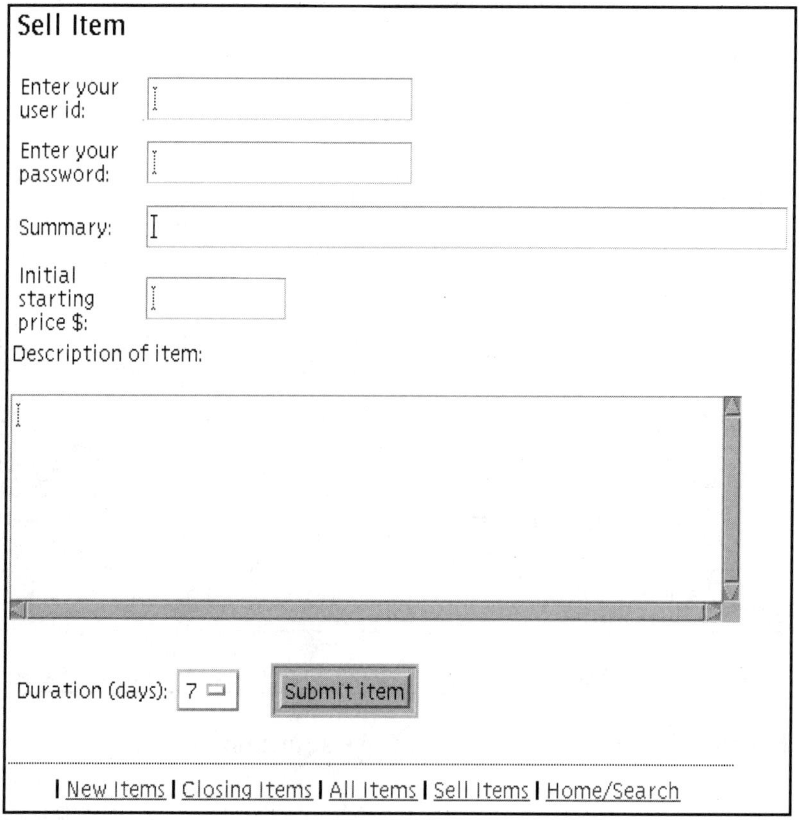

Sell Item

Enter your user id:

Enter your password:

Summary:

Initial starting price $:

Description of item:

Duration (days): 7   Submit item

| New Items | Closing Items | All Items | Sell Items | Home/Search

Figure 1.9 Sell item at Duke's Auction

2
Auction House Application

The proliferation of Internet- and intranet-based applications has created a great need for distributed transactional applications that leverage the speed, security, and reliability of server-side technology. One way to meet this need is to use a multitiered model in which a thin client application invokes business logic that executes on the server. Normally, thin client multitiered applications are hard to write because they involve many lines of intricate code to handle transaction and state management, multithreading, resource pooling, and other complex low-level details. And to add to the difficulties, you have to rework this intricate code every time you write a new application because the code is so low-level it cannot be reused.

If you could use prebuilt and pretested transaction management code or even reuse some of your own code, you would save a lot of time and energy that you could better spend solving the business problem. Well, Enterprise JavaBeans technology can give you the help you need. Enterprise JavaBeans technology makes distributed transactional applications easy to write because it separates the low-level details from the business logic. You concentrate on creating the best business solution and leave the rest to the underlying architecture.

This chapter describes how to create an example auction with the services provided by the Enterprise JavaBeans platform. Later chapters show how to customize these services.

Covered in this Chapter

A Multitiered Application with Enterprise Beans

An enterprise bean is a small set of interfaces and classes that provide two types of methods: business logic and life cycle. A client program calls the business logic methods to interact with the data on the server. Every enterprise bean has a system-level container that calls the life-cycle methods to manage the bean on the server. In addition to these two types of methods, an enterprise bean has an associated configuration file, called a *deployment descriptor*, to configure the bean at deployment time.

As well as being responsible for creating and deleting beans, the Enterprise JavaBeans server also manages transactions, concurrency, security, and data persistence (storing and retrieving data). Even the connections between the client and server are provided using the Remote Method Invocation (RMI) and Java Naming and Directory Interface™ (JNDI) APIs, and servers can optionally provide scalability through thread management and caching.

The auction house example implements a complete Enterprise JavaBeans solution by providing only the business logic and using the underlying services provided by the architecture. However, you may find that the container-managed services, although providing maximum portability, do not meet all your application requirements. The next chapters show how to provide these services in your bean.

Thin Client Programs and Multitiered Architecture

A *thin client* is a client program that invokes business logic running on the server. It is called thin because most of the processing happens on the server. The auction house application shown in Figure 2.1 has a user interface that is a set of HTML pages. The HTML pages get input from and show information to the user in the browser. Behind the HTML pages is a servlet that passes data between the browser and the Enterprise JavaBeans server. The Enterprise JavaBeans server handles reading from and writing to the underlying database.

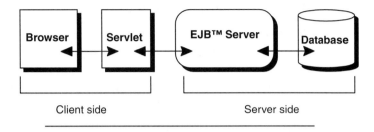

Figure 2.1 Client and server sides

Multitiered architecture or three-tier architecture extends the standard two-tier client-and-server model by placing a multithreaded application server between the client and the database. The application server is where the enterprise beans reside and where the application's business logic executes.

Figure 2.2 shows that client programs (on the first tier) communicate with the database (third tier) through the application server (second tier). The application server responds to the client requests and makes database calls as needed into the underlying database.

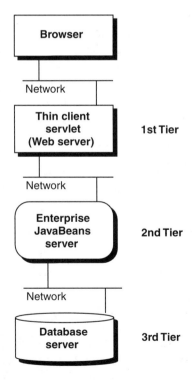

Figure 2.2 Multitiered communications

Entity and Session Bean Differences

There are two types of enterprise beans: entity beans and session beans. A *session bean* is created on behalf of a client and usually exists only for the duration of a single client and server session. A session bean performs operations, such as calculations or accessing a database, for the client. The data in a session bean is not recoverable in the event its container crashes.

An *entity bean* is a persistent object that represents data maintained in a database. An entity bean can manage its own persistence, or it can delegate this function to its container. An entity bean can live as long as the data it represents. An entity bean is identified by a primary key. If the container in which an entity bean is hosted crashes, the entity bean, its primary key, and any remote references survive the crash.

Typically, an entity bean represents one row of persistent data stored in a database table. In the auction house example, `RegistrationBean` is an entity bean that represents data for one registered user, and `AuctionItemBean` is an entity bean that represents the data for one auction item. Entity beans are transactional and long-lived. As long as the data remains, the entity bean can access and update that data. This does not mean you need a bean running for every table row. Instead, entity beans are loaded and saved as needed.

A session bean might execute database reads and writes, but it is not required. A session bean might invoke JDBC calls itself or it might use an entity bean to make the call, in which case the session bean is a client to the entity bean. A session bean's fields contain the state of the conversation and are transient (are not saved). If the server or client crashes, the session bean is gone. A session bean is often used with one or more entity beans to perform complex operations on the data.

Session Beans	Entity Beans
Fields contain conversation state.	Represents data in a database.
Handles database access for client.	Shares access for multiple users.
Life of client is life of Bean.	Persists as long as data exists.
Can be transaction aware.	Transactional.
Does not survive server crashes.	Survives server crashes.
No fine-grained data handling.	Fine-grained data handling.

NOTE   In the Enterprise JavaBeans specification, Enterprise JavaBeans server support for session beans is mandatory. Enterprise JavaBeans server support for entity beans is optional, but is mandatory for version 2.0 of the specification.

Auction House Workings

Figure 2.3 shows the enterprise beans for the auction house application and their relationship to the Enterprise JavaBeans server. The thin-client server invokes business logic in the four enterprise beans through their home and remote interfaces (described below). The Enterprise JavaBeans server in this example handles the low-level details including database read and write operations. The four enterprise beans in the example can be described as follows:

- `AuctionItemBean` is an entity bean that maintains information for an auction item.
- `RegistrationBean` is an entity bean that stores user registration information.
- `BidderBean` is a session bean that uses `AuctionItemBean` to retrieve a list of all auction items, only new items, items due to close, and items

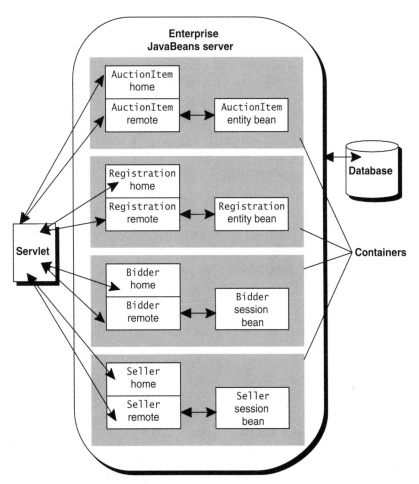

Figure 2.3 Parts of a Bean

whose summary matches a search string from the database. It also checks the user ID and password when someone places a bid, and it stores new bids in the database.

- SellerBean is a session bean that uses RegistrationBean to check the user ID and password when someone posts an auction item, and it uses AuctionItemBean to add new auction items to the database.

An entity or session bean is really a collection of interfaces and classes. All entity and session beans consist of a remote interface, home interface, and the bean class. The servlet looks up the beans's home interface running in the Enterprise JavaBeans server, uses the home interface to create the remote interface, and invokes bean methods through the remote interface. An enterprise bean's interfaces and container do the following:

- An enterprise bean's remote interface describes the bean's methods, or what the bean does. A client program or another enterprise bean calls the methods defined in the remote interface to invoke the business logic implemented by the bean.

- An enterprise bean's home interface describes how a client program or another enterprise bean creates, finds (entity beans only), and removes that enterprise bean from its container.

- The container provides the interface between the enterprise bean and the low-level implementations in a given Enterprise JavaBeans server.

Developing and Running Applications

Deployment tools and an Enterprise JavaBeans server are essential to running Enterprise JavaBeans applications. Deployment tools generate containers. The server provider can include containers and deployment tools for their own server and will typically publish their low-level interfaces so other vendors can develop containers and deployment tools for their server. The auction house example uses the Enterprise JavaBeans server and deployment tools created by BEA Weblogic (http://www.beasys.com/weblogic.html).

Because everything is written to specification, all enterprise beans are interchangeable with containers, deployment tools, and servers created by other vendors. In fact, you might or might not write your own enterprise beans because it is possible, and sometimes desirable, to use enterprise beans written by one or more providers that you assemble into an Enterprise JavaBeans application.

How Multitiered Applications Work

The goal in a multitiered application is for the client to be able to work on application data without knowing at build time where the data is stored in the third tier. To make this level of transparency possible, the underlying services in a multitiered architecture use lookup services to locate remote server objects (the bean's remote interface object), and data communication services to move data from the client, through the remote server object, to its final destination in a storage medium.

Lookup Service.   To find remote server objects at runtime, the client program needs a way to look them up. One way to look remote server objects up at runtime is to use the JNDI API. JNDI is a common interface to existing naming and directory interfaces. The Enterprise JavaBeans containers use JNDI as an interface to the RMI naming service.

At deployment time, the JNDI service registers (binds) the remote interface with a name. As long as the client program uses the same naming service and asks for the remote interface by its registered name, it will be able to find it. The client program calls the lookup method on a `javax.naming.Context` object to ask for the remote interface by its registered name. The `javax.naming.Context` object stores the bindings; it is a different object from the Enterprise JavaBeans context, which is covered later in this book.

Data Communication.   Once the client program gets a reference to a remote server object, it makes calls on the remote server object's methods. Because the client program has a reference to the remote server object, a technique called data marshaling is used to make it appear as if the remote server object is local to the client program.

In *data marshaling*, methods that are called on the remote server object are wrapped with their data and sent to the remote server object. The remote server object unwraps (unmarshals) the methods and data, and calls the enterprise bean. The results of the call to the enterprise bean are wrapped again, passed back to the client through the remote server object, and unmarshaled.

The Enterprise JavaBeans containers use RMI services to marshal data. When the bean is compiled, stub and skeleton files are created. The stub file provides the data wrapping and unwrapping configuration on the client, and the skeleton provides the same information for the server. The data is passed between the client program and the server using serialization. *Serialization* is a way to represent Java objects as bytes that can be sent over the network as a stream and reconstructed on the other side in the same state they were in when first sent.

How Enterprise Beans Are Used in the Example

The example uses two entity beans and two session beans. The entity beans, `AuctionItemBean` and `RegistrationBean`, represent persistent items stored in a database, and the session beans, `SellerBean`, and `BidderBean`, represent short-lived operations with the client and data.

The session beans are the client interface to the entity beans. The `SellerBean` object processes requests to add new auction items for sale. The `BidderBean` object processes requests to retrieve auction items and place bids on those items. Changing and adding to the database data in a container-managed bean is left to the entity beans.

Entity and session beans are distributed objects that use the RMI API. This means that when an error occurs, an RMI remote exception is thrown.

AuctionServlet

`AuctionServlet` is essentially the second tier in the application and the focal point for auction activities. It accepts end-user input from the browser by way of hypertext transfer protocol (HTTP), passes the input to the appropriate enterprise bean for processing, and displays the processed results to the end user in the browser.

Figure 2.4 presents a Unified Modeling Language (UML) class diagram for the `AuctionServlet` class.

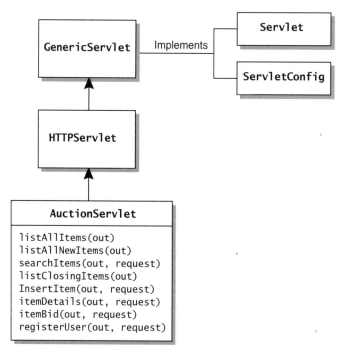

Figure 2.4 UML class diagram

The `AuctionServlet` methods shown above invoke business logic that executes on the server by looking up an enterprise bean and calling one or more of its methods. When the servlet adds HTML codes to a page for display to the user, that logic executes on the client.

For example, the `listAllItems(out)` method executes code on the client to dynamically generate an HTML page to be viewed by the client in a browser. The HTML page is populated with the results of a call to `BidderBean` that executes logic on the server to generate a list of all auction items.

```
private void listAllItems(ServletOutputStream out) throws IOException{
//Put text on HTML page
  setTitle(out, "Auction results");
  String text = "Click Item number for description and to place bid.";
  try{
     addLine("<BR>"+ text, out);
//Look up Bidder bean home interface.
     BidderHome bhome=(BidderHome) ctx.lookup("bidder");
//Create Bidder bean remote interface.
     Bidder bid=bhome.create();
//Call Bidder bean method through remote interface.
     Enumeration enum=(Enumeration)bid.getItemList();

     if(enum != null) {
//Put retrieved items on servlet page.
        displayitems(enum, out);
        addLine("", out);
     }
  } catch (Exception e) {
//Print error on servlet page.
     addLine("AuctionServlet List All Items error",out);
     System.out.println("AuctionServlet <list>:"+e);
  }
     out.flush();
}
```

Entity Bean Classes

`AuctionItemBean` and `RegistrationBean` are entity beans. `AuctionItemBean` adds new auction items to the database and updates the bid amount as users bid on the item. `RegistrationBean` adds information to the database on registered users. Both beans consist of the classes described here.

AuctionItem Entity Bean

These are the `AuctionItemBean` interfaces and classes:

- `AuctionItem`
- `AuctionItemHome`

- AuctionItemBean
- AuctionItemPK

AuctionItem is the remote interface. It describes what the bean does by declaring the developer-defined methods that provide the business logic for this bean. These methods are the ones used by the client to interact with the bean over the remote connection. Its name maps to the AUCTIONITEMS table shown just below.

```
package auction;

import javax.ejb.*;
import java.rmi.*;
import java.util.*;

//Interface that contains the methods that can be called
//in the auction bean
public interface AuctionItem extends EJBObject {
  String getDescription() throws RemoteException;
  String getSeller() throws RemoteException;
  int getId() throws RemoteException;
  String getSummary() throws RemoteException;
  double getIncrement() throws RemoteException;
  double getHighBid() throws RemoteException;
  int getBidCount() throws RemoteException;
  String getHighBidder() throws RemoteException;
  Date getStartDate() throws RemoteException;
  Date getEndDate() throws RemoteException;
  double getStartPrice() throws RemoteException;
  int setHighBid(String buyer, double amount, double increment)
                  throws RemoteException;
}
```

AuctionItemHome is the home interface. It describes how the bean is created in, found in, and removed from its container. The enterprise bean server deployment tools will provide the implementation for this interface.

```
package auction;

import javax.ejb.*;
import java.rmi.*;
import java.util.*;

//Interface that is called by the client to create and return Beans
public interface AuctionItemHome extends EJBHome {
  AuctionItem create(String theseller, String thedescription, int duration,
                  double thestartprice, String thesummary)
                  throws CreateException, RemoteException;
  AuctionItem create(int id, String theseller, String thedescription,
                  int duration, double thestartprice,
                  String thesummary, double increment)
                  throws CreateException, RemoteException;
```

```
AuctionItem findByPrimaryKey(AuctionItemPK id)
                    throws FinderException, RemoteException;
public Enumeration findAllItems() throws FinderException, RemoteException;
public Enumeration findAllNewItems(java.sql.Date newtoday)
                    throws FinderException, RemoteException;
public Enumeration findAllClosedItems(java.sql.Date closedtoday)
                    throws FinderException, RemoteException;
public Enumeration findAllMatchingItems(String searchString)
                    throws FinderException, RemoteException;
}
```

`AuctionItemBean` (page 51) is the enterprise bean. It implements `EntityBean`, provides the business logic for the developer-defined methods, and implements `EntityBean` methods for creating the bean and setting the session context. This is a class that the bean developer needs to implement. Its field variables map to fields in the AUCTIONITEMS table shown just below.

`AuctionItemPK` is the primary key class. The Enterprise JavaBeans server requires a container-managed entity bean to have a primary key class with a public primary key field (or fields, if using composite primary keys). The bean developer implements this class. The ID field is the primary key in the AUCTIONITEMS table shown just below, so the ID field is a public field in this class. The ID field is assigned a value when the primary key class is constructed.

```
package auction;

//Class that is used to find auction items by their unique id
public class AuctionItemPK implements java.io.Serializable {
  public int id;
}
```

You can request the container manage database persistence for an enterprise bean or write the code to manage the persistence yourself. In this chapter, all beans (entity and session) are container-managed. With container-managed beans, all you do is specify which fields are container managed and let the Enterprise JavaBeans server do the rest. This is great for simple applications, but if you are coding something that is fairly complex, you might need more control. How to override the underlying Enterprise JavaBeans services to gain more control or provide similar services for non-Enterprise JavaBean applications is covered in Chapter 3, Data and Transaction Management (page 37).

Auction Items Table

This is the schema for the AUCTIONITEMS database table. Some application servers create the table for you, but others require you to create it yourself. The BEA Weblogic application server does not create the database table.

```
create table AUCTIONITEMS (SUMMARY VARCHAR(80) ,
ID              INT ,
COUNTER         INT ,
```

```
DESCRIPTION          VARCHAR(1000) ,
STARTDATE            DATE ,
ENDDATE              DATE ,
STARTPRICE           DOUBLE PRECISION ,
INCREMENT            DOUBLE PRECISION ,
SELLER               VARCHAR(30) ,
MAXBID               DOUBLE PRECISION,
BIDCOUNT             INT,
HIGHBIDDER           VARCHAR(30) )
```

Registration Entity Bean

RegistrationBean consists of the same kinds of interfaces and classes and database table as the AuctionItem bean, but the actual business logic, database table fields, and primary key are different. Rather than describe the classes, you can browse them and refer back to the AuctionItem bean discussion if you have questions.

- Registration
- RegistrationHome
- RegistrationBean
- RegistrationPK

Registration Table

This is the schema for the REGISTRATION database table. Some application servers create the table for you, but others require you to create it yourself. The BEA Weblogic application server does not create the database table.

```
create table REGISTRATION (THEUSER VARCHAR(40) ,
PASSWORD             VARCHAR(40) ,
EMAILADDRESS         VARCHAR(80) ,
CREDITCARD           VARCHAR(40) ,
BALANCE              DOUBLE PRECISION )
```

Session Bean Classes

BidderBean and SellerBean are the session beans. BidderBean retrieves lists of auction items, searches for an item, checks the user ID and password when someone places a bid, and stores new bids in the database. SellerBean checks the user ID and password when someone posts an auction item, and adds new auction items to the database.

Both session beans are initially deployed as stateless beans. A *stateless bean* does not keep a record of what the client did in a previous call; whereas, a *stateful bean* does. Stateful beans are very useful if the operation is more than a simple lookup and the client operation depends on something that happened in a previous call.

Bidder Session Bean

These are the `BidderBean` interfaces and classes. There is no primary key class because these beans are transient and no database access is involved. To retrieve auction items from the database, `BidderBean` creates an instance of `AuctionItemBean`, and to process bids, it creates an instance of `RegistrationBean`.

- `Bidder`
- `BidderHome`
- `BidderBean`

`Bidder` is the remote interface. It describes what the bean does by declaring the developer-defined methods that provide the business logic for this bean. These methods are the ones that the client calls remotely.

```
package bidder;

import javax.ejb.*;
import java.rmi.*;
import java.util.*;

//Interface that contains the methods that can be called
//on the bidder bean for placed auction bids
public interface Bidder extends EJBObject {
  int placeBid(int item, String user, String password, double amount)
          throws RemoteException;
  Enumeration getItemList() throws RemoteException;
  Enumeration getNewItemList() throws RemoteException;
  Enumeration getClosedItemList() throws RemoteException;
   Enumeration getMatchingItemsList(String searchString) throws
   RemoteException;
}
```

`BidderHome` is the home interface. It describes how the bean is created in, found in, and removed from its container. `BidderBean` (page 57) is the enterprise bean. It implements `SessionBean`, provides the business logic for the developer-defined methods, and implements `SessionBean` methods for creating the bean and setting the session context.

```
package bidder;

import javax.ejb.*;
import java.rmi.*;
import java.util.*;

//Interface that is called by the client to create Beans
public interface BidderHome extends EJBHome {
  Bidder create() throws CreateException, RemoteException;
}
```

Seller Session Bean

`SellerBean` consists of the same kinds of interfaces and classes as `Bidder-Bean`, except the business logic is different. Rather than describe the classes, you can browse them and refer back to the `BidderBean` discussion if you have questions.

- `Seller`
- `SellerHome`
- `SellerBean`

Container Classes

The container needs classes to deploy an enterprise bean onto a particular Enterprise JavaBeans server, and those classes are generated with a deployment tool. Container classes include `*_Stub.class` and `*_Skel.class` classes that provide the RMI hooks on the client and server sides for marshaling (moving) data between the client program and the Enterprise JavaBeans server. In addition, implementation classes are created for the interfaces and deployment rules defined for each bean.

- The stub object is installed on or downloaded to the client system and provides a local proxy object for the client. It implements the remote interfaces and transparently delegates all method calls across the network to the remote object.

- The skel object is installed on or downloaded to the server system and provides a local proxy object for the server. It unwraps data received over the network from the stub object for processing by the server.

Examining a Container-Managed Bean

This section walks through the `RegistrationBean` code to show how easy it is to have the container manage persistent data storage to an underlying medium such as a database (the default). Chapter 3, Data and Transaction Management modifies `RegistrationBean` to use bean-managed persistence to handle database access and manage transactions.

Member Variables

A container-managed environment needs to know which variables are for persistent storage and which are not. In the Java programming language, the `transient` keyword indicates variables to not include when data in an object is serialized and written to persistent storage. In the `RegistrationBean` class, the `EntityContext` variable is marked transient to indicate that its data not be written to the underlying storage medium.

`EntityContext` data is not written to persistent storage because its purpose is to provide information on the container's run-time context. It, therefore, does not contain data on the registered user and should not be saved to the underlying storage medium. The other variables are declared `public` so the container can use the Reflection API to discover them.

```
protected transient EntityContext ctx;
public String theuser, password, creditcard, emailaddress;
public double balance;
```

Create Method

The bean's `ejbCreate` method is called by the container after the client program calls the `create` method on the remote interface and passes in the registration data. This method assigns the incoming values to the member variables that represent user data. The container handles storing and loading the data, and creating new entries in the underlying storage medium.

```
public RegistrationPK ejbCreate(String theuser,String password,
                                String emailaddress,String creditcard)
                                throws CreateException, RemoteException {
  this.theuser=theuser;
  this.password=password;
  this.emailaddress=emailaddress;
  this.creditcard=creditcard;
  this.balance=0;
```

Entity Context Methods

An entity bean has an associated `EntityContext` instance that gives the bean access to container-managed run-time information such as the transaction context.

```
//API Ref: void setEntityContext(EntityContext ectx)
  public void setEntityContext(javax.ejb.EntityContext ctx)
                               throws RemoteException {
    this.ctx = ctx;
  }

//API Ref: void unsetEntityContext(EntityContext ectx)
  public void unsetEntityContext() throws RemoteException{
    ctx = null;
  }
```

Load Method

The bean's `ejbLoad` method is called by the container to load data from the underlying storage medium. This would be necessary when `BidderBean` or `SellerBean` need to check a user's ID or password against the stored values.

You do not implement the `ejbLoad` method because the Enterprise JavaBeans container seamlessly loads the data from the underlying storage medium for you.

```
//API Ref: void ejbLoad()
  public void ejbLoad() throws RemoteException {}
```

Store Method

The bean's `ejbStore` method is called by the container to save user data. This method is not implemented because the Enterprise JavaBeans container seamlessly stores the data to the underlying storage medium.

```
//API Ref: void ejbStore()
  public void ejbStore() throws RemoteException {}
```

Connection Pooling

Loading data from and storing data to a database can take a lot of time and reduce an application's overall performance. To reduce database connection time, the BEA Weblogic server uses a JDBC connection pool to cache database connections so connections are always available when the application needs them.

However, you are not limited to the default JDBC connection pool. You can override the bean-managed connection pooling behavior and substitute your own. Chapter 8, Performance Techniques, explains how.

Deployment Descriptor

The remaining configuration for a container-managed bean occurs at deployment time. The following is the text-based deployment descriptor used in a BEA Weblogic Enterprise JavaBeans server for deploying the `Registration` Bean.

```
Text Deployment Descriptor
  (environmentProperties

    (persistentStoreProperties
     persistentStoreType        jdbc

      (jdbc
        tableName               registration
        dbIsShared              false
```

```
        poolName                    ejbPool
        (attributeMap
          creditcard                creditcard
          emailaddress              emailaddress
          balance                   balance
          password                  password
          theuser                   theuser
        ); end attributeMap
      ); end jdbc
    ); end persistentStoreProperties
  ); end environmentProperties
```

The deployment descriptor indicates that storage is a database whose connection is held in a JDBC connection pool called `ejbPool`. The `attributeMap` contains the enterprise bean variable on the left and the associated database field on the right.

XML Deployment Descriptor

In Enterprise JavaBeans 1.1, the deployment descriptor uses XML. Below is the equivalent configuration in XML for the `Registration` Bean.

The container-managed fields map directly to their counterpart names in the database table. The container resource authorization (res-auth) means the container handles the database login for the REGISTRATION table.

```
<persistence-type>Container</persistence-type>
<cmp-field><field-name>creditcard
    </field-name></cmp-field>
<cmp-field><field-name>emailaddress
    </field-name></cmp-field>
<cmp-field><field-name>balance
    </field-name></cmp-field>
<cmp-field><field-name>password
    </field-name></cmp-field>
<cmp-field><field-name>theuser
    </field-name></cmp-field>
<resource-ref>
<res-ref-name>registration</res-ref-name>
<res-type>javax.sql.DataSource</res-type>
<res-auth>Container</res-auth>
</resource-ref>
```

Container-Managed Finder Methods

The auction house search facility is implemented as a container-managed finder method. It starts when the end user types in a search string and clicks the Submit button on the home page to locate an auction item. This section walks through the different parts of the finder-based search code. Chapter 3 describes how to create a bean-managed search to handle complex queries and searches that span more than one bean type (entity and session beans) or database tables.

Finder-Based Search

Figure 2.5 shows how the browser passes the search string to the `AuctionServlet.searchItem` method, which then passes it to the `BidderBean.getMatchingItemsList` method. At this point, `BidderBean.getMatchingItemsList` passes the search string to the `findAllMatchingItems` method declared in the `AuctionItemHome` interface.

The `findAllMatchingItems` method is a finder method, and container implementations vary in how they handle calls to `finder` methods. BEA Weblogic containers look in the bean's deployment descriptor for information on a bean's `finder` methods. In the case of the search, the deployment descriptor maps the search string passed to `AuctionItemHome.findAllMatchingItems` to the `summary` field in the underlying `AuctionItems` database table. This tells the Enter-

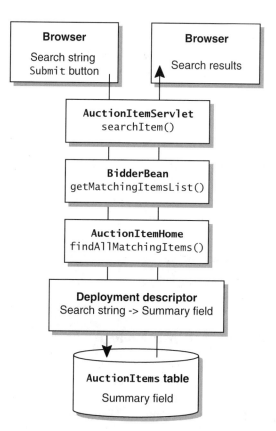

Figure 2.5 Searching for auction items

prise JavaBeans server to retrieve data for all auction items with a summary field that contains text that matches the search string.

AuctionServlet.searchItems

The searchItems method retrieves the text string from the browser, creates an HTML page to display the search results, and passes the search string to the BidderBean.getMatchingItemsList method. BidderBean is a session bean that retrieves lists of auction items and checks the user ID and password for end users seeking to bid on auction items. The search results are returned to this method in an Enumeration variable.

```
private void searchItems(ServletOutputStream out, HttpServletRequest request)
                         throws IOException {
//Retrieve search string
  String searchString=request.getParameter("searchString");
//Create HTML page
  String text = "Click Item number for description and to place bid.";
  setTitle(out, "Search Results");
  try {
     addLine("<BR>"+text, out);
//Look up home interface for BidderBean
     BidderHome bhome=(BidderHome) ctx.lookup("bidder");
//Create remote interface for BidderBean Bidder bid=bhome.create();
//Pass search string to BidderBean method
     Enumeration enum=(Enumeration) bid.getMatchingItemsList(searchString);
        if(enum != null) {
          displayitems(enum, out);
          addLine("", out);
        }
  } catch (Exception e) {
    addLine("AuctionServlet Search Items error", out);
    System.out.println("AuctionServlet <newlist>: "+e);
  }
    out.flush();
}
```

BidderBean.getMatchingItemsList

The BidderBean.getMatchingItemsList method calls the AuctionItemHome.findAllMatchingItems method and passes it the search string. AuctionItemBean is an entity bean that handles auction item updates and retrievals. The search results return an Enumeration.

```
public Enumeration getMatchingItemsList(String searchString)
                                       throws RemoteException {
  Enumeration enum=null;
  try{
//Create Home interface for AuctionItemBean
    AuctionItemHome home = (AuctionItemHome) ctx.lookup("auctionitems");
//Pass search string to Home interface method
    enum=(Enumeration)home.findAllMatchingItems(searchString);
```

```
    }catch (Exception e) {
      System.out.println("getMatchingItemList: "+e);
      return null;
    }
    return enum;
}
```

AuctionItemHome.findAllMatchingItems

The `AuctionItemHome.findAllMatchingItems` method is not implemented in `AuctionItemBean`. Instead, the `AuctionItemBean` finder-method implementations are defined in the `AuctionItemBean` deployment descriptor when BEA Weblogic containers are used.

When the bean is using these containers, even if the bean has finder-method implementations, they are ignored, and the deployment-descriptor settings are consulted instead.

```
//Declare method in Home interface
  public Enumeration findAllMatchingItems(String searchString)
                        throws FinderException, RemoteException;
```

AuctionItemBean Deployment Descriptor

When a bean's finder method is called, the container consults the deployment descriptor for that bean to find out what data the finder method needs to retrieve from the underlying database table. The container passes this information to the Enterprise JavaBeans server, which does the actual retrieval.

The deployment descriptor for `AuctionItemBean` provides `finderDescriptors` for all finder methods declared in the `AuctionItemHome` interface. The `finderDescriptor` for the `findAllMatchingItems` method maps the search string to the summary field in the underlying AuctionItems database table. This tells the Enterprise JavaBeans server to retrieve the data for all table rows with a summary field that matches the text in the search string.

```
(finderDescriptors
  "findAllItems()"          "(= 1 1)"
  "findAllNewItems(java.sql.Date newtoday)" "(= startdate $newtoday)"
  "findAllClosedItems(java.sql.Date closedtoday)" "(= enddate $closedtoday)"
  "findAllMatchingItems(String searchString)" "(like summary $searchString)"
); end finderDescriptors
```

AuctionItemBean

```
    package auction;

    import java.rmi.RemoteException;
    import javax.ejb.*;
    import java.util.*;
    import java.text.NumberFormat;
```

```
//Implementation of the auction bean on the server side
public class AuctionItemBean implements EntityBean {
  //one line summary of auction item
  public String summary;
  //username of person selling the item
  public String seller;
  //auction item identification number
  public int id;
  //auction item description
  public String description;
  //initial price of auction item
  public double startprice=0;
  //Date auction started
  public java.sql.Date startdate;
  //Date auction finishes
  public java.sql.Date enddate;
  //current maximum bid amount and bid increment
  public double maxbid,increment;
  //number of bids
  public int bidcount;
  //username of highest bidder
  public String highbidder;
  protected transient EntityContext ctx;
  //next available auction number
  public static int counter=400000;

  public String getDescription() throws RemoteException {
    return description;
  }
  public String getSummary() throws RemoteException {
    return summary;
  }
  public int getId() throws RemoteException {
    return id;
  }
  public String getSeller() throws RemoteException {
    return seller;
  }
  public double getIncrement() throws RemoteException {
    return increment;
  }
  public double getHighBid() throws RemoteException {
    return maxbid;
  }
  public int getBidCount() throws RemoteException {
    return bidcount;
  }
  public String getHighBidder() throws RemoteException {
    return highbidder;
  }
  public Date getStartDate() throws RemoteException {
    return startdate;
  }
  public Date getEndDate() throws RemoteException {
    return enddate;
```

```
    }
    public double getStartPrice() throws RemoteException {
      return startprice;
    }
    public boolean isAuctionStillRunning() {
      Date now = (Calendar.getInstance()).getTime();
      if(enddate.getTime()>=now.getTime()) {
        return true;
      } else {
        return false;
      }
    }
    public int setHighBid(String buyer, double amount, double increment)
                        throws RemoteException{
      if(isAuctionStillRunning()) {
        highbidder=buyer;
        maxbid=amount;
        this.increment=increment;
        bidcount++;
        return(0);
      } else {
        return (-1);
      }
    }
  public void ejbCreate(String theseller, String thedescription, int duration,
                   double thestartprice, String thesummary)
                   throws CreateException, RemoteException {
    double inc=0;
    try {
      inc=Math.round((thestartprice)/10);
    } catch(Exception e) {
      System.out.println("error parsing money"+e);
    }
    ejbCreate(counter++, theseller, thedescription, duration, thestartprice,
            thesummary, inc);
    }
    public void ejbCreate(int theid, String theseller, String thedescription,
                int duration, double thestartprice, String thesummary,
                   double theincrement)  throws CreateException,
                   RemoteException {
      id=theid;
      seller=theseller;
      description=thedescription;
      Calendar currenttime=Calendar.getInstance();
      Date currentdate=currenttime.getTime();
      startdate=new java.sql.Date(currentdate.getTime());
      currenttime.add(Calendar.DATE,duration);
      enddate=new java.sql.Date((currenttime.getTime()).getTime());
      startprice=thestartprice;
      summary=thesummary;
      maxbid=startprice;
      increment=theincrement;
  }
  public void ejbPostCreate(int id, String theseller, String thedescription,
              int duration, double thestartprice, String thesummary,
```

```
                   double increment) throws CreateException, RemoteException {
    }
    public void ejbPostCreate(String theseller, String thedescription,
                int duration, double thestartprice, String thesummary)
                throws CreateException, RemoteException {
    }
    public void setEntityContext(javax.ejb.EntityContext ctx)
                throws RemoteException {
      this.ctx = ctx;
    }
    public void unsetEntityContext() throws RemoteException {
      ctx = null;
//API Ref: void ejbRemove()
    public void ejbRemove() throws RemoteException, RemoveException { }
//API Ref: void ejbActivate()
    public void ejbActivate() throws RemoteException { }
//API Ref: void ejbPassivate()
    public void ejbPassivate() throws RemoteException { }
    public void ejbLoad() throws RemoteException { }
    public void ejbStore() throws RemoteException { }
```

BidderBean

```
    package bidder;

    import java.rmi.RemoteException;
    import javax.ejb.*;
    import java.util.*;
    import java.text.NumberFormat;
    import java.io.Serializable;
    import javax.naming.*;
    import auction.*;
    import registration.*;

    //Implementation of the session Bidder Bean
    public class BidderBean implements SessionBean {
      protected SessionContext sctx;
      Properties p = new Properties();
      Context ctx;

      public int placeBid(int item, String buyer, String password, double amount)
                    throws RemoteException {
        double highbid, increment=0;
        int bidcount=0;

        try {
          //Find bidder details from Registration database and
          //verify that the password supplied for that bidder matches what
          //is in the database
          RegistrationHome rhome = (RegistrationHome) ctx.lookup("registration");
          RegistrationPK rpk=new RegistrationPK();
          rpk.theuser=buyer;
          Registration newbidder=rhome.findByPrimaryKey(rpk);
```

```
      if ((newbidder == null) || (!newbidder.verifyPassword(password))) {
         return(Auction.INVALID_USER);
      }
      //Now find the auction item receiving bids, and retrieve and set
      //the highest bid number of bids on that item. The next bid
      //increment is calculated based on a simple formula applied to
      //the current bid price

      AuctionItemHome home = (AuctionItemHome) ctx.lookup("auctionitems");
      AuctionItemPK pk=new AuctionItemPK();
      pk.id=item;
      AuctionItem aitem=home.findByPrimaryKey(pk);
      if (aitem !=null) {
        increment=aitem.getIncrement();
        highbid=aitem.getHighBid();
        bidcount=aitem.getBidCount();
          if ((amount >= (highbid+increment)) ||
                       (bidcount == 0 && amount >=highbid )) {
            if(aitem.setHighBid(buyer, amount, (amount)/10)>=0 ) {
              //bid beat other bids!
              return Auction.HIGH_BID;
            } else {
              return Auction.AUCTION_OVER;
            }
          } else { // amount < highbid+increment
            return Auction.OUT_BID;
          }
      } else { aitem = null
        //Item does not exist
        return Auction.INVALID_ITEM;
      }
    } catch(Exception e) {
      System.out.println("placeBid: "+e);
      return Auction.INVALID_ITEM;
    }
}
public Enumeration getItemList() throws RemoteException {
  //Return list of all items in the auction database
  Enumeration enum=null;
  try {
    AuctionItemHome home = (AuctionItemHome) ctx.lookup("auctionitems");
    enum=(Enumeration)home.findAllItems();
  } catch (Exception e) {
    System.out.println("getItemList: "+e);
    return null;
  }
  return enum;
}
public Enumeration getNewItemList() throws RemoteException {
  //Return list of all new items in the auction database
  Enumeration enum=null;
  try {
    AuctionItemHome home = (AuctionItemHome) ctx.lookup("auctionitems");
    Calendar currenttime=Calendar.getInstance();
    enum = (Enumeration)home.findAllNewItems(
```

```
                     new java.sql.Date((currenttime.getTime()).getTime()));
        } catch (Exception e) {
          System.out.println("getNewItemList: "+e);
          return null;
        }
        return enum;
  }
  public Enumeration getClosedItemList() throws RemoteException {
    //Return list of all completed auction items in the auction database
    Enumeration enum=null;
    try {
      AuctionItemHome home = (AuctionItemHome) ctx.lookup("auctionitems");
      Calendar currenttime=Calendar.getInstance();
      enum = (Enumeration)home.findAllClosedItems(
              new java.sql.Date((currenttime.getTime()).getTime()));
    } catch (Exception e) {
      System.out.println("getClosedItemList: "+e);
      return null;
    }
      return enum;
  }
  public Enumeration getMatchingItemsList(String searchString)
                                       throws RemoteException {
    //Return list of all items matching searchString in the auction database
    Enumeration enum=null;
    try {
      AuctionItemHome home = (AuctionItemHome) ctx.lookup("auctionitems");
      enum=(Enumeration)home.findAllMatchingItems(searchString);
    } catch (Exception e) {
      System.out.println("getMatchingItemList: "+e);
      return null;
    }
    return enum;
  }
  public void ejbCreate() throws CreateException, RemoteException {
    Properties p = new Properties();
    p.put(Context.INITIAL_CONTEXT_FACTORY,
                        "weblogic.jndi.TengahInitialContextFactory");
    try {
      ctx = new InitialContext(p);
    } catch(Exception e) {
      System.out.println("create exception: "+e);
    }
  }
  public void setSessionContext(SessionContext sctx) throws RemoteException
{
    this.sctx = sctx;
  }
  public void unsetSessionContext() throws RemoteException {
    sctx = null;
  }
  public void ejbRemove() {}
  public void ejbActivate() throws RemoteException { }
  public void ejbPassivate() throws RemoteException { }
}
```

3
Data and Transaction Management

When you use the Enterprise JavaBeans architecture, data is written to and read from the database without your writing any SQL code to do it. But what if you want to write your own SQL commands or manage transactions? You can override the built-in container-managed persistence and implement bean-managed persistence using your own data storage and transaction-management code.

Bean-managed persistence comes in handy when you want more control than the container-managed persistence provides. For example, you might want to override the default of most containers to map the data in one bean to one row in a table, implement your own finder methods, or customize caching.

This chapter converts the `RegistrationBean` class from Chapter 2, Auction House Application, to provide its own SQL commands for reading from and writing to the database. It also explains how you can write your own transaction-management code and implement a more complex search than you can get with the finder-based search described in Chapter 2.

Covered in this Chapter

Bean-Managed Persistence and the JDBC Platform

There might be times when you want to override container-managed persistence and implement entity or session bean methods to use the SQL commands you provide. This type of bean-managed persistence can be useful if you need to improve performance or need to map data in multiple beans to one row in a database table. This section shows you how to convert the `RegistrationBean` class to access the database with the JDBC `PreparedStatement` class.

Connect to Database

This version of the `RegistrationBean` (SQL) class establishes a connection to the database by instantiating a static `Driver` class and providing the `getConnection` method. The `getConnection` method queries the static `DriverManager` class for a registered database driver that matches the Uniform Resource Locator (URL). In this case, the URL is `weblogic.jdbc.jts.Driver`.

```
//Create static instance of database driver
static {
  new weblogic.jdbc.jts.Driver();
}

//Get registered driver from static instance
public Connection getConnection() throws SQLException{
  return DriverManager.getConnection( "jdbc:weblogic:jts:ejbPool");
}
```

Create Method

The `ejbCreate` method assigns values to data member variables, gets a connection to the database, and creates an instance of the `java.sql.PreparedStatement` class to execute the SQL statement for writing the data to the `registration` table in the database.

A `PreparedStatement` object is created from a SQL statement, which is sent to the database and precompiled before any data is sent. You call the appropriate `set<type>` statements on the `PreparedStatement` object to send the data. Keeping the `PreparedStatement` and `Connection` objects as private instance variables greatly reduces overhead because the SQL statement does not have to be compiled every time data is sent.

The last thing the `ejbCreate` method does is to create a primary key class with the user ID, and then return it to the container.

```
public RegistrationPK ejbCreate(String theuser, String password,
                    String emailaddress, String creditcard)
                    throws CreateException, RemoteException {
  this.theuser=theuser;
  this.password=password;
```

```
        this.emailaddress=emailaddress;
        this.creditcard=creditcard;
        this.balance=0;
        try {
          con=getConnection();
//API Ref: PrepareStatement prepareStatement(String sql)
          ps=con.prepareStatement("insert into registration (theuser, password,
                                    emailaddress, creditcard, balance)
          values ( ?, ?, ?, ?, ?)");
          ps.setString(1, theuser);
          ps.setString(2, password);
          ps.setString(3, emailaddress);
          ps.setString(4, creditcard);
          ps.setDouble(5, balance);
          if (ps.executeUpdate() != 1) {
            throw new CreateException ("JDBC did not create a row");
          }
          RegistrationPK primaryKey = new RegistrationPK();
          primaryKey.theuser = theuser;
          return primaryKey;
        } catch (CreateException ce) {
          throw ce;
        } catch (SQLException sqe) {
          throw new CreateException (sqe.getMessage());
        } finally {
          try {
            ps.close();
          } catch (Exception ignore) {}
          try {
            con.close();
          } catch (Exception ignore) {}
        }
    }
```

Load Method

The ejbLoad method gets the primary key from the entity context and passes it to the refresh method, which loads the data.

```
    public void ejbLoad() throws RemoteException {
      try {
        refresh((RegistrationPK) ctx.getPrimaryKey());
      } catch (FinderException fe) {
        throw new RemoteException (fe.getMessage());
      }
    }
```

Refresh Method

The refresh method is programmer-supplied code to load the data from the database. It checks the primary key value, gets a connection to the database, and creates a PreparedStatement object for querying the database for the user specified in the primary key. Data is read from the database into a ResultSet and assigned to the global member variables so the `RegistrationBean` has the most up-to-date information for the user.

```
private void refresh(RegistrationPK pk)throws FinderException,
RemoteException {
  if (pk == null) {
    throw new RemoteException ("primary key cannot be null");
  }
  Connection con = null;
  PreparedStatement ps = null;
  try {
    con=getConnection();
    ps=con.prepareStatement("select password, emailaddress, creditcard,
                      balance from registration where theuser = ?");
    ps.setString(1, pk.theuser);
    ps.executeQuery();
//API Ref: ResultSet getResultSet()
    ResultSet rs = ps.getResultSet();
    if (rs.next()) {
      theuser = pk.theuser;
//API Ref: String getString(String columnName)
      password = rs.getString(1);
      emailaddress = rs.getString(2);
      creditcard = rs.getString(3);
      balance = rs.getDouble(4);
    } else {
      throw new FinderException
              ("Refresh: Registration ("+ pk.theuser + ") not found");
    }
  } catch (SQLException sqe) {
    throw new RemoteException (sqe.getMessage());
  }
  finally {
    try {
      ps.close();
    } catch (Exception ignore) {}
    try {
      con.close();
    } catch (Exception ignore) {}
  }
}
```

Store Method

This method gets a database connection and creates a `PreparedStatement` to update the database.

```
public void ejbStore() throws RemoteException {
  Connection con = null;
  PreparedStatement ps = null;
  try {
    con = getConnection();
//API Ref: PrepareStatement prepareStatement(String sql)
```

```
      ps = con.prepareStatement("update registration set password = ?,
                    emailaddress = ?, creditcard = ?,
                    balance = ? where theuser = ?");
//API Ref: void setString(int index, String s)
      ps.setString(1, password);
      ps.setString(2, emailaddress);
      ps.setString(3, creditcard);
//API Ref: void setDouble(int index, double doublevalue)
      ps.setDouble(4, balance);
      ps.setString(5, theuser);
//API Ref: int executeUpdate()
      int i = ps.executeUpdate();
      if (i == 0) {
        throw new RemoteException ("ejbStore: Registration
          (" + theuser + ") not updated");
      }
    } catch (RemoteException re) {
        throw re;
    } catch (SQLException sqe) {
        throw new RemoteException (sqe.getMessage());
    } finally {
      try {
        ps.close();
      } catch (Exception ignore) {}
      try {
        con.close();
      } catch (Exception ignore) {}
    }
  }
```

Find Method

The ejbFindByPrimaryKey method matches the signature of the findByPrimaryKey method in the RegistrationHome interface. It calls the refresh
method to get or refresh the user data for the user specified by the primary key.
The container-managed version of RegistrationBean does not implement this
method because the container handles getting and refreshing the user data.

```
public RegistrationPK ejbFindByPrimaryKey(RegistrationPK pk)
                  throws FinderException, RemoteException {
  if ((pk == null) || (pk.theuser == null)) {
    throw new FinderException ("primary key cannot be null");
  }
  refresh(pk);
  return pk;
}
```

Managing Transactions

Wouldn't it be great if every operation your application attempts succeeds?
Unfortunately, in the multithreaded world of distributed applications and

shared resources, this is not always possible. Why? First of all, shared resources must maintain a consistent view of the data to all users. This means reads and writes have to be managed so users do not overwrite each other's changes, or transaction errors do not corrupt data integrity. Also, if you factor in intermittent network delays or dropped connections, the potential for operations to fail in a Web-based application increases as the number of users increases.

If operation failures are unavoidable, the next best thing is to recover safely, and that is where transaction management fits in. Modern databases and transaction managers let you undo and restore the state of a failed sequence of operations to ensure the data is consistent for access by multiple threads.

This section adds code to the container-managed `SellerBean` so it can manage its auction item insertion transaction beyond the default transaction management provided by its container.

Why Manage Transactions?

When you access databases using the JDBC API, all operations are run with an explicit auto commit by default. This means any other application viewing this data will see the updated data after each JDBC call. For simple applications this may be acceptable, but consider the auction application and the sequences that occur when `SellerBean` inserts an auction item. The user's account is first charged for listing the item, and the item is then added to the list of items up for auction. These operations require `RegistrationBean` to debit the account and `AuctionItemBean` to add the item to the auction list.

In auto-commit mode, if the auction item insertion fails, only the listing is backed out, and you have to manually adjust the user's account to refund the listing charge. In the meantime, another thread might try to deduct from the same user's account, find no credit left, and abort when perhaps a few milliseconds later it would have completed. There are two ways to ensure the debit is backed out if the auction item insertion fails:

- Add session synchronization code to a container-managed session bean to gain control over transaction commits and roll backs.
- Configure JDBC services to transaction commit mode and add code to start, stop, commit, and roll back the transaction. This is a bean-managed transaction and can be used with an entity or session bean.

Session Synchronization

A container-managed session bean can optionally include session synchronization code to manage the default auto commit provided by the container. Session synchronization code lets the container notify the bean when important points in the transaction are reached. Upon receiving the notification, the bean can take any needed actions before the transaction proceeds to the next point.

NOTE   A session bean using bean-managed transactions does not need session synchronization because the bean is in full control of the commit.

Container-Managed Example

`SellerBean` is a session bean that uses `RegistrationBean` and `AuctionItem-Bean` in the following ways:

- `RegistrationBean` checks the user ID and password when someone posts an auction item, and debits the seller's account for a listing.
- `AuctionItemBean` adds new auction items to the database.

The transaction begins in the `SellerBean.insertItem` method with the account debit and ends when the entire transaction either commits or rolls back. The entire transaction, including the 50-cents debit, rolls back if the auction item is null (the insertion failed), or if an exception is caught. If the auction item is not null and the insertion succeeds, the entire transaction including the 50-cents debit commits.

Session Synchronization Code

To use session synchronization, a session bean implements the `SessionSynchronzation` interface and its three methods, `afterBegin`, `beforeCompletion`, and `afterCompletion`. This example adapts the `SellerBean` (Session Synchronization) code to use session synchronization.

```
public class SellerBean implements SessionBean, SessionSynchronization {
  private transient SessionContext ctx;
  private transient Properties p = new Properties();
  private transient boolean success = true;

  public void afterBegin() {}
  public void beforeCompletion() {
    if (!success ) {
      ctx.setRollbackOnly();
    }
  }
  public void afterCompletion(boolean state) {}
```

afterBegin.   The container calls the `afterBegin` method before the debit to notify the session bean that a new transaction is about to begin. You can implement this method to do any preliminary database work that might be needed for the transaction. In this example, no preliminary database work is needed, so this method has no implementation.

beforeCompletion.   The container calls the `beforeCompletion` method when it is ready to write the auction item and debit to the database, but before it actually does so (commits). You can implement this method to write out any cached database updates or roll back the transaction. In this example, the method calls the `setRollbackOnly` method on its session context in the event the success variable is set to `false` during the transaction.

afterCompletion.   The container calls the `afterCompletion` method when the transaction commits. A Boolean value of `true` means the data committed and `false` means the transaction rolled back. The method uses the Boolean value to determine if it needs to reset the bean's state in the case of a rollback. In this example, there is no need to reset the state in the event of a failure. The `insertItem` method shown here has comments to indicate where `SessionSynchronization` methods are called.

```
public int insertItem(String seller, String password, String description,

int auctiondays, double startprice, String summary) throws RemoteException {
  try {
    Context jndiCtx = new InitialContext(p);
    RegistrationHome rhome = (RegistrationHome) sCtx.lookup("registration");
    RegistrationPK rpk=new RegistrationPK();
    rpk.theuser=seller;
    Registration newseller=rhome.findByPrimaryKey(rpk);
    if((newseller == null) || (!newseller.verifyPassword(password))) {
      return(Auction.INVALID_USER);
    }
//Call to afterBegin
    newseller.adjustAccount(-0.50);
    AuctionItemHome home = (AuctionItemHome) jndiCtx.lookup("auctionitems");
    AuctionItem ai= home.create(seller, description, auctiondays,
                            startprice, summary);
    if(ai == null) {
      success=false;
      return Auction.INVALID_ITEM;
    } else {
      return(ai.getId());
    }
  } catch(Exception e){
      System.out.println("insert problem="+e);
      success=false;
      return Auction.INVALID_ITEM;
    }
//Call to beforeCompletion
//Call to afterCompletion

  }
```

Transaction Commit Mode

If you configure the JDBC services to transaction commit mode, you can have the bean manage the transaction. To set the JDBC services to commit, call `con.setAutoCommit(false)` on your JDBC connection. Not all JDBC drivers support commit mode, but to have the bean control and manage transactions, you need a JDBC driver that does.

Transaction commit mode lets you add code that creates a safety net around a sequence of dependent operations. The Java Transaction API (JTA) provides the hooks you need to create that safety net. But, if you are using the Enterprise JavaBeans architecture, you can do it with a lot less code. You only have to configure the Enterprise JavaBeans server, and specify where the transaction starts, stops, rolls back, and commits in your code.

Server Configuration.   Configuring the Enterprise JavaBeans server involves specifying the following settings in a configuration file for each bean:

- An isolation level to specify how exclusive a transaction's access to shared data is
- A transaction attribute to specify how to handle bean-managed or container-managed transactions that continue in another bean
- A transaction type to specify whether the transaction is managed by the container or the bean.

For example, you would specify these settings for the BEA Weblogic server in a `DeploymentDescriptor.txt` file for each bean. Here is the part of the `DeploymentDescriptor.txt` file for `SellerBean` that specifies the isolation level and transaction attribute. A description of the settings follows.

```
(controlDescriptors
  (DEFAULT
     isolationLevel           TRANSACTION_SERIALIZABLE
     transactionAttribute     REQUIRED
     runAsMode                CLIENT_IDENTITY
     runAsIdentity            guest
  ); end DEFAULT
); end controlDescriptors
```

Here is the equivalent Enterprise JavaBeans 1.1 extensible markup language (XML) description that specifies the transaction type. In this example, `Seller-Bean` is container-managed.

```
<container-transaction>
    <method>
        <ejb-name>SellerBean</ejb-name>
        <method-name>*</method-name>
    </method>
```

```
    <transaction-type>Container</transaction-type>
    <trans-attribute>Required</trans-attribute>
</container-transaction>
```

In this example, SellerBean is bean-managed.

```
<container-transaction>
    <method>
        <ejb-name>SellerBean</ejb-name>
        <method-name>*</method-name>
    </method>
    <transaction-type>Bean</transaction-type>
    <trans-attribute>Required</trans-attribute>
</container-transaction>
```

Transaction-Attribute Descriptions.   An enterprise bean uses a transaction attribute to specify whether a bean's transactions are managed by the bean itself or by the container, and how to handle transactions that started in another bean.

The Enterprise JavaBeans server can control only one transaction at a time. This model follows the example set by the OMG Object Transaction Service (OTS), which means that the current Enterprise JavaBeans specification does not provide a way to nest transactions. A *nested transaction* is a new transaction that starts from within an existing transaction. While transaction nesting is not allowed, continuing an existing transaction in another bean is allowed.

When a bean is entered, the server creates a transaction context to manage the transaction. When the transaction is managed by the bean, you access the context to begin, commit, and roll back the transaction as needed.

The following table lists the transaction attributes with a brief description for each one. Note that the attribute names changed between the 1.0 and 1.1 versions of the Enterprise JavaBeans specification.

1.1 Specification	1.0 Specification
REQUIRED	TX_REQUIRED
Container-managed transaction. The server either starts and manages a new transaction on behalf of the user or continues using the transaction that was started by the code that called this bean.	
REQUIRESNEW	TX_REQUIRED_NEW
Container-managed transaction. The server starts and manages a new transaction. If an existing transaction starts this transaction, it suspends until this transaction completes.	

(continues)

1.1 Specification	1.0 Specification
Specified as bean transaction-type in deployment descriptor.	TX_BEAN_MANAGED

Bean-managed transaction. You access the transaction context to begin, commit, or roll back the transaction as needed.

SUPPORTS	TX_SUPPORTS

If the code calling this bean has a transaction running, include this bean in that transaction.

NEVER	TX_NOT_SUPPORTED

If the code calling a method in this bean has a transaction running, suspend that transaction until the method called in this bean completes. No transaction context is created for this bean.

MANDATORY	TX_MANDATORY

The transaction attribute for this bean is set when another bean calls one of its methods. In this case, this bean gets the transaction attribute of the calling bean. If the calling bean has no transaction attribute, the method called in this bean throws a TransactionRequired exception.

Isolation-Level Descriptions.   An enterprise bean uses an isolation level to negotiate its own interaction with shared data, and to negotiate the interaction of other threads with the same shared data. As the name implies, there are various levels of isolation with TRANSACTION_SERIALIZABLE providing the highest level of data integrity.

> **NOTE**   Be sure to verify that your database can handle the level you choose. In the Enterprise JavaBeans 1.1 specification, only bean-managed session beans can set the isolation level. If the database cannot handle the isolation level, the Enterprise JavaBeans server will get a failure when it tries to call the setTransaction-Isolation JDBC method.

TRANSACTION_SERIALIZABLE.   This level provides maximum data integrity. The bean gets what amounts to exclusive access to the data. No other transaction can read or write this data until the serializable transaction completes.

In this context, serializable means to process the data as a serial operation; it should not be confused with serializing objects to preserve and restore their states. Running transactions as a single serial operation is the slowest setting. If performance is an issue, use another isolation level that meets your application requirements but provides better performance.

TRANSACTION_REPEATABLE_READ. At this level, data read by a transaction can be read, but not modified, by another transaction. The data is guaranteed to have the same value it had when first read, unless the previous transaction changes it and writes the changed value back.

TRANSACTION_READ_COMMITTED. At this level, data read by a transaction cannot be read by other transactions until the previous transaction either commits or rolls back. However, if another transaction alters the data after this transaction starts, a second read would retrieve the modified data. To prevent this type of inconsistent data, use TRANSACTION_REPEATABLE_READ.

TRANSACTION_READ_UNCOMMITTED. At this level, data involved in a transaction can be read by other threads before the previous transaction either completes or rolls back. The other transactions cannot tell whether the data was finally committed or rolled back.

Bean-Managed Example. SellerBean is a session bean that uses RegistrationBean and AuctionItemBean in the following ways:

- RegistrationBean checks the user ID and password when someone posts an auction item, and debits the seller's account for a listing.
- AuctionItemBean adds new auction items to the database.

The transaction begins in the SellerBean.insertItem method with the account debit and ends when the entire transaction either commits or rolls back. The entire transaction including the 50-cents debit rolls back if the auction item is null (the insertion failed) or if an exception is caught. If the auction item is not null and the insertion succeeds, the entire transaction including the 50-cents debit commits.

For this example, the isolation level is TRANSACTION_SERIALIZABLE, and the transaction attribute is TX_BEAN_MANAGED. The other beans in the transaction, RegistrationBean and AuctionItemBean, have an isolation level of TRANSACTION_SERIALIZABLE and a transaction attribute of REQUIRED. Changes to this version of SellerBean.insertItem over the container-managed version are flagged with comments.

```
public int insertItem(String seller, String password, String description,
                int auctiondays, double startprice, String summary)
                throws RemoteException {
//Declare transaction context variable using the
```

```
        //javax.transaction.UserTransaction class
          UserTransaction uts= null;
          try {
            Context ectx = new InitialContext(p);
        //Get the transaction context
            uts=(UserTransaction)ctx.getUserTransaction();
            RegistrationHome rhome = (RegistrationHome)ectx.lookup("registration");
            RegistrationPK rpk=new RegistrationPK();
            rpk.theuser=seller;
            Registration newseller=rhome.findByPrimaryKey(rpk);
            if((newseller == null)|| (!newseller.verifyPassword(password))) {
                return(Auction.INVALID_USER);
            }
        //Start the transaction
//API Ref: void begin()
            uts.begin();
        //Deduct 50 cents from seller's account
            newseller.adjustAccount(-0.50);
            AuctionItemHome home = (AuctionItemHome) ectx.lookup("auctionitems");
            AuctionItem ai= home.create(seller, description, auctiondays,
                                        startprice, summary);
            if(ai == null) {
        //Roll transaction back
//API Ref: void rollback()
                uts.rollback();
                return Auction.INVALID_ITEM;
            } else {
        //Commit transaction
//API Ref: void commit()
                uts.commit();
                return(ai.getId());
            }
            } catch(Exception e){
            System.out.println("insert problem="+e);
        //Roll transaction back if insert fails
                uts.rollback();
                return Auction.INVALID_ITEM;
            }
        }
```

Bean-Managed Finder Methods

The container-managed search described in Chapter 2, Auction House Application, is based on a finder-method mechanism in which the deployment descriptor, rather than the bean, specifies the finder-method behavior. While the finder mechanism works well for simple queries and searches, it cannot handle complex operations that span more than one bean type or database table. Also, the Enterprise JavaBeans 1.1 specification currently provides no specification for putting finder rules in the deployment descriptor.

So, for more complex queries and searches, you have to write bean-managed queries and searches. This section explains how to write a bean-managed version of the auction house search facility of Chapter 2. The bean-managed search involves changes to the `AuctionServlet.searchItems` method and a new session bean, `SearchBean`.

AuctionServlet.searchItems

The search begins when the end user submits a search string to the search facility on the auction house home page and clicks the Submit button. This invokes `AuctionServlet`, which retrieves the search string from the HTTP header and passes it to the `searchItem` method.

NOTE   The search logic for this example is fairly simple. The idea here is to show you how to move the search logic into a separate enterprise bean so you can create a more complex search on your own.

Figure 3.1 shows how the `searchItem` operation is in the following two parts: (1) Using the search string to retrieve primary keys, and (2) Using primary keys to retrieve auction items. Parts 1 and 2 are described in more detail below the figure.

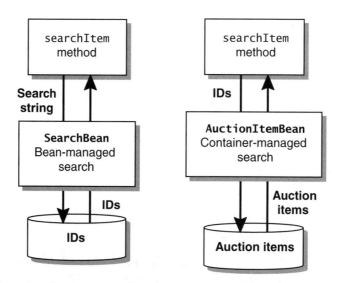

Figure 3.1 Search items operation

Part 1: The first thing the `searchItems` method does is pass the search string submitted by the end user to the `SearchBean` session bean. `SearchBean` implements a bean-managed search that retrieves a list of primary keys for all auction items whose `Summary` fields contain characters matching the search string. This list is returned to the `searchItems` method in an `Enumeration` variable.

```
private void searchItems(ServletOutputStream out,
                         HttpServletRequest request)
                         throws IOException {
  String searchString=request.getParameter("searchString");
  String text = "Click Item number for description and to place bid.";
  setTitle(out, "Search Results");
  try {
    addLine("<BR>"+text, out);
//Look up Home interfaces
    AuctionItemHome ahome = (
    AuctionItemHome) ctx.lookup("auctionitems");
    SearchHome shome=(SearchHome) ctx.lookup("search");
//Create remote interface for search Bean
    Search search=shome.create();
//Call search method and pass the search string
    Enumeration enum=(Enumeration) search.getMatchingItemsList(
                                  searchString);
    addLine("<TABLE BORDER=1 CELLPADDING=1 CELLSPACING=0>
      <TR> <TH>Item<TH> <TH>Summary<TH><TH>Current High bid<TH>
      <TH>Number of bids<TH><TH>Closing Date<TH><TR>", out);
//Iterate through search results
    while ((enum != null) && (enum.hasMoreElements())) {
      while(enum.hasMoreElements(in)) {
//Locate auction items
        AuctionItem ai=ahome.findByPrimaryKey((AuctionItemPK)enum.
                                      nextElement());
        displayLineItem(ai, out);
      }
  }
    addLine("<TABLE>", out);
  } catch (Exception e) {
    addLine("AuctionServlet Search Items error", out);
    System.out.println("AuctionServlet <searchItems>:"+e);
  }
  out.flush();
}
```

Part 2: The searchItems method then uses the returned Enumeration list from Part 1 and AuctionItemBean (page 51) to retrieve each bean in turn by calling findByPrimaryKey on each primary key in the list. This is a container-managed search based on the finder mechanism described in Auction House Application (Chapter 2).

```
//Iterate through search results
while ((enum != null) && enum.hasMoreElements()) {
  while(enum.hasMoreElements(in)) {
    //Locate auction items
    AuctionItem ai=ahome.findByPrimaryKey((
    AuctionItemPK)enum.nextElement());
    displayLineItem(ai, out);
  }
}
```

SearchBean

The SearchBean class (page 54) defines a bean-managed search for the primary keys of auction items with summary fields that contain characters matching the search string. This bean establishes a database connection and provides the getMatchingItemsList and EJBCreate methods. A custom SearchBean is written because the default finder rules supplied by the EJB server do not allow a wild card SQL search string. This technique can also be used for more complex queries or queries that could be better optimized by the developer than those search queries generated by the EJB server.

Database Connection

Because this bean manages its own database access and search, it has to establish its own database connection. It cannot rely on the container to do this. The database connection is established by instantiating a static Driver class and providing the getConnection method. The getConnection method queries the static DriverManager class for a registered database driver that matches the Uniform Resource Locator (URL). In this case, the URL is weblogic.jdbc.jts.Driver.

```
//Establish database connection
  static {
    new weblogic.jdbc.jts.Driver();
  }
  public Connection getConnection() throws SQLException {
    return DriverManager.getConnection("jdbc:weblogic:jts:ejbPool");
  }
```

Get Matching Items List

The getMatchingItemsList method looks up AuctionItemBean and creates a PreparedStatement object for querying the database for summary fields that contain the search string. Data is read from the database into a ResultSet, stored in a Vector, and returned to AuctionServlet.

```
    public Enumeration getMatchingItemsList(String searchString)
                    throws RemoteException {
      ResultSet rs = null;
      PreparedStatement ps = null;
      Vector v = new Vector();
      Connection con = null;
      try {
  //Get database connection
      con=getConnection();
//API Ref: PreparedStatement prepareStatement(String sql)
      ps=con.prepareStatement("select id from auctionitems where" +
                      "summary like ?");
      ps.setString(1, "%"+searchString+"%");
```

```
//Execute database query
    ps.executeQuery();
//Get results set
    rs = ps.getResultSet();
//Get information from results set
    AuctionItemPK pk;
    while (rs.next()) {
       pk = new AuctionItemPK();
       pk.id = (int)rs.getInt(1);
//Store retrieved data in vector
       v.addElement(pk);
    }
    rs.close();
    return v.elements();
  } catch (Exception e) {
    System.out.println("getMatchingItemsList: "+e);
    return null;
  } finally {
    try {
    if (rs != null) {
       rs.close();
    }
    if (ps != null) {
       ps.close();
    }
    if (con != null) {
       con.close();
    }
    } catch (Exception ignore) {}
  }
}
```

Create Method

The ejbCreate method creates a javax.naming.InitialContext object. This is a JNDI class that lets SearchBean access the database without relying on the container.

```
public void ejbCreate() throws CreateException,
  RemoteException {
  Properties p = new Properties();
  p.put(Context.INITIAL_CONTEXT_FACTORY,
             "weblogic.jndi.TengahInitialContextFactory");
  try {
    ctx = new InitialContext(p);
  } catch(Exception e) {
    System.out.println("create exception: "+e);
  }
}
```

SearchBean

```
package search;

import java.rmi.RemoteException;
import javax.ejb.*;
import java.util.*;
import java.text.NumberFormat;
import java.io.Serializable;
import javax.naming.*;
import auction.*;
import registration.*;
import java.sql.*;

public class SearchBean implements SessionBean {
    protected SessionContext sctx;
    Properties p = new Properties();
    Context ctx;
    static {
      new weblogic.jdbc.jts.Driver();
    }

  public Connection getConnection() throws SQLException {
    return DriverManager.getConnection("jdbc:weblogic:jts:ejbPool");
  }
  public Enumeration getMatchingItemsList(String searchString)
                                    throws RemoteException {
    //Search for matching item by comparing searchString to
    //the database summary field and returning an enumerated
    //list of the primary key auction id values.

    ResultSet rs = null;
    PreparedStatement ps = null;
    Vector v = new Vector();
    Connection con = null;
    try {
      AuctionItemHome home = (AuctionItemHome)
      ctx.lookup("auctionitems");
      con = getConnection();
      ps = con.prepareStatement(
          "select id from auctionitems where summary like ?");
      ps.setString(1, "%"+searchString+"%");
      ps.executeQuery();
      rs = ps.getResultSet();
      AuctionItemPK pk;
      while(rs.next()) {
        pk = new AuctionItemPK();
        pk.id = (int)rs.getInt(1);
        v.addElement(pk);
      }
      return v.elements();
    } catch (Exception e) {
      System.out.println("getMatchingItemsList: "+e);
      return null;
    } finally {
```

```
            try {
              if(rs != null) {
                rs.close();
              }
              if(ps != null) {
                ps.close();
              }
              if(con != null) {
                con.close();
              }
            } catch (Exception ignore) {
                //An exception was thrown trying to
                //close the used connections. The exception is ignored
                //because there is no further need for the used connection.
            }
          }
        }
      public void ejbCreate() throws CreateException, RemoteException {
        Properties p = new Properties();
        p.put(Context.INITIAL_CONTEXT_FACTORY,
                      "weblogic.jndi.TengahInitialContextFactory");
        try {
          ctx = new InitialContext(p);
        } catch(Exception e) {
          System.out.println("create exception: "+e);
        }
      }
      public void setSessionContext(SessionContext sctx) throws RemoteException {
        this.sctx = sctx;
      }
      public void unsetSessionContext() throws RemoteException {
        sctx = null;
      }
//API Ref: void ejbRemove()
      public void ejbRemove() {}
//API Ref: void ejbActivate()
      public void ejbActivate() throws RemoteException { }
//API Ref: void ejbPassivate()
      public void ejbPassivate() throws RemoteException { }
    }
```

4

Distributed Computing

As recently as 10 years ago, distributed computing generally meant you had client PCs in one room with a server in another room. The problem here is if the server machine is down, the clients cannot update the payroll, sales, or other distributed company databases. Preventing this kind of down-time requires different distributed models. One example is the master and slave model in which, if the master fails, the slaves take over.

The problem with the different distributed network models is they all require some form of manual intervention and are often tied to one operating system or language. And while these approaches meet some of the short-term requirements for decreasing down-time, they do not apply to heterogeneous distributed systems with mixed network protocols and machines.

The Java platform and other advances such as Common Object Request Broker Architecture (CORBA), multitiered servers, and wireless networks have brought the realization of fully distributed computing another step ahead of the traditional client and server approach. Today, you can build applications that include service redundancy by default. If one server connection fails, you can seamlessly use a service on another server. CORBA and Distributed Component Object Model (DCOM) bridges mean that objects can be transferred between virtually all machines and languages. And with the new Jini™ System software, the distributed computing environment can soon be part of everything in your home, office or school. In short, distributed computing has never been as important as it is today.

The first part of this chapter shows you how to write lookup code using JNDI, CORBA, Interoperable Object Reference (IOR), and RMI over Internet Inter-ORB Protocol (RMI-IIOP). The second part describes how to use lookup code with RMI and CORBA, and concludes with a discussion of JDBC and servlet technologies.

Covered in this Chapter

- Lookup Services (page 58)
- Java Naming and Directory Interface (page 59)
- RMI Lookup Service (page 64)
- RMI Registration Server (page 67)
- Common Object Request Broker Architecture (page 83)
- JDBC Technology (page 103)
- Servlets (page 118)

Lookup Services

Lookup (naming) services enable communications over a network. A client program can use a lookup protocol to get information on remote programs or machines and use that information to establish a communication.

- One common lookup service you might already be familiar with is Directory Name Service (DNS). It maps Internet Protocol (IP) addresses to machine names. Programs use the DNS mapping to look up the IP address associated with a machine name and use the IP address to establish a communication.

- In the same way, the AuctionServlet presented in Chapter 2, Auction House Application, uses the naming service built into the Enterprise JavaBeans architecture to look up and reference enterprise beans registered with the Enterprise JavaBeans server.

In addition to naming services, some lookup protocols provide directory services. Directory services such as Lightweight Directory Access Protocol (LDAP) and Sun's NIS+ provide other information and services beyond what is available with simple naming services. For example, NIS+ associates a work-group attribute with a user account. This attribute can be used to restrict access to a machine so only the users in the specified workgroup have access.

This chapter describes how JNDI is used in the auction application to look up enterprise beans. It also explains how to use some of the many other lookup services that have become available over time. The code to use these other services is not as simple as the lookup code in the auction application in Chapter 2, but the advantages to these other services can outweigh the need for more complex code in some situations.

Java Naming and Directory Interface

The JNDI API makes it easy to plug lookup services from various providers into a program written in the Java programming language. As long as the client and server both use the same lookup service, the client can easily look up information registered with the server and establish communication.

The auction application session beans use JNDI and a special JNDI naming factory from BEA Weblogic to look up entity beans. JNDI services normally initialize the naming factory as a property on the command line or as an initialization value. First, the naming factory weblogic.jndi.TengahInitialContextFactory is put into a java.util.Property object, then the Property object is passed as a parameter to the InitialContext constructor. Here is an example ejbCreate method.

```
Context ctx; //JNDI context
public void ejbCreate() throws CreateException, RemoteException {
  Hashtable env = new Hashtable();
  env.put(Context.INITIAL_CONTEXT_FACTORY,
                      "weblogic.jndi.TengahInitialContextFactory");
  try {
    ctx = new InitialContext(env);
  } catch(Exception e) {
    System.out.println("create exception: "+e);
  }
}
```

Once created, the JNDI context is used to look up enterprise bean home interfaces. In this example, a reference to the enterprise bean bound to the name registration is retrieved and used for further operations.

```
RegistrationHome rhome = (RegistrationHome) ctx.lookup("registration");
RegistrationPK rpk=new RegistrationPK();
rpk.theuser=buyer;
Registration newbidder = rhome.findByPrimaryKey(rpk);
```

On the server side, the deployment descriptor for the RegistrationBean has its bean homename value set to registration. Enterprise JavaBeans tools generate the rest of the naming code for the server.

The server calls ctx.bind to bind the name registration to the JNDI context. The this parameter references the _stub class that represents the RegistrationBean.

```
ctx.bind("registration", this);
```

JNDI is not the only way to look up remote objects. Lookup services are also available in the RMI, JINI, and CORBA platforms. You can use these platform-specific lookup services directly or from the JNDI API.

JNDI allows the application to change the name service with little effort. For example, here are the code changes to have the `BidderBean.ejbCreate` method use the `org.omb.CORBA` lookup services instead of the default BEA Weblogic lookup services.

```
Hashtable env = new Hashtable();
env.put("java.naming.factory.initial", "com.sun.jndi.cosnaming.CNCtxFactory");
Context ic = new InitialContext(env);
```

CORBA Naming Service

CORBA defines a specification for objects in a distributed system to communicate with each other. Objects that use the CORBA specification to communicate are called *CORBA objects*, and consist of client and server objects.

CORBA objects can be written in any language with Interface Definition Language (IDL) mapping. These languages include the Java programming language, C++, and many traditional non–object-orientated languages.

The naming lookup service, like all other CORBA specifications, is defined in terms of IDL. The IDL module for the CORBA lookup service is called `Cos-Naming`. Any platform with an IDL mapping can use this service to look up and discover CORBA objects. The IDL module for the CORBA lookup service is available in the Java 2 Platform in the `org.omg.CosNaming` package and the mapping to the Java programming language is created by a tool called `idlto-java`.

The key interface in the `CosNaming` module is `NamingContext`. The `Naming-Context` interface defines methods to bind objects to a name, list those bidding, and retrieve bound object references.

In addition to these public interfaces are helper classes. The `NameComponent` helper class is used in CORBA client and server programs to build the full name for the object reference name. The full name is an array of one or more `NameComponents` that indicate where to find the objects. The naming scheme can be application specific.

Figure 4.1 shows how the full name for the auction application can be defined to use `auction` as the root naming context with `RegistrationBean` and `Auc-tionItemBean` as children of the root context. This, in effect, employs a similar naming scheme as that used for the application class packaging.

In this example, the auction application has adapted `SellerBean` to a CORBA naming service to look up the CORBA `RegistrationBean`. The following

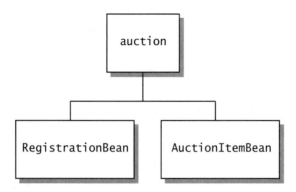

Figure 4.1 Full name and root naming context

code is extracted from the SellerBean class, which acts as the CORBA client, and the RegistrationServer CORBA server.

CORBA RegistrationServer.   The RegistrationServer (lookup) code creates a NameComponent object that uses the auction and RegistrationBean strings as a full name indicating where to locate the RegistrationBean.

```
NameComponent[] fullname = new NameComponent[2];
fullname[0] = new NameComponent("auction", "");
fullname[1] = new NameComponent( "RegistrationBean", "");
```

This next code binds the fullname as a new name context. The first elements in the full name (auction, in this example) are placeholders for building the context-naming tree. The last element of the full name (RegistrationBean, in this example) is the name submitted as the binding to the object.

```
    public static void main(String args[]) {
    String[] orbargs = { "-ORBInitialPort 1050"};
//API Ref: status ORB init(String[] args, Properties props)
    ORB orb = ORB.init(orbargs, null)
    RegistrationServer rs= new RegistrationServer();
    try{
//API Ref: void connect(Object object)
        orb.connect(rs);
        org.omg.CORBA.Object nameServiceObj =
                        orb.resolve_initial_references("NameService");
        NamingContext nctx = NamingContextHelper.narrow(nameServiceObj);
//API Ref: NameComponent(String nameid, String kind)
        NameComponent[] fullname = new NameComponent[2];
        fullname[0] = new NameComponent("auction", "");
        fullname[1] = new NameComponent("RegistrationBean", "");
        NameComponent[] tempComponent = new NameComponent[1];
        for (int i=0; i < fullname.length-1; i++ ) {
          tempComponent[0]= fullname[i];
          try {
//API Ref: NamingContext bind_new_context(NameComponent[] nc)
```

```
          nctx=nctx.bind_new_context(tempComponent);
        } catch (org.omg.CosNaming.NamingContextPackage.AlreadyBound e){
          //If this part of the tree is already bound then ignore this exception
        }
      }
        tempComponent[0]=fullname[fullname.length-1];
      //Finally bind the object to the full context path
//API Ref: static void rebind(String rminame, Remote obj)
        nctx.rebind(tempComponent, rs);
```

Once the `RegistrationServer` object is bound, it can be looked up with a JNDI lookup using a `CosNaming` service provider as described in Java Naming and Directory Interface (page 59) or using the CORBA name lookup service. Either way, the CORBA name server must be started before any lookups can take place. In the Java 2 platform, the CORBA `name server` is started as follows to start the CORBA `RegistrationServer` on the default TCP port 900:

```
tnameserv
```

If you need to use a different port, you can start the server like this:

```
tnameserv -ORBInitialPort 1050
```

CORBA SellerBean.   On the client side, the CORBA lookup uses the `Name-Component` object to construct the name. Start the object server like this:

```
java registration.RegistrationServer
```

The difference in the client is that the name is passed to the `resolve` method, which returns the CORBA object. The following code from the `SellerBean` object illustrates this point.

```
public static void main(String args[]) {
  java.util.Properties props=System.getProperties();
  props.put("org.omg.CORBA.ORBInitialPort", "1050");
  System.setProperties(props);
  ORB orb = ORB.init(args, props);
```

```
//API Ref: Object resolve_initial_references(String servicename)
    org.omg.CORBA.Object nameServiceObj = orb.resolve_initial_references(
                                          "NameService") ;
    nctx= NamingContextHelper.narrow(nameServiceObj);
    NameComponent[] fullname = new NameComponent[2];
    fullname[0] = new NameComponent("auction", "");
    fullname[1] = new NameComponent("RegistrationBean", "");
//API Ref: Object resolve(NameComponent[] nc)
    org.omg.CORBA.Object cobject= nctx.resolve(fullname);
  }
```

The narrow method from the `Helper` class is generated by the IDL compiler, which provides a detailed mapping to translate each CORBA field into its respective Java programming language field. For example, the `Seller-`

`Bean.insertItem` method looks up a registration CORBA object using the name `RegistrationBean`, and returns a `RegistrationHome` object. With the `RegistrationHome` object, you can return a `Registration` record by calling its `findByPrimaryKey` method.

```
public int insertItem(String seller, String password, String description,
                      int auctiondays, double startprice, String summary)
                      throws RemoteException {
try{
  NameComponent[] fullname = new NameComponent[2];
  fullname[0] = new NameComponent("auction", "");
  fullname[1] = new NameComponent("RegistrationBean", "");
  org.omg.CORBA.Object cobject= nctx.resolve(fullname);
  RegistrationHome regHome = RegistrationHomeHelper.narrow(cobject);
  RegistrationHome regRef =
          RegistrationHomeHelper.narrow(nctx.resolve(fullname));
  RegistrationPKImpl rpk = new RegistrationPKImpl();
  rpk.theuser(seller);
  Registration newseller =
          RegistrationHelper.narrow(regRef.findByPrimaryKey(rpk));
  if ((newseller == null) || (!newseller.verifyPassword(password))) {
      return(Auction.INVALID_USER);
  }
  } catch(Exception e) {
      System.out.println("insert problem="+e);
      return Auction.INVALID_ITEM;
  }
}
```

Interoperable Object References

Using a CORBA name service works for most CORBA applications especially when the object request brokers (ORBs) are supplied by one vendor. However, you might find the name service is not completely compatible among all ORBs, and you could get a frustrating `COMM_FAILURE` message when the CORBA client tries to connect to the CORBA server.

The solution is to use an Interoperable Object Reference (IOR) instead. An IOR is available in ORBs that support the Internet Inter-ORB protocol (IIOP). It contains the information a naming service keeps for each object such as the host and port where the object resides, a unique lookup key for the object on that host, and what version of IIOP is supported.

IOR Server. To create an IOR all you do is call the `object_to_string` method from the ORB class and pass it an instance of the object. For example, to convert the `RegistrationServer` object to an IOR, you need to add the line `String ref = orb.object_to_string(rs);` to the main program:

```
String[] orbargs= {"-ORBInitialPort 1050"};
ORB orb = ORB.init(orbargs, null);
```

```
    RegistrationServer rs = new RegistrationServer();
    //Add this line
//API Ref: String object_to_String(Object object)
    String ref = orb.object_to_string(rs);
```

So, instead of retrieving this object information from a naming service, there is another way for the server to send information to the client. You can register the returned String with a substitute name server, which can be a simple HTTP Web server because the object is already in a transmittable format.

IOR Client.   This example uses an HTTP connection to convert the IOR string back to an object. You call the string_to_object method from the ORB class. This method requests the IOR from the RegistrationServer and returns the IOR string. The String is passed to the ORB using the ORB.string_to_object method, and the ORB returns the remote object reference:

```
URL iorserver = new URL("http://server.com/servlet?object=registration");
URLConnection con = ioserver.openConnection();
BufferedReader br = new BufferReader(new InputStreamReader(
                                      con.getInputStream));
String ref = br.readLine();
//API Ref: Object string_to_object(String stringvalue)
org.omg.CORBA.Object cobj = orb.string_to_object(ref);
RegistrationHome regHome = RegistrationHomeHelper.narrow(cobj);
```

The substitute name server can keep persistent IOR records that can survive a restart if needed.

RMI Lookup Service

The RMI API originally used its own communication protocol called Java Remote Method Protocol (JRMP), which resulted in having its own lookup service. Newer releases of RMI can now use the more ubiquitous IIOP protocol, in addition to JRMP.

The JRMP RMI naming service is similar to other lookup and naming services. The actual lookup is achieved by calling Naming.lookup and passing a URL parameter to that method. The URL specifies the machine name, an optional port where the RMI naming server that knows about the object is running (rmiregistry) and the remote object you want to reference and call methods on. For example:

```
//API Ref: static Remote lookup(String rminame)
    SellerHome shome = (SellerHome)Naming.lookuup("rmi://appserver:1090/seller");
```

The above code returns the remote SellerHome reference _stub from the object bound to the name seller on the machine called appserver. The rmi part of the URL is optional and you may have seen RMI URLs without it, but if you are using JNDI or RMI-IIOP, including rmi in the URL will save confusion later. Once you have a reference to SellerHome, you can call its methods.

In contrast to the JNDI lookup performed by AuctionServlet (page 59), which requires a two-stage lookup to create a context and then the actual lookup, RMI initializes the connection to the RMI name server, rmiregistry, and also gets the remote reference with one call. This remote reference is leased to the client from the rmiregistry. The lease means that unless the client informs the server it still needs a reference to the object, the lease expires and the memory is reclaimed. This leasing operation is automatic and transparent to the user, but can be tuned by setting the server property java.rmi.dgc.leaseValue value in milliseconds when starting the server as follows:

```
java -Djava.rmi.dgc.leaseValue=120000 myAppServer
```

You can find more information on leasing in Distributed Garbage Collection (page 75).

RMI over Internet Inter-ORB Protocol

RMI over Internet Inter-ORB Protocol lets existing RMI code reference and look up an object using the CORBA CosNaming service. This gives you greater interoperability between architectures with little change to your existing RMI code.

NOTE   The rmic compiler provides the -iiop option to generate the stub and the classes necessary for RMI-IIOP.

IIOP Server.   The RMI-IIOP protocol is implemented as a JNDI plug-in, so as before, you need to create an InitialContext:

```
Hashtable env = new Hashtable();
env.put("java.naming.factory.initial", "com.sun.jndi.cosnaming." +
                                "CNCtxFactory");
env.put("java.naming.provider.url","iiop://localhost:1091");
Context ic = new InitialContext(env);
```

The naming factory should look familiar because it is the same CORBA naming service used in CORBA Naming Service (page 60). The main difference is the addition of a URL value specifying the naming service to which to connect. The naming service used here is the tnameserv program started on port 1091.

```
tnameserv -ORBInitialPort 1091
```

The other main change to the server side is to replace calls to `Naming.rebind` to use the JNDI `rebind` method in the `InitialContext` instance. For example:

Old RMI lookup code:
```
SellerHome shome= new SellerHome("seller");
Naming.rebind("seller", shome);
```

New RMI code:
```
Hashtable env = new Hashtable();
env.put("java.naming.factory.initial","com.sun.jndi.cosnaming.CNCtxFactory");
env.put("java.naming.provider.url", "iiop://localhost:1091");
Context ic = new InitialContext(env);
SellerHome shome= new SellerHome("seller");
ic.rebind("seller", shome);
```

IIOP Client.   On the client side, the RMI lookup is changed to use an instance of the `InitialContext` in place of RMI `Naming.lookup`. The returned object is mapped to the requested object by using the `narrow` method of the `javax.rmi.PortableRemoteObject` class. `PortableRemoteObject` replaces `UnicastRemoteObject` that was previously available in the RMI server code.

Old RMI code:
```
//API Ref: static Remote lookup(String rminame)
SellerHome shome = (SellerHome)Naming.lookup("rmi://appserver:1090/seller");
```

New RMI code:
```
Hashtable env = new Hashtable();
env.put("java.naming.factory.initial", "com.sun.jndi.cosnaming.CNCtxFactory");
env.put("java.naming.provider.url", iiop://localhost:1091");
Context ic = new InitialContext(env);
SellerHome shome =
//API Ref: static object narrow(Object narrowFrom, Class narrowTo
        (SellerHome)PortableRemoteObject.narrow(ic.lookup("seller"), SellerHome)
```

The `PortableRemoteObject` replaces `UnicastRemoteObject` previously available in the RMI server code. The RMI code would either extend `UnicastRemoteObject` or call the `exportObject` method from the `UnicastRemoteObject` class. The `PortableRemoteObject` also contains an equivalent `exportObject` method. In the current implementation, it is best to explicitly remove unused objects by calling `PortableRemoteObject.unexportObject`.

Improving Lookup Performance

When you run your application, if you find it would be faster to walk the object to the other computer on a floppy, you have a network configuration problem. The source of the problem is how host names and IP addresses are resolved, and there is a workaround.

RMI and other naming services use the `InetAddress` class to obtain resolved host name and IP addresses. `InetAddress` caches look up results to improve subsequent calls, but when it is passed a new IP address or host name, it performs a cross-reference between the IP address and the host name to prevent address spoofing. If you supply the host name as an IP address, `InetAddress` still tries to verify the name of the host. To work around this problem, include the host name and IP address in a `hosts` file on the client.

Unix Systems.   On Unix, the host file is usually `/etc/hosts`.

Windows.   On Windows 95 or 98, the `hosts` file is `c:\windows\hosts`, (`hosts.sam` is a sample file). On Windows NT, the `hosts` file is `c:\winnt\system32\drivers\etc\hosts`. All you do is put these lines in the host file. The `myserver1` and `myserver2` entries are the hosts running the remote server and `rmiregistry`.

```
127.0.0.1  localhost
129.1.1.1  myserver1
129.1.1.2  myserver2
```

RMI Registration Server

RMI API enables client and server communications over the Net between programs written in the Java programming language. The Enterprise JavaBeans server transparently implements the necessary RMI code so the client program can reference the enterprise beans running on the server and access them as if they are running locally to the client program.

Having RMI built into the Enterprise JavaBeans server is very convenient and saves you coding time, but if you need to use advanced RMI features or integrate RMI with an existing application, you need to override the default RMI implementation and write your own RMI code.

This section replaces the container-managed `RegistrationBean` from the section How Enterprise Beans Are Used in the Example (from Chapter 2) with an RMI-based registration server. The container-managed `SellerBean` (Chapter 2) is also changed to call the new RMI registration server using a Java 2 RMI lookup call.

About RMI

The RMI API lets you access a remote server object from a client program by making simple method calls on the server object. While other distributed architectures for accessing remote server objects such as Distributed Component

Object Model (DCOM) and Common Object Request Broker Architecture (CORBA) return references to the remote object, the RMI API not only returns references, but provides these additional benefits.

- The RMI API handles remote object references (call by reference) and can also return a copy of the object (call by value).
- If the client program does not have local access to the class from which a local or remote object was instantiated, RMI services can download the class file.

Serialization and Data Marshaling.   To transfer objects, the RMI API uses the Serialization API to wrap (marshal) and unwrap (unmarshal) the objects. To marshal an object, the Serialization API converts the object to a stream of bytes, and to unmarshal an object, the Serialization API converts a stream of bytes into an object. You can find more informationon data marshaling in Data Marshaling (page 73).

RMI over IIOP.   One of the initial disadvantages to RMI was that its sole reliance on the Java platform to write the interfaces made integration into existing legacy systems difficult. However, RMI over IIOP discussed in the section Lookup Services earlier in this chapter lets RMI communicate with any system or language that CORBA supports.

If you combine improved integration with the ability of RMI to burrow through firewalls using HTTP firewall proxying, you might find distributing your business logic using RMI is easier than a socket-based solution.

NOTE   Transferring code and data are key parts of the Jini System software specification. In fact, adding a discovery and join service to the RMI services would create something very similar to what you get in the Jini architecture.

RMI in the Auction Application

The RMI-based `RegistrationServer` (RMI) has the following new methods:

- A new `create` method for creating a new user.
- A new `find` method for finding a user.
- A new `search` method for the custom search of users in the database.

The new custom search passes results back to the calling client by way of an RMI callback. The RMI callback custom search is similar to the finder methods used in the bean- and container-managed examples from Auction House Application (Chapter 2) and Data and Transaction Management (Chapter 3), except in the RMI version, it can take more time to generate the results because the remote registration server calls a remote method exported by the RMI-based `SellerBean` (RMI) client.

If the calling client is written in the Java programming language, and is not, for example, a Web page, the server can update the client as soon as the results are ready. But, the HTTP protocol used in most browsers does not allow results to be pushed to the client without a request for those results. This means the resulting Web page is not created until the results are ready, which can add a small delay.

Class Overview.   The two main classes in the RMI-based auction implementation are `SellerBean` (RMI) and `RegistrationServer` (RMI). `SellerBean` is called from `AuctionServlet` (RMI) to insert an auction item into the database and check for low account balances.

The example models the Enterprise JavaBeans architecture in that a user's registration details are separate from the code to create and find the registration details. That is, the user's registration details provided by the `Registration` (RMI) class are separate from the code to create and find a `Registration` object, which is in the `RegistrationHome` (RMI) class.

The remote interface implementation in `RegistrationHome` is bound to the `rmiregistry`. When a client program wants to manipulate a user's registration details, it must first look up the reference to the `RegistrationHome` object in the `rmiregistry`.

File Summary.   All the source code files for the RMI-based example are described in the bullet list below.

- `SellerBean` (RMI): Client program that calls the `Registration-Server.verifypasswd` and `RegistrationServer.findLowCreditAc-counts` remote methods. `SellerBean` also exports its `updateResults` method that `RegistrationServer` calls when it completes its `Registra-tionServer.findLowCreditAccounts` search.

- `RegistrationServer` (RMI): Remote server object that implements the `RegistrationHome` and `Registration` remote interfaces.

- `Registration` (RMI): Remote interface that declares the `getUser`, `ver-ifypasswd`, and other remote methods for managing a user's registration details.

- `RegistrationHome` (RMI): Remote interface that declares the `create`, `findByPrimaryKey`, and `findLowCreditAccounts` remote methods that create or return instances of registration details.

- `RegistrationImpl.java`: The `RegistrationServer` (RMI) source file includes the implementation for the `Registration` remote interface as class `RegistrationImpl`.
- `RegistrationPK` (RMI): Class that represents a user's registration details using just the primary key of the database record.
- `ReturnResults` (RMI): Remote interface that declares the `updateResults` method the `SellerBean` class implements as a callback.
- `AuctionServlet` (RMI): Modified version of the original `AuctionServlet` class where registration accounts are created by calling the RMI `RegistrationServer` directly. The auction servlet also calls the `SellerBean.auditAccounts` method, which returns a list of users with a low account balance.

The `auditAccounts` method is called with the following URL, which does a simple check to verify the request came from the local host.

`http://phoenix.eng.sun.com:7001/AuctionServlet?action=auditAccounts`

You also need the following `java.policy` security policy file to grant the permissions needed to run the example on the Java 2 Platform.

```
grant {
  permission java.net.SocketPermission "*:1024-65535", "connect,accept,resolve";
  permission java.net.SocketPermission "*:80", "connect";
  permission java.lang.RuntimePermission "modifyThreadGroup";
  permission java.lang.RuntimePermission "modifyThread";
};
```

Most RMI applications need the two socket permissions for socket and HTTP access to the specified ports. The two thread permissions were listed in a stack trace as being needed for the `RegistrationImpl` class to create a new inner thread.

In the Java 2 platform, when a program does not have all the permissions it needs, the Java virtual machine generates a stack trace that lists the permissions that need to be added to the security policy file. See Signed Applets and Security Managers (page 305) for more information on this and other security topics.

Compile the Example.   Before describing the RMI-based code for the above classes, here is the command sequence to compile the example on the Unix and Win32 platforms:

Unix:
```
javac registration/Registration.java
javac registration/RegistrationPK.java
```

```
javac registration/RegistrationServer.java
javac registration/ReturnResults.java
javac seller/SellerBean.java
rmic -d . registration.RegistrationServer
rmic -d . registration.RegistrationImpl
rmic -d . seller.SellerBean
```

Win32:
```
javac registration\Registration.java
javac registration\RegistrationPK.java
javac registration\RegistrationServer.java
javac registration\ReturnResults.java javac seller\SellerBean.java
rmic -d . registration.RegistrationServer
rmic -d . registration.RegistrationImpl
rmic -d . seller.SellerBean
```

Start the RMI Registry.   Because you are using your own RMI code, you have to explicitly start the RMI Registry so the SellerBean object can find the remote enterprise beans. The RegistrationServer uses the RMI Registry to register or bind enterprise beans that can be called remotely. The SellerBean client contacts the registry to look up and get references to the remote AuctionItem and Registration enterprise beans.

Because RMI allows code and data to be transferred, you must be sure the system classloader does not load extra classes that could be mistakenly sent to the client. In this example, extra classes would be the stub and skel class files and the RegistrationSever and RegistrationImpl classes. To prevent them being mistakenly sent, they should not appear anywhere in the CLASSPATH when you start the RMI Registry, and because the current path could be included automatically, you need to start the RMI Registry away from the code workspace, too.

The following commands prevent the sending of extra classes by unsetting the CLASSPATH before starting the RMI Registry on the default 1099 port. You can specify a different port by adding the port number as follows: rmiregistry 4321 &. If you specify a different port number, you must specify the same port number in both your client lookup and server rebind calls.

Unix:
```
export CLASSPATH=""
rmiregistry &
```

Win32:
```
unset CLASSPATH
start rmiregistry
```

Start the Remote Server.   Once the rmiregistry is running, you can start the remote server, RegistrationServer. The RegistrationServer program

registers the name `registration2` with the `rmiregistry` name server, and any
client can use this name to retrieve a reference to the remote server object, `Reg-
istrationHome`.

To run the example, copy the `RegistrationServer` and `RegistrationImpl`
classes and the associated stub classes to a remotely accessible area and start
the server program.

Unix:
```
cp *_Stub.class /home/zelda/public_html/registration
cp RegistrationImpl.class /home/zelda/public_html/registration
cd /home/zelda/public_html/registration
java -Djava.server.hostname=phoenix.sun.com registration.RegistrationServer
```

Windows:
```
copy *_Stub.class  \home\zelda\public_html\registration
copy RegistrationImpl.class  \home\zelda\public_html\registration
cd \home\zelda\public_html\registration
java -Djava.server.hostname=phoenix.sun.com registration.RegistrationServer
```

The following key properties are used to configure RMI servers and clients.
These properties can be set inside the program or supplied as command line
properties to the Java virtual machine.

- The `java.rmi.server.codebase` property specifies where the publicly
  accessible classes are located. On the server this can be a simple file URL
  to point to the directory or JAR file that contains the classes. If the URL
  points to a directory, the URL must terminate with a file separator character, "/". If you are not using a file URL, you will either need an HTTP
  server to download the remote classes or have to manually deliver the
  remote client stub and remote interface classes in, for example, a JAR file.

- The `java.rmi.server.hostname` property is the complete host name of
  the server where the publicly accessible classes reside. This is only
  needed if the server has problems generating a fully qualified name by
  itself.

- The `java.rmi.security.policy` property specifies the policy file with
  the permissions needed to run the remote server object and access the
  remote server classes for download.

Establishing Remote Communications

Client programs communicate with each other through the server. The server
program consists of three files. The `Registration.java` and `Registra-
tionHome.java` remote interface files define the methods that can be called
remotely, and the `RegistrationServer.java` class file defines the `Registra-
tionServer` and `RegistrationImpl` classes that implement the methods.

To establish remote communications, both the client and server programs need to access the remote interface classes. The server needs the interface classes to generate the interface implementation, and the client uses the remote interface class to call the remote server method implementation. For example, `Seller-Bean` creates a reference to `RegistrationHome`, the interface, and not `RegistrationServer`, the implementation, when it needs to create a user registration.

Besides the server interfaces and classes, you need stub and skeleton classes to establish remote communications. The stub and skeleton classes needed in this example are generated when you run the `rmic` compiler command on the `RegistrationServer` and `SellerBean` classes.

The generated `SellerBean`, `SellerBean_Stub.class`, and `SellerBean_Skel.class` files are needed for the callback from the server to the `SellerBean` client. It is the `_Stub.class` file on the client that marshals data to and unmarshals it from the server, while the `_Skel.class` class does the same for the server.

NOTE In the Java 2 platform, the server side, `_Skel.class` file is not used.

Data Marshaling. An example of marshaling and unmarshaling data is when you call the `RegistrationHome.create` method from `SellerBean`, this call is forwarded to the `RegistrationServer_Stub.create` method. The `RegistrationServer_Stub.create` method wraps the method arguments and sends a serialized stream of bytes to the `RegistrationServer_Skel.create` method.

As shown in Figure 4.2, the `RegistrationServer_Skel.create` method unwraps the serialized bytestream, recreates the arguments to the original `RegistrationHome.create` call, and returns the result of calling the real `RegistrationServer.create` method back along the same route, but this time wrapping the data on the server side.

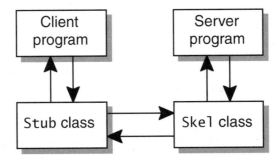

Figure 4.2 Data marshaling

Marshaling and unmarshaling data is not without its complications. The first issue is that serialized objects might be incompatible across JDK releases. A Serialized object has an identifier stored with the object that ties the serialized object to its release. If the RMI client and server complain about incompatible serial IDs, you might need to generate backward-compatible stubs and skeletons using the -vcompat option to the rmic compiler. Another issue is not all objects are serialized by default.

Fortunately, in the Java 2 Platform the Collections API offers alternatives to previously unmarshalable objects. In this example, an ArrayList from the Collections API replaces the Vector. If the Collections API is not an option for you, you can create a wrapper class that extends Serializable and provides readObject and writeObject method implementations to convert the object into a bytestream.

RegistrationServer Class

The RegistrationServer (RMI) class extends java.rmi.server.UnicastRemoteObject and implements the create, findByPrimaryKey, and findLowCreditAccounts methods declared in the RegistrationHome interface. The RegistrationServer.java source file also includes the implementation for the Registration remote interface as class RegistrationImpl. RegistrationImpl also extends UnicastRemoteObject.

Exporting a Remote Object.   Any object you want to be accessible remotely needs to either extend java.rmi.server.UnicastRemoteObject or use the exportObject method from the UnicastRemoteObject class. If you extend UnicastRemoteObject, you also get the equals, toString and hashCode methods for the exported object.

Passing by Value and Passing by Reference.   Although the RegistrationImpl class is not bound to the registry, it is still referenced remotely because it is associated with the RegistrationHome return results. Because RegistrationImpl extends UnicastRemoteObject, its results are passed by reference, and so only one copy of that user's registration bean exists in the Java virtual machine at any one time.

In the case of reporting results such as in the RegistrationServer.findLowCreditAccounts method, the RegistrationImpl class copy of the remote object could be used instead. By simply not extending UnicastRemoteObject in the RegistrationImpl class definition, a new Registration object would be returned for each request. In effect the values were passed, but not the reference to the object on the server.

Distributed Garbage Collection.   Using remote references to objects on the server from a client outside the server's garbage collector introduces some potential problems with memory leaks. How does the server know it is holding onto a reference to a `Registration` object that is no longer being used by any clients because they aborted or a network connection was dropped?

To avoid potential memory leaks on the server from clients, RMI uses a leasing mechanism when giving out references to exported objects. When exporting an object, the Java virtual machine increases the count for the number of references to this object and sets an expiration time, or lease time, for the new reference to this object.

When the lease expires, the reference count of this object is decreased and if it reaches 0, the object is set for garbage collection by the Java virtual machine. It is up to the client that maintains this weak reference to the remote object to renew the lease if it needs the object beyond the lease time. A weak reference is a way to refer to an object in memory without keeping it from being garbage collected.

This lease-time value is a configurable property measured in milliseconds. If you have a fast network, you could shorten the default value and create a large number of transient object references. The following code sets the lease time-out to 2 minutes.

```
Property prop = System.getProperties();
prop.put("java.rmi.dgc.leaseValue", 120000);
```

The `create` and `findByPrimaryKey` methods are practically identical to the other versions of the `Registration` Server. The main difference is that on the server side, the registration record is referenced as `RegistrationImpl`, which is the implementation of `Registration`. On the client side, `Registration` is used instead.

The `findLowCreditAccounts` method builds an `ArrayList` of serializable `RegistrationImpl` objects and calls a remote method in the `SellerBean` class to pass the results back. The results are generated by an inner `Thread` class so the method returns before the results are complete. The `SellerBean` object waits for the `updateAccounts` method to be called before displaying the HTML page. In a client written with the Java programming language, it would not need to wait, but could display the update in real time.

```
public class RegistrationServer extends UnicastRemoteObject
                            implements RegistrationHome {
  public registration.RegistrationPK create(String theuser,
        String password, String emailaddress, String creditcard)
        throws registration.CreateException{
```

```
  double balance=0;
  Connection con = null;
  PreparedStatement ps = null;;

  try {
    con=getConnection();
    ps=con.prepareStatement("insert into registration (theuser, password,
          emailaddress, creditcard, balance) values (?, ?, ?, ?, ?)");
    ps.setString(1, theuser);
    ps.setString(2, password);
    ps.setString(3, emailaddress);
    ps.setString(4, creditcard);
    ps.setDouble(5, balance);

    if (ps.executeUpdate() != 1) {
      throw new CreateException ();//JDBC did not create any row;
    }
    RegistrationPK primaryKey = new RegistrationPK();
    primaryKey.setUser(theuser);
    return primaryKey;
  } catch (CreateException ce) {
    throw ce;
  } catch (SQLException sqe) {
    throw new CreateException ();
  } finally {
    try {
        ps.close();
        con.close();
    } catch (Exception ignore) {
      //Ignore the exception as we are no longer interested
      //in this connection
    }
  }
}
public registration.Registration findByPrimaryKey(
                              registration.RegistrationPK pk)
                              throws registration.FinderException {
  //Return a Registration object that is created from reading
  //values from the database by calling refresh()
  if ((pk == null) || (pk.getUser() == null)) {
    throw new FinderException ();
  }
  return(refresh(pk));
}

private Registration refresh(RegistrationPK pk) throws FinderException {
  //Read the appropriate registration fields from the database
  //based on the database item that the primary key (pk) contains
  if(pk == null) {
    throw new FinderException ();
  }
  Connection con = null;
  PreparedStatement ps = null;
  try {
    con=getConnection();
```

```
        ps=con.prepareStatement("select password, emailaddress, creditcard,
                            balance from registration where theuser = ?");
        ps.setString(1, pk.getUser());
        ps.executeQuery();
        ResultSet rs = ps.getResultSet();
        if(rs.next()) {
          RegistrationImpl reg=null;
          try{
            reg= new RegistrationImpl();
          }catch (RemoteException e) {}
            reg.theuser = pk.getUser();
            reg.password = rs.getString(1);
            reg.emailaddress = rs.getString(2);
            reg.creditcard = rs.getString(3);
            reg.balance = rs.getDouble(4);
            return reg;
        } else{
          throw new FinderException ();
        }
      } catch (SQLException sqe) {
            throw new FinderException();
      } finally {
        try {
          ps.close();
          con.close();
        } catch (Exception ignore) {}
      }
    }

    public void findLowCreditAccounts(final ReturnResults client)
                                      throws FinderException {
      //This method finds accounts with less than 3 dollars in
      //a US domain. It then creates a RegistrationImpl object and
      //calls a callback method called updateResults from the
      //ReturnResults class. It runs as a thread so the client
      //does not have to block to wait for the results to return
      Runnable bgthread = new Runnable() {
        public void run() {
          Connection con = null;
          ResultSet rs = null;
          PreparedStatement ps = null;
          ArrayList ar = new ArrayList();
          try {
            con=getConnection();
            ps=con.prepareStatement("select theuser,
                    balance from registration where balance < ?");
            ps.setDouble(1, 3.00);
            ps.executeQuery();
            rs = ps.getResultSet();
            RegistrationImpl reg=null;
            while (rs.next()) {
              try {
                reg= new RegistrationImpl();
              } catch (RemoteException e) {}
                reg.theuser = rs.getString(1);
```

```
                  reg.balance = rs.getDouble(2);
                  ar.add(reg);
              }
            rs.close();
            client.updateResults(ar);
          } catch (Exception e) {
            System.out.println("findLowCreditAccounts: "+e);
            return;
          }
          finally {
            try {
              if(rs != null) {
                rs.close();
              }
              if(ps != null) {
                ps.close();
              }
              if(con != null) {
                con.close();
              }
            }catch (Exception ignore) {}
        }
      } //run
    };
    Thread t = new Thread(bgthread);
    t.start();
  }
```

The main method loads the JDBC pool driver. This version uses the Postgres database, installs the RMISecurityManager, and contacts the RMI registry to bind the RegistrationHome remote object to the name registration2. It does not need to bind the remote interface, Registration, because that class is loaded when it is referenced by RegistrationHome.

By default, the server uses port 1099. If you want to use a different port number, you can add it to the machine name with a colon as follows: phoenix:4321. If you change the port here, you must start the RMI Registry with the same port number.

The main method also installs a RMIFailureHandler. If the server fails to create a server socket, the failure handler returns true, which instructs the RMI server to retry the operation.

```
public static void main(String[] args){
  try {
    new pool.JDCConnectionDriver("postgresql.Driver",
                        "jdbc:postgresql:ejbdemo","postgres", "pass");
  } catch (Exception e){
    System.out.println("error in loading JDBC driver");
    System.exit(1);
  }
  try {
```

```
              Properties env=System.getProperties();
              env.put("java.rmi.server.codebase",
                              "http://phoenix.sun.com/registration");
              RegistrationServer rs= new RegistrationServer();
//API Ref: static SecurityManager getSecurityManager()
          if(System.getSecurityManager() == null ) {
//API Ref: static SecurityManager setSecurityManager(SecurityManager s)
              System.setSecurityManager(new RMISecurityManager());
          }
//API Ref: static void setFailureHandler(RMIFailureHandler fh)
          RMISocketFactory.setFailureHandler(new RMIFailureHandlerImpl());
//API Ref: static void rebind(String rminame, Remote obj)
          Naming.rebind("//phoenix.sun.com/registration2",rs);
      } catch (Exception e) {
        System.out.println("Exception thrown "+e);
      }
    } //End of Main
  class RMIFailureHandlerImpl implements RMIFailureHandler {
    public boolean failure(Exception ex ){
      System.out.println("exception "+ex+" caught");
      return true;
    }
  }
```

Registration Interface

The Registration (RMI) (page 169) interface declares the methods implemented by the RegistrationImpl class in the RegistrationServer.java source file.

```
package registration;

import java.rmi.*;
import java.util.*;

public interface Registration extends Remote {
  boolean verifyPassword(String password) throws RemoteException;
  String getEmailAddress() throws RemoteException;
  String getUser() throws RemoteException;
  int adjustAccount(double amount) throws RemoteException;
  double getBalance() throws RemoteException;
}
```

RegistrationHome Interface

The RegistrationHome (RMI) interface declares the methods implemented by the RegistrationServer class. These methods mirror the Home interface defined in the Enterprise JavaBeans example. The findLowCreditAccounts method takes a remote interface as its only parameter.

```
package registration;

import java.rmi.*;
import java.util.*;
```

```
public interface RegistrationHome extends Remote {
  RegistrationPK create(String theuser, String password, String emailaddress,
            String creditcard) throws CreateException, RemoteException;
  Registration findByPrimaryKey(RegistrationPK theuser)
            throws FinderException, RemoteException;
  public void findLowCreditAccounts(ReturnResults rr)
            throws FinderException, RemoteException;
}
```

ReturnResults Interface

The ReturnResults (RMI) interface declares the method implemented by the
SellerBean class. The updateResults method is called from Registration-
Server to return data and frees the client from blocking while the results are
generated.

```
package registration;
import java.rmi.*;
import java.util.*;

public interface ReturnResults extends Remote {
  public void updateResults(ArrayList results)
            throws FinderException, RemoteException;
}
```

SellerBean Class

The SellerBean (RMI) class includes the callback method implementation
and calls the RegistrationServer object using RMI. The updateResults
method in the SellerBean class is made accessible to other services in the auction application with a call to the UnicastRemoteObject.exportObject
method.

The call to UnicastRemoteObject in this example makes all public methods in
the SellerBean class available to other RMI clients. When the auction administrator wishes to retrieve the list of accounts that have a low balance, the Sell-
erBean.auditAccounts method is called, which calls the remote RMI method
findLowCreditAccounts from the RegistrationServer and waits on a Boolean object called ready.

When the remote findLowCreditAccounts method has finished processing the
search results, it calls the updateResults method from the RMI exported SellerBean. The updateResults method updates ArrayList of Auction user IDs
from the passed-in value and notifies all methods waiting on the Boolean object
ready that the results have been updated. This enables the auditAccounts
method to continue and forward the results to the Auction administrator.

```
package seller;

import java.rmi.RemoteException;
```

```java
import java.rmi.*;
import javax.ejb.*;
import java.util.*;
import java.text.NumberFormat;
import java.io.Serializable;
import javax.naming.*;
import auction.*;
import registration.*;
import java.rmi.server.UnicastRemoteObject;
import java.util.ArrayList;

public class SellerBean implements SessionBean, ReturnResults {
  protected SessionContext ctx;
  javax.naming.Context ectx;
  Hashtable env = new Hashtable();
  Boolean ready=new Boolean("false");
  ArrayList returned;

  public int insertItem(String seller, String password, String description,
                        int auctiondays, double startprice, String summary)
                        throws RemoteException {
    //Insert an item into the Auction items for sale. First
    //the seller details are verified with the Registration Database
    //before calling the AuctionItem Bean.
    try {
      RegistrationHome regRef = (RegistrationHome)Naming.lookup(
                                "//phoenix.sun.com/registration2");
      RegistrationPK rpk= new RegistrationPK();
      rpk.setUser(seller);
      Registration newseller = (
      Registration)regRef.findByPrimaryKey(rpk);
      if ((newseller == null) || (!newseller.verifyPassword(password))) {
        return(Auction.INVALID_USER);
      }
      AuctionItemHome home = (AuctionItemHome) ectx.lookup("auctionitems");
      AuctionItem ai = home.create(seller, description, auctiondays,
                                   startprice, summary);
      if (ai == null) {
        return Auction.INVALID_ITEM;
       } else{
        return(ai.getId());
       }
    } catch(Exception e){
      System.out.println("insert problem="+e);
      return Auction.INVALID_ITEM;
    }
  }
  public void updateResults(java.util.ArrayList ar) throws RemoteException {
    //Method called from remote rmi client as a callback
    returned=ar;
    synchronized(ready) {
      ready.notifyAll();
    }
  }
```

```java
    public ArrayList auditAccounts() {
      //Call the findLowCreditAccounts method from the RegistrationServer
      //and wait for the results to be sent via the updateResults method
      try {
        RegistrationHome regRef = (RegistrationHome)Naming.lookup(
                          "//phoenix.eng.sun.com/registration2");
        regRef.findLowCreditAccounts(this);
        synchronized(ready) {
          try {
            ready.wait();
          } catch (InterruptedException e){}
        }
        return (returned);
      } catch (Exception e) {
        System.out.println("error in creditAudit "+e);
      }
      return null;
    }

    public void ejbCreate() throws javax.ejb.CreateException,
                                              RemoteException {
      //Initialize the Bean by creating the RMI connection
      //and exporting this object to the rmi registry.
      env.put(javax.naming.Context.INITIAL_CONTEXT_FACTORY,
              "weblogic.jndi.TengahInitialContextFactory");
      try {
        ectx = new InitialContext(env);
      } catch (NamingException e) {
        System.out.println("problem contacting EJB server");
        throw new javax.ejb.CreateException();
      }
      Properties env=System.getProperties();
      env.put("java.rmi.server.codebase",
              "http://phoenix.sun.com/registration");
      env.put("java.security.policy","java.policy");
      UnicastRemoteObject.exportObject(this);
    }
    public void setSessionContext(SessionContext ctx) throws RemoteException {
      this.ctx = ctx;
    }
    public void unsetSessionContext() throws RemoteException {
      ctx = null;
    }
    public void ejbRemove() {}
    public void ejbActivate() throws RemoteException {
      System.out.println("activating seller bean");
    }
    public void ejbPassivate() throws RemoteException {
      System.out.println("passivating seller bean");
    }
}
```

Common Object Request Broker Architecture

Both the RMI and Enterprise JavaBeans auction application implementations use the Java programming language to implement the different auction service tiers. However, you might need to integrate with applications written in C, C++, or other languages and running on a myriad of operating systems and machines.

One way to integrate with other applications is to transmit data in a common format such as eight-bit characters over a TCP/IP socket. The disadvantage is you have to spend a fair amount of time deriving a messaging protocol and mapping the various data structures to and from the common transmission format so the data can be sent and received over the TCP/IP connection.

This is exactly where CORBA and its Interface Definition Language (IDL) can help. IDL provides a common format to represent an object that can be distributed to other applications. The other applications might not even understand objects, but as long as they can provide a mapping between the common IDL format and their own data representations, the applications can share data.

This section describes the Java programming language to IDL mapping scheme, and how to replace the original container-managed `RegistrationBean` with its CORBA server equivalent. The `SellerBean` and `AuctionServlet` classes are changed to interoperate with the CORBA `RegistrationServer` program.

IDL Mapping Scheme

Many programming languages provide a mapping between their data types to the common denominator IDL format, and the Java programming language is no exception. The Java programming language can send objects defined by IDL to other CORBA distributed applications, and it can receive objects defined by IDL from other CORBA distributed applications.

This section describes the Java language to IDL mapping scheme and, where appropriate, discusses issues you should take into consideration.

Quick Reference

Tables 4.1 through 4.3 are quick reference tables of the Java programming language to CORBA IDL data types, and the runtime exceptions thrown when conversions fail. Data types in these tables that need explanation are covered next.

Table 4.1 Java Data Type	Table 4.2 IDL Format	Table 4.3 Run-Time Exception
byte	octet	
boolean	boolean	
char	char	DATA_CONVERSION
char	wchar	
double	double	
float	float	
int	long	
int	unsigned long	
long	long long	
long	unsigned long long	
short	short	
short	unsigned short	
java.lang.String	string	DATA_CONVERSION
java.lang.String	wstring	MARSHAL

Unsigned Values.   The primitive types byte, short, int, and long are represented by 8-bit, 16-bit, 32-bit, and 64-bit two's-complement integers. So, a Java short value represents the range -2^{15} to $2^{15}-1$ or $-32,768$ to $32,767$ inclusive. The equivalent signed IDL type for a short, matches that range, but the unsigned IDL short type uses the range 0 to 2^{16} or 0 to 65,535.

This means that in the case of a short, if an unsigned short value greater than 32,767 is passed to a program written in the Java programming language, the short value is represented in the Java programming language as a negative number. This can cause confusion in boundary tests for a value greater than 32,767 or less than 0.

IDL char Types.   The Java programming language uses 16-bit unicode, but the IDL char and string types are 8-bit characters. You can map a Java char to an 8-bit IDL char to transmit multibyte characters if you use an array to do it. However, the IDL wide char type wchar is specifically designed for languages with multibyte characters and allocates a fixed number of bytes as needed to contain that language set for each and every letter.

When mapping between the Java programming language char type and the IDL char type, a DATA_CONVERSION exception is thrown if the character does not fit into eight bits.

IDL string Types.   The IDL string type can be thought of as a sequence of IDL char types, and also raises the DATA_CONVERSION exception. The IDL wstring type is equivalent to a sequence of wchars terminated by a wchar NULL.

An IDL string and wstring type can either have a fixed size or no maximum defined size. If you try to map a java.lang.String to a fixed size or bounded IDL string and the java.lang.String is too large, a MARSHAL exception is raised.

Setting Up IDL Mappings.   Java programming language to IDL mappings are placed in a file with an .idl extension. The file is compiled so it can be accessed by CORBA programs that need to send and receive data. This section explains how to construct the mappings for package statements and the Java data types. The section CORBA in the Auction Application (page 89) describes how to use this information to set up an IDL mapping file for the CORBA Registration server.

Java Packages and Interfaces.   Java package statements are equivalent to the module type in IDL. The module types can be nested, which results in generated Java classes being created in nested subdirectories. IDL is compiled and the compiler maps IDL interfaces to Java interfaces.

For example, if a CORBA program contains this package statement:

```
package registration;
```

the mappings file would have this IDL module mapping for it:

```
module registration {
};
```

If a CORBA program contains a package hierarchy like this

```
package registration.corba;
```

the equivalent IDL module mapping is this:

```
module registration {
  module corba {
  };
};
```

Distributed classes are defined as Java interfaces and map to the IDL interface type. IDL does not define access such as public or private as you find in the Java programming language. It does, however, allow inheritance from other interfaces. This example adds the Java Registration interface to an IDL registration module.

```
module registration {
  interface Registration {
  };
}
```

This example adds the Java `Registration` interface to an IDL registration module, and indicates the `Registration` interface inherits from the `User` interface.

```
module registration {
    interface Registration: User {
    };
}
```

Java Methods. IDL operations map to Java methods. The IDL operation looks similar to a Java method except there is no concept of access control. You also have to tell the IDL compiler which parameters are `in`, `inout`, or `out`. An `inout` parameter is marshaled four times, and `in` and `out` parameters are marshaled twice. Because marshling takes time, you want to specify the parameters exactly. Specifying parameters to be `inout` when they really are not will only generate a lot of time consuming code.

- `in`: parameter is passed into the method but not changed.
- `inout`: parameter is passed into the method and might be returned changed.
- `out`: parameter might be returned changed.

This IDL mapping includes the `Registration` and `RegistrationHome` interface methods to IDL operations using one IDL module type.

```
module registration {
  interface Registration {
    boolean verifyPassword(in string password);
    string getEmailAddress();
    string getUser();
    long adjustAccount(in double amount);
    double getBalance();
  };
  interface RegistrationHome {
    Registration findByPrimaryKey( in RegistrationPK
                                    theuser) raises (FinderException);
  }
}
```

Java Arrays. Arrays in the Java programming language are mapped to the IDL array or IDL sequence type using a type definition. This example maps the Java array `double balances[10]` to an IDL array type of the same size.

```
typedef double balances[10];
```

These examples map the Java array `double balances[10]` to an IDL sequence type. The first `typedef` sequence is an example of an unbounded sequence, and the second `typedef` sequence has the same size as the array.

```
typedef sequence<double> balances;
typedef sequence<double,10> balances;
```

Java Exception.   Java exceptions are mapped to IDL exceptions. Operations use IDL exceptions by including the `raises` keyword. This example maps the `CreateException` from the auction application to the IDL exception type, and adds the IDL `raises` keyword to the operation as follows. IDL exceptions follow C++ syntax, so instead of throwing an exception (as you would in the Java programming language), the operation raises an exception.

```
exception CreateException {
};
interface RegistrationHome {
  RegistrationPK create(in string theuser, in string password,
    in string emailaddress, in string creditcard)
    raises (CreateException);
}
```

Other IDL Keywords and Types

These other basic IDL types do not have an exact equivalent in the Java programming language. Many of these should be familiar if you have used C or C++. The Java programming language provides a mapping for these types so a program written in the Java programming language can receive data from programs written in C or C++.

- IDL attribute keyword
- IDL `enum`
- IDL `struct`
- IDL `union`
- IDL `Any`
- IDL `Principal`
- IDL `Object`

IDL Attribute.   The required IDL attribute keyword is similar to the `get` and `set` methods used to access fields in the JavaBeans™ software. In the case of a value declared as an IDL attribute, the IDL compiler generates two methods of the same name as the IDL attribute. One method returns the field and the other method sets it. For example, this `attribute definition`:

```
interface RegistrationPK {
  attribute string theuser;
};
```

defines these methods

```
//Return user
  String theuser();
//Set user
  void theuser(String arg);
```

IDL enum.   The Java programming language has an Enumeration class for representing a collection of data. The IDL enum type is different because it is declared as a data type and not a data collection. The IDL enum type is a list of values that can be referenced by name instead of by their position in the list. In the example, you can see that referring to an IDL enum status code by name is more readable than referring to it by its number. This next example maps static final int values in the final class LoginError.

```
enum LoginError { INVALID_USER, WRONG_PASSWORD, TIMEOUT};
```

You can reference the values as you would reference a static field: Login-Error.INVALID_USER:

```
switch (problem) {
  case LoginError.INVALID_USER:
    System.out.println("please login again");
    break;
}
```

IDL struct.   An IDL struct type can be compared to a Java class that has only fields, which is how it is mapped by the IDL compiler. This example declares an IDL struct. Note that IDL types can reference other IDL types. In this example LoginError is from the enum type declared above.

```
struct ErrorHandler {
  LoginError errortype;
  short retries;
};
```

IDL union.   An IDL union can represent one type from a list of types defined for that union. The IDL union maps to a Java class of the same name with a discriminator method used for determining the type of this union.

This example maps the GlobalErrors union to a Java class by the name of GlobalErrors. A default case: DEFAULT could be added to handle any elements that might be in the LoginErrors enum type, and not specified with a case statement here.

```
union GlobalErrors switch (LoginErrors) {
  case: INVALID_USER: string message;
  case: WRONG_PASSWORD: long attempts;
  case: TIMEOUT: long timeout;
};
```

In a program written in the Java programming language, the GlobalErrors union class is created as follows:

```
GlobalErrors ge = new GlobalErrors();
ge.message("please login again");
```

```
//The INVALID_USER value is retrieved like this:
switch (ge.discriminator().value()) {
  case: LoginError.INVALID_USER
    System.out.println(ge.message());
    break;
}
```

Any type. If you do not know what type is going to be passed or returned to an operation, you can use the Any type mapping, which can represent any IDL type. The following operation returns and passes an unknown type:

```
interface RegistrationHome {
  Any customSearch(Any searchField, out count);
};
```

To create a type of Any, first request the type from the Object Request Broker (ORB). To set a value in a type of Any, use an insert_<*type*> method. To retrieve a value, use the extract_<*type*> method. This example requests an object of type Any, and uses the insert<*type*> method to set a value.

```
Any sfield = orb.create_any();
sfield.insert_long(34);
```

The Any type has an assigned TypeCode value that you can query using type().kind().value() on the object. The following example shows a test for the TypeCode double. This example includes a reference to the IDL Type-Code to find out which type the Any object contains. The TypeCode is used for all objects. You can analyze the type of a CORBA object using the _type or type methods as shown here.

```
public Any customSearch(Any searchField, IntHolder count){
  if(searchField.type().kind().value() == TCKind._tk_double){
//Return number of balances greater than supplied amount
    double findBalance=searchField.extract_double();
```

Principal. The Principal type identifies the owner of a CORBA object, for example, a user name. The value can be interrogated from the request_principal field of the CORBA RequestHeader class to make the identification. More comprehensive security and authorization is available in the CORBA security service.

Object. The Object type is a CORBA object. If you need to send Java objects, you have to either translate them into an IDL type or use a mechanism to serialize them when they are transferred.

CORBA in the Auction Application

In this section, the container-managed RegistrationBean from the auction application in Chapter 2 is completely replaced with a standalone CORBA

Registration Server that implements the registration service. The CORBA `RegistrationServer` is built by creating and compiling an IDL mappings file so client programs can communicate with the registration server.

The SellerBean (CORBA) and AuctionServlet (CORBA) sources are updated to look up the CORBA registration server.

CORBA `RegistrationServer` Implementation.   This section describes the `Registration.idl` (CORBA) file, which maps the `RegistrationHome` and `Registration` remote interfaces from the Enterprise JavaBean auction application to their IDL equivalents and shows how to compile the `Registration.idl` file into CORBA registration server classes.

The CORBA registration server implements the `create` and `findByPrimaryKey` methods from the original `RegistrationBean` class, and is enhanced with the following two new methods to help illustrate CORBA callbacks and how to use the Any type.

- `findLowCreditAccounts` (in `ReturnResults` rr), which uses a callback to return a list of accounts with a low balance.

- Any `customSearch` (in Any searchfield, out `long` count), which returns a different search result depending on the search field type submitted.

IDL Mappings File.   Here is the `Registration.idl` (CORBA) file that maps the data types and methods used in the `RegistrationHome` and `Registration` programs to their IDL equivalents.

```
module registration {
  interface Registration {
    boolean verifyPassword(in string password);
    string getEmailAddress();
    string getUser();
    long adjustAccount(in double amount);
    double getBalance();
  };
  interface RegistrationPK {
   attribute string theuser;
  };
  enum LoginError {INVALIDUSER, WRONGPASSWORD, TIMEOUT};
  exception CreateException {
  };
  exception FinderException {
  };
  typedef sequence<Registration> IDLArrayList;
  interface ReturnResults  {
    void updateResults(in IDLArrayList results) raises (FinderException);
  };
  interface RegistrationHome {
    RegistrationPK create(in string theuser, in string password,
```

```
                        in string emailaddress, in string creditcard)
                        raises (CreateException);
        Registration findByPrimaryKey(in RegistrationPK theuser)
                        raises (FinderException);

    void findLowCreditAccounts(in ReturnResults rr) raises (FinderException);
      Any customSearch(in Any searchfield, out long count);
    };
};
```

Compiling the IDL Mappings File. The IDL file has to be converted into Java classes that can be used in the CORBA distributed network. The Java 2 Platform compiles .idl files using the program idltojava. This program will be replaced with the idltoj command. The -fno-cpp arguments indicate there is no C++ compiler installed.

```
idltojava -fno-cpp Registration.idl
```

Other Java IDL compilers should also work, for example, jidl from ORBacus can generate classes that can be used by the Java 2 ORB.

Stubs and Skeletons. CORBA and RMI are similar in that compilation generates a stub file for the client and a skeleton file for the server. As shown in Figure 4.3, the stub (or proxy) and skeleton (or servant) are used to marshal and unmarshal data between the client and server. The skeleton is used by the server. In this example, the IDL RegistrationHome interface mapping generates a _RegistrationHomeImplBase class (the skeleton or servant class) that the generated RegistrationServer class extends.

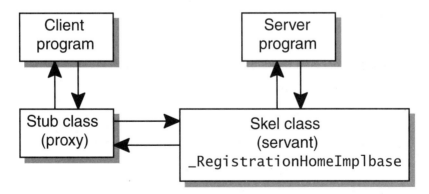

Figure 4.3 Marshaling Data

When requesting a remote CORBA object or calling a remote method, the client call passes through the stub class before reaching the server. This proxy class invokes CORBA requests for the client program. The following example is the code automatically generated for the `RegistrationHomeStub.java` class.

```
org.omg.CORBA.Request r = _request("create");
r.set_return_type(registration.RegistrationPKHelper.type());
org.omg.CORBA.Any _theuser = r.add_in_arg();
```

Object Request Broker

The center of the CORBA distributed network is the Object Request Broker, or ORB. The ORB is involved in marshaling and unmarshaling objects between the client and server. Other services such as the Naming Service and Event Service work with the ORB.

The Java 2 Platform includes an ORB in the distribution called the IDL ORB. This ORB is different from many other ORBs because it does not include a distinct Basic Object Adapter (BOA) or Portable Object Adapter (POA).

An object adapter manages the creation and life cycle of objects in the CORBA distributed space. This can be compared to the container in the Enterprise Java-Beans server managing the life cycle of the session and entity beans.

The `AuctionServlet` (CORBA) and `Seller` (CORBA) programs create and initialize a Java 2 ORB like this:

```
//API Ref: status ORB init(String{} args, Properties props)
    ORB orb = ORB.init(args, null);
```

In the `RegistrationServer` (CORBA) program, the server object to be distributed is bound to the ORB using the `connect` method:

```
    RegistrationServer rs = new RegistrationServer();
//API Ref: void connect(Object object)
    orb.connect(rs);
```

An object connected to an ORB can be removed with the `disconnect` method:

```
//API Ref: void disconnect(Object object)
    orb.disconnect(rs);
```

Once connected to a CORBA server object, the Java 2 ORB keeps the server alive and waits for client requests to the CORBA server.

```
java.lang.Object sync = new java.lang.Object();
synchronized(sync) {
  sync.wait();
}
```

Making the CORBA Server Accessible.   Although this object is now being managed by the ORB, the clients do not yet have a mechanism to find the remote object. This can be solved by binding the CORBA server object to a naming service.

The Java 2 naming service is called `tnameserv`. The naming service by default uses port 900; however, this value can be changed by setting the argument -`ORBInitialPort` port number when starting `tnameserv` or setting the property `org.omg.CORBA.ORBInitialPort` when starting the client and server processes.

```
java.util.Properties props=System.getProperties();
props.put("org.omg.CORBA.ORBInitialPort", "1050");
System.setProperties(props);
ORB orb = ORB.init(args, props);
```

The next lines from the `main` method in the `RegistrationServer` (CORBA) class show how this naming reference is created. The first step is to request the service called `NameService` by calling the `resolve_initial_references` method from the ORB with the value `NameService`. This technique is used to find other services from the ORB, not just the NameService.

The `NamingContext` is retrieved by narrowing the returned `Object` to the `NameComponent` type. The name is built up and bound to the naming service as a list of `NameComponent` elements. The name in this example has a root called `auction` with this object being bound at the next level of the name tree as `RegistrationBean`. The naming scheme could be used to mirror the package and class that the object came from; in this example it could be used to describe that the object was also the class `auction.RegistrationBean`.

```
org.omg.CORBA.Object nameServiceObj = orb.resolve_initial_references(
                              NameService");
NamingContext nctx = NamingContextHelper.narrow(nameServiceObj);
NameComponent[] fullname = new NameComponent[2];
fullname[0] = new NameComponent("auction", "");
fullname[1] = new NameComponent("RegistrationBean", "");
//API Ref: NameComponent(String nameid, String kind)
NameComponent[] tempComponent = new NameComponent[1];
for(int i=0; i < fullname.length-1; i++ ) {
    tempComponent[0]= fullname[i];
    try {
      nctx=nctx.bind_new_context(tempComponent);
    } catch (org.omg.CosNaming.NamingContextPackage.AlreadyBound e){
    //It may already be bound, so ignore
}
tempComponent[0]=fullname[fullname.length-1];
try {
  nctx.rebind(tempComponent, rs);
} catch (Exception e){
  System.out.println("rebind failed"+e);
}
```

Plugging in a New ORB. The Java 2 IDL ORB does not currently include some of the services available in many other commercial ORBs such as security or event notification services. However, you can use another ORB in the

Java 2 run time by configuring two properties and including any necessary object adapter code.

Using a new ORB in the registration server requires the `org.omg.CORBA.ORB-Class` and `org.omg.CORBA.ORBSingletonClass` properties point to the appropriate ORB classes. In this example the ORBacus ORB is used instead of the Java 2 IDL ORB. To use another ORB, the code below should be plugged into the `RegistrationServer.main` method.

In the example code, a `SingletonClass` ORB is used. The `SingletonClass` ORB is not a full ORB and is primarily used as a factory for `TypeCodes`. The call to `ORB.init()` in the last line creates the `Singleton` ORB.

```
Properties props= System.getProperties();
props.put("org.omg.CORBA.ORBClass", "com.ooc.CORBA.ORB");
props.put("org.omg.CORBA.ORBSingletonClass","com.ooc.CORBA.ORBSingleton");
System.setProperties(props);
ORB orb = ORB.init(args, props) ;
```

In the Java 2 IDL, there is no distinct object adapter. As shown in the example code segment below, using the Basic Object Adapter (BOA) from ORBacus requires an explicit cast to the ORBacus ORB. The BOA is notified that the object is ready to be distributed by calling the `impl_is_ready(null)` method.

```
BOA boa = ((com.ooc.CORBA.ORB)orb).BOA_init(args, props);
  ...
boa.impl_is_ready(null);
```

Although both the `ORBSingletonClass` and `ORBClass` ORBs build the object name using `NameComponent`, you have to use a different ORBacus naming service. The `CosNaming.Server` service is started as follows where the `-OAhost` parameter is optional:

```
java com.ooc.CosNaming.Server -OAhost localhost -OAport 1060
```

Once the naming service is started, the server and client programs find the naming service using the IIOP protocol to the host and port named when starting the naming service:

```
java registration.RegistrationServer -ORBservice NameService
                    iiop://localhost:1060/DefaultNamingContext
```

Naming Service Access by CORBA Clients. CORBA clients access the naming service in a similar way to the server, except that instead of binding a name, the client resolves the name built from the `NameComponents`. The `AuctionServlet` and `SellerBean` classes use the following code to look up the CORBA server:

```
//API Ref: NameComponent(String nameid, String kind)
   NameComponent[] fullname = new NameComponent[2];
```

```
fullname[0] = new NameComponent("auction", "");
fullname[1] = new NameComponent("RegistrationBean", "");

RegistrationHome regRef = RegistrationHomeHelper.narrow(nctx.resolve(
                                                    fullname));
```

In the case of the ORBacus ORB, the clients also need a Basic Object Adapter if callbacks are used as in the `SellerBean.auditAccounts` method. The naming context helper is also configured differently for the ORBacus server started earlier:

```
Object obj = ((com.ooc.CORBA.ORB)orb).get_inet_object ("localhost",
                                    1060, "DefaultNamingContext");
NamingContext nctx = NamingContextHelper.narrow(obj);
```

Helper and Holder Classes

References to remote objects in CORBA use a `Helper` class to retrieve a value from that object. A commonly used method is the `Helper narrow` method, which ensures the object is cast correctly.

`Holder` classes hold values returned when using `inout` or `out` parameters in a method. The caller first instantiates the appropriate `Holder` class for that type and passes the `Holder` class to the method call as one of the parameters. On return from the method call, the application retrieves the value that has been changed in the `Holder`.

In the next example, the count of how many occurrences of the search term is held in a instance of an `int` type `Holder` object. The `Holder` object, count is passed to the `customSearch` method where the field called `value` in the `Holder` object is changed on the remote end. On return from the `customSearch` method, the count value is retrieved by accessing the `value` field.

```
//API Ref: IntHolder()
    IntHolder count= new IntHolder();
    sfield=regRef.customSearch(sfield,count);
    System.out.println("count now set to "+count.value);
```

Garbage Collection

Unlike RMI, CORBA does not have a distributed garbage collection mechanism. References to an object are local to the client proxy and the server servant. This means each Java virtual machine is free to reclaim that object and garbage collect it if there are no longer references to it. If an object is no longer needed on the server, the `orb.disconnect(object)` needs to be called to allow the object to be garbage collected.

CORBA Callbacks

The new `findLowCreditAccounts` method is called from the `AuctionServlet` when the user uses the URL `http://localhost:7001/AuctionServlet?action=auditAccounts`. The `AuctionServlet.auditAccounts` method calls the `SellerBean.auditAccounts` method, which returns an `ArrayList` of Registration records.

```
//From file AuctionServlet.java
  private void auditAccounts(ServletOutputStream out,HttpServletRequest
                               request) throws IOException{
//   ...
    SellerHome home = (SellerHome) ctx.lookup("seller");
    Seller si= home.create();
    if(si != null) {
       //Call the auditAccounts method in SellerBean and return
       //an ArrayList of Registration records. Call the getUser
       //and getBalance methods on each Registration Object.
       ArrayList ar=si.auditAccounts();
//API Ref: Interator iterator()
//API Ref: boolean hasNext()
       for(Iterator i=ar.iterator(); i.hasNext();) {
         Registration user=(Registration)(i.next());
         addLine("<TD>"+user.getUser() + "<TD><TD>"+user.getBalance() +
              "<TD><TR>", out);
       }
         addLine("<TABLE>", out);
       }
```

The `SellerBean` object calls the CORBA `RegistrationHome.findLowCreditAccounts` method implemented in the `RegistrationServer` class, and passes a reference to itself as a parameter in the `findLowCreditAccounts` method call. The reference can be passed because the `SellerBean` class implements the `ReturnResults` interface declared in the `Registration.idl` file.

```
//From file SellerBean.java
  public ArrayList auditAccounts() {
    try {
//API Ref: NameComponent(String nameid, String kind)
       NameComponent[] fullname = new NameComponent[2];
       fullname[0] = new NameComponent("auction", "");
       fullname[1] = new NameComponent("RegistrationBean", "");
       RegistrationHome regRef = RegistrationHomeHelper.narrow(
                             nctx.resolve(fullname));
       //Pass a reference to this SellerBean object to the
       //Registration CORBA method findLowCreditAccounts
       regRef.findLowCreditAccounts(this);
       synchronized(ready) {
         try {
           ready.wait();
         } catch (InterruptedException e){}
       }
```

```
        return (returned);
      } catch (Exception e) {
        System.out.println("error in auditAccounts "+e);
      }
      return null;
  }
```

The `RegistrationServer.findLowCreditAccounts` method retrieves user records from the database registration table that have a credit value less than three. It then returns the list of `Registration` records in an `ArrayList` by calling the `SellerBean.updateResults` method to which it has a reference.

```
//From file RegistrationServer.java
  public void findLowCreditAccounts(final ReturnResults client)
                                  throws FinderException {
    //Start a new thread to do the search because it might
    //take a while to complete
    Runnable bgthread = new Runnable() {
      public void run() {
        Connection con = null;
        ResultSet rs = null;
        PreparedStatement ps = null;
        ArrayList ar = new ArrayList();
        try {
          con=getConnection();
          //Search for the records we are interested in using
          //a simple JDBC call
//API Ref: PrepareStatement prepareStatement(String sql)
          ps=con.prepareStatement("select theuser,
                balance from registration where balance < ?");
//API Ref: void setDouble(int index, double doublevalue)
          ps.setDouble(1, 3.00);
          //Execute the prepared statement query
//API Ref: ResultSet executeQuery()
          ps.executeQuery();
          rs = ps.getResultSet();
          RegistrationImpl reg=null;
          while(rs.next()) {
            //Create a Registration object for each row and add each
            //Registration to an ArrayList
            try {
              reg= new RegistrationImpl();
            } catch (Exception e) {
              System.out.println("Problem creating registration record"+e);
            }
//API Ref: String getString(String columnName)
            reg.theuser = rs.getString(1);
//API Ref: double getDouble(String columnName)
            reg.balance = rs.getDouble(2);
//API Ref: boolean add(Object object)
            ar.add(reg);
          }
          rs.close();
```

```
//API Ref: Object[] toArray(Object[] objarray)
         RegistrationImpl[] regarray = (RegistrationImpl [])ar.toArray(
                                     new RegistrationImpl[0]);
         //Convert the ArrayList to an array of RegistrationImpl objects
         //and pass the results back by calling the updateResults method
         //from the SellerBean client
         client.updateResults(regarray);
       } catch (Exception e) {
       System.out.println("findLowCreditAccounts: "+e);
       return;
       } finally {
       try {
         if(rs != null) {
           rs.close();
         }
         if(ps != null) {
           ps.close();
         }
         if(con != null) {
           con.close();
         }
       } catch (Exception ignore) {}
       }
     }//run
   };
  Thread t = new Thread(bgthread);
  t.start();
  }
```

The SellerBean.updateResults method updates the global ArrayList of
Registration records returned by the RegistrationServer object and notifies the SellerBean.auditAccounts method that it can return that ArrayList
of Registration records to the AuctionServlet.

```
//From file SellerBean.java
ArrayList returned =new ArrayList();

  public void updateResults(Registration[] ar)
                             throws registration.FinderException {
     if (ar == null) {
       throw new registration.FinderException();
     }
     try {
       for(int i=0; i< ar.length; i++) {
         returned.add(ar[i]);
       }
     } catch (Exception e) {
       System.out.println("updateResults error:"+e);
       throw new registration.FinderException();
     }
     synchronized(ready) {
       ready.notifyAll();
     }
   }
}
```

Using the Any Type

The `RegistrationServer.customSearch` method uses the IDL Any type to pass in and return results. Users can call the `customSearch` method from the `AuctionServlet` as follows:

```
http://phoenix.sun.com:7001/
AuctionServlet?action=customSearch&searchfield=2
```

The `searchfield` parameter can be set to a number or a string. The `AuctionServlet.customFind` method passes the search field directly to the `SellerBean.customFind` method and retrieves a `String` that is then displayed to the user.

```
//From file AuctionServlet.java
private void customSearch(ServletOutputStream out,HttpServletRequest
                          request) throws IOException{
    String text = "Custom Search";
    String searchField=request.getParameter("searchfield");
    setTitle(out, "Custom Search");
    if(searchField == null ) {
      addLine("Error: SearchField was empty", out);
      out.flush();
      return;
    }
    try {
      addLine("<BR>"+text, out);
      SellerHome home = (SellerHome)ctx.lookup("seller");
      Seller si= home.create();
      if(si != null) {
        //Call customFind method from SellerBean and display results
        String displayMessage=si.customFind(searchField);
        if(displayMessage != null ) {
          addLine(displayMessage+"<BR>", out);
        }
      }
    } catch (Exception e) {
      addLine("AuctionServlet customFind error",out);
      System.out.println("AuctionServlet " + "<customFind>:"+e);
    }
    out.flush();
  }
```

The `SellerBean.customFind` method calls the `RegistrationHome` object implemented in the `RegistrationServer` (CORBA) class, and because the `searchField` might be a number or a string, an object of the CORBA type Any is used to transfer the value.

The convenience of not needing to specify the type of the object incurs an extra cost because special methods are required to set and retrieve values from an object of type Any. The Any object is created by a call to the ORB, `orb.create_any` method.

The `customFind` method also uses an out parameter, `count`, of type `int` that returns the number of records found. The number of records found is retrieved from `count.value` when the `customFind` method returns. The `return` type of the `customFind` method also is type `String` and is described after the code sample.

```java
//From file SellerBean.java
  public String customFind(String searchField)
                             throws javax.ejb.FinderException, RemoteException{
    int total=-1;
    IntHolder count= new IntHolder();
    try {
//API Ref: NameComponent(String nameid, String kind)
      NameComponent[] fullname = new NameComponent[2];
      fullname[0] = new NameComponent("auction", "");
      fullname[1] = new NameComponent(
                        "RegistrationBean", "");
      RegistrationHome regRef =
                  RegistrationHomeHelper.narrow(nctx.resolve(fullname));
      if(regRef == null ) {
        System.out.println("cannot contact RegistrationHome");
        throw new javax.ejb.FinderException();
      }
//API Ref: Any create_any()
      Any sfield=orb.create_any();
      Double balance;
      try {
        //Treat the search value as an account balance. If it cannot
        //be converted to a number then its an email address so send it
        //as a String
//API Ref: static Double valueOf(double doublevalue)
        balance=Double.valueOf(searchField);
        try {
          //Insert the double value held as balance into the Any object
//API Ref: void insert_double(double doublevalue)
          sfield.insert_double(balance.doubleValue());
        } catch (Exception e) {
          return("Problem with search value"+balance);
        }
        sfield=regRef.customSearch(sfield,count);
        //The number of records is available in the count out parameter
        //and in the return object.
        if(sfield != null ) {
          total=sfield.extract_long();
        }
        return(total+" accounts are below optimal level from" +
             count.value+" records");
      } catch (NumberFormatException e) {
        //The value could not be converted to a double so search
        //with the value of type String
//API Ref: void insert_string(String stringvalue)
        sfield.insert_string(searchField);
        Registration reg;
```

```
        //The returned object contains a Registration record stored
        //as a type Any.
        if((reg=RegistrationHelper.extract(
          regRef.customSearch(sfield,count))) != null ) {
            return("Found user "+reg.getUser() +" who has email address "+
                    reg.getEmailAddress());
        } else {
          return("No users found who have email address " + searchField);
        }
      }
    } catch(Exception e){
      System.out.println("customFind problem="+e);
      throw new javax.ejb.FinderException();
    }
  }
}
```

The `return` value from the call to `customFind` is extracted into an object of type Any and the results of the search are then displayed to the user in the Auc-`tionServlet`. For simple types, the `extract_<type>` method of the Any object can be used. However, for the `Registration` type, the `RegistrationHelper` class is used.

```
Registration reg = RegistrationHelper.extract(
                        regRef.customSearch(sfield,count));
```

The `RegistrationServer.customSearch` method determines the type of Object being passed in the `searchField` parameter by checking the `.type().kind().value()` of the Any object.

```
if(searchField.type().kind().value() == TCKind._tk_double)
```

Finally, because the `customSearch` method returns an object of type Any, a call to `orb.create_any()` is required. For simple types like `double`, the `insert_<type>` method is used. For a `Registration` record, the `RegistrationHelper` class is used like this: `RegistrationHelper.insert(returnResults, regarray[0])`.

```
//From file RegistrationServer.java
  public Any customSearch(Any searchField, IntHolder count){
    Any returnResults= orb.create_any();
    int tmpcount=count.value;
    if(searchField.type().kind().value() == TCKind._tk_double){
      // Search database for number of accounts where the balance is
      //less than supplied amount
      double findBalance=searchField.extract_double();
      Connection con = null;
      ResultSet rs = null;
      PreparedStatement ps = null;
      try {
        con=getConnection();
//API Ref: PrepareStatement prepareStatement(String sql)
```

```
                 ps=con.prepareStatement("select count(*) from
                                 registration where balance < ?");
//API Ref: void setDouble(int index, double doublevalue)
                 ps.setDouble(1, findBalance);
//API Ref: ResultSet executeQuery()
                 ps.executeQuery();
                 rs = ps.getResultSet();
//API Ref: boolean next()
                 if(rs.next()) {
//API Ref: int getInt(String ColumnName)
                     tmpcount = rs.getInt(1);
                 }
               count.value=tmpcount;
               rs.close();
             } catch (Exception e) {
               System.out.println("custom search: "+e);
               returnResults.insert_long(-1);
               return(returnResults);
             } finally {
               try {
                 if(rs != null) { rs.close(); }
                 if(ps != null) { ps.close(); }
                 if(con != null) { con.close(); }
               } catch (Exception ignore) {}
             }
               returnResults.insert_long(tmpcount);
               return(returnResults);
         } else if(searchField.type().kind().value() == TCKind._tk_string) {
             // If the any value is of type string then the admin was
             //looking for an email address so return the
             //email addresses that match supplied address
             String findEmail=searchField.extract_string();
             Connection con = null;
             ResultSet rs = null;
             PreparedStatement ps = null;
             ArrayList ar = new ArrayList();
             RegistrationImpl reg=null;
             try {
               con=getConnection();
               ps=con.prepareStatement("select theuser, emailaddress from
                         registration where emailaddress like ?");
               ps.setString(1, findEmail);
               ps.executeQuery();
               rs = ps.getResultSet();
               while (rs.next()) {
                 reg= new RegistrationImpl();
                 reg.theuser = rs.getString(1);
                 reg.emailaddress = rs.getString(2);
                 //Add each entry to an ArrayList in readiness to convert
                 //an array of RegistrationImpl records
                 ar.add(reg);
               }
               rs.close();
             RegistrationImpl[] regarray = (RegistrationImpl [])ar.toArray(
             new RegistrationImpl[0]);
```

```
        RegistrationHelper.insert(returnResults, regarray[0]);
        return(returnResults);
      } catch (Exception e) {
        System.out.println("custom search: "+e);
        return(returnResults);
      }
      finally {
        try {
          if(rs != null) { rs.close(); }
          if(ps != null) { ps.close(); }
          if(con != null) { con.close(); }
        } catch (Exception ignore) {}
      }
  }
  return(returnResults);
}
```

In Conclusion

As you have seen, converting the application to use RMI or CORBA requires very little change to core programs. The main differences are the initialization and naming service. By abstracting these two areas in your application away from the business logic you ease migration between different distributed object architectures for the Java platform.

JDBC Technology

The bean-managed Enterprise JavaBeans auction application with its RMI and CORBA variants has used simple JDBC calls to retrieve and update information from a database using a JDBC connection pool. By default, JDBC database access involves opening a database connection, running SQL commands in a statement, processing the returned results, and closing the database connection.

Overall, the default approach works well for low-volume database access, but how do you manage a large number of requests that update many related tables at once and still ensure data integrity? This section explains how.

JDBC Drivers

The connection to the database is handled by the JDBC Driver class. The Java 2 SDK contains only one JDBC driver, a `jdbc-odbc` bridge that can communicate with an existing Open DataBase Connectivity (ODBC) driver. Other databases need a JDBC driver specific to that database.

To get a general idea of what the JDBC driver does, you can examine the JDC-ConnectionDriver class. The JDCConnectionDriver class implements the java.sql.Driver class and acts as a pass-through driver by forwarding JDBC requests to the real database JDBC Driver. The JDBC driver class is loaded with a call to `Class.forName(drivername)`. These next code lines show how to load three different JDBC driver classes:

```
Class.forName("sun.jdbc.odbc.JdbcOdbcDriver");
Class.forName("postgresql.Driver");
Class.forName("oracle.jdbc.driver.OracleDriver");
```

Each JDBC driver is configured to understand a specific URL so multiple JDBC drivers can be loaded at any one time. When you specify a URL at connect time, the first matching JDBC driver is selected.

The `jdbc-odbc` bridge accepts URLs starting with `jdbc:odbc:` and uses the next field in that URL to specify the data source name. The data source name identifies the particular database scheme you wish to access. The URL can also include more details on how to contact the database and enter the account.

```
//access the ejbdemo tables
  String url = "jdbc:odbc:ejbdemo";
```

This next example contains the Oracle SQL*net information on the particular database called `ejbdemo` on machine `dbmachine`.

```
String url = "jdbc:oracle:thin:user/password@(description=(address_list=(
       address=(protocol=tcp (host=dbmachine)(port=1521)))(source_route=yes)
       (connect_data=(sid=ejbdemo)))";
```

This next example uses `mysql` to connect to the `ejbdemo` database on the local machine. The login user name and password details are also included.

```
String url = "jdbc:mysql://localhost/ejbdemo?user=user;password=pass";
```

JDBC drivers are divided into four types. Drivers may also be categorized as pure Java or thin drivers to indicate if they are used for client applications (pure Java drivers) or applets (thin drivers). Newer drivers are usually Type 3 or 4. The four types are as follows:

Type 1 Drivers. Type 1 JDBC drivers are the bridge drivers such as the `jdbc-odbc` bridge. These drivers rely on an intermediary such as ODBC to transfer the SQL calls to the database. Bridge drivers often rely on native code, although the `jdbc-odbc` library native code is part of the Java 2 virtual machine.

Type 2 Drivers. Type 2 Drivers use the existing database API to communicate with the database on the client. Although Type 2 drivers are faster than Type 1 drivers, Type 2 drivers use native code and require additional permissions to work in an applet. A Type 2 driver might need client-side database code to connect over the network.

Type 3 Drivers.   Type 3 Drivers call the database API on the server. JDBC requests from the client are first proxied to the JDBC Driver on the server to run. Type 3 and 4 drivers can be used by thin clients because they need no native code.

Type 4 Drivers.   The highest level of driver reimplements the database network API in the Java programming language. Type 4 drivers can also be used on thin clients because they also have no native code.

Database Connections

A database connection can be established with a call to the `DriverManager.getConnection` method. The call takes a URL that identifies the database and, optionally, the database login user name and password.

```
//API Ref: static Connection getConnection(String url)
    Connection con = DriverManager.getConnection(url);
//API Ref: static Connection getConnection(String url, String user,
                                           String password)
    Connection con = DriverManager.getConnection(url, "user", "password");
```

After a connection is established, a statement can be run against the database. The results of the statement can be retrieved and the connection closed.

One useful feature of the `DriverManager` class is the `setLogStream` method. You can use this method to generate tracing information to help you diagnose connection problems that would normally not be visible. To generate tracing information, just call the method like this:

```
//API Ref: static void setLogStream(PrintStream out)
    DriverManager.setLogStream(System.out);
```

Connection Pooling (page XX) shows you how to improve the throughput of JDBC connections by not closing the connection once the statement completes. Each JDBC connection to a database incurs overhead in opening a new socket and using the username and password to log into the database. Reusing the connections reduces the overhead. The `Connection Pool` keeps a list of open connections and clears any connections that cannot be reused.

Statements

There are three basic types of SQL statements used in the JDBC API: `CallableStatement`, `Statement`, and `PreparedStatement`. When a `Statement` or `PreparedStatement` is sent to the database, the database driver translates it into a format that the underlying database can recognize.

Callable Statements.   Once you have established a connection to a database, you can use the `Connection.prepareCall` method to create a callable statement. A callable statement lets you execute SQL stored procedures. This next example creates a `CallableStatement` object with three parameters for storing account login information.

```
//API Ref: CallableStatement prepareCall(String sql)
      CallableStatement cs = con.prepareCall("{call accountlogin(?,?,?)}");
//API Ref: void setString(int index, String s)
      cs.setString(1,theuser);
      cs.setString(2,password);
//API Ref: void registerOutParameter(int index, int sqltype)
      cs.registerOutParameter(3,Types.DATE);
      cs.executeQuery();
//API Ref: Date getDate(int index)
      Date lastLogin = cs.getDate(3);
```

Statements.   The `Statement` interface lets you execute a simple SQL statement with no parameters. The SQL instructions are inserted into the `Statement` object when the `Statement.execute<type>` method is called.

Query Statement.   This code segment creates a `Statement` object and calls the `Statement.executeQuery` method to select text from the dba database table. The results of the query are returned in a `ResultSet` object. How to retrieve results from a `ResultSet` object is explained in Result Sets (page XX) below.

```
//API Ref: Statement createStatement()
    Statement stmt = con.createStatement();
//API Ref: int executeQuery(String sql)
    ResultSet results = stmt.executeQuery("SELECT TEXT FROM dba ");
```

Update Statement.   This next code segment creates a `Statement` object and calls the `Statement.executeUpdate` method to add an e-mail address to a table in the dba database table.

```
    String updateString = "INSERT INTO dba VALUES ('some text')";
//API Ref: int executeUpdate(String sql)
    int count = stmt.executeUpdate(updateString);
```

Prepared Statement.   The `PreparedStatement` interface descends from the `Statement` interface and uses a template to create a SQL request. Use a `PreparedStatement` to make multiple database operations where only the values change. The advantage to using a `PreparedStatement` is that the statement is compiled the first time and subsequent calls are optimized by inserting only the changed data.

NOTE   Not all database drivers compile prepared statements.

Query `PreparedStatement`. You create a `PreparedStatement` object by specifying the template definition and parameter placeholders. The parameter data is inserted into the `PreparedStatement` object by calling its `set<type>` methods and specifying the parameter and its data. The SQL instructions and parameters are sent to the database when the `execute<type>` method is called.

This next code segment creates a `PreparedStatement` object to select user data based on the user's e-mail address. The question mark ("?") indicates this statement has one parameter.

```
//API Ref: PrepareStatement prepareStatement(String sql)
    PreparedStatement pstmt = con.prepareStatement(select theuser from
                                registration where emailaddress like ?");
    //Initialize first parameter with email address
//API Ref: void setString(int index, String s)
    pstmt.setString(1, emailAddress);
//API Ref: ResultSet executeQuery()
    ResultSet results = ps.executeQuery();
```

Once the `PreparedStatement` template is initialized, only the changed values are inserted for each call.

```
pstmt.setString(1, anotherEmailAddress);
```

Update `PreparedStatement`. This code segment creates a `Prepared-Statement` object to update a seller's registration record. The template has five parameters, which are set with five calls to the appropriate `PreparedStatement.set<type>` methods.

```
PreparedStatement ps = con.prepareStatement(
                "insert into registration(theuser, password,
                emailaddress, creditcard, balance) values (?, ?, ?, ?, ?)");
ps.setString(1, theuser);
ps.setString(2, password);
ps.setString(3, emailaddress);
ps.setString(4, creditcard);
ps.setDouble(5, balance);
ps.executeUpdate();
```

Caching Database Results

The `PreparedStatement` concept of reusing requests can be extended to caching the results of a JDBC call. For example, an auction item description remains the same until the seller changes it. If the item receives thousands of requests, the results of the query statement "`select description from auctionitems where item_id='4000343'`" might be stored more efficiently in a hash table.

Storing results in a hash table requires the JDBC call be intercepted before creating a real statement to return the cached results, and it requires that the cache entry be cleared if there is a corresponding update to that `item_id`.

Result Sets

The ResultSet interface manages access to data returned from a query. The data returned equals one row in a database table. Some queries return one row of data while many queries return multiple rows of data.

You use get<*type*> methods to retrieve data from specific columns for each row returned by the query. The SELECT TEXT FROM dba query selects the TEXT column from the dba table.

```
    Statement stmt = con.createStatement();
    ResultSet results = stmt.executeQuery("SELECT TEXT FROM dba ");
//API Ref: boolean next()
      while(results.next()){
//API Ref: String getString(String columnName)
        String s = results.getString("TEXT");
        displayText.append(s + "\n");
      }
    stmt.close();
```

Scrolling Result Sets

Before JDBC 2.0, JDBC drivers returned read-only result sets with cursors that moved in one direction, forward. Each element was retrieved by calling the next method on the result set. JDBC 2.0 introduces scrollable results sets whose values can be read and updated if reading and updating is supported by the underlying database. With scrollable result sets, any row can be selected at random, and the result set can be traversed forward and backward.

One advantage to the new result set is you can update a set of matching rows without having to issue an additional executeUpdate call. The updates are made using JDBC calls, so no custom SQL commands need to be generated. This improves the portability of the database code you create.

Both Statements and PreparedStatements have an additional constructor that accepts a scroll and an update type parameter. The scroll type value can be any one of the following:

- ResultSet.TYPE_FORWARD_ONLY: Default behavior in JDBC 1.0. The application can only call next() on the result set.
- ResultSet.SCROLL_SENSITIVE: ResultSet is fully navigable, and updates are reflected in the result set as they occur.
- ResultSet.SCROLL_INSENSITIVE: Result set is fully navigable, but updates are only visible after the result set is closed. You need to create a new result set to see the results.

The update type parameter can be one of the following two values:

- `ResultSet.CONCUR_READ_ONLY`: The result set is read only.
- `ResultSet.CONCUR_UPDATABLE`: The result set can be updated.

You can verify that your database supports these types by calling `con.get-MetaData().supportsResultSetConcurrency()` method as shown here.

```
Connection con = getConnection();
//API Ref: DatabaseMetaData getMetaData()
//API Ref: boolean supportsResultSetConcurrency(int type, int concurrency)
    if(con.getMetaData().supportsResultSetConcurrency(
    ResultSet.SCROLL_INSENSITIVE,
    ResultSet.CONCUR_UPDATABLE)) {
//API Ref: PrepareStatement prepareStatement(String sql)
    PreparedStatement pstmt = con.prepareStatement("select password,
                        emailaddres, creditcard, balance from registration
                        where theuser = ?", ResultSet.SCROLL_INSENSITIVE,
                        ResultSet.CONCUR_UPDATABLE);
    }
```

Navigating the `ResultSet`.   The fully scrollable result set returns a cursor that can be moved using simple commands. By default, the result set cursor points to the row before the first row of the result set. A call to the next method retrieves the first result set row. The cursor can also be moved by calling one of the following `ResultSet` methods:

- `beforeFirst()`: Default position. Puts the cursor before the first row of the result set.
- `first()`: Puts the cursor on the first row of the result set.
- `last()`: Puts the cursor before the last row of the result set.
- `afterLast()`: Puts the cursor beyond last row of the result set. Calls to `previous` moves backward through the `ResultSet`.
- `absolute(pos)`: Puts the cursor at the row number position, where `absolute(1)` is the first row and `absolute(-1)` is the last row.
- `relative(pos)`: Puts the cursor at a row relative to its current position, where relative(1) moves row cursor one row forward.

Updating the Result Set.   You can update a value in a result set by calling the `ResultSet.update<type>` method on the row in which the cursor is positioned. The type value here is the same value used when retrieving a value from the result set. For example, `updateString` updates a `String` value in the result set.

These next code lines update the balance for a user from the result set created earlier. The update applies only to the result set until the call to `rs.updateRow()`, which updates the underlying database. Closing the result set before calling updateRow will lose any edits applied to the result set.

```
//API Ref: boolean first()
    rs.first();
//API Ref: double updateDouble(String columnName)
//API Ref: double getDouble(String columnName, double d)
    updateDouble("balance", rs.getDouble("balance") - 5.00);
```

Inserting a new row uses the same update<*type*> methods. The only difference being that the method rs.moveToInsertRow is called before, and rs.insertRow is called after the fields have been initialized. You can delete the current row with a call to rs.deleteRow.

Batch Jobs.   By default, every JDBC statement is sent to the database individually. Apart from the additional network requests, this process incurs additional delays if a transaction spans several statements. JDBC 2.0 lets you submit multiple statements at one time with the addBatch method.

This next code segment shows how to use the addBatch statement. The calls to stmt.addBatch append statements to the original Statement, and the call to executeBatch submits the entire statement with all the appends to the database.

```
        Statement stmt = con.createStatement();
        stmt.addBatch("update registration set balance=balance-5.00
            where theuser="+theuser);
        stmt.addBatch("insert into auctionitems(description, startprice)
            values("+description+","+startprice+")");
//API Ref: int executeBatch()
        int[] results = stmt.executeBatch();
```

The addBatch method return result is an array of row counts affected for each statement executed in the batch job. If a problem occurs, a java.sql.BatchUpdateException is thrown. An incomplete array of row counts can be obtained from BatchUpdateException by calling its getUpdateCounts method.

Storing Classes, Images, and Other Large Objects.   Many databases can store binary data as part of a row if the database field is assigned a long raw, longvarbinary, or other similar type. These fields can accommodate up to two gigabytes of data. This means if you can convert the data into a binary stream or array of bytes, it can be stored and retrieved from the database in the same way you would store a String or double. This technique can be used to store and retrieve images and Java objects.

Storing and Retrieving an Image.   It is very easy to store an object that can be serialized or converted to a byte array. Unfortunately, java.awt.Image is not `Serializable`. However, as shown in this next code example, you can store the image data to a file and store the information in the file as bytes in a database binary field.

```
int itemnumber=400456;
//Each image is assumed to be in the format <auctionitem>.jpg
//400456.jpg
File file = new File(itemnumber+".jpg");
FileInputStream fis = new FileInputStream(file);
PreparedStatement pstmt = con.prepareStatement("update auctionitems
        set theimage=? where id= ?");
//The FileInputStream fis and the length of that stream are used
//as parameters to the setBinaryStream method
```
//API **Ref:** void setBinaryStream(int index, InputStream stream, int length)
```
pstmt.setBinaryStream(1, fis, (int)file.length()):
pstmt.setInt(2, itemnumber);
```
//API **Ref:** int executeUpdate()
```
pstmt.executeUpdate();
```
//API **Ref:** void close()
```
pstmt.close();
fis.close();
```

To retrieve this image and create a byte array that can be passed to `createImage`, do the following:

```
int itemnumber=400456;
byte[] imageBytes;
PreparedStatement pstmt = con.prepareStatement(
                    "select theimage from auctionitems where id= ?");
```
//API **Ref:** void setInt(int index, int intvalue)
```
pstmt.setInt(1, itemnumber);
ResultSet rs = pstmt.executeQuery();
if(rs.next()) {
   //Retrieve the image as bytes and convert to an image using the
   //method createImage from the awt Toolkit
```
//API **Ref:** byte[] getBytes(String ColumnName)
```
   imageBytes = rs.getBytes(1);
}
pstmt.close();
rs.close();
Image auctionimage = Toolkit.getDefaultToolkit().createImage(imageBytes);
```

Storing and Retrieving an Object.   A class can be serialized to a binary database field in much the same way as the image was in the previous example. In this example, the `RegistrationImpl` class is changed to support default serialization by adding `implements Serializable` to the class declaration.

Next, a `ByteArrayInputStream` is created to be passed as the JDBC binary stream. To create the `ByteArrayInputStream`, `RegistrationImpl` is first piped through an `ObjectOutputStream` to an underlying `ByteArrayInput-Stream` with a call to `RegistrationImpl.writeObject`. The `ByteArrayInputStream` is converted to a byte array, which can then be used to create the

ByteArrayInputStream. The create method in RegistrationServer.java
is changed as follows:

```
public registration.RegistrationPK create(String theuser, String password,
                                String emailaddress, String creditcard)
                                throws registration.CreateException{
    double balance=0;
    Connection con = null;
    PreparedStatement ps = null;;
    try {
      con=getConnection();
      //Create a Registration Bean from the parameters supplied
      RegistrationImpl reg= new RegistrationImpl();
      reg.theuser = theuser;
      reg.password = password;
      reg.emailaddress = emailaddress;
      reg.creditcard = creditcard;
      reg.balance = balance;
      //Getting this Bean into the database requires an input stream,
      //which in this case is a ByteArrayInputStream that is created from
      //a byte array. The byte array is created from a bytearrayoutput
      //stream of the object that is to be stored.
      //Create a ByteArray stream and write the object to that stream
      ByteArrayOutputStream regStore = new ByteArrayOutputStream();
      ObjectOutputStream regObjectStream = new ObjectOutputStream(regStore);
      regObjectStream.writeObject(reg);
      //Create an array of bytes from the bytearray stream
      byte[] regBytes=regStore.toByteArray();
      regObjectStream.close();
      regStore.close();
      //Finally, create the byte array input stream from the array of bytes
      ByteArrayInputStream regArrayStream = new
                                      ByteArrayInputStream(regBytes);
      ps=con.prepareStatement("insert into registration (theuser, theclass)
                          values (?, ?)");
      ps.setString(1, theuser);
      ps.setBinaryStream(2, regArrayStream, regBytes.length);
      if(ps.executeUpdate() != 1) {
        throw new CreateException ();
      }
      RegistrationPK primaryKey = new RegistrationPKImpl();
      primaryKey.theuser(theuser);
      return primaryKey;
    } catch (IOException ioe) {
      throw new CreateException ();
    } catch (CreateException ce) {
      throw ce;
    } catch (SQLException sqe) {
      System.out.println("sqe="+sqe);
      throw new CreateException ();
    } finally {
      try {
        ps.close();
        con.close();
```

```
        } catch (Exception ignore) {
        }
      }
  }
```

The object is retrieved and reconstructed by extracting the bytes from the database, creating a `ByteArrayInputStream` from those bytes to be read from an `ObjectInputStream`, and by calling `readObject` to create the instance again.

This next example shows the changes needed to the `Registration-Server.refresh` method to retrieve the registration instance from the database.

```
private Registration refresh(RegistrationPK pk) throws FinderException {
    if(pk == null) {
        throw new FinderException ();
    }
    ResultSet rs = null;
    Connection con = null;
    PreparedStatement ps = null;
    try {
        con=getConnection();
        ps=con.prepareStatement("select theclass from registration
                            where theuser = ?");
        ps.setString(1, pk.theuser());
        ps.executeQuery();
        rs = ps.getResultSet();
        if(rs.next()){
            byte[] regBytes = rs.getBytes(1);
            ByteArrayInputStream regArrayStream =
                new ByteArrayInputStream(regBytes);
            ObjectInputStream regObjectStream =
                new ObjectInputStream(regArrayStream);
            RegistrationImpl reg=
                (RegistrationImpl)regObjectStream.readObject();
            return reg;
        } else {
            throw new FinderException ();
        }
    } catch (Exception sqe) {
        System.out.println("Exception when loading image: "+sqe);
        throw new FinderException ();
    } finally {
        try {
            rs.close();
            ps.close();
            con.close();
        } catch (Exception ignore) {}
    }
}
```

BLOBs and CLOBs.   Storing large fields in a table with the other data is not necessarily optimal, especially if the data has a variable size. One way to handle large, variable-sized objects is with the Large Objects (LOBs) type. LOBs use a locator, essentially a pointer, in the database record that points to the real database field.

There are two types of LOBs: Binary Large Objects (BLOBs) and Character Large Objects (CLOBs). When you access a BLOB or CLOB, the data is not copied to the client. To retrieve the actual data from a result set, you have to retrieve the pointer with a call to `BLOB`, `blob = getBlob(1)`, or `CLOB`, `clob = getClob(1)`, and then retrieve the data with a call to `blob.getBinaryStream()` or `clob.getBinaryStream()`. Both `getBlob` and `getClob` are in the `java.sql` package.

Controlling Transactions

By default, JDBC statements are processed in full auto-commit mode. This mode works well for a single database query, but if an operation depends on several database statements that all have to complete successfully or the entire operation is cancelled, a finer transaction is needed.

A description of transaction isolation levels is covered in more detail in Data and Transaction Management (Chapter 3). To use transaction management in the JDBC platform, you first need to disable the full auto-commit mode by calling:

```
Connection con= getConnection();
con.setAutoCommit(false);
```

At this point, you can either commit any following JDBC statements or undo any updates by calling the `Connection.rollback` method. The roll back call is commonly placed in the `Exception` handler, although it can be placed anywhere in the transaction flow.

This next example inserts an auction item and decrements the user's balance. If the balance is less than zero, the entire transaction is rolled back and the auction item is removed.

```
//New insertItem code to add to file SellerBean.java
static {
    try{
        new pool.JDCConnectionDriver("COM.cloudscape.core.JDBCDriver",
                                     "jdbc:cloudscape:ejbdemo","none",
                                     "none");
    } catch(Exception e) {
        System.out.println("new pool error"+e);
    }
}

public Connection getConnection() throws SQLException {
    return DriverManager.getConnection("jdbc:jdc:jdcpool");
}
public int insertItem(String seller, String password, String description,
                      int auctiondays, double startprice, String summary) {
```

```
        Connection con = null;
        int count=0;
        double balance=0;
        java.sql.Date enddate, startdate;
        Statement stmt=null;
//API Ref: PrepareStatement prepareStatement(String sql)
        PreparedStatement ps = null;

        try {
          con = getConnection();
          //Disable auto commit of jdbc transactions for this connection
//API Ref: void setAutoCommit(boolean autoCommit)
          con.setAutoCommit(false);
//API Ref: Statement createStatement()
          stmt = con.createStatement();
          stmt.executeQuery("select counter from auctionitems");
//API Ref: ResultSet getResultSet()
          ResultSet rs = stmt.getResultSet();
          if(rs.next()) {
            count=rs.getInt(1);
          }
          //Calculate the end date of the auction
//API Ref: static Calendar getInstance()
          Calendar currenttime = Calendar.getInstance();
//API Ref: long getTime()
          java.util.Date currentdate = currenttime.getTime();
          startdate=new java.sql.Date(currentdate.getTime());
//API Ref: void add(int partofdate, int dateamount)
          currenttime.add(Calendar.DATE, auctiondays);
          enddate = new java.sql.Date((currenttime.getTime()).getTime());

          //Insert auction item
          ps = con.prepareStatement("insert into auctionitems(id, description,
              startdate, enddate, startprice, summary) values (?,?,?,?,?,?)");
          ps.setInt(1, count);
          ps.setString(2, description);
//API Ref: void setDate(int index, Date datavalue)
          ps.setDate(3, startdate);
          ps.setDate(4, enddate);
//API Ref: void setDouble(int index, double doublevalue)
          ps.setDouble(5, startprice);
          ps.setString(6, summary);
          ps.executeUpdate();
          ps.close();

          //Update users balance to deduct a listing fee
//API Ref: PrepareStatement prepareStatement(String sql)
          ps = con.prepareStatement("update registration set" +
                              "balance=balance -0.50 where theuser= ?");
          ps.setString(1, seller);
          executeUpdate(ps);
          ps.close();
          stmt = con.createStatement();
          stmt.executeQuery("select balance from registration
                      where theuser='"+seller+"'");
```

```
//API Ref: ResultSet getResultSet()
            rs = stmt.getResultSet();
            if(rs.next()) {
               balance=rs.getDouble(1);
            }
            stmt.close();
            //Finally, check the users balance, its is less than 0 rollback
            //the whole transaction else update the auction id number and
            //commit everything to the database
            if(balance <0) {
//API Ref: void rollback()
                con.rollback();
                con.close();
                return (-1);
            }
            stmt= con.createStatement();
            //Counter is the next auction item id number that can be
            //used for a auction listing
//API Ref: int executeUpdate(String sql)
            stmt.executeUpdate("update auctionitems set counter=counter+1");
            stmt.close();
            con.commit();
            con.close();
            return(0);
          } catch(SQLException e) {
          try {
             //Always roll the transaction back if something unexpected happens
             con.rollback();
             con.close();
             stmt.close();
             ps.close();
          } catch (Exception ignore){}
        }
        return (0);
     }
```

Escaping Characters

The JDBC API provides the escape keyword so you can specify the character
you want to use to escape characters. For example, if you want to use the percent sign (%) as the percent sign and not have it interpreted as the SQL wild
card used in SQL LIKE queries, you have to escape it with the *escape character*
you specify with the escape keyword. This next statement shows how you
would use the escape keyword to look for the value 10%.

```
stmt.executeQuery("select tax from sales where tax like '10\%' {escape '\'}");
```

If your program stores names and addresses entered from the command line or
by way of a user interface to the database, the single quotes (') symbol might
appear in the data. Passing single quotes directly into a SQL string causes problems when the SQL statement is parsed because SQL gives this symbol another
meaning unless it is escaped.

To solve this problem, the following method escapes any single quote (') symbol found in the input line. This method can be extended to escape any other
characters such as commas that the database or database driver might interpret
another way.

```
static public String escapeLine(String s) {
  String retvalue = s;
  if(s.indexOf ("'") != -1 ) {
    StringBuffer hold = new StringBuffer();
    char c;
    for(int i=0; i < s.length(); i++ ) {
      if((c=s.charAt(i)) == '\'' ) {
      hold.append ("'");
    } else {
      hold.append(c);
    }
  }
  retvalue = hold.toString();
  }
  return retvalue;
}
```

However, if you use a `PreparedStatement` instead of a simple `Statement`,
most of these escape problems go away. For example, instead of this line with
the escape sequence:

```
stmt.executeQuery("select tax from sales where tax like '10\%' {escape '\'}");
```

You could use this line:

```
preparedstmt = C.prepareStatement("update tax set tax = ?");
```

Mapping Database Types

Apart from a few JDBC types such as `INTEGER` that are represented as an integer in most popular databases, you might find that the JDBC type for a table
column does not match the type as it is represented in the database. This means
calls to `ResultSet.getObject`, `PreparedStatement.setObject`, and `Call-
ableStatement.getObject()` will very likely fail.

Your program can determine the database column type from the database meta
data and use that information to check the value before retrieving it. This next
code checks that the value is, in fact, type `INTEGER` before retrieving its value.

```
int count=0;
Connection con=getConnection();
Statement stmt= con.createStatement();
stmt.executeQuery("select counter from auctionitems");
ResultSet rs = stmt.getResultSet();
if(rs.next()) {
//API Ref: DatabaseMetaData getMetaData()
  if(rs.getMetaData().getColumnType(1) == Types.INTEGER) {
    Integer i=(Integer)rs.getObject(1);
```

```
        count=i.intValue();
    }
}
rs.close();
```

Mapping Date Types

The DATE type is where most mismatches occur. This is because the java.util.Date class represents both date and time, but SQL has the following three types to represent data and time information:

- A DATE type that represents the date only (as in 03/23/99).
- A TIME type that specifies the time only (as in 12:03:59).
- A TIMESTAMP that represents time value in nanoseconds.

These three additional types are provided in the java.sql package as java.sql.Date, java.sql.Time, and java.sql.Timestamp and are all subclasses of java.util.Date. This means you can use convert java.util.Date values to the type you need to be compatible with the database type.

NOTE   The Timestamp class loses precision when it is converted to a java.util.Date because java.util.Date does not contain a nanosecond field. It is better to not convert a Timestamp instance if the value will be written back to the database.

This example uses the java.sql.Date class to convert the java.util.Date value returned by the call to Calendar.getTime to a java.sql.Date.

```
Calendar currenttime = Calendar.getInstance();
java.sql.Date startdate = new java.sql.Date((currenttime.getTime()).getTime());
```

You can also use the java.text.SimpleDateFormat class to do the conversion. This example uses the java.text.SimpleDateFormat class to convert a java.util.Date object to a java.sql.Date object:

```
SimpleDateFormat template = new SimpleDateFormat("yyyy-MM-dd");
java.util.Date enddate = new java.util.Date("10/31/99");
java.sql.Date sqlDate = java.sql.Date.valueOf(template.format(enddate));
```

If you find a database date representation cannot be mapped to a Java type with a call to getObject or getDate, retrieve the value with a call to getString and format the string as a Date value using the SimpleDateFormat class shown above.

Servlets

A servlet is a server-side program written in the Java programming language that interacts with clients and is usually tied to a HyperText Transfer Protocol

(HTTP) server. One common use for a servlet is to extend a Web server by providing dynamic Web content.

Servlets have an advantage over other technologies such as Perl scripts in that they are compiled, have threading capability built in, and provide a secure programming environment. Even Web sites that previously did not provide servlet support can do so now by using programs such as `JRun` or the Java module for the Apache Web server.

The Web-based auction application described in Duke's Auction Demonstration (page 7) uses a servlet to accept and process buyer and seller input through the browser and to dynamically return auction item information to the browser. The `AuctionServlet` program is created by extending the `HttpServlet` class. The `HttpServlet` class provides a framework for handling HTTP requests and responses.

This section examines the `AuctionServlet` and includes information on how to use `Cookie` and `Session` objects in a servlet.

HttpServlet

The `AuctionServlet` class extends `HttpServlet`, which is an abstract class.

```
public class AuctionServlet extends HttpServlet {
```

A servlet can be either loaded when the Web server starts up or when requested by way of an HTTP URL that specifies the servlet. The servlet is usually loaded by a separate classloader in the Web server because this allows the servlet to be reloaded by unloading the classloader that loaded the servlet class. However, if the servlet depends on other classes and one of those classes changes, you will need to update the date stamp on the servlet for it to reload.

After a servlet loads, the first stage in its life cycle is the Web server calls the servlet's `init` method. Once loaded and initialized, the next stage in the servlet's life cycle is to serve requests. The servlet serves requests through its `service`, `doGet`, or `doPost` method implementations.

The servlet can optionally implement a `destroy` method to perform clean-up operations before the Web server unloads the servlet.

The `init` Method

The `init` method is called only once by the Web server when the servlet is first started. The `init` method is passed a `ServletConfig` object containing initialization information pertaining to the Web server where the application is running.

The `ServletConfig` object is used to access information maintained by the Web server including values from the `initArgs` parameter in the servlet properties file.

Code in the `init` method uses the `ServletConfig` object to retrieve the `initArgs` values by calling the `config.getInitParameter("parameter")` method.

The `AuctionServlet.init` method also contacts the Enterprise JavaBeans server to create a `Context` (ctx) object. The `ctx` object is used in the `service` method to establish a connection with the Enterprise JavaBeans server.

```
public class AuctionServlet extends HttpServlet {
Context ctx=null;
private String pageTemplate;

public void init(ServletConfig config) throws ServletException{
  super.init(config);
  try {
    ctx = getInitialContext();
  } catch (Exception e){
    System.err.println("failed to contact EJB server"+e);
  }
  try {
    //The pagetemplate parameter contains the name of the file
    //that contains the default HTML page layout.
    //The readFile method is a convenience method in AuctionServlet
    //to read a file as into a string.
    pageTemplate=readFile(config.getInitParameter("pagetemplate"));
  } catch(IOException e) {
    System.err.println("Error in AuctionServlet <init>"+e);
  }
}
```

The destroy Method

The `destroy` method is a life-cycle method implemented by servlets that need to save their state between servlet loading and unloading. For example, the `destroy` method would save the current servlet state, and the next time the servlet is loaded, that saved state would be retrieved by the `init` method. You should be aware that the `destroy` method might not be called if the server machine crashes.

```
public void destroy() {
  saveServletState();
}
```

The service Method

The `AuctionServlet` is an HTTP servlet that handles client requests and generates responses through its service method. It accepts as parameters the `HttpServletRequest` and `HttpServletResponse` request and response objects.

- `HttpServletRequest` contains the headers and input streams sent from the client to the server.
- `HttpServletResponse` is the output stream that is used to send information from the servlet back to the client.

The `service` method handles standard HTTP client requests received by way of its `HttpServletRequest` parameter by delegating the request to one of the following methods designed to handle that request. The different types of requests are described in HTTP Requests (page 122).

- `doGet` for GET, conditional GET, and HEAD requests.
- `doPost` for POST requests.
- `doPut` for PUT requests.
- `doDelete` for DELETE requests.
- `doOptions` for OPTIONS requests.
- `doTrace` for TRACE requests.

The `AuctionServlet` program provides its own `service` method implementation that calls one of the following methods based on the value returned by the call to `cmd = request.getParameter("action")`. These method implementations match the default implementations provided in the `doGet` and `doPost` methods called by the default `service` method, but add some auction application-specific functionality for looking up enterprise beans.

- `listAllItems(out)`
- `listAllNewItems(out)`
- `listClosingItems(out)`
- `insertItem(out, request)`
- `itemDetails(out, request)`
- `itemBid(out, request)`
- `registerUser(out, request)`

```
//API Ref: void service (HTTPServletRequest request,
                         HttpServletResponse response)
public void service(HttpServletRequest request, HttpServletResponse response)
                  throws IOException {
  String cmd;
  response.setContentType("text/html");
  ServletOutputStream out = response.getOutputStream();
  if(ctx == null ) {
    try {
      ctx = getInitialContext();
    } catch (Exception e){
      System.err.println("failed to contact EJB server"+e);
    }
  }

  //The action parameter is part of the posted URL. For example
  //http://phoenix.sun.com/AuctionServlet?action=details&item=4000001
  cmd =request.getParameter("action");
  if(cmd !=null)  {
    if(cmd.equals("list")) {
      listAllItems(out);
    } else if(cmd.equals("newlist")) {
```

```
        listAllNewItems(out);
      } else if(cmd.equals("search")) {
        searchItems(out, request);
      } else if(cmd.equals("close")) {
        listClosingItems(out);
      } else if(cmd.equals("insert")) {
        insertItem(out, request);
      } else if (cmd.equals("details")) {
        itemDetails(out, request );
      } else if (cmd.equals("bid")) {
        itemBid(out, request) ;
      } else if (cmd.equals("register")) {
        registerUser(out, request);
      }
    } else{
      // no command set
      setTitle(out, "error");
    }
    setFooter(out);
    out.flush();
}
```

HTTP Requests

A request is a message sent from a client program such as a browser to a server program. The first line of the request message contains a method that indicates the action to perform on the incoming URL. The two commonly used mechanisms for sending information to the server are GET and POST.

- GET requests might pass parameters to a URL by appending them to the URL. GET requests can be bookmarked and e-mailed and add the information to the URL of the response.

- POST requests might pass additional data to a URL by directly sending it to the server separately from the URL. POST requests cannot be bookmarked or e-mailed and do not change the URL of the response.

- PUT requests are the reverse of GET requests. Instead of reading the page, PUT requests write (or store) the page.

- DELETE requests are for removing Web pages.

- OPTIONS requests are for getting information about the communication options available on the request/response chain.

- TRACE requests are for testing or diagnostic purposes because they let the client see what is being received at the other end of the request chain.

Using Cookies in Servlets

HTTP cookies are essentially custom HTTP headers passed between a client and a server. Although cookies are not overwhelmingly popular, they do enable state to be shared between the two machines. For example, when a user logs into a site, a cookie can maintain a reference verifying the user has passed the pass-word check and can use that reference to identify that same user on future visits.

Cookies are normally associated with a server. If you set the domain to .java.sun.com, then the cookie is associated with the domain. If no domain is set, the cookie is only associated with the server that created the cookie.

Setting a Cookie.   The Java Servlet API includes a Cookie class that you can use to set or retrieve the cookie from the HTTP header. HTTP cookies include a name and value pair. The startSession method shown here is in the Login Servlet program. In this method, the name in the name and value pair used to create the Cookie is JDCAUCTION, and a unique identifier generated by the server is the value.

```
          protected Session startSession(String theuser, String password,
                                         HttpServletResponse response) {
              Session session = null;
              if( verifyPassword(theuser, password) ) {
                //The user was validated in the user database,
                //create a session
                session = new Session (theuser);
                //Set a timeout for this session that we control
                session.setExpires (sessionTimeout + System.currentTimeMillis());
                sessionCache.put (session);
              //Create a client cookie
//API Ref: Cookie(String name, String value)
                Cookie c = new Cookie("JDCAUCTION", String.valueOf(session.getId()));
//API Ref: void setPath(String path)
                c.setPath ("/");
//API Ref: void setMaxAge(int expire)
                c.setMaxAge (-1);
//API Ref: void setDomain(String domainstring)
                c.setDomain (domain);
//API Ref: void addCookie(Cookie cookie)
                response.addCookie (c);
              }
              return session;
          }
```

Later versions of the Servlet API include a Session API, to create a session using the Servlet API in the previous example you can use the getSession method.

```
HttpSession session = new Session (true);
```

The startSession method is called by requesting the login action from a POST to the LoginServlet as follows:

```
<FORM ACTION="/LoginServlet" METHOD="POST">
<TABLE>
<INPUT TYPE="HIDDEN" NAME="action" VALUE="login">
<TR><TD>Enter your user id:</TD>
```

```
<TD><INPUT TYPE="TEXT" SIZE=20 NAME="theuser"></TD>
</TR>
<TR><TD>Enter your password:<TD>
<TD><INPUT TYPE="PASSWORD" SIZE=20 NAME="password"></TD>
</TR>
</TABLE>
<INPUT TYPE="SUBMIT" VALUE="Login" NAME="Enter">
</FORM>
```

The cookie is created with an maximum age of −1, which means the cookie is not stored but remains alive while the browser runs. The value is set in seconds, although when using values smaller than a few minutes you need to be careful of machine times being slightly out of sync.

The path value can be used to specify that the cookie applies only to files and directories under the path set on that machine. In this example the root path / means the cookie is applicable to all directories.

The domain value in the example is read from the initialization parameters for the servlet. If the domain is null, the cookie is applied to that machine's domain only.

Retrieving a Cookie.   The cookie is retrieved from the HTTP headers with a call to the getCookies method on the request:

```
//API Ref: Cookie[] getCookies()
    Cookie c[] = request.getCookies();
```

You can later retrieve the name and value pair settings by calling the Cookie.get-Name method to retrieve the name and by calling the Cookie.getValue method to retrieve the value. LoginServlet has a validateSession method that checks the user's cookies to find a JDCAUCTION cookie that was set in this domain:

```
    private Session validateSession(HttpServletRequest request,
                                    HttpServletResponse response) {
      //Request the users cookies for this domain
      Cookie c[] = request.getCookies();
      Session session = null;
      if( c != null ) {
        for(int i=0; i < c.length && session == null; i++ ) {
          //Look for a cookie whose name is JDCAUCTION in this
          //domain. This cookie was previously set by us.
          //The cookie value is the session id number stored in the
          //session cache.
          if(c[i].getName().equals("JDCAUCTION")) {
            String key = String.valueOf (c[i].getValue());
            session=sessionCache.get(key);
          }
        }
      }
      return session;
    }
```

If you use the Servlet Session API, you can use the following method. Note that the parameter is false to specify that the session value is returned and a new session not created.

```
HttpSession session = request.getSession(false);
```

Generating Sessions.   The `LoginServlet.validateSession` method returns a `Session` object represented by the `Session` (Servlets) class. The `Session` class uses an identifier generated from a numeric sequence. This numbered session identifier is the value part of the name and value pair stored in the cookie.

The only way to reference the user name on the server is with this session identifier, which is stored in a simple memory cache with the other session IDs. When a user terminates a session, the `LoginServlet` logout action is called like this:

```
http://phoenix.sun.com:7001/LoginServlet?action=logout
```

The session cache implemented in the `SessionCache` (Servlets) program includes a reaper thread to remove sessions older than a preset time. The preset timeout could be measured in hours or days, depending on how many visitors visit the site.

Preventing Page Caching.   The `LoginServlet.setNoCache` method sets the `Cache-Control` or `Pragma` values (depending on which version of the HTTP protocol is being used) in the response header to `no-cache`. The `Expires` expiration header is also set to 0. Alternately, you can set the time to be the current system time. Even if the client does not cache the page, there are often proxy servers in a corporate network that would. Only pages using Secure Socket Layer (SSL) are not cached by default.

```
    private void setNoCache (HttpServletRequest request,
                             HttpServletResponse response) {
//API Ref: String getProtocol()
        if(request.getProtocol().compareTo ("HTTP/1.0") == 0) {
//API Ref: void setHeader(String name, String value)
        response.setHeader ("Pragma", "no-cache");
        } else if (request.getProtocol().compareTo("HTTP/1.1") == 0) {
        response.setHeader ("Cache-Control", "no-cache");
        }
//API Ref: void setDateHeader(String name, long datevalue)
        response.setDateHeader ("Expires", 0);
    }
```

Restricting Access and Redirections.   If you install the `Login` servlet as the default servlet or servlet to run when serving any page under the document root, you can use cookies to restrict users to certain sections of the site. For example, you can allow users who have cookies that state they have logged in to access sections of the site that require a login password and keep all others out.

The `Login` servlet checks for a restricted directory in its `init` method. The `init` method shown below sets the `protectedDir` variable to `true` if the `config` variable passed to it specifies a protected directory. The Web server configuration file provides the settings passed to a servlet in the `config` variable.

```
    public void init(ServletConfig config) throws ServletException  {
      super.init(config);
//API Ref: String getInitParameter(String parametername)
      domain = config.getInitParameter("domain");
      restricted = config.getInitParameter("restricted");
      if(restricted != null) {
        protectedDir=true;
      }
    // ..
```

Later on in the `validateSession` and `service` methods, the `protectedDir` variable is checked, and the `HttpResponse.sendRedirect` method is called to send the user to the correct page based on the user's login and session status.

```
//API Ref: void sendRedirect(String urlstring)
    if(protectedDir) {
      response.sendRedirect (restricted+"/index.html");
    } else{
      response.sendRedirect (defaultPage);
    }
```

The `init` method also retrieves the servlet context for the `FileServlet` servlet so methods can be called on the `FileServlet` in the `validateSession` method. The advantage, to calling methods on `FileServlet` to serve the files rather than serving the files from within the `LoginServlet`, is that you get the full advantage of all the functionality added into `FileServlet` such as memory mapping or file caching. The downside is that the code may not be portable to other servers that do not have `FileServlet`. This code retrieves the `FileServlet` context.

```
    FileServlet fileServlet = (FileServlet)
//API Ref: ServletContext getServletContext()
                        config.getServletContext().getServlet("file");
```

The `validateSession` method prevents users without a logon session from accessing the restricted directory.

HTTP Error Codes

You can return an HTTP error code by using the `sendError` method. For example, two common HTTP error codes are error 500, which indicates an internal server error, and the 404 error code, in which indicates page not found.

This next code segment returns the HTTP 500 error code.

```
protected void service(HttpServletRequest request,HttpServletResponse
                       response) throws ServletException {
   response.sendError (500);
}
```

Reading GET and POST Values

The Servlet API has a getParameter method in the HttpServletRequest class that returns the GET or POST value for the name you supply.

- The HTTP GET request handles name and value pairs as part of the URL. The getParameter method parses the URL passed in, retrieves the name=value pairs delimited by the ampersand (&) character, and returns the value.
- The HTTP POST request reads the name and value pairs from the input stream from the client. The getParameter method parses the input stream for the name and value pairs.

The getParameter method works well for simple servlets, but if you need to retrieve the POST parameters in the order they were placed on the Web page or handle multipart posts, you can write your own code to parse the input stream.

The next example returns POST parameters in the order they were received from the Web page. Normally, the parameters are stored in a Hashtable that does not maintain the sequence order of elements stored in it. The example keeps a reference to each name and value pair in a vector that can be traversed to return the values in the order they were received by the server.

```
//File auction.PostServlet.java
package auction;

import java.io.*;
import java.util.*;
import javax.servlet.*;
import javax.servlet.http.*;

public class PostServlet extends HttpServlet {

  public void init(ServletConfig config) throws ServletException  {
    super.init(config);
  }

  public void service(HttpServletRequest request, HttpServletResponse
                      response) throws IOException {
    private Vector paramOrder;
    private Hashtable parameters;
```

```
//API Ref: void setContentType(String type)
       response.setContentType("text/html");
//API Ref: PrintWriter getWriter()
       PrintWriter out = response.getWriter();
       if(request.getMethod().equals("POST") && request.getContentType().equals(
                    "application/x-www-form-urlencoded")) {
         //If this is a POST request and the content type from the post is
         //a url encoded form, build a hash table with the extracted parameter
         //values and generate an associated vector that just records the
         //name of the parameters in ascending order
         //
         parameters = parsePostData(request.getContentLength(),
                   request.getInputStream(), paramOrder);
       }
       //Parse through the list of posted parameters by getting the name
       //of each parameter from the vector and extracting the value
       //of that parameter by calling getParameter on the Hashtable of
       //value pairs
       for(int i=0;i<paramOrder.size();i++) {
         String name = (String)paramOrder.elementAt(i);
         String value = getParameter((String)paramOrder.elementAt(i),
                               parameters);
         out.println("name="+name+" value="+value);
       }
       out.println("</body></html>");
       out.close();
     }

     private Hashtable parsePostData(int length, ServletInputStream instream,
                            Vector paramOrder) {
       String valArray[] = null;
       int inputLen, offset;
       byte[] postedBytes = null;
       boolean dataRemaining=true;
       String postedBody;
       Hashtable ht = new Hashtable();
       paramOrder= new Vector(10);
       StringBuffer sb = new StringBuffer();
       if(length <=0) {
         return null;
       }
       postedBytes = new byte[length];
       //Read the posted form into a byte array

       try {
         offset = 0;
         while(dataRemaining) {
           inputLen = instream.read (postedBytes, offset, length - offset);
           if(inputLen <= 0) {
             throw new IOException ("read error");
           }
           offset += inputLen;
           if((length-offset) ==0) {
             dataRemaining=false;
           }
         }
       }
```

```
    } catch (IOException e) {
      System.out.println("Exception ="+e);
      return null;
    }
    //Create a string from the byte array and parse the name/value
    //pairs.
    postedBody = new String (postedBytes);
    StringTokenizer st = new StringTokenizer(postedBody, "&");
    String key=null;
    String val=null;
    while (st.hasMoreTokens()) {
      String pair = (String)st.nextToken();
      int pos = pair.indexOf('=');
      if(pos == -1) {
        throw new IllegalArgumentException();
      }
      try {
        //Spaces and other http sensitive characters are url encoded
        //before posting so convert the posted string into its original
        //form
        key = java.net.URLDecoder.decode(pair.substring(0, pos));
        val = java.net.URLDecoder.decode(pair.substring(pos+1,
                                          pair.length()));
      } catch (Exception e) {
        throw new IllegalArgumentException();
      }
      if(ht.containsKey(key)) {
        String oldVals[] = (String []) ht.get(key);
        valArray = new String[oldVals.length + 1];
        for(int i = 0; i < oldVals.length; i++) {
          valArray[i] = oldVals[i];
        }
        valArray[oldVals.length] = val;
      } else {
        valArray = new String[1];
        valArray[0] = val;
      }
      ht.put(key, valArray);
      paramOrder.addElement(key);
    }
    return ht;
  }

  public String getParameter(String name, HashTable parameters) {
    String vals[] = (String []) parameters.get(name);
    if(vals == null) {
      return null;
    }
    String vallist = vals[0];
    for(int i = 1; i < vals.length; i++) {
      vallist = vallist + "," + vals[i];
    }
    return vallist;
  }
}
```

To find out whether the request is POST or GET, call the getMethod in the HttpServletRequest class. To determine the format of the data being posted, call the getContentType method in the HttpServletRequest class. For simple HTML Web pages, the type returned by this call will be application/x-www-form-urlencoded.

If you need to create a post with more than one part such as the one created by the following HTML form, the servlet will need to read the input stream from the post to reach individual sections. Each section is distinguished by a boundary defined in the post header.

```
<FORM ACTION="/PostMultiServlet" METHOD="POST" ENCTYPE="multipart/form-data">
<INPUT TYPE="TEXT" NAME="desc" value="">
<INPUT TYPE="FILE" NAME="filecontents" value="">
<INPUT TYPE="SUBMIT" VALUE="Submit" NAME="Submit">
</FORM>
```

The next example extracts a description and a file from the client browsers. It reads the input stream looking for a line matching the boundary string, reads the content line, skips a line and then reads the data associated with that part. The uploaded file is simply displayed, but could also be written to disk.

```
//File auction.PostMultiServlet.java
package auction;

import java.io.*;
import java.util.*;
import javax.servlet.*;
import javax.servlet.http.*;

public class PostMultiServlet extends HttpServlet {
    public void init(ServletConfig config) throws ServletException  {
      super.init(config);
    }

    public void service(HttpServletRequest request, HttpServletResponse
                        response) throws ServletException, IOException {
      response.setContentType("text/html");
      PrintWriter out = response.getWriter();
      if(request.getMethod().equals("POST") &&
              request.getContentType().startsWith("multipart/form-data")) {
        int index = request.getContentType().indexOf("boundary=");
        if(index < 0) {
          System.out.println("can't find boundary type");
          return;
        }
        //Look for the data past the identifying string boundary=
        String boundary = request.getContentType().substring(index+9);
        ServletInputStream instream = request.getInputStream();
        byte[] tmpbuffer = new byte[8192];
        int length=0;
        String inputLine=null;
        boolean moreData=true;
```

```
//Skip http header fields until form data is reached
        length = instream.readLine(tmpbuffer, 0, tmpbuffer.length);
        inputLine = new String (tmpbuffer, 0, 0, length);
        while(inputLine.indexOf(boundary)  >0 && moreData) {
            length = instream.readLine(tmpbuffer, 0, tmpbuffer.length);
            inputLine = new String (tmpbuffer, 0, 0, length);
            if(inputLine !=null)
              System.out.println("input name="+inputLine);
              if(length<0) {
                moreData=false;
              }
        }
        if(moreData) {
            length = instream.readLine(tmpbuffer, 0, tmpbuffer.length);
            inputLine = new String (tmpbuffer, 0, 0, length);
            if(inputLine.indexOf("desc") >=0) {
                length = instream.readLine(tmpbuffer, 0, tmpbuffer.length);
                inputLine = new String (tmpbuffer, 0, 0, length);
                length = instream.readLine(tmpbuffer, 0, tmpbuffer.length);
                inputLine = new String (tmpbuffer, 0, 0, length);
                System.out.println("description ="+inputLine);
            }
        }
        while(inputLine.indexOf(boundary)  >0 && moreData) {
            length = instream.readLine(tmpbuffer, 0, tmpbuffer.length);
            inputLine = new String (tmpbuffer, 0, 0, length);
        }
        if(moreData) {
            length = instream.readLine(tmpbuffer, 0, tmpbuffer.length);
            inputLine = new String (tmpbuffer, 0, 0, length);
            if(inputLine.indexOf("filename") >=0) {
                //We know what the file name is now
                int startindex=inputLine.indexOf("filename");
                System.out.println("file name=" +
                              "inputLine.substring(startindex+10," +
                              "inputLine.indexOf("\"", startindex+10)));
                length = instream.readLine(tmpbuffer, 0, tmpbuffer.length);

                inputLine = new String (tmpbuffer, 0, 0, length);
            }
        }
        byte fileBytes[]=new byte[50000];
        int offset=0;
        if(moreData) {
            //Read the contents of the posted file into fileBytes
            while(inputLine.indexOf(boundary) >0 && moreData) {
                length = instream.readLine(tmpbuffer,0, tmpbuffer.length);
                inputLine = new String (tmpbuffer, 0, 0, length);
                if(length >0 && (inputLine.indexOf(boundary) <0)) {
                    System.arraycopy(tmpbuffer, 0, fileBytes, offset, length);
                    offset+=length;
                } else {
                    moreData=false;
                }
            }
        }
```

```
//Trim last two newline/return characters before using data
      for(int i=0;i<offset-2;i++) {
         System.out.print((char)fileBytes[i]);
      }
   }
}
out.println("</body></html>");
out.close();
   }
}
```

Threading

A servlet must be able to handle multiple concurrent requests. Any number of end users at any given time could invoke the servlet, and while the `init` method is always run single-threaded, the service method is multithreaded to handle multiple requests.

This means any fields accessed by the service method should be restricted to simple thread access. The example below uses the synchronized keyword to restrict access to a counter so it can only be updated by one thread at a time:

```
static int counter;
Boolean lock = new Boolean(true);
synchronized(lock){
   counter++;
}
```

HTTPS

Many servers, browsers, and the Java Plug-In can support the secure HTTP protocol called HTTPS. HTTPS is similar to HTTP except the data is transmitted over a secure socket layer (SSL) instead of a normal socket connection. Web servers often listen for HTTP requests on one port while listening for HTTPS requests on another.

SSL has checks to find out if encrypted data sent over the network has been tampered with in transit. SSL also authenticates the Web server to its clients by providing a public key certificate. In SSL 3.0 the client can also authenticate itself with the server by using a public key certificate.

Public key cryptography (also called asymmetric key encryption) uses a public and private key pair. Any message encrypted with the private key in the pair can be decrypted only with the corresponding public key. Certificates are digitally signed statements generated from a trusted third-party Certificate Authority. The Certificate Authority needs proof that you are who you say you are because clients will be trusting the certificate they receive.

It is this certificate that contains the public key in the public and private key pair. The certificate is signed by the private key of the Certificate Authority, and most browsers know the public key for the main Certificate Authorities.

While public key encryption is good for authentication purposes, it is not as fast as symmetric key encryption and so the SSL protocol uses both types of keys in the life cycle of an SSL connection. The client and server begin an HTTPS transaction with a connection initialization or handshaking phase.

It is in the handshaking stage that the server is authenticated using the certificate that the client has received. The client uses the server's public key to encrypt messages sent to the server. After the client has been authenticated and the encryption algorithm or cipher has been agreed between the two parties, new symmetric session keys are used to encrypt and decrypt any further communication.

The encryption algorithm or cipher can be one of many popular algorithms like Rivest, Shamir and Adleman (RSA) or Data Encryption Standard (DES). The greater the number of bits used to make the key, the more difficult it is to break into using brute-force search techniques.

Using public key cryptography and certificates lets you provide the amount of privacy your application needs for safe and secure transactions. Servers, browsers, and Java Plug-In have their own setup for enabling HTTPS using SSL communications. In general, the steps involve the following:

- Get a private key and a digitally signed certificate with the matching public key.
- Install the certificate in a location specified by the software you are using (server, browser, or Java Plug-In).
- Enable SSL features and specify your certificate and private key files as instructed in your documentation.

You should enable SSL features according to your specific application requirements depending on the level of security you need. For example, you do not need to verify the identity of customers browsing auction items, but you will want to encrypt credit card and other personal information supplied when buyers and sellers register to participate.

HTTPS can be used for any data not just HTTP Web pages. Programs written in the Java programming language can be downloaded over an HTTPS connection, and you can open a connection to an HTTPS server in the Java Plug-in. To write a program in the Java programming language that uses SSL, you need an SSL library and a detailed knowledge of the HTTPS handshaking process. Your SSL library should provide all the functionality you need because this information is restricted by export security control.

5

JNI Technology

The Java platform is relatively new, which means there could be times when you will need to integrate programs written in the Java programming language with existing non–Java language services, API toolkits, and programs. The Java platform provides the Java Native Interface (JNI) to help ease this type of integration.

The JNI defines a standard naming and calling convention so the Java virtual machine can locate and invoke native methods. In fact, JNI is built into the Java virtual machine so that the Java virtual machine can invoke local system calls to perform input and output, graphics, networking, and threading operations on the host operating system.

This chapter explains how to use JNI in programs written in the Java programming language to call libraries on the local machine, call Java methods from inside native code, and it explains how to create and run a Java virtual machine instance. To show how you can put JNI to use, the examples in this chapter include integrating JNI with the Xbase C++ database API, and show how you can call a mathematical function. Xbase (`http://www.startech.keller.tx.us/xbase/xbase.html`) has sources you can download.

Covered in this Chapter

JNI Example

The `ReadFile` example program shows how you can use the JNI to invoke a native method that makes C function calls to map a file into memory.

About the Example

You can call code written in any programming language from a program written in the Java programming language by declaring a native Java method, loading the library that contains the native code, and calling the native method. The `ReadFile` source code below does exactly that.

However, successfully running the program requires a few additional steps beyond compiling the Java programming language source file. After you compile, but before you run the example, you have to generate a header file. The native code implements the function definitions contained in the generated header file and implements the business logic as well. The following sections walk through all the steps.

```
import java.util.*;

class ReadFile {
//Native method declaration
  native byte[] loadFile(String name);
//Load the library
  static {
    System.loadLibrary("nativelib");
  }

  public static void main(String args[]) {
    byte buf[];
//Create class instance
    ReadFile mappedFile=new ReadFile();
//Call native method to load ReadFile.java
    buf=mappedFile.loadFile("ReadFile.java");
//Print contents of ReadFile.java
    for(int i=0;i<buf.length;i++) {
      System.out.print((char)buf[i]);
    }
  }
}
```

Native Method Declaration. The `native` declaration provides the bridge to run the `native` function in the Java virtual machine. In this example, the `loadFile` function maps to a C function called `Java_ReadFile_loadFile`. The function implementation accepts a `String` that represents a file name and returns the contents of that file in the byte array.

```
native byte[] loadFile(String name);
```

Load the Library. The library containing the native code implementation is loaded by a call to `System.loadLibrary()`. Placing this call in a static initializer ensures this library is only loaded once per class. The library can be loaded outside of the `static` block if your application requires it.

> **NOTE** You might need to configure your environment so the `loadLibrary` method can find your native code library. See the section Compile the Dynamic or Shared Object Library for this information.

```
//API Ref: static void loadLibrary(String libraryname)
    static {
        System.loadLibrary("nativelib");
    }
```

Compile the Program. To compile the program, run the `javac` compiler command as you normally would:

```
javac ReadFile.java
```

Next, you need to generate a header file with the `native` method declaration and implement the `native` method to call the C functions for loading and reading a file.

Generate the Header File

To generate a header file, run the `javah` command on the `ReadFile` class. In this example, the generated header file is named `ReadFile.h`. It provides a method signature that you have to use when you implement the loadfile `native` function.

```
javah -jni ReadFile
```

Method Signature

The `ReadFile.h` header file defines the interface to map the Java method to the native C function. It uses a method signature to map the arguments and return value of the Java mappedfile.loadFile method to the loadFile native method in the nativelib library. Here is the loadFile native method mapping (method signature):

```
/*
 * Class:      ReadFile
 * Method:     loadFile
 * Signature: (Ljava/lang/String;)[B
 */
JNIEXPORT jbyteArray JNICALL Java_ReadFile_loadFile
  (JNIEnv *, jobject, jstring);
```

The method signature parameters function as follows:

- JNIEnv *: A pointer to the JNI environment. This pointer is a handle to the current thread in the Java virtual machine; it contains mapping and other housekeeping information.

- jobject: A reference to the object that called this native code. If the calling method is static, this parameter would be type jclass instead of jobject.

- jstring: The parameter supplied to the native method. In this example, it is the name of the file to be read.

Implement the native Method

In this native C source file, the loadFile definition is a copy and paste of the C declaration contained in ReadFile.h. The definition is followed by the native method implementation. JNI provides a mapping for both C and C++ by default.

```
/* file nativelib.c */
#include <jni.h>
#include <sys/types.h>
#include <sys/ipc.h>
#include <sys/shm.h>
#include <sys/mman.h>
#include <sys/stat.h>
#include <fcntl.h>
#include <unistd.h>

JNIEXPORT jbyteArray JNICALL Java_ReadFile_loadFile
  (JNIEnv * env, jobject jobj, jstring name) {
    caddr_t m;
    jbyteArray jb;
    jboolean iscopy;
    struct stat finfo;
//API Ref: const char* GetStringUTFChars(JNIEnv *env, jstring string,
                                         jboolean *iscopy)
    const char *mfile = (*env)->GetStringUTFChars(env, name, &iscopy);
    int fd = open(mfile, O_RDONLY);
    if (fd == -1) {
```

```
        printf("Could not open %s\n", mfile);
    }
    lstat(mfile, &finfo);
    m = mmap((caddr_t) 0, finfo.st_size,
                PROT_READ, MAP_PRIVATE, fd, 0);
    if (m == (caddr_t)-1) {
      printf("Could not mmap %s\n", mfile);
      return(0);
    }
//API Ref: jbyteArray NewByteArray(JNIEnv *env, jsize length)
    jb=(*env)->NewByteArray(env, finfo.st_size);
//API Ref: SetByteArrayRegion(JNIEnv *env, jbyteArray array, jsize startelement,
                        jsize length, jbyte *buffer)
    (*env)->SetByteArrayRegion(env, jb, 0, finfo.st_size, (jbyte *)m);
    close(fd);
    (*env)->ReleaseStringUTFChars(env, name, mfile);
    return (jb);
}
```

You can approach calling an existing C function instead of implementing one in one of two ways:

1. Map the name generated by JNI to the existing C function name. The Other Programming Issues section (page 148) shows how to map between Xbase database functions and Java programming language code.

2. Use the shared stubs code available from the JNI page (http://java.sun.com/products/jdk/faq/jnifaq.html) on the java.sun.com Web site.

Compile the Dynamic or Shared Object Library

The library needs to be compiled as a dynamic or shared object library so it can be loaded at run time. Static or archive libraries are compiled into an executable and cannot be loaded at run time. The shared object or dynamic library for the loadFile example is compiled on various platforms as follows:

GNU C/Linux:
```
gcc  -o libnativelib.so -shared -Wl,-soname,libnative.so
    -I/export/home/jdk1.2/
include -I/export/home/jdk1.2/include/linux nativelib.c -static -lc
```

SunPro C/Solaris:
```
cc -G -so libnativelib.so -I/export/home/jdk1.2/include
    -I/export/home/jdk1.2/include/solaris nativelib.c
```

GNU C++/Linux with Xbase:
```
g++ -o libdbmaplib.so -shared -Wl,-soname,libdbmap.so
    -I/export/home/jdk1.2/include
    -I/export/home/jdk1.2/include/linux dbmaplib.cc
    -static -lc -lxbase
```

Win32/WinNT/Win2000:
```
cl -Ic:/jdk1.2/include -Ic:/jdk1.2/include/win32 -LD nativelib.c
   -Felibnative.dll
```

Run the Example

To run the example, the Java virtual machine needs to find the native JNI library that was created. To do this, set the library path to the current directory as follows:

Unix or Linux:
```
LD_LIBRARY_PATH=.
export LD_LIBRARY_PATH
```

Windows NT/2000/95:
```
set PATH=%path%;.
```

With the library path properly specified for your platform, invoke the program as you normally would with the interpreter command:

```
java ReadFile
```

Strings and Arrays

This section explains how to pass string and array data between a program written in the Java programming language and a program written in another language.

Passing Strings

The String object in the Java programming language, which is represented as jstring in JNI, is a 16-bit unicode string. In C a string is by default constructed from 8-bit characters. So, to access a Java String object passed to a C or C++ function or return a C or C++ string to a Java method, you need to use JNI conversion functions in your native method implementation.

The GetStringUTFChar function retrieves 8-bit characters from a 16-bit jstring using the Unicode Transformation Format (UTF). UTF represents Unicode as a string of 8- or 16-bit characters without losing any information. The third parameter GetStringUTFChar returns the result JNI_TRUE if it made a local copy of the jstring, or it returns JNI_FALSE otherwise.

C Version:
```
(*env)->GetStringUTFChars(env, name, iscopy)
```

C++ Version:
```
env->GetStringUTFChars(name, iscopy)
```

The following C JNI function converts an array of C characters to a jstring:

```
//API Ref: jstring NewStringUTF(JNIEnv *env, const char *bytes)
    (*env)->NewStringUTF(env, lastfile)
```

The example below converts the lastfile[80] C character array to a jstring, which is returned to the calling Java method:

```
    static char lastfile[80];

    JNIEXPORT jstring JNICALL Java_ReadFile_lastFile
      (JNIEnv *env, jobject jobj) {
//API Ref: jstring NewStringUTF(JNIEnv *env, const char *bytes)
        return((*env)->NewStringUTF(env, lastfile));
    }
```

To let the Java virtual machine know you are finished with the UTF representation, call the ReleaseStringUTFChars conversion function as shown below. The second argument is the original jstring value used to construct the UTF representation, and the third argument is the reference to the local representation of that String.

```
(*env)->ReleaseStringUTFChars(env, name, mfile);
```

If your native code can work with Unicode without needing the intermediate UTF representation, call the GetStringChars function to retrieve the Unicode string, and release the reference with a call to ReleaseStringChars:

```
    JNIEXPORT jbyteArray JNICALL Java_ReadFile_loadFile
      (JNIEnv * env, jobject jobj, jstring name) {
        caddr_t m;
        jbyteArray jb;
        struct stat finfo;
        jboolean iscopy;
//API Ref: const jchar *GetStringChars(JNIEnv *env, jstring string,
                                        jboolean *iscopy)
        const jchar *mfile = (*env)->GetStringChars(env, name, &iscopy);
        //...
//API Ref: void ReleaseStringChars(JNIEnv *env, jstring string,
                                    const jchar *chars)
        (*env)->ReleaseStringChars(env, name, mfile);
```

Passing Arrays

In the example presented in the last section, the loadFile native method returns the contents of a file in a byte array, which is a primitive type in the Java programming language. You can retrieve and create primitive types in the Java programming language by calling the appropriate TypeArray function.

For example, to create a new array of floats, call NewFloatArray, or to create a new array of bytes, call NewByteArray. This naming scheme extends to retrieving elements from, adding elements to, and changing elements in the array. To get elements from an array of bytes, call GetByteArrayElements. To add elements to or change elements in the array, call Set<*type*>ArrayElements.

The GetByteArrayElements function affects the entire array. To work on a portion of the array, call GetByteArrayRegion instead. There is only a Set<*type*>ArrayRegion function for changing array elements. However the region could be of size array.length, which is equivalent to the nonexistent Set<*type*>ArrayElements.

Native Code Type	Functions Used
jboolean	NewBooleanArray GetBooleanArrayElements GetBooleanArrayRegion/SetBooleanArrayRegion ReleaseBooleanArrayRegion
jbyte	NewByteArray GetByteArrayElements GetByteArrayRegion/SetByteArrayRegion ReleaseByteArrayRegion
jchar	NewCharArray GetCharArrayElements GetCharArrayRegion/SetCharArrayRegion ReleaseCharArrayRegion
jdouble	NewDoubleArray GetDoubleArrayElements GetDoubleArrayRegion/SetDoubleArrayRegion ReleaseDoubleArrayRegion
jfloat	NewFloatArray GetFloatArrayElements GetFloatArrayRegion/SetFloatArrayRegion ReleaseFloatArrayRegion
jint	NewIntArray GetIntArrayElements GetIntArrayRegion/SetIntArrayRegion ReleaseIntArrayRegion
jlong	NewLongArray GetLongArrayElements GetLongArrayRegion/SetLongArrayRegion ReleaseLongArrayRegion

(continues)

Native Code Type	Functions Used
jobject	NewObjectArray GetObjectArrayElement/SetObjectArrayElement
jshort	NewShortArray GetShortArrayElements GetShortArrayRegion/SetShortArrayRegion ReleaseShortArrayRegion

In the loadFile native method from the example in the previous section, the entire array is updated by specifying a region that is the size of the file being read in:

```
jbyteArray jb;
//API Ref: jbyteArray NewByteArray(JNIEnv *env, jsize length)
    jb=(*env)->NewByteArray(env, finfo.st_size);
//API Ref: SetByteArrayRegion(JNIEnv *env, jbyteArray array, jsize startelement,
                    jsize length, jbyte *buffer)
    (*env)->SetByteArrayRegion(env, jb, 0, finfo.st_size, (jbyte *)m);
    close(fd);
```

The array is returned to the calling Java programming language method, which in turn, garbage collects the reference to the array when it is no longer used. The array can be explicitly freed with the following call.

```
//API Ref: void ReleaseByteArrayElements(JNIEnv *env, jbyteArray array,
                    jbyte *elems, jint mode)
    (*env)-> ReleaseByteArrayElements(env, jb, (jbyte *)m, 0);
```

The last argument to the ReleaseByteArrayElements function above can have the following values:

- 0: Updates to the array from within the C code are reflected in the Java programming language copy.
- JNI_COMMIT: The Java programming language copy is updated, but the local jbyteArray is not freed.
- JNI_ABORT: Changes are not copied back, but the jbyteArray is freed. The value is used only if the array is obtained with a get mode of JNI_TRUE, meaning the array is a copy.

See Memory Issues (page 155) for more information on memory management.

Pinning Arrays

When retrieving an array, you can specify if this is a copy (JNI_TRUE) or a reference to the array residing in your Java program (JNI_FALSE). If you use a reference to the array, you will want the array to stay where it is in the Java heap and not get moved by the garbage collector when it compacts heap memory. To prevent the array references from being moved, the Java virtual machine pins the array into memory. Pinning the array ensures that when the array is released, the correct elements are updated in the Java virtual machine.

In the loadfile native method example from the previous section, the array is not explicitly released. One way to ensure the array is garbage collected when it is no longer needed is to call a Java method, pass the byte array instead, and free the local array copy. This technique is shown in the section on Multidimensional Arrays (page 145).

Object Arrays

You can store any Java object in an array with the `NewObjectArray` and `SetObjectArrayElement` function calls. The main difference between an object array and an array of primitive types is that when constructing a `jobjectArray`, the Java class is used as a parameter.

This next C++ example shows how to call `NewObjectArray` to create an array of `String` objects. The size of the array is set to five, the class definition is returned from a call to `FindClass`, and the elements of the array are initialized with an empty string. The elements of the array are updated by calling `SetObjectArrayElement` with the position and value to put in the array.

```
/*  ReturnArray.C  */
#include <jni.h>
#include "ArrayHandler.h"

    JNIEXPORT jobjectArray JNICALL Java_ArrayHandler_returnArray
                                        (JNIEnv *env, jobject jobj){
        jobjectArray ret;
        int i;
        char *message[5]= {"first", "second", "third", "fourth", "fifth"};
        ret = (jobjectArray)env->NewObjectArray(5,
//API Ref: jclass FindClass(JNIenv *env, const char *name)
            env->FindClass("java/lang/String"),
//API Ref: jstring NewStringUTF(JNIEnv *env, const char *bytes)
            env->NewStringUTF(""));
        for(i=0;i<5;i++) {
//API Ref: void SetObjectArrayElement(JNIEnv *env, jobjectArray array,
                                    jsize index, jobject value)
            env->SetObjectArrayElement(ret,i,env->NewStringUTF(message[i]));
        }
        return(ret);
    }
```

The Java class that calls this native method is as follows:

```
//ArrayHandler.java
```

```
    public class ArrayHandler {
        public native String[] returnArray();
        static{
//API Ref: static void loadLibrary(String libraryname)
            System.loadLibrary("nativelib");
        }
        public static void main(String args[]) {
          String ar[];
          ArrayHandler ah= new ArrayHandler();
          ar = ah.returnArray();
          for(int i=0; i<5; i++) {
             System.out.println("array element"+i+ "=" + ar[i]);
          }
        }
    }
```

Multidimensional Arrays

You might need to call existing numerical and mathematical libraries such as the linear algebra library CLAPACK/LAPACK or other matrix-crunching programs from your Java program using native methods. Many of these libraries and programs use two-dimensional and higher-order arrays.

In the Java programming language, any array that has more than one dimension is treated as an array of arrays. For example, a two-dimensional integer array is handled as an array of integer arrays. The array is read horizontally, or in what is also termed as row order.

Other languages such as FORTRAN use column ordering, so extra care is needed if your program hands a Java array to a FORTRAN function. Also, the array elements in an application written in the Java programming language are not guaranteed to be contiguous in memory. Some numerical libraries use the knowledge that the array elements are stored next to each other in memory to perform speed optimizations, so you might need to make an additional local copy of the array to pass to those functions.

The next example passes a two-dimensional array to a native method, which then extracts the elements, performs a calculation, and calls a Java method to return the results. The array is passed as an object array that contains an array of jints. The individual elements are extracted by first retrieving a jintArray instance from the object array by calling GetObjectArrayElement, and then extracting the elements from the jintArray row.

The example uses a fixed-size matrix. If you do not know the size of the array being used, the GetArrayLength(array) function returns the size of the outermost array. You will need to call the GetArrayLength(array) function on each dimension of the array to discover the total size of the array. The new array sent back to the program written in the Java language is built in reverse.

First, a jintArray instance is created and that instance is set in the object array by calling SetObjectArrayElement.

```java
public class ArrayManipulation {
  private int arrayResults[][];
  Boolean lock=new Boolean(true);
  int arraySize=-1;

  public native void manipulateArray(int[][] multiplier, Boolean lock);
  static{
//API Ref: static void loadLibrary(String libraryname)
    System.loadLibrary("nativelib");
  }
  public void sendArrayResults(int results[][]) {
    arraySize=results.length;
    arrayResults=new int[results.length][];
    System.arraycopy(results,0,arrayResults, 0, arraySize);
  }
  public void displayArray() {
    for (int i=0; i<arraySize; i++) {
      for(int j=0; j <arrayResults[i].length;j++) {
        System.out.println("array element "+i+","+j+ "= " + arrayResults[i][j
]);
      }
    }
  }
  public static void main(String args[]) {
    int[][] ar = new int[3][3];
    int count=3;
    for(int i=0;i<3;i++) {
      for(int j=0;j<3;j++) {
        ar[i][j]=count;
      }
      count++;
    }
    ArrayManipulation am= new ArrayManipulation();
    am.manipulateArray(ar, am.lock);
    am.displayArray();
  }
}
```

```c
#include <jni.h>
#include <iostream.h>
#include "ArrayManipulation.h"

JNIEXPORT void
    JNICALL Java_ArrayManipulation_manipulateArray
            (JNIEnv *env, jobject jobj, jobjectArray elements, jobject lock){
  jobjectArray ret;
  int i,j;
  jint arraysize;
  int asize;
  jclass cls;
  jmethodID mid;
  jfieldID fid;
```

```
      long localArrayCopy[3][3];
      long localMatrix[3]={4,4,4};

      for(i=0; i<3; i++) {
//API Ref: jobject GetObjectArrayElement(JNIEnv *env, jobjectArray array,
                                          jsize index)
         jintArray oneDim= (jintArray)env->GetObjectArrayElement(elements, i);
//API Ref: jint* GetIntArrayElements(JNIEnv *env, jintArray array, jboolean
                                     *iscopy)
         jint *element=env->GetIntArrayElements(oneDim, 0);
         for(j=0; j<3; j++) {
            localArrayCopy[i][j]= element[j];
         }
      }
   // With the C++ copy of the array,
   // process the array with LAPACK, BLAS, etc.

      for (i=0;i<3;i++) {
        for (j=0; j<3 ; j++) {
          localArrayCopy[i][j]=
             localArrayCopy[i][j]*localMatrix[i];
        }
      }
   // Create array to send back
//API Ref: jintArray NewIntArray(JNIEnv *env, jsize length)
      jintArray row= (jintArray)env->NewIntArray(3);
//API Ref: jclass GetObjectClass(JNIEnv *env, jobject obj)
      ret=(jobjectArray)env->NewObjectArray(3, env->GetObjectClass(row), 0);

      for(i=0;i<3;i++) {
        row= (jintArray)env->NewIntArray(3);
//API Ref: SetIntArrayRegion(JNIEnv *env, jintArray array, jsize startelement,
                             jsize length, jint *buffer)
        env->SetIntArrayRegion((jintArray)row,(jsize)0,3,
                               (jint *)localArrayCopy[i]);
        env->SetObjectArrayElement(ret,i,row);
      }
      cls=env->GetObjectClass(jobj);
//API Ref: jmethodID GetMethodId(JNIEnv *env, jclass class,
                                 const char *methodname, const char *methodsig)
      mid=env->GetMethodID(cls, "sendArrayResults",
                                "([[I)V");
      if (mid == 0) {
        cout <<"Can't find method sendArrayResults";
        return;
      }
//API Ref: void ExceptionClear(JNIEnv *env)
      env->ExceptionClear();
//API Ref: jint MonitorEnter(JNIEnv *env, jobject object)
      env->MonitorEnter(lock);
//API Ref: CallVoidMethod(JNIEnv *env, jobject object, jmethodId methodid,
                          object arg1)
      env->CallVoidMethod(jobj, mid, ret);
//API Ref: jint MonitorExit(JNIEnv *env, jobject object)
      env->MonitorExit(lock);
```

```
//API Ref: jthrowable ExceptionOccurred(JNIEnv *env)
      if(env->ExceptionOccurred()) {
        cout << "error occured copying array back" << endl;
//API Ref: void ExceptionDescribe(JNIEnv *env)
        env->ExceptionDescribe();
        env->ExceptionClear();
      }
//API Ref: jfieldID GetFieldID(JNIEnv *env, jclass class, const char *fieldname,
                            const char *fieldsig)
      fid=env->GetFieldID(cls, "arraySize", "I");
      if (fid == 0) {
        cout <<"Can't find field arraySize";
        return;
      }
      asize=env->GetIntField(jobj,fid);
      if(!env->ExceptionOccurred()) {
        cout<< "Java array size=" << asize << endl;
      } else {
        env->ExceptionClear();
      }
      return;
    }
```

Other Programming Issues

This section presents information on accessing classes, methods, and fields, and covers threading, memory, and Java virtual machine issues.

Language Issues

So far, the native method examples have covered calling standalone C and C++ functions that either return a result or modify parameters passed into the function. However, C++—like the Java programming language—uses instances of classes. If you create a class in one native method, the reference to this class does not have an equivalent class in the Java programming language. This makes it difficult to call functions on the C++ class that was first created.

One way to handle this situation is to keep a record of the C++ class reference and pass that back to a proxy or to the calling program. To ensure the C++ class persists across native method calls, use the C++ new operator to create a reference to the C++ object on the heap.

The following code provides a mapping between the Xbase database and Java code. The Xbase database has a C++ API and uses an initialization class to perform subsequent database operations. When the class object is created, a pointer to this object is returned as a Java int value. You can use a long or larger value for machines with greater than 32 bits.

```
public class CallDB {
  public native int initdb();
```

```
      public native short opendb(String name, int ptr);
      public native short GetFieldNo(String fieldname, int ptr);

      static {
//API Ref: static void loadLibrary(String libraryname)
         System.loadLibrary("dbmaplib");
      }
      public static void main(String args[]) {
        String prefix=null;
        CallDB db=new CallDB();
        int res=db.initdb();
        if(args.length>=1) {
          prefix=args[0];
        }
        System.out.println(db.opendb("MYFILE.DBF", res));
        System.out.println(db.GetFieldNo("LASTNAME", res));
        System.out.println(db.GetFieldNo("FIRSTNAME", res));
      }
   }
```

The return result from the call to the initdb native method, the int value, is passed to subsequent native method calls. The native code included in the dbmaplib.cc library dereferences the Java object passed in as a parameter and retrieves the object pointer. The line xbDbf* Myfile=(xbDbf*)ptr; casts the int pointer value to be a pointer of Xbase type xbDbf.

```
#include <jni.h>
#include <xbase/xbase.h>
#include "CallDB.h"

JNIEXPORT jint JNICALL Java_CallDB_initdb(JNIEnv *env, jobject jobj) {
  xbXBase* x;
  x= new xbXBase();
  xbDbf* Myfile;
  Myfile =new xbDbf(x);
  return ((jint)Myfile);
}
JNIEXPORT jshort JNICALL Java_CallDB_opendb(JNIEnv *env, jobject jobj,
                                            jstring dbname, jint ptr) {
  xbDbf* Myfile=(xbDbf*)ptr;
  return((*Myfile).OpenDatabase( "MYFILE.DBF"));
}
JNIEXPORT jshort JNICALL Java_CallDB_GetFieldNo(JNIEnv *env, jobject jobj,
                                                jstring fieldname, jint ptr) {
  xbDbf* Myfile=(xbDbf*)ptr;
  return((*Myfile).GetFieldNo(env->GetStringUTFChars(fieldname,0)));
}
```

Calling Methods

The section on arrays highlighted some reasons for calling Java programming language methods from within native code; for example, when you need to free the result you intend to return. Other uses for calling Java native methods from within your native code are if you need to return more than one result or you just simply want to modify Java programming language values from within native code. Calling a Java programming language method from within native code involves the following three steps:

1. Retrieve a class reference
2. Retrieve a method identifier
3. Call the methods

1. Retrieve a Class Reference.   The first step is to retrieve a reference to the class that contains the methods you want to access. To retrieve a reference, you can either use the FindClass method or access the jobject or jclass argument to the native method.

Use the FindClass method:

```
JNIEXPORT void JNICALL Java_ArrayHandler_returnArray(JNIEnv *env,
                                                     jobject jobj){
  jclass cls = (*env)->FindClass(env, "ClassName");
}
```

Use the jobject argument:

```
JNIEXPORT void JNICALL Java_ArrayHandler_returnArray(JNIEnv *env,
                                                     jobject jobj){
  jclass cls=(*env)->GetObjectClass(env, jobj);
}
```

or

Use the jclass argument:

```
JNIEXPORT void JNICALL Java_ArrayHandler_returnArray(JNIEnv *env,
                                                     jclass jcls){
  jclass cls=jcls;
}
```

2. Retrieve a Method Identifier.   Once the class has been obtained, the second step is to call the GetMethodID function to retrieve an identifier for a method you select in the class. The identifier is needed when calling the method of that class instance. Because the Java programming language supports method overloading, you also need to specify the method signature you want to call. To find out what signature your Java method uses, run the javap command as follows:

```
javap -s Class
```

The method signature used is displayed as a comment after each method declaration as shown here:

```
bash# javap -s ArrayHandler
Compiled from ArrayHandler.java
```

```
public class ArrayHandler extends java.lang.Object {
  java.lang.String arrayResults[];
  /*   [Ljava/lang/String;    */
  static {};
  /*    ()V   */
  public ArrayHandler();
  /*    ()V   */
  public void displayArray();
  /*    ()V   */
  public static void main(java.lang.String[]);
  /*    ([Ljava/lang/String;)V   */
  public native void returnArray();
  /*    ()V   */
  public void sendArrayResults(java.lang.String[]);
  /*    ([Ljava/lang/String;)V   */
}
```

Use the `GetMethodID` function to call instance methods in an object instance, or use the `GetStaticMethodID` function to call static methods. Their argument lists are the same.

3. Call the Methods.   Third, the matching instance method is called using a `Call<type>Method` function. The `type` value can be `Void`, `Object`, `Boolean`, `Byte`, `Char`, `Short`, `Int`, `Long`, `Float`, or `Double`.

The parameters to the method can be passed as a comma-separated list, an array of values to the `Call<type>MethodA` function, or as a `va_list`. The `va_list` is a construct often used for variable argument lists in C. `Call<type>MethodV` is the function used to pass a `va_list()`.

Static methods are called in a similar way except the method naming includes an additional `Static` identifier, `CallStaticByteMethodA`, and the `jclass` value is used instead of `jobject`.

The next example returns the object array by calling the `sendArrayResults` method from the `ArrayHandler` class.

```
// ArrayHandler.java
public class ArrayHandler {
  private String arrayResults[];
  int arraySize=-1;

  public native void returnArray();
  static{
//API Ref: static void loadLibrary(String libraryname)
    System.loadLibrary("nativelib");
  }
  public void sendArrayResults(String results[]) {
    arraySize=results.length;
    arrayResults=new String[arraySize];
    System.arraycopy(results,0,arrayResults,0,arraySize);
  }
```

```
    public void displayArray() {
      for (int i=0; i<arraySize; i++) {
        System.out.println("array element "+i+ "= " + arrayResults[i]);
      }
    }
    public static void main(String args[]) {
      String ar[];
      ArrayHandler ah= new ArrayHandler();
      ah.returnArray();
      ah.displayArray();
    }
}
```

The native C++ code is defined as follows:

```
//file: nativelib.cc
#include <jni.h>
#include <iostream.h>
#include "ArrayHandler.h"

JNIEXPORT void JNICALL Java_ArrayHandler_returnArray(JNIEnv *env,
                                                        jobject jobj){
    jobjectArray ret;
    int i;
    jclass cls;
    jmethodID mid;
    char *message[5]= {"first", "second", "third", "fourth", "fifth"};
//API Ref: jarray NewObjectArray(JNIEnv *env, jsize length, jclass elementClass,
                                jobject initialElement)
    ret=(jobjectArray)env->NewObjectArray(5,
        env->FindClass("java/lang/String"),
        env->NewStringUTF(""));
    for(i=0;i<5;i++) {
      env->SetObjectArrayElement(ret,i,env->NewStringUTF(message[i]));
    }
    cls=env->GetObjectClass(jobj);
    mid=env->GetMethodID(cls, "sendArrayResults", "([Ljava/lang/String;)V");
    if (mid == 0) {
      cout <<"Can't find method sendArrayResults";
      return;
    }
    env->ExceptionClear();
    env->CallVoidMethod(jobj, mid, ret);
    if(env->ExceptionOccurred()) {
      cout << "error occured copying array back" <<endl;
      env->ExceptionDescribe();
      env->ExceptionClear();
    }
    return;
}
```

To build this on Linux, run the following commands:

```
javac ArrayHandler.java
javah -jni ArrayHandler
```

```
g++  -o libnativelib.so -shared -Wl,-soname,libnative.so -I/export/home/
jdk1.2/include -I/export/home/jdk1.2/include/linux nativelib.cc  -lc
```

If you want to specify a super class method to, for example, call the parent constructor, you can do so by calling the `CallNonvirtual<type>Method` functions. One important point when calling Java methods or fields from within native code is that you need to catch any raised exceptions. The `ExceptionClear` function clears any pending exceptions while the `ExceptionOccured` function checks to see if an exception has been raised in the current JNI session.

Accessing Fields

Accessing Java fields from within native code is similar to calling Java methods. However, the set or field is retrieved with a field ID, instead of a method ID.

The first thing you need to do is retrieve a field ID. You can use the `GetFieldID` function, but specify the field name and signature in place of the method name and signature. Once you have the field ID, call a `Get<type>Field` function to set the field value. The `<type>` is the same as the native type being returned except the `j` is dropped and the first letter is capitalized. For example, the `<type>` value is `Int` for native type `jint`, and `Byte` for native type `jbyte`.

The `Get<type>Field` function result is returned as the native type. For example, to retrieve the `arraySize` field in the `ArrayHandler` class, call `GetIntField` as shown in the following example.

The field can be set by calling the `env->SetIntField(jobj, fid, arraysize)` functions. Static fields can be set by calling `SetStaticIntField(jclass, fid, arraysize)` and retrieved by calling `GetStaticIntField(jclass, fid)`.

```
#include <jni.h>
#include <iostream.h>
#include "ArrayHandler.h"

JNIEXPORT void JNICALL Java_ArrayHandler_returnArray(JNIEnv *env,
                                                     jobject jobj){
    jobjectArray ret;
    int i;
    jint arraysize;
    jclass cls;
    jmethodID mid;
    jfieldID fid;
    char *message[5]= {"first", "second", "third", "fourth", "fifth"};

    ret=(jobjectArray)env->NewObjectArray(5,
        env->FindClass("java/lang/String"),
        env->NewStringUTF(""));
    for(i=0;i<5;i++) {
```

```
        env->SetObjectArrayElement(ret,i,env->NewStringUTF(message[i]));
    }
    cls=env->GetObjectClass(jobj);
    mid=env->GetMethodID(cls, "sendArrayResults", "([Ljava/lang/String;)V");
    if (mid == 0) {
        cout <<"Can't find method sendArrayResults";
        return;
    }
    env->ExceptionClear();
    env->CallVoidMethod(jobj, mid, ret);
    if(env->ExceptionOccurred()) {
        cout << "error occured copying array back" << endl;
        env->ExceptionDescribe();
        env->ExceptionClear();
    }
    fid=env->GetFieldID(cls, "arraySize",  "I");
    if (fid == 0) {
        cout <<"Can't find field arraySize";
        return;
    }
    arraysize=env->GetIntField(jobj, fid);
    if(!env->ExceptionOccurred()) {
        cout<< "size=" << arraysize << endl;
    } else {
        env->ExceptionClear();
    }
    return;
}
```

Threads and Synchronization

Although the native library is loaded once per class, individual threads in an application written in the Java programming language use their own interface pointer when calling the native method. If you need to restrict access to a Java object from within native code, you can either ensure that the Java methods you call have explicit synchronization or you can use the JNI MonitorEnter and MonitorExit functions.

In the Java programming language, code is protected by a monitor whenever you specify the synchronized keyword, and the monitor enter and exit routines are normally hidden from the application developer. In JNI, you need to explicitly delineate the entry and exit points of thread safe code.

The following example uses a Boolean object to restrict access to the Call-VoidMethod function.

```
env->ExceptionClear();
env->MonitorEnter(lock);
env->CallVoidMethod(jobj, mid, ret);
env->MonitorExit(lock);
if(env->ExceptionOccurred()) {
  cout << "error occured copying array back" << endl;
```

```
    env->ExceptionDescribe();
    env->ExceptionClear();
}
```

You may find that in cases where you want access to a local system resource like a Microsoft Foundation Classes (MFC) window handle or message queue, it is better to use one `Java.lang.Thread` and access the local threaded native event queue or messaging system from within the native code.

Memory Issues

By default, JNI uses local references when creating objects inside a native method. This means that when the method returns, the references are eligible to be garbage collected. If you want an object to persist across native method calls, use a global reference instead. A global reference is created from a local reference by calling `NewGlobalReference` on the local reference.

You can explicitly mark a reference for garbage collection by calling `Delete-GlobalRef` on the reference. You can also create a weak style `Global` reference that is accessible outside the method but that can be garbage collected. To create one of these references, call `NewWeakGlobalRef` and `DeleteWeak-GlobalRef` to mark the reference for garbage collection.

You can even explicitly mark a local reference for garbage collection by calling the `env->DeleteLocalRef(localobject)` method. This is useful if you are using a large amount of temporary data.

```
static jobject stringarray=0;

JNIEXPORT void JNICALL Java_ArrayHandler_returnArray(JNIEnv *env,
                                                        jobject jobj){
    jobjectArray ret;
    int i;
    jint arraysize;
    int asize;
    jclass cls, tmpcls;
    jmethodID mid;
    jfieldID fid;
    char *message[5]= {"first", "second", "third", "fourth", "fifth"};
    ret=(jobjectArray)env->NewObjectArray(5,
        env->FindClass("java/lang/String"),
        env->NewStringUTF(""));
    //Make the array available globally
//API Ref: jobject NewGlobalRef(JNIEnv *env, jobject object)
    stringarray=env->NewGlobalRef(ret);
    //Process array
    // ...
    //clear local reference when finished..
//API Ref: void DeleteLocalRef(JNIEnv *env, jobject localref)
    env->DeleteLocalRef(ret);
    }
```

Invocation

The section on calling methods showed you how to call a method or field in a Java program using the JNI interface and a class loaded using the FindClass function. With a little more code, you can create a standalone program that invokes a Java virtual machine and includes its own JNI interface pointer that can be used to create instances of Java classes. In the Java 2 release, the run-time program named java is a small JNI application that does exactly that.

You can create a Java virtual machine with a call to JNI_CreateJavaVM and shut the created Java virtual machine down with a call to JNI_DestroyJavaVM. A Java virtual machine might also need some additional environment properties. These properties can be passed to the JNI_CreateJavaVM function in a JavaVMInitArgs structure.

The JavaVMInitArgs structure contains a pointer to a JavaVMOption value used to store environment information such as the classpath and Java virtual machine version, or system properties that would normally be passed on the command line to the program.

When the JNI_CreateJavaVM function returns, you can call methods and create instances of classes using the FindClass and NewObject functions the same way you would for embedded native code.

NOTE   The Java virtual machine invocation was only used for native thread Java virtual machines. Some older Java virtual machines have a green threads option that is stable for invocation use. On a Unix platform, you may also need to explicitly link with -lthread or -lpthread.

This next program invokes a Java virtual machine, loads the ArrayHandler class, and retrieves the arraySize field, which should contain the value −1. The Java virtual machine options include the current path in the classpath and turning the Just-In-Time (JIT) compiler off with the option -Djava.compiler=NONE.

```
#include <jni.h>

void main(int argc, char *argv[], char **envp) {
  JavaVMOption options[2];
  JavaVMInitArgs vm_args;
  JavaVM *jvm;
  JNIEnv *env;
  long result;
  jmethodID mid;
```

```
      jfieldID fid;
      jobject jobj;
      jclass cls;
      int i, asize;

      options[0].optionString = ".";
      options[1].optionString = "-Djava.compiler=NONE";
      vm_args.version = JNI_VERSION_1_2;
      vm_args.options = options;
      vm_args.nOptions = 2;
      vm_args.ignoreUnrecognized = JNI_FALSE;
//API Ref: jint JNI_CreateJavaVM(JavaVM **pvm, void **penv, void *args)
      result = JNI_CreateJavaVM(&jvm,(void **)&env, &vm_args);
      if(result == JNI_ERR ) {
        printf("Error invoking the JVM");
        exit (-1);
      }
      cls = (*env)->FindClass(env,"ArrayHandler");
      if( cls == NULL ) {
        printf("can't find class ArrayHandler\n");
        exit (-1);
      }
      (*env)->ExceptionClear(env);
      mid=(*env)->GetMethodID(env, cls, "<init>", "()V");
      jobj=(*env)->NewObject(env, cls, mid);
      fid=(*env)->GetFieldID(env, cls, "arraySize", "I");
      asize=(*env)->GetIntField(env, jobj, fid);
      printf("size of array is %d",asize);
      (*jvm)->DestroyJavaVM(jvm);
    }
```

Attaching Threads

After the Java virtual machine is invoked, there is one local thread running the Java virtual machine. You can create more threads in the local operating system and attach the Java virtual machine to those new threads. You might want to do this if your native application is multithreaded.

Attach the local thread to the Java virtual machine with a call to AttachCurrentThread. You need to supply pointers to the Java virtual machine instance and JNI environment. In the Java 2 platform, you can also specify in the third parameter the thread name and/or group you want this new thread to live under. It is important to detach any thread that has been previously attached; otherwise, the program will not exit when you call DestroyJavaVM.

```
#include <jni.h>
#include <pthread.h>

JavaVM *jvm;

void *native_thread(void *arg) {
  JNIEnv *env;
```

```
        jclass cls;
        jmethodID mid;
        jfieldID fid;
        jint result;
        jobject jobj;
        JavaVMAttachArgs args;
        jint asize;

        args.version= JNI_VERSION_1_2;
        args.name="user";
        args.group=NULL;
        result=(*jvm)->AttachCurrentThread(jvm, (void **)&env, &args);
        cls = (*env)->FindClass(env,"ArrayHandler");
        if( cls == NULL ) {
          printf("can't find class ArrayHandler\n");
          exit (-1);
        }
        (*env)->ExceptionClear(env);
        mid=(*env)->GetMethodID(env, cls, "<init>", "()V");
        jobj=(*env)->NewObject(env, cls, mid);
        fid=(*env)->GetFieldID(env, cls, "arraySize", "I");
        asize=(*env)->GetIntField(env, jobj, fid);
        printf("size of array is %d\n",asize);
        (*jvm)->DetachCurrentThread(jvm);
}
void main(int argc, char *argv[], char **envp) {
        JavaVMOption *options;
        JavaVMInitArgs vm_args;
        JNIEnv *env;
        jint result;
        pthread_t tid;
        int thr_id;
        int i;
        options = (void *)malloc(3 * sizeof(JavaVMOption));
        options[0].optionString = "-Djava.class.path=.";
        options[1].optionString = "-Djava.compiler=NONE";
        vm_args.version = JNI_VERSION_1_2;
        vm_args.options = options;
        vm_args.nOptions = 2;
        vm_args.ignoreUnrecognized = JNI_FALSE;
        result = JNI_CreateJavaVM(&jvm,(void **)&env, &vm_args);
        if(result == JNI_ERR ) {
          printf("Error invoking the JVM");
          exit (-1);
        }
        thr_id=pthread_create(&tid, NULL, native_thread, NULL);
//If you don't have join, sleep instead
//sleep(1000);
        pthread_join(tid, NULL);
        (*jvm)->DestroyJavaVM(jvm);
        exit(0);
}
```

6

Project Swing:
Building a User Interface

The Java Foundation Classes (JFC) Project Swing and Enterprise JavaBeans architectures share one key design element: the separation of data from the display or manipulation of that data. In Enterprise JavaBeans applications, the entity bean provides a view of the data. The underlying data storage mechanism can be swapped out and replaced without changing the entity bean view or recompiling any code that uses the view.

Project Swing separates the view and control of a visual component from its contents, or data model. However, although Project Swing does have the components that make up a Model-View-Controller (MVC) architecture, it is more accurately described as a model-delegate architecture. This is because the controller part of the Project Swing interface, often the mouse and keyboard events the component responds to, is combined with the physical view in one User Interface (UI) delegate object.

Each component, for example, a `JButton` or a `JScrollBar`, has a separate UI delegate class that inherits from the `ComponentUI` class and is under the control of a separate UI manager. Although each component has a basic UI delegate, it is no longer tied to the underlying data, so a new set of delegates—a set of metal-styled components, for example—can be swapped in while the application is still running. The ability to change the look and behavior reflects the pluggable look and feel (PLAF) feature available in Project Swing.

Covered in this Chapter

Components and Data Models

This section explains Project Swing in terms of the `AuctionClient` (page 193) program shown in Figure 6.1. It is a simple GUI application that lets auction administrators list and browse auction items.

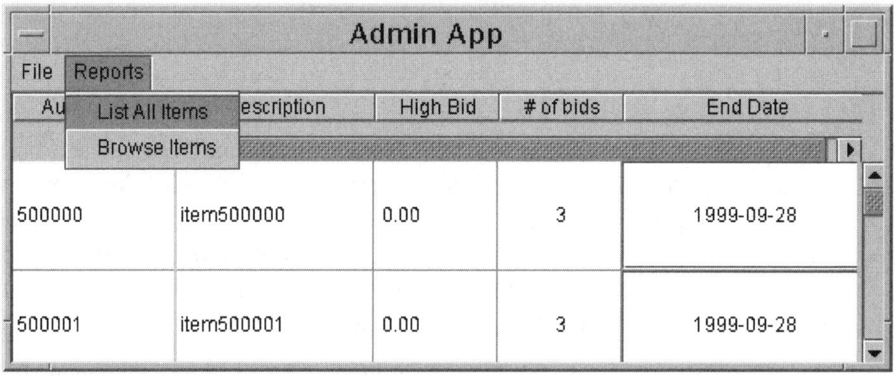

Figure 6.1 Administration applet

Lightweight Components

All components in Project Swing, except `JApplet`, `JDialog`, `JFrame`, and `JWindow` are lightweight components. Lightweight components, unlike their Abstract Window Toolkit (AWT) counterparts, do not depend on the local windowing toolkit.

For example, a heavyweight `java.awt.Button` running on the Java platform for the Unix platform maps to a real `Motif` button. In this relationship, the `Motif` button is called the peer to the `java.awt.Button`. If you create two `java.awt.Buttons` in an application, two peers and hence two `Motif` buttons are also created. The Java platform communicates with the `Motif` buttons using the Java Native Interface (JNI). For each and every component added to the application, there is additional overhead tied to the local windowing system, which is why these components are called heavyweight.

Lightweight components are termed peerless components and emulate the local window system components. A lightweight button is represented as a rectangle with a label inside that accepts mouse events. Adding more lightweight buttons means drawing more rectangles.

A lightweight component needs to be drawn on something, and an application written in the Java programming language needs to interact with the local window manager so that the main application window can be closed or minimized. This is why the top-level parent components mentioned above (JFrame, JApplet, and others) are implemented as heavyweight components—they need to be mapped to a component in the local window toolkit.

A JButton is a very simple shape to draw. For more complex components like JList or JTable, the elements or cells of the list or table are drawn by a CellRenderer object. A CellRenderer object provides flexibility because it makes it possible for any type of object to be displayed in any row or column.

For example, a JTable can use a different CellRenderer for each column. This code segment sets the second column, which is referenced as index 1, to use a CustomRenderer object to create the cells for that column.

```
    JTable scrollTable=new JTable(rm);
    TableColumnModel scrollColumnModel = scrollTable.getColumnModel();
    CustomRenderer custom = new CustomRenderer();
//API Ref: TableColumn getColumn(int index)
    scrollColumnModel.getColumn(1).setCellRenderer(custom);
```

Ordering Components

Each Project Swing applet or application needs at least one heavyweight container component (a JFrame, JWindow, JApplet, or JDialog). Each of these containers with JFrame's lightweight multiple document interface (MDI) counterpart, JInternalFrame, contains a component called a root pane. The JRootPane manages the additional layers used in the container such as the JLayeredPane, JContentPane, GlassPane, and the optional JMenuBar. It also lets all emulated (lightweight) components interact with the AWT event queue to send and receive events. Interacting with the event queue gives emulated components indirect interaction with the local window manager.

JLayeredPane. The JLayeredPane sits on top of the JRootPane, and as its name implies, controls the layers of the components contained within the boundary of the heavyweight container. The components are not added to the JLayeredPane, but to the JContentPane instead. The JLayeredPane determines the Z-ordering of the components in the JRootPane. The Z-order can be thought of as the order of overlay among the various components. If you drag-and-drop a component or request a dialog to pop up, you want that component to appear in front of the others in the application window. The `JLayeredPane` lets you layer components.

The `JLayeredPane` divides the depth of the container into different bands that can be used to assign a component to a type-appropriate level. The `DRAG_LAYER` band, value 400, appears above all other defined component layers. The lower-most level of `JLayeredPane`, the `DEFAULT_FRAME_LAYER` band, has value −3,000 and is the level of the heavyweight containers, including the `MenuBar`. The bands are as follows:

Value	Layer Name	Component Types
−3,000	DEFAULT_FRAME_LAYER	JMenubar
0	DEFAULT_LAYER	JButton, JTable, ...
	PALETTE_LAYER	Floating components such as JToolBar
	MODAL_LAYER	Modal dialogs
400	DRAG_LAYER	Drag-and-drop over all layers

Within these general depth bands, components can be further arranged with another numbering system to order the components in a particular band, but this system reverses the numbering priority.

For example, in a specific band such as `DEFAULT_LAYER`, components with a value of 0 appear in front of others in that band; whereas, components with a higher number or −1 appear behind them. The highest number in this scheme is the number of components minus 1, so one way to visualize it is shown in Figure 6.2, which shows a vector of components that steps through painting the components with a higher number first, finishing with the one at position 0.

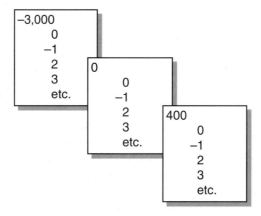

Figure 6.2 Painting components

For example, the following code adds a `JButton` to the default layer and specifies that it appear in front of the other components in that same layer:

```
JButton enterButton = new JButton("Enter");
layeredPane.add(enterButton, LayeredPane.Default_Layer, 0);
```

You can achieve the same effect by calling the `LayeredPane.moveToFront` method within a layer or by using the `LayeredPane.setLayer` method to move to a different layer.

JContentPane. The `JContentPane` manages adding components to heavyweight containers. So, you have to call the `getContentPane` method to add a component to the `ContentPane` of the `RootPane`. By default, a `ContentPane` is initialized with a `BorderLayout` layout manager. There are two ways to change the layout manager. You can call the `setLayout` method like this:

```
getContentPane()).setLayout(new BoxLayout())
```

Or you can replace the default `ContentPane` with your own `ContentPane`, such as a `JPanel`, like this:

```
JPanel pane= new JPanel();
pane.setLayout(new BoxLayout());
setContentPane(pane);
```

GlassPane. The `GlassPane` is usually completely transparent and just acts as a sheet of glass in front of the components. You can implement your own `GlassPane` by using a component like `JPanel` and installing it as the `GlassPane` by calling the `setGlassPane` method. The `RootPane` is configured with a `GlassPane` that can be retrieved by calling `getGlassPane`.

One way to use a `GlassPane` is to implement a component that invisibly handles all mouse and keyboard events, effectively blocking user input until an event completes. The `GlassPane` can block the events, but currently the cursor will not return to its default state if you have set the cursor to be a busy cursor in the `GlassPane`. An additional mouse event is required for the refresh.

```
MyGlassPane  glassPane = new MyGlassPane();
setGlassPane(glassPane);
glassPane.setVisible(true); //before worker thread
  ..
glassPane.setVisible(false); //after worker thread

private class MyGlassPane extends JPanel {

  public MyGlassPane() {
    addKeyListener(new KeyAdapter() { });
    addMouseListener(new MouseAdapter() { });
    super.setCursor(Cursor.getPredefinedCursor(Cursor.WAIT_CURSOR));
  }
}
```

Data Models.   Numerous model layers are combined to form the tables of the `AuctionClient` GUI. At a foundational level, the `TableModel` interface and its two implementations `AbstractTableModel` and `DefaultTableModel` provide the most basic means for storage, retrieval, and modification of the underlying data.

The `TableModel` defines and categorizes the data by its class. It also determines if the data can be edited and how the data is grouped into columns and rows. It is important to note, however, that while the `TableModel` interface is used most often in the construction of a `JTable`, it is not fundamentally tied to their display. Implementations could just as easily form the basis of a spreadsheet component, or even a non-GUI class that calls for the organization of data in tabular format.

The `ResultsModel` class is at the heart of the `AuctionClient` tables. It defines a dynamic data set, dictates whether class users can edit the data through its `ResultsModel.isCellEditable` method, and provides the `update` method to keep the data current. The model underlies the scrolling and fixed tables and lets modifications be reflected in each view.

At a higher level, representing an intermediate layer between data and its graphical representation, is the `TableColumnModel`. At this level the data is grouped by column in anticipation of its ultimate display in the table. The visibility and size of these columns, their headers, and the component types of their cell renderers and editors are all managed by the `TableColumnModel` class.

For example, freezing the leftmost columns in the `AuctionClient` GUI is possible because column data is easily exchanged among multiple `TableColumn-Model` and `JTable` objects. This translates to the `fixedTable` and `scrollTable` objects of the `AuctionClient` program.

Higher still lie the various renderers, editors, and header components whose combination defines the look and organization of the `JTable` component. This level is where the fundamental layout and display decisions of the `JTable` are made.

The creation of the inner classes `CustomRenderer` and `CustomButtonRenderer` within the `AuctionClient` application allows users of those classes to redefine the components upon which the appearance of table cells are based. Likewise, the `CustomButtonEditor` class takes the place of the table's default editor. In true object-oriented style, the default editors and renderers are easily replaced, affecting neither the data they represent nor the function of the component in which they reside.

Finally, the various component user interfaces are responsible for the ultimate appearance of the `JTable`. It is here the look-and-feel specific representation of the `AuctionClient` tables and their data are rendered in final form to the user. The end result is that adding a Project Swing front end to existing services requires little additional code. In fact, coding the model is one of the easier tasks in building a Project Swing application.

Table Model.   The `JTable` class has an associated `DefaultTableModel` class that internally uses a `Vector` of vectors to store data. The data for each row is stored in a single `Vector` object while another `Vector` object stores each of those rows as its constituent elements. The `DefaultTableModel` object can be initialized with data in several different ways. This code shows the `DefaultTableModel` created with a two-dimensional array and with a second array representing column headings. The `DefaultTableModel` in turn converts the `Object` arrays into the appropriate `Vector` objects:

```
        Object[][] data = new Object[][]{{"row 1 col1", "row 1 col2" },
                                {"row 2 col 1", "row 2 col 2"}};
        Object[] headers = new Object[] {"first header","second header"};
        DefaultTableModel model = new DefaultTableModel(data, headers);
        table = new JTable(model);
//API Ref: void setAutoResizeMode(int mode)
        table.setAutoResizeMode(JTable.AUTO_RESIZE_OFF);
```

Creating a custom table model is nearly as easy as using `DefaultTableModel` and requires little additional coding. You can implement a table model by implementing a method to return the number of entries in the model and a method to retrieve an element at a specific position in that model. For example, the `JTable` model can be implemented from `javax.swing.table.AbstractTableModel` by implementing the methods `getColumnCount`, `getRowCount`, and `getValueAt`, as shown here:

```
final Object[][] data = new Object[][]{ {"row 1 col1","row 1 col2" },
                                {"row 2 col 1","row 2 col 2"} };
final Object[] headers = new Object[] {"first header","second header"};
TableModel model = new AbstractTableModel(){
  public int getColumnCount() {
    return data[0].length;
  }
  public int getRowCount() {
    return data.length;
  }
  public String getColumnName(int col) {
    return (String)headers[col];
  }
  public Object getValueAt(int row,int col) {
      return data[row][col];
  }
};
table = new JTable(model);
table.setAutoResizeMode(JTable.AUTO_RESIZE_OFF);
```

This table is read-only and its data values are already known. In fact, the data are even declared final so they can be retrieved by the inner `TableModel` class. This is not normally the situation when working with live data.

You can create an editable table by adding the `isCellEditable` verification method, which is used by the default cell editor and the `AbstractTableModel` class for setting a value at a position. Up until this change, the `AbstractTableModel` has been handling the repainting and resizing of the table by firing different table changed events. Because the `AbtractTableModel` does not know that something has occurred to the table data, you need to inform it by calling the `fireTableCellUpdated` method. The following lines are added to the `AbstractTableModel` inner class to allow editing of the data:

```
        public void setValueAt (Object value, int row, int col) {
          data[row][col] = value;
          fireTableCellUpdated (row, col);
        }
//API Ref: boolean isCellEditable(int row, int column)
        public boolean isCellEditable(int row, int col) {
          return true;
        }
```

More Table Models. A common requirement for the display of tabular data is the inclusion of a nonscrolling column. This column provides a set of anchor data that remains stationary and visible while its neighboring columns are scrolled horizontally (and often out of view). This is particularly important in cases where row data can be identified by a unique value in the fixed column, such as a name or identification number. The next code example uses a fixed table column to display a list of the auction items.

The base table model in this example implements the `AbstractTableModel` class. Its update method dynamically populates the table data from a call to the database. It sends an event that the table has been updated by calling the `fireTableStructureChanged` method to indicate that the number of rows or columns in the table have changed.

```
package auction;

import javax.swing.table.AbstractTableModel;
import javax.swing.event.TableModelEvent;
import java.text.NumberFormat;
import java.util.*;
import java.awt.*;

public class ResultsModel extends AbstractTableModel{
  String[]  columnNames={};
  Vector rows = new Vector();

  public String getColumnName(int column) {
    if(columnNames[column] != null) {
```

```
          return columnNames[column];
        } else {
          return "";
        }
      }
      public boolean isCellEditable(int row, int column){
        return false;
      }
      public int getColumnCount() {
        return columnNames.length;
      }
      public int getRowCount() {
        return rows.size();
      }
      public Object getValueAt(int row, int column){
        Vector tmprow = (Vector)rows.elementAt(row);
        return tmprow.elementAt(column);
      }
      public  void update(Enumeration enum) {
        try {
          //Create the column headers which are later accessed through
          //the getColumnName method
          columnNames = new String[5];
          columnNames[0]=new String("Auction Id #");
          columnNames[1]=new String("Description");
          columnNames[2]=new String("High Bid");
          columnNames[3]=new String("# of bids");
          columnNames[4]=new String("End Date");
          //Create each vector row from the AuctionItem data
          while((enum !=null) && (enum.hasMoreElements())) {
              AuctionItem auctionItem=(AuctionItem)enum.nextElement();
              Vector items=new Vector();
              items.addElement(new Integer(auctionItem.getId()));
              items.addElement(auctionItem.getSummary());
              int bidcount= auctionItem.getBidCount();
              if(bidcount >0) {
                items.addElement(NumberFormat.getCurrencyInstance().format(
                            auctionItem.getHighBid())));
              } else {
                items.addElement("-");
              }
              items.addElement(new Integer(bidcount));
              items.addElement(auctionItem.getEndDate());
              rows.addElement(items);
          }
//API Ref: void fireTableStructureChanged()
          fireTableStructureChanged();
        } catch (Exception e) {
          System.out.println("Exception e"+e);
        }
      }
    }
  }
```

The table is created from the ResultsModel model. Then, the first table column is removed from that table and added to a new table. Because there are now two

tables, the only way the selections can be kept in sync is to use a ListSelec-
tionModel object to set the selection on the table row in the other tables that
were not selected by calling the setRowSelectionInterval method. The full
example can be found in the AuctionClient source file:

```
private void listAllItems() throws IOException{
   ResultsModel rm=new ResultsModel();
   try {
      BidderHome bhome=(BidderHome)ctx.lookup("bidder");
      Bidder bid=bhome.create();
      Enumeration enum=(Enumeration)bid.getItemList();
      if (enum != null) {
         rm.update(enum);
      }
   } catch (Exception e) {
      System.out.println("AuctionServlet <list>:"+e);
   }
   //Create a new table using the ResultsModel object as the table model
   scrollTable=new JTable(rm);
   //Force the End Date and Description columns to have
   //a set width
   adjustColumnWidth(scrollTable.getColumn("End Date"), 150);
   adjustColumnWidth(scrollTable.getColumn("Description"), 120);
   //The scroll column model is initially mapped to
   //display all the table data. The fixed column model
   //is initially empty
   scrollColumnModel = scrollTable.getColumnModel();
   fixedColumnModel = new DefaultTableColumnModel();

   //Get the first column, remove it from the scroll column, and
   //add it to the fixed table
   TableColumn col = scrollColumnModel.getColumn(0);
   scrollColumnModel.removeColumn(col);
   fixedColumnModel.addColumn(col);

   //Create a new table based on the fixed column model (1 column)
   fixedTable = new JTable(rm,fixedColumnModel);

   //Keep the heights of the fixed and scroll tables the same
   fixedTable.setRowHeight(scrollTable.getRowHeight());

   headers = new JViewport();
   //Get the selection model used in this table and override it
   //so we can also update the scroll table if the fixed table
   //is selected and vice versa
   ListSelectionModel fixedSelection = fixedTable.getSelectionModel();
   fixedSelection.addListSelectionListener(
      new ListSelectionListener() {
         public void valueChanged(ListSelectionEvent e) {
            ListSelectionModel lsm = (ListSelectionModel)e.getSource();
            if (!lsm.isSelectionEmpty())  {
               setScrollableRow();
            }
         }
      }
```

```
        });
//API Ref: ListSelectionMode getSelectionModel()
        ListSelectionModel scrollSelection = scrollTable.getSelectionModel();
        scrollSelection.addListSelectionListener(new ListSelectionListener() {
          public void valueChanged(ListSelectionEvent e) {
            ListSelectionModel lsm = (ListSelectionModel)e.getSource();
            if (!lsm.isSelectionEmpty())  {
              setFixedRow();
            }
          }
        });
        //Create a custom renderer and use it on column 2
        CustomRenderer custom = new CustomRenderer();
        custom.setHorizontalAlignment(JLabel.CENTER);
//API Ref: void setCellRenderer(TableCellRenderer renderer)
        scrollColumnModel.getColumn(2).setCellRenderer(custom);
        //Use the custom button renderer on column 3
        scrollColumnModel.getColumn(3).setCellRenderer(new
                                                CustomButtonRenderer());
        //Add the custom button editor to column 3
        CustomButtonEditor customEdit=new CustomButtonEditor(frame);
        scrollColumnModel.getColumn(3).setCellEditor(customEdit);

        //Add the scrolling column headers to the header viewport
        //the headers viewport is later added to the headerPanel with
        //an associated scroll bar
//API Ref: JTableHeader getTableHeader()
        headers.add(scrollTable.getTableHeader());

        //Create a panel for the top left of the display that contains
        //the headers for the column that does not move
        JPanel topPanel = new JPanel();
        topPanel.setLayout(new BoxLayout(topPanel, BoxLayout.X_AXIS));
        adjustColumnWidth(fixedColumnModel.getColumn(0), 100);
        JTableHeader fixedHeader=fixedTable.getTableHeader();
        fixedHeader.setAlignmentY(Component.TOP_ALIGNMENT);
        topPanel.add(fixedHeader);
//API Ref: Component createRigidArea(Dimension d)
        topPanel.add(Box.createRigidArea(new Dimension(2, 0)));
        topPanel.setPreferredSize(new Dimension(400, 40));

        //Create a panel to contain the scroll headers that will
        //be displayed at the top right
        JPanel headerPanel = new JPanel();
        headerPanel.setAlignmentY(Component.TOP_ALIGNMENT);
        headerPanel.setLayout(new BorderLayout());
        JScrollPane scrollpane = new JScrollPane();
//API Ref: JScrollBar getHorizontalScrollBar()
        scrollBar = scrollpane.getHorizontalScrollBar();
        headerPanel.add(headers, "North");
        headerPanel.add(scrollBar, "South");
        topPanel.add(headerPanel);
        //Set the scrollable part of both the table views
        scrollTable.setPreferredScrollableViewportSize(new Dimension(300,180));
        fixedTable.setPreferredScrollableViewportSize( new Dimension(100,180));
```

```
            fixedTable.setPreferredSize(new Dimension(100,180));
            innerPort = new JViewport();

            //If the user moves the scrollbar at the top
            //of the scrollable data update the header and table
            //data positions so they are viewable
//API Ref: void setView(Component view)
            innerPort.setView(scrollTable);
            scrollpane.setViewport(innerPort);
             scrollBar.getModel().addChangeListener(new ChangeListener()  {
              public void stateChanged(ChangeEvent e) {
//API Ref: Point getViewPosition()
                Point q = headers.getViewPosition();
                Point p = innerPort.getViewPosition();
                int val = scrollBar.getModel().getValue();
                p.x = val;
                q.x = val;

//API Ref: void setView(Component view)
                headers.setViewPosition(p);
                headers.repaint(headers.getViewRect());
                innerPort.setViewPosition(p);
                innerPort.repaint(innerPort.getViewRect());
              }
            });

            //Disable continuous update of the scroll table. Needed to
            //improve performance of a scrolling table in SDK 1.2
            scrollTable.getTableHeader().setUpdateTableInRealTime(false);

            //The bottom panel is where both tables data is positioned
            JPanel bottomPanel = new JPanel();
            bottomPanel.setLayout(new BoxLayout(bottomPanel, BoxLayout.X_AXIS));
            fixedTable.setAlignmentY(Component.TOP_ALIGNMENT);
            bottomPanel.add(fixedTable);
            bottomPanel.add(Box.createRigidArea(new Dimension(2, 0)));
            innerPort.setAlignmentY(Component.TOP_ALIGNMENT);
            bottomPanel.add(innerPort);
            bottomPanel.add(Box.createRigidArea(new Dimension(2, 0)));

            //Only allow vertical scrollbars as we are managing the
            //horizontal scroll ourselves
            scrollPane = new JScrollPane(bottomPanel,
                        JScrollPane.VERTICAL_SCROLLBAR_ALWAYS,
                        JScrollPane.HORIZONTAL_SCROLLBAR_NEVER);
            JViewport outerPort = new JViewport();
            outerPort.add(bottomPanel);
            //Workaround to affix the headers to the top of the scrollpane
            //uses setColumnHeaderView
//API Ref: void setColumnHeaderView(Component view)
             scrollPane.setColumnHeaderView(topPanel);
//API Ref: void setViewport(JViewport viewport)
            scrollPàne.setViewport(outerPort);
            scrollTable.setAutoResizeMode(JTable.AUTO_RESIZE_OFF);
            frame.getContentPane().add(scrollPane);
```

```
      scrollTable.validate();
      frame.setSize(450,200);
  }
  void setFixedRow() {
    int index=scrollTable.getSelectedRow();
    fixedTable.setRowSelectionInterval(index, index);
  }
  void setScrollableRow() {
    //Highlight the row by calling setRowSelectionInterval with a
    //range of 1
    int index=fixedTable.getSelectedRow();
    scrollTable.setRowSelectionInterval(index, index);
  }
  void adjustColumnWidth(TableColumn c, int size) {
    c.setPreferredWidth(size);
    c.setMaxWidth(size);
    c.setMinWidth(size);
  }
```

JList Model.   The JList component displays a vertical list of data elements
and uses a ListModel to hold and manipulate the data. It also uses a ListSe-
lectionModel object to enable selection and subsequent retrieval of elements
in the list.

Default implementations of the AbstractListModel and AbstractListSe-
lectionModel classes are provided in the Project Swing API in the form of the
DefaultListModel and DefaultListSelectionModel classes. If you use
these two default models and the default cell renderer, you get a list that displays model elements by calling the toString method on each object. The list
uses the MULTIPLE_INTERVAL_SELECTION list selection model to select each
element from the list.

Three selection modes are available to DefaultListSelectionModel:
SINGLE_SELECTION, where only one item is selected at a time;
SINGLE_INTERVAL_SELECTION, in which a range of sequential items can be
selected; and MULTIPLE_INTERVAL_SELECTION, which allows any or all elements to be selected. The selection mode can be changed by calling the setSe-
lectionMode method in the JList class.

```
public SimpleList() {
  JList list;
  DefaultListModel deflist;

  deflist= new DefaultListModel();
  deflist.addElement("element 1");
  deflist.addElement("element 2");
  list = new JList(deflist);
  JScrollPane scroll = new JScrollPane(list);
  getContentPane().add(scroll, BorderLayout.CENTER);
}
```

JTree Model.   The JTree class models and displays a vertical list of elements or nodes arranged in a tree-based hierarchy as shown in Figure 6.3.

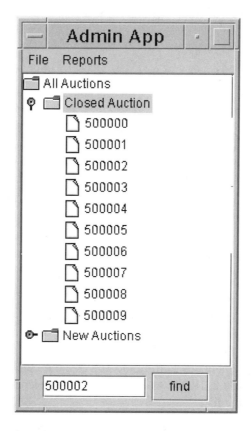

Figure 6.3 Vertical list of elements in a tree

A JTree object has one root node and one or more child nodes, which can contain further child nodes. Each parent node can be expanded to show all its children similar to directory trees familiar to Windows users.

Like the JList and JTable components, the JTree consists of more than one model. The selection model is similar to the one detailed for the JList model. The selection modes have the following slightly different names: SINGLE_TREE_SELECTION, DISCONTIGUOUS_TREE_SELECTION, and CONTIGUOUS_TREE_SELECTION.

While DefaultTreeModel maintains the data in the tree and is responsible for adding and removing nodes, it is the DefaultTreeMutableTreeNode class that defines the methods used for node traversal. The DefaultTreeModel is often used to implement custom models because there is no AbstractTreeModel in the JTree package. However, if you use custom objects, you must implement TreeModel. This code example creates a JTree using the DefaultTreeModel so the administrator can search and browse the auction numbers and details for reporting.

```java
import java.awt.*;
import java.awt.event.*;
import javax.swing.*;
import javax.swing.tree.*;

public class SimpleTree extends JFrame {
  public SimpleTree() {
    String[] treelabels =   {"All Auctions", "Closed Auction",
                            "Open Auctions"};
    Integer[] closedItems = {new Integer(500144), new Integer(500146),
                            new Integer(500147)};
    Integer[] openItems = { new Integer(500148), new Integer(500149)};
    //Create an array of nodes based on the size of the labels and
    //open and closed items
    DefaultMutableTreeNode[] nodes = new
                            DefaultMutableTreeNode[treelabels.length];
    DefaultMutableTreeNode[] closednodes = new
                            DefaultMutableTreeNode[closedItems.length];
    DefaultMutableTreeNode[] opennodes = new
                            DefaultMutableTreeNode[openItems.length];
    //Populate the labels with the data label elements
    for (int i=0; i < treelabels.length; i++) {
      nodes[i] = new DefaultMutableTreeNode(treelabels[i]);
    }

    //Arrange the tree so that from the top level All Auctions
    //closed and open auctions are children from that top level
    nodes[0].add(nodes[1]);
    nodes[0].add(nodes[2]);

    for (int i=0; i < closedItems.length; i++) {
        //Populate the closed items nodes with the closed item data
        //ie auction ids
        closednodes[i] = new DefaultMutableTreeNode(closedItems[i]);
        //Add the closed items under the Closed Auction parent node
        nodes[1].add(closednodes[i]);
    }

    for (int i=0; i < openItems.length; i++) {
        //Populate the open items nodes with the open item data
        //ie auction ids
        opennodes[i] = new DefaultMutableTreeNode(openItems[i]);
        //Add the open items under the Open Auction parent node
        nodes[2].add(opennodes[i]);
    }
    //Finally create the tree model from the nodes created above
    //and then create the tree
    DefaultTreeModel model=new DefaultTreeModel(nodes[0]);
    JTree tree = new JTree(model);
```

```
      JScrollPane scroll = new JScrollPane(tree);
      getContentPane().add(scroll, BorderLayout.CENTER);
  }

  public static void main(String[] args) {
    SimpleTree frame = new SimpleTree();
    frame.addWindowListener( new WindowAdapter() {
      public void windowClosing( WindowEvent e ) {
        System.exit(0);
      }
    });
    frame.setVisible(true);
    frame.pack();
    frame.setSize(150,150);
  }
}
```

The toString method is used to retrieve the value for the Integer objects in the tree. And although the DefaultTreeModel is used to maintain the data in the tree and to add or remove nodes, the DefaultMutableTreeNode class defines the methods used to traverse through the nodes in the tree.

A primitive search of the nodes in a JTree is accomplished with the depth-FirstEnumeration method, which is the same as the postorderEnumeration method and works its way from the end points of the tree first. You can also call the preorderEnumeration method, the reverse of the postorderEnumeration method, which starts from the root and descends each tree in turn. Or you can call the breadthFirstEnumeration method, which starts from the root and visits all the child nodes in one level before visiting the child nodes at a lower depth.

The following code expands the parent node if it contains a child node that matches the search field entered. It uses a call to Enumeration e = nodes[0].depthFirstEnumeration() to return a list of all the nodes in the tree. Once it has found a match, it builds the TreePath from the root node to the node that matched the search. It passes the TreePath to the makeVisible method in the JTree class that ensures the node is expanded in the tree.

```
import java.awt.*;
import java.util.*;
import java.awt.event.*;
import javax.swing.*;
import javax.swing.tree.*;

public class SimpleSearchTree extends JFrame {
  JPanel findPanel;
  JTextField findField;
  JTree tree;
  JButton findButton;
  DefaultMutableTreeNode[] nodes;
```

```
      public SimpleSearchTree() {
        String[] treelabels = { "All Auctions", "Closed Auction",
                               "Open Auctions"};
        Integer[] closedItems = { new Integer(500144), new Integer(500146),
                                 new Integer(500147) };
        Integer[] openItems ={ new Integer(500148), new Integer(500149)};
        //Create an array of nodes based on the size of the labels and
        //open and closed items

        nodes = new DefaultMutableTreeNode[treelabels.length];
```
//API Ref: DefaultMutableTreeNode(Object node)
```
        DefaultMutableTreeNode[] closednodes = new
                              DefaultMutableTreeNode[closedItems.length];
        DefaultMutableTreeNode[] opennodes = new
                              DefaultMutableTreeNode[openItems.length];

        //Populate the labels with the data label elements
        for (int i=0; i < treelabels.length; i++) {
           nodes[i] = new DefaultMutableTreeNode(treelabels[i]);
        }

        //Arrange the tree so that from the top level, all
        //closed and open auctions are children from that top level
        nodes[0].add(nodes[1]);
        nodes[0].add(nodes[2]);
        for (int i=0; i < closedItems.length; i++) {
           //Populate the closed items nodes with the closed item data,
           //i.e., auction ids
           closednodes[i] = new DefaultMutableTreeNode(closedItems[i]);
           //Add the closed items under the Closed Auction parent node
           nodes[1].add(closednodes[i]);
        }

        for (int i=0; i < openItems.length; i++) {
           //Populate the open item nodes with the open item data,
           //i.e., auction ids
           opennodes[i] = new DefaultMutableTreeNode(openItems[i]);
           //Add the open items under the Open Auction parent node
           nodes[2].add(opennodes[i]);
        }
        //Finally, create the tree model from the nodes created above
        //and then create the tree

        DefaultTreeModel model=new DefaultTreeModel(nodes[0]);
        tree = new JTree(model);
        JScrollPane scroll = new JScrollPane(tree);
        getContentPane().add(scroll, BorderLayout.CENTER);
        findPanel= new JPanel();
        findField= new JTextField(10);
        findButton= new JButton("find");
```
//API Ref: void addActionListener(ActionListener l)
```
        findButton.addActionListener (new ActionListener() {
```
//API Ref: void actionPerformed(ActionEvent e)
```
          public void actionPerformed (ActionEvent e) {
            String field=findField.getText();
```

```
            if (field != null) {
              //Search for the node whose label matches the search string
              findNode(findField.getText());
            } else {
              return;
            }
          }
        });
        findPanel.add(findField);
        findPanel.add(findButton);
        getContentPane().add(findPanel, BorderLayout.SOUTH);
      }
      public void findNode(String field) {
        //Get an enumeration list of all the nodes.
        //The ordering is generated by starting from the root
        //to the end of each branch, and to the end of
        //the next branch including any nodes not visited before.
```
//API Ref: Enumeration depthFirstEnumeration()
```
        Enumeration e = nodes[0].depthFirstEnumeration();
        Object currNode;
        while (e.hasMoreElements()) {
          currNode = e.nextElement();
          if (currNode.toString().equals(field)) {
            //Does the node match our search string? If so, generate
            //a path object to highlight the matching node
            //with a call to setSelectionRow.
```
//API Ref: TreePath(Object singlePath)
```
            TreePath path=new
                      TreePath(((DefaultMutableTreeNode)currNode).getPath());
```
//API Ref: void makeVisible(TreePath path)
```
            tree.makeVisible(path);
```
//API Ref: void setSelectionRow(int row)
```
            tree.setSelectionRow(tree.getRowForPath(path));
            return;
          }
        }
      }

      public static void main(String[] args) {
        SimpleSearchTree frame = new SimpleSearchTree();
```
//API Ref: void addWindowListener(WindowListener l)
```
        frame.addWindowListener( new WindowAdapter() {
```
//API Ref: void windowClosing(WindowEvent e)
```
          public void windowClosing( WindowEvent e ) {
            System.exit(0);
          }
        });
        frame.setVisible(true);
        frame.pack();
        frame.setSize(300,150);
      }
    }
```

JTree, JTable, and JList are probably the most common components you
will want to customize. But you can use models such as SingleSelection-

Model for general data manipulation. The SingleSelectionModel class lets you specify how data is selected in a component.

Custom Cell Rendering.   As you learned above, many components have a default cell renderer to paint each element in a table, tree, or list. The default cell renderer is usually a JLabel and displays a String representation of the data element.

A simple custom cell renderer can extend the Default<*type*>CellRenderer class to provide additional customization in the get<*type*>CellRenderer. The DefaultTableCellRenderer and DefaultTreeCellRenderer components both use a JLabel to render the cell. This means any customization that can be applied to a JLabel can also be used in the JTable or JTree cell.

For example, the following renderer sets the background color of the component if the auction item has received a high number of bids:

```
class CustomRenderer extends DefaultTableCellRenderer {
//API Ref: Component getTableCellRendererComponent(JTable table, Object value,
        boolean isSelected, boolean hasFocus, int row, int column)
    public Component getTableCellRendererComponent(JTable table,Object value,
                    boolean isSelected, boolean hasFocus, int row,
                    int column) {
        Component comp = super.getTableCellRendererComponent(table,
                    value,isSelected, hasFocus, row,column);
        JLabel label = (JLabel)comp;
        //Does the auction item have 30 or more bids. If so display
        //a hot item image
        if(((Integer)value).intValue() >= 30) {
//API Ref: void setIcon(Icon icon)
            label.setIcon(new ImageIcon("Hot.gif"));
        } else {
            label.setIcon(new ImageIcon("Normal.gif"));
        }
        return label;
    }
}
```

The renderer is set on a column like this:

```
CustomRenderer custom = new CustomRenderer();
custom.setHorizontalAlignment(JLabel.CENTER);
scrollColumnModel.getColumn(2).setCellRenderer(custom);
```

If the component being displayed inside the JTable column requires more functionality than is available using a JLabel, you can create your own Table-CellRenderer. This next code example uses a JButton as the renderer cell.

```
class CustomButtonRenderer extends JButton implements TableCellRenderer {
    public CustomButtonRenderer() {
        setOpaque(true);
    }
```

```
//API Ref: Component getTableCellRendererComponent(JTable table, Object value,
        boolean isSelected, boolean hasFocus, int row, int column)
    public Component getTableCellRendererComponent(JTable table, Object value,
                    boolean isSelected, boolean hasFocus, int row, int column) {
    if(isSelected) {
      ((JButton)value).setForeground(table.getSelectionForeground());
      ((JButton)value).setBackground(table.getSelectionBackground());
    } else {
      ((JButton)value).setForeground(table.getForeground());
      ((JButton)value).setBackground(table.getBackground());
    }
    return (JButton)value;
}
```

Like the default `JLabel` cell renderer, this class relies on an underlying component (in this case, `JButton`) to do the painting. Selection of the cell toggles the button colors. As before, the cell renderer is secured to the appropriate column of the auction table with the `setCellRenderer` method:

```
//API Ref: void setCellRenderer(TableCellRenderer renderer)
    scrollColumnModel.getColumn(3).setCellRenderer(new CustomButtonRenderer());
```

Alternately, all `JButton` components can be configured to use the `CustomButtonRenderer` in the table with a call to `setDefaultRenderer` as follows:

```
//API Ref: void setDefaultRenderer(Class columnClass, TableCellRenderer renderer)
    table.setDefaultRenderer(JButton.class, new CustomButtonRenderer());
```

Custom Cell Editing.   In the same way that you can configure how a cell is painted in a `JTable` or `JTree` component, you can also configure how an editable cell responds to edits. One difference between using cell editors and cell renderers is that there is a `DefaultCellEditor` for all components, but no `DefaultTableCellEditor` for table cells.

While separate renderers exist for `JTree` and `JTable`, a single `DefaultCellEditor` class implements both the `TableCellEditor` and `TreeCellEditor` interfaces. However, the `DefaultCellEditor` class has constructors for only the `JComboBox`, `JCheckBox`, and `JTextField` components. The `JButton` class does not map to any of these constructors, so a dummy `JCheckBox` is created to satisfy the requirements of the `DefaultCellEditor` class.

This next example from `AuctionClient` contains code to create a custom button editor that displays the number of days left in the auction when the button is double-clicked. The double-click to trigger the action is specified by setting the value `clickCountToStart` to 2. An exact copy of the `getTableCellEditorComponent` method paints the button in edit mode. A `JDialog` component that displays the number of days left appears when the `getCellEditorValue` method is called. The value for the number of days left is calculated by moving the current calendar date toward the end date. The `Calendar` class does not have a method that expresses a difference in two dates in anything other than the milliseconds between those two dates.

```
//From AuctionClient.java
class CustomButtonEditor extends DefaultCellEditor {
  final JButton mybutton;
  JFrame frame;

  CustomButtonEditor(JFrame frame) {
    super(new JCheckBox());
    mybutton = new JButton();
    this.editorComponent = mybutton;
    //To activate this button requires to mouse clicks (double click)
    this.clickCountToStart = 2;
    this.frame=frame;
    mybutton.setOpaque(true);
    mybutton.addActionListener(new ActionListener() {
      public void actionPerformed(ActionEvent e) {
//API Ref: void fireEditingStopped()
        fireEditingStopped();
      }
    });
  }

  protected void fireEditingStopped() {
    super.fireEditingStopped();
  }

//API Ref: Object getCellEditorValue()
  public Object getCellEditorValue() {
    JDialog jd= new JDialog(frame, "Time left");
    Calendar today=Calendar.getInstance();
    Calendar end=Calendar.getInstance();
    SimpleDateFormat in=new SimpleDateFormat("yyyy-MM-dd");
    try {
      //Get the button text from the table row. This value is the end date
      //of the auction and was previously initialized when the table
      //was populated with data.
//API Ref:  void setTime(Date date)
      end.setTime(in.parse(mybutton.getText()));
    } catch (Exception e){
      System.out.println("Error in date"+mybutton.getText()+e);
    }
    int days = 0;
    //To work out if the date in the button is later or earlier than
    //today, roll the date forward a day at a time until it is later
    //than today.
//API Ref: boolean before(Object when)
    while(today.before(end)) {
//API Ref: void roll(int datefield, boolean up)
      today.roll(Calendar.DATE, true);
      days++;
    }
    jd.setSize(200,100);
    //If the end date was originally after today, mark the auction as
```

```
            //completed. Otherwise, display the number of days remaining.
            if (today.after(end)) {
               jd.getContentPane().add(new JLabel("Auction completed"));
            } else {
               jd.getContentPane().add(new JLabel("Days left="+days));
            }
            jd.setVisible(true);
             return new String(mybutton.getText());
         }
```
```
//API Ref: Component getTableCellEditorComponent(JTable table, Object value,
            boolean isSelected, int row, int column)
      public Component getTableCellEditorComponent(JTable table, Object value,
                   boolean isSelected, int row, int column) {
         ((JButton) editorComponent).setText(((JButton)value).getText());
         if (isSelected) {
           ((JButton)
             editorComponent).setForeground(table.getSelectionForeground());
           ((JButton)
             editorComponent).setBackground(table.getSelectionBackground());
         } else {
           ((JButton) editorComponent).setForeground(table.getForeground());
           ((JButton) editorComponent).setBackground(table.getBackground());
         }
         return editorComponent;
         }
     }
```

Specialized Event Handling

Project Swing uses the event handling classes that have been available in the AWT API since JDK 1.1. However, some new APIs are available in the Swing-Utilities class that are used to add some control over the event queue. The two new event handling methods are invokeLater and invokeAndWait. The invokeAndWait method waits for the event to be processed in the event queue.

These methods are often used to request focus on a component after another event has occurred that might affect the component focus. You can return the focus by calling the invokeLater method and passing a Thread:

```
JButton button =new JButton();
//API Ref: static void invokeLater(Runnable run)
   SwingUtilities.invokeLater(new Runnable() {
     public void run() {
       button.requestFocus();
     }
});
```

Project Swing Directions

While the basic architecture of Project Swing has stayed true to its original design, many optimizations and improvements have been made to components like JTable and in areas such as scrolling. Add to this the Java HotSpot™ technology, which greatly reduces the cost of object creation, and Project Swing can boast its best performance to date.

However, as seen in the Analyze a Program section (page 270), a simple 700 × 300 table requires nearly half a megabyte of memory when double buffered. The creation of ten tables would probably require swapping memory to disk, severely affecting performance on low-end machines.

Printing API

The Java 2 Platform java.awt.print package lets you print anything that can be rendered to a Graphics or Graphics2D context—including AWT components, Project Swing components, and 2D graphics.

The printing API is easy to use. Your application tells the printing system what to print, and the printing system determines when each page is rendered. This callback printing model enables printing support on a wide range of printers and systems. The callback model also lets users print to a bitmap printer from a computer that does not have enough memory or disk space to hold the bitmap for an entire page.

A graphics context lets a program paint to a rendering device such as a screen, printer, or off-screen image. Because Project Swing components are rendered through a Graphics object using AWT graphics support, it is easy to print Project Swing components with the new printing API. However, AWT components are not rendered to a graphics device, so you must extend the AWT component class and implement the AWT component paint method.

What Is in the Package?

The java.awt.print package consists of the following interfaces, classes, and exceptions.

- Interfaces
  - Pageable
  - Printable
  - PrinterGraphics
- Classes
  - Book
  - PageFormat
  - Paper
  - PrinterJob

- Exceptions
  - PrinterAbortException
  - PrinterException
  - PrinterIOException

Printing an AWT Component

The PrintButton (AWT) application displays the panel with MyButton on it, shown in Figure 6.4. When you click the button, the application prints the MyButton component.

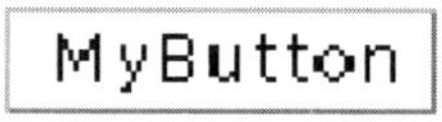

Figure 6.4 AWT button

In the code, the Button class is extended to implement Printable and includes the paint and print method implementations. The print method is required because the class implements Printable, and the paint method is needed to describe how the button shape and label text looks when printed.

To see the button, the printer graphics context is translated into the imageable area of the printer, and to see the label text, a font is set on the printer graphics context.

In this example, the button is printed at a 164/72-inch inset from the left-imageable margin (there are 72 pixels per inch) and 5/72 inches from the top-imageable margin. This is where the button is positioned in the frame by the layout manager, and those same numbers are returned by the following calls:

```
int X = (int)this.getLocation().getX();
int Y = (int)this.getLocation().getY();
```

And here is the MyButton class code:

```
class MyButton extends Button implements Printable {
  public MyButton() {
    super("MyButton");
  }
  public void paint(Graphics g) {
  //To see the label text, you must specify a font for
  //the printer graphics context
    Font  f = new Font("Monospaced", Font.PLAIN,12);
    g.setFont (f);
  //Using "g" render anything you want.
  //Get the button's location, width, and height
    int X = (int)this.getLocation().getX();
    int Y = (int)this.getLocation().getY();
```

```
            int W = (int)this.getSize().getWidth();
            int H = (int)this.getSize().getHeight();
        //Draw the button shape
//API Ref: void drawRect(int x, int y, int width, int height)
            g.drawRect(X, Y, W, H);
        //Draw the button label
        //For simplicity code to center the label inside the
        //button shape is replaced by integer offset values
            g.drawString(this.getLabel(), X+10, Y+15);
        }
//API Ref: int print(Graphics graphics, PageFormat pageFormat, int pageIndex)
        public int print(Graphics g, PageFormat pf,
                            int pi) throws PrinterException {
            if (pi >= 1) {
              return Printable.NO_SUCH_PAGE;
            }
            Graphics2D g2 = (Graphics2D) g;
        //To see the button on the printed page,translate the printer graphics
        //context into the imageable area
//API Ref: double getImageableX()
//API Ref: double getImageableY()
            g2.translate(pf.getImageableX(), pf.getImageableY());
            g2.setColor(Color.black);
            paint(g2);
            return Printable.PAGE_EXISTS;
          }
    }
```

> **NOTE**   The printing `Graphics2D` is based on the `BufferedImage` class; on some platforms it does not default to a foreground color of black. If this is the case on your platform, you have to add `g2.set-Color(Color.black)` to the `print` method before the `paint` invocation.

The `PrintButton` class creates a `MyButton` instance and implements an `action-Performed` method to create a printer job for `MyButton` when it is clicked.

Printing a Project Swing Component

Printing the Project Swing component shown in Figure 6.5 is almost the same as printing an AWT component, except the `MyButton` subclass does not need a `paint` method implementation. It does, however, have a `print` method that calls the `paint` method for the component. The `paint` method implementation is not needed because Project Swing components know how to paint themselves.

Figure 6.5 Project Swing button

The `PrintButton` (Project Swing) application for Project Swing displays a panel with a `MyButton` on it.

```
class MyButton extends JButton implements Printable {
  public MyButton() {
    super("MyButton");
  }
  public int print(Graphics g, PageFormat pf,
                   int pi) throws PrinterException {
    if (pi >= 1) {
      return Printable.NO_SUCH_PAGE;
    }
    Graphics2D g2 = (Graphics2D) g;
    g2.translate(pf.getImageableX(),  pf.getImageableY());
    Font  f = new Font("Monospaced", Font.PLAIN,12);
    g2.setFont (f);
    paint(g2);
    return Printable.PAGE_EXISTS;
  }
  //...
}
```

If you extend a `JPanel` and implement `Printable`, you can print a panel component and all of its contents.

```
public class printpanel extends JPanel implements ActionListener, Printable {
```

The `PrintPanel` code prints a `JPanel` object and the `JButton` it contains, and the `ComponentPrinterFrame` code prints a `JFrame` object and the `JButton`, `JList`, `JCheckBox`, and `JComboBox` components it contains.

Printing Graphics in Project Swing

In the same way the AWT example subclassed a `Button` component and implemented the `paint` method to draw the button, you can subclass an AWT or Project Swing component and implement the `paint` method to render 2D graphics to the screen or printer. The `ShapesPrint` (Project Swing) application borrowed from *The Java Tutorial* shows how this is done. It is modified for this text to include a `TextLayout` object.

The `paintComponent` method calls the `drawShapes` method to render the 2D graphics to the screen when the application starts. When you click the `Print` button, a printer graphics context is created and passed to the `drawShapes` method for the printing shown in Figure 6.6.

Print Dialog

It is easy to display a `Print` dialog (Figure 6.7) so that the end user can interactively change the print job properties. The `actionPerformed` method of the previous Project Swing example is modified here to do just that.

Figure 6.6 Printing graphical shapes

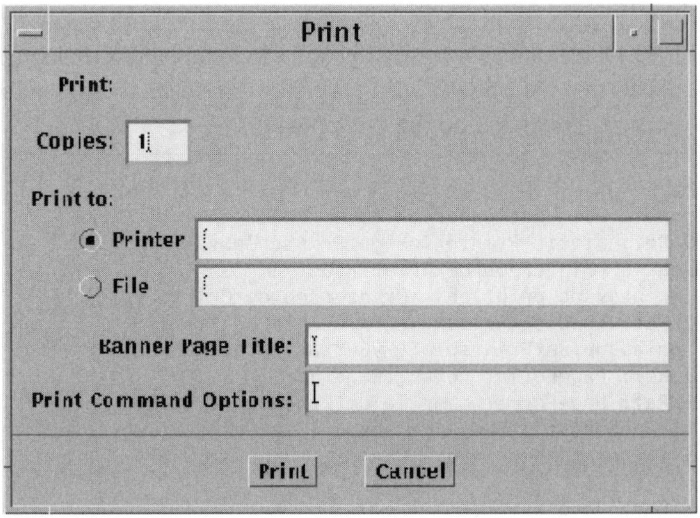

Figure 6.7 Print dialog box

```
    public void actionPerformed(ActionEvent e) {
      PrinterJob printJob = PrinterJob.getPrinterJob();
      printJob.setPrintable((MyButton) e.getSource());
//API Ref: boolean printDialog()
      if(printJob.printDialog()){
        try { printJob.print(); }
        catch (Exception PrinterExeption) { }
      }
    }
```

NOTE   In Project Swing, the `printJob.setPageable((MyBut-ton) e.getSource())` statement can be written as `printJob.set-Printable((MyButton)  e.getSource())`. The difference is that `setPrintable` is for applications that do not know the number of pages they are printing. If you use `setPrintable`, you need to add `if(pi >= 1){return  Printable.NO_SUCH_PAGE;}` to the beginning of the `print` method. Pages are numbered starting with zero, so `pi >= 1` tests if the page index has two or more pages.

Page Setup Dialog

You can add a line of code that tells the `PrinterJob` object to display a `Page` dialog so that the user can interactively modify the page format for printing in portrait, landscape, or reverse landscape mode. The `actionPerformed` method of the previous Project Swing example is modified here to display `Page` and `Print` dialogs.

NOTE   Some platforms do not support a `Page` dialog. On those platforms, the `pageDialog` call simply returns the passed-in `Page-Format` object and no dialog appears.

```
    public void actionPerformed(ActionEvent e) {
//API Ref: static PrinterJob getPrinterJob()
    static PrinterJob getPrinterJob()
      PrinterJob printJob = PrinterJob.getPrinterJob();
//API Ref: void setPrintable(Printable painter)
      printJob.setPrintable((MyButton) e.getSource());
//API Ref: PageFormat defaultPage()
//API Ref: PageFormat pageDialog(PageFormat page)
      PageFormat pf = printJob.pageDialog(printJob.defaultPage());
      if(printJob.printDialog()){
        try {
//API Ref: void print()
          printJob.print();
        } catch (Exception ex) {}
      }
    }
```

Printing a Collection of Pages

You can use the Book class to print a collection of pages that you append to the book. The pages can be in any order and have different page formats.

The Print2Button example puts the Print and Print 2 buttons of type MyButton on the panel shown in Figure 6.8. It creates a book that contains the pages to print. When you click either button, the book prints one copy of the Print button in landscape mode and two copies of the Print 2 button in portrait mode, as specified in the actionPerformed method implementation shown below.

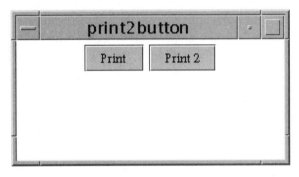

Figure 6.8 Printing a collection of pages

NOTE   Currently a bug restricts the Solaris platform to print only in portrait mode.

```
    public void actionPerformed(ActionEvent e) {
      PrinterJob printJob = PrinterJob.getPrinterJob();
    /* Set up Book */
      PageFormat landscape = printJob.defaultPage();
      PageFormat portrait = printJob.defaultPage();
//API Ref: void setOrientation(int orientation)
      landscape.setOrientation(PageFormat.LANDSCAPE);
      portrait.setOrientation(PageFormat.PORTRAIT);
      Book bk = new Book();
//API Ref: void append(Printable painter, PageFormat page)
      bk.append((Printable)b, landscape);
//API Ref: void append(Printable painter, PageFormat page, int numPages)
      bk.append((Printable)b2, portrait, 2);
//API Ref: void setPageable(Pageable document)
      printJob.setPageable(bk);
      try {
        printJob.print();
      } catch (Exception ex) { }
    }
```

Advanced Printing

The previous section explained how to print simple components and covered techniques that can be used to print screen captures. However, if you want to print more than one component per page, or if your component is larger in size than one page, you need to do some additional work inside your `print` method. This section explains what you need to do and concludes with an example of how to print the contents of a `JTable` component.

Multiple Components per Page

There are times when printing one component on a page does not meet your printing needs. For example, you might want to include a header on each page or print a footer with the page number—something that isn't necessarily displayed on the screen. Unfortunately, printing multiple customized components on a page is not as easy as adding additional `paint` calls because each `paint` call overwrites the output of the previous call.

The key to printing more than one component on a page is to use the `translate(double, double)` and `setClip` methods in the `Graphics2D` class. The `translate` method moves an imaginary pen to the next position of the print output where the component can be painted and then printed. There are two `translate` methods in the `Graphics2D` class. To print multiple components you need the one that takes `double` arguments because this `translate` method allows relative positioning. Be sure to cast any integer values to `double` or `float`. Relative positioning in this context means that previous calls to `translate` are taken into account when calculating the new translated point.

The `setClip` method is used to restrict the component to be painted only, and therefore printed, in the area specified. This lets you print multiple components on a page by moving the imaginary pen to different points on the page and painting each component in the clip area.

Example.   You can replace the `print` method in the `PrintButton` (AWT) and `PrintButton` (Project Swing) examples with the following code to add the footer message `Company Confidential` to the page.

```
public int print(Graphics g, PageFormat pf, int pi) throws PrinterException {
    if (pi >= 1) {
        return Printable.NO_SUCH_PAGE;
    }
    Graphics2D g2 = (Graphics2D) g;
    Font f= Font.getFont("Courier");
//API Ref: double getImageableWidth()
//API Ref: double getImageableHeight()
    double height=pf.getImageableHeight();
    double width=pf.getImageableWidth();
```

```
            g2.translate(pf.getImageableX(), pf.getImageableY());
            g2.setColor(Color.black);
            g2.drawString("Company Confidential", (int)width/2,
                          (int)height-g2.getFontMetrics().getHeight());
            g2.translate(0f,0f);
//API Ref: void setClip(int x, int y, int width, int height)
            g2.setClip(0,0,(int)width,(int)(height-
                                    g2.getFontMetrics().getHeight()*2));
            paint (g2);
            return Printable.PAGE_EXISTS;
      }
```

In the new `print` method, the `Graphics2D` context is clipped before calling the parent `JButton paint` method. This prevents the `JButton paint` method from overwriting the bottom of the page. The `translate` method is used to point the `JButton paint` method to start the `paint` at offset 0,0 from the visible part of the page. The visible area was already calculated by the previous `translate` call:

```
//API Ref: void translate(double x, double y)
      g2.translate(pf.getImageableX(), pf.getImageableY());
```

For some components, you might need to set the foreground color to see your results. In this example the text is printed in black.

Useful Methods to Call in the `print` Method. The following methods are useful for calculating the number of pages required and for shrinking components to fit on a page:

`PageFormat` methods:
```
getImageableHeight()
```

 Returns the page height you can use for printing your output.

```
getImageableWidth()
```

 Returns the page width you can use for printing your output.

`Graphics2D` methods:
```
//API Ref: void scale(double sx, double sy)
      scale(xratio, yratio)
```

Scales the 2D graphics context by this size. A ratio of 1 maintains the size, less than 1 shrinks the graphics context.

Components Larger Than One Page

The Java 2 Printing API has a Book API that provides the concept of pages. However, the Book API only adds printable objects to a collection of printable objects. It does not calculate page breaks or split components over multiple pages.

When printing a simple component on a page, you only have to check for the index value being greater or equal to one and return NO_SUCH_PAGE when this value is reached. To print multiple pages, you have to calculate the number of pages needed to contain the component. You can calculate the total number of pages needed by subtracting the space taken by the component from the value returned by getImageableHeight. Once the total number of pages is calculated, you can run the following check inside the print method:

```
if(pageIndex >=TotalPages) {
   return NO_SUCH_PAGE;
}
```

The Printing framework calls the print method multiple times until pageIndex is less than or equal to TotalPages. All you need to do is create a new page from the same component on each print loop. This is done by treating the printed page like a sliding window over the component.

The part of the component that is to be printed is selected by a translate call to mark the top of the page and a setClip call to mark the bottom of the page. Figure 6.9 illustrates this process. The left side of the diagram represents the page sent to the printer. The right side contains the long component being printed in the print method. The first page can be represented as follows:

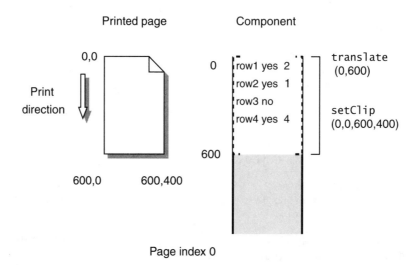

Figure 6.9 translate calls

Figure 6.10 shows how the printed page window slides along the component to print the second page, page index 1. This process continues until the last page is reached.

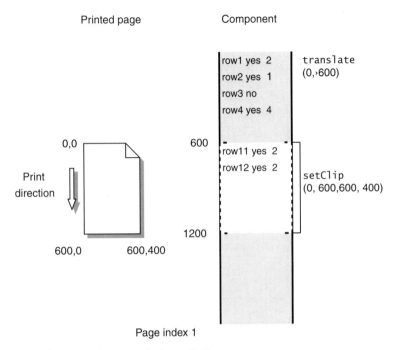

Figure 6.10 Printed page window sliding

Printing a JTable Component

The Report class (page 202) uses many of the advanced techniques covered in this section to print out the data and header of a JTable component (Figure 6.11) that can span many pages. The printed output also includes a footer at the bottom with the page number.

Description	open price	latest price	End Date	Quantity
Box of Biros	1.00	4.99	Mar 18, 1...	2
Blue Biro	0.10	0.14	Mar 18, 1...	1
legal pad	1.00	2.49	Mar 18, 1...	1
tape	1.00	1.49	Mar 18, 1...	1
stapler	4.00	4.49	Mar 18, 1...	1
legal pad	1.00	2.29	Mar 18, 1...	5

Sales Report

print me!

Figure 6.11 Sales report

Figure 6.12 shows how the report looks when it prints:

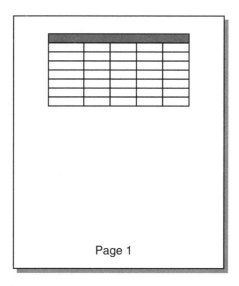

Page 1

Figure 6.12 Printed page

Printing a Sales Report

The SalesReport class (page 204) prints a sales report with the rows split over multiple pages with numbers at the bottom of each page. Figure 6.13 shows how the application looks when launched:

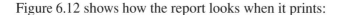

Figure 6.13 Sales report

You need this policy file to launch the applet:

```
grant {
  permission java.lang.RuntimePermission "queuePrintJob";
};
```

To launch the applet assuming a policy file named `printpol` and an HTML file named `SalesReport.html`, you would type:

```
appletviewer -J-Djava.security.policy=printpol SalesReport.html
```

Figure 6.14 shows how the report prints:

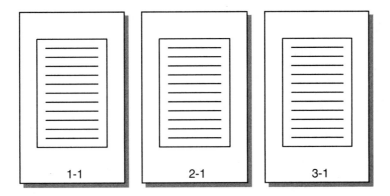

Figure 6.14 Printed sales report

AuctionClient

```
package auction;

import java.io.*;
import javax.naming.*;
import javax.ejb.*;
import java.rmi.RemoteException;
import java.util.*;
import java.text.NumberFormat;
import bidder.*;
import registration.*;
import seller.*;
import search.*;
import javax.swing.*;
import javax.swing.event.*;
import java.awt.event.*;
import java.awt.*;
import java.text.*;
import javax.swing.table.*;
import javax.swing.tree.*;

public class AuctionClient implements ActionListener{
  javax.naming.Context ctx=null;
```

```java
JMenuBar mb = new JMenuBar();
JMenu file = new JMenu("File");
JMenu reports = new JMenu("Reports");
JMenuItem filePrint = new JMenuItem("Print");
JSeparator separator = new JSeparator();
JMenuItem fileQuit = new JMenuItem("Quit");
JMenuItem itemList = new JMenuItem("List All Items");
JMenuItem browseItems = new JMenuItem("Browse Items");
JFrame frame=new JFrame();
JViewport innerPort, headers;
JScrollBar scrollBar;
JScrollPane scrollPane;
JTable fixedTable, scrollTable;
TableColumnModel fixedColumnModel, scrollColumnModel;
int rowHeight=64;
JTree tree;
DefaultMutableTreeNode[] nodes;
JTextField findField;
JPanel homePanel=null;
JPanel browsePanel=null;
JPanel scrollPanel=null;

public AuctionClient() {
  try {
    ctx = getInitialContext();
  } catch (Exception e) {
    System.out.println("error contacting EJB server"+e);
  }

  //Add menu items to menus
  file.add(filePrint);
  file.add(separator);
  file.add(fileQuit);
  reports.add(itemList);
  reports.add(browseItems);
  mb.add(file);
  mb.add(reports);
  frame.setJMenuBar(mb);

  filePrint.addActionListener(this);
  fileQuit.addActionListener(this);
  itemList.addActionListener(this);
  browseItems.addActionListener(this);
  homePanel = new JPanel();
  homePanel.setLayout(new CardLayout());
  browsePanel = new JPanel();
  browsePanel.setLayout(new BorderLayout());
  scrollPanel = new JPanel();
  scrollPanel.setLayout(new BorderLayout());
  homePanel.add(scrollPanel, "List All Items");
  homePanel.add(browsePanel, "Browse Items");
  frame.getContentPane().add(homePanel, BorderLayout.CENTER);
  frame.setSize(200,100);
  frame.setVisible(true);
}
```

```
public void actionPerformed(ActionEvent evt) {
  Object obj = evt.getSource();
  if (obj == itemList) {
    try {
      listAllItems();
      ((CardLayout)homePanel.getLayout()).show(homePanel,
                                    ((JMenuItem)obj).getText());
    } catch (Exception e) {
      System.out.println("Exception: "+e);
    }
  } else if (obj == browseItems) {
    try {
      browseItems();
      ((CardLayout)homePanel.getLayout()).show(homePanel,
                                    ((JMenuItem)obj).getText());
    } catch (Exception e) {
      System.out.println("Exception: "+e);
    }
  } else if (obj == fileQuit) {
    frame.dispose();
    System.exit(0);
  }
}
static public javax.naming.Context getInitialContext() throws Exception {
  Properties p = new Properties();
  p.put(javax.naming.Context.INITIAL_CONTEXT_FACTORY,
                      "weblogic.jndi.TengahInitialContextFactory");
  return new InitialContext(p);
}
private void listAllItems() throws IOException{
  ResultsModel rm=new ResultsModel();
    try {
      BidderHome bhome=(BidderHome)ctx.lookup("bidder");
      Bidder bid=bhome.create();
      Enumeration enum=(Enumeration)bid.getItemList();
      if (enum != null) {
        rm.update(enum);
      }
    } catch (Exception e) {
        System.out.println("AuctionServlet <list>:"+e);
    }
  //Create a new table using the ResultsModel object as the table model
  scrollTable=new JTable(rm);
  //Force the End Date columns and Description columns to have
  //a set width
  adjustColumnWidth(scrollTable.getColumn("End Date"), 150);
  adjustColumnWidth(scrollTable.getColumn("Description"), 120);
  //The scroll column model is initially mapped to
  //display all the table data. The fixed column model
  //is initially empty
  scrollColumnModel = scrollTable.getColumnModel();
  fixedColumnModel = new DefaultTableColumnModel();

  //Get the first column, remove it from the scroll column and
  //add it to the fixed table
```

```
      TableColumn col = scrollColumnModel.getColumn(0);
      scrollColumnModel.removeColumn(col);
      fixedColumnModel.addColumn(col);

      //Create a new table based on the fixed column model (1 column)
      fixedTable = new JTable(rm,fixedColumnModel);

      //Keep the heights of the fixed and scroll tables the same
      fixedTable.setRowHeight(scrollTable.getRowHeight());

      headers = new JViewport();
      //Get the selection model used in this table and override it
      //so we can also update the scroll table if the fixed table
      //is selected and vice-versa
      ListSelectionModel fixedSelection = fixedTable.getSelectionModel();
```
//**API Ref**: void addListSelectionListener(ListSelectionListener l)
```
      fixedSelection.addListSelectionListener(
          new ListSelectionListener() {
              public void valueChanged(ListSelectionEvent e) {
                ListSelectionModel lsm = (ListSelectionModel)e.getSource();
                if (!lsm.isSelectionEmpty())  {
                   setScrollableRow();
                }
              }
          });
```
//**API Ref**: ListSelectionMode getSelectionModel()
```
      ListSelectionModel scrollSelection = scrollTable.getSelectionModel();
      scrollSelection.addListSelectionListener(new ListSelectionListener() {
         public void valueChanged(ListSelectionEvent e) {
           ListSelectionModel lsm = (ListSelectionModel)e.getSource();
           if (!lsm.isSelectionEmpty())  {
             setFixedRow();
           }
         }
      });
      //Create a custom renderer and use it on column 2
      CustomRenderer custom = new CustomRenderer();
      custom.setHorizontalAlignment(JLabel.CENTER);
```
//**API Ref**: void setCellRenderer(TableCellRenderer renderer)
```
      scrollColumnModel.getColumn(2).setCellRenderer(custom);
      //Use the custom button renderer on column 3
      scrollColumnModel.getColumn(3).setCellRenderer(new
                                             CustomButtonRenderer());
      //Add the custom button editor to column 3
      CustomButtonEditor customEdit=new CustomButtonEditor(frame);
      scrollColumnModel.getColumn(3).setCellEditor(customEdit);

      //Add the scrolling column headers to the header viewport
      //the headers viewport is later added to the headerPanel with
      //an associated scroll bar
```
//**API Ref**: JTableHeader getTableHeader()
```
      headers.add(scrollTable.getTableHeader());

      //Create a panel for the top left of the display that contains
      //the headers for the column that does not move
```

```
                JPanel topPanel = new JPanel();
                topPanel.setLayout(new BoxLayout(topPanel, BoxLayout.X_AXIS));
                adjustColumnWidth(fixedColumnModel.getColumn(0), 100);
                JTableHeader fixedHeader=fixedTable.getTableHeader();
//API Ref: void setAlignmentY()
                fixedHeader.setAlignmentY(Component.TOP_ALIGNMENT);
                topPanel.add(fixedHeader);
//API Ref: Component createRigidArea(Dimension d)
                topPanel.add(Box.createRigidArea(new Dimension(2, 0)));
                topPanel.setPreferredSize(new Dimension(400, 40));

                //Create a panel to contain the scroll headers that will
                //displayed at the top right
                JPanel headerPanel = new JPanel();
                headerPanel.setAlignmentY(Component.TOP_ALIGNMENT);
                headerPanel.setLayout(new BorderLayout());
                JScrollPane scrollpane = new JScrollPane();
//API Ref: JScrollBar getHorizontalScrollBar()
                scrollBar = scrollpane.getHorizontalScrollBar();
                headerPanel.add(headers, "North");
                headerPanel.add(scrollBar, "South");
                topPanel.add(headerPanel);
                //set the scrollable part of both the table views
                scrollTable.setPreferredScrollableViewportSize(new Dimension(300,180));
                fixedTable.setPreferredScrollableViewportSize( new Dimension(100,180));
                fixedTable.setPreferredSize(new Dimension(100,180));
                innerPort = new JViewport();

                //If the user moves the scrollbar at the top
                //of the scrollable data update the header and table
                //data positions so they are viewable
//API Ref: void setView(Component view)
                innerPort.setView(scrollTable);
                scrollpane.setViewport(innerPort);
                 scrollBar.getModel().addChangeListener(new ChangeListener()  {
                  public void stateChanged(ChangeEvent e) {
//API Ref: Point getViewPosition()
                    Point q = headers.getViewPosition();
                    Point p = innerPort.getViewPosition();
                    int val = scrollBar.getModel().getValue();
                    p.x = val;
                    q.x = val;

//API Ref: void setView(Component view)
                    headers.setViewPosition(p);
                    headers.repaint(headers.getViewRect());
                    innerPort.setViewPosition(p);
                    innerPort.repaint(innerPort.getViewRect());
                  }
                });

                //Disable continuous update of the scroll table. Needed to
                //improve performance of a scrolling table in SDK 1.2
                scrollTable.getTableHeader().setUpdateTableInRealTime(false);
```

```
            //The bottom panel is where both tables data is positioned
            JPanel bottomPanel = new JPanel();
            bottomPanel.setLayout(new BoxLayout(bottomPanel, BoxLayout.X_AXIS));
            fixedTable.setAlignmentY(Component.TOP_ALIGNMENT);
            bottomPanel.add(fixedTable);
            bottomPanel.add(Box.createRigidArea(new Dimension(2, 0)));
            innerPort.setAlignmentY(Component.TOP_ALIGNMENT);
            bottomPanel.add(innerPort);
            bottomPanel.add(Box.createRigidArea(new Dimension(2, 0)));

            //Only allow vertical scrollbars as we are managing the
            //horizontal scroll ourselves
            scrollPane = new JScrollPane(bottomPanel,
                          JScrollPane.VERTICAL_SCROLLBAR_ALWAYS,
                          JScrollPane.HORIZONTAL_SCROLLBAR_NEVER);
            JViewport outerPort = new JViewport();
            outerPort.add(bottomPanel);
            //Workaround to affix the headers to the top of the scrollpane
            //uses setColumnHeaderView
```
//**API Ref**: void setColumnHeaderView(Component view)
```
            scrollPane.setColumnHeaderView(topPanel);
```
//**API Ref**: void setViewport(JViewport viewport)
```
            scrollPane.setViewport(outerPort);
            scrollTable.setAutoResizeMode(JTable.AUTO_RESIZE_OFF);
            frame.getContentPane().add(scrollPane);
            scrollTable.validate();
            frame.setSize(450,200);
        }
        void setFixedRow() {
          int index=scrollTable.getSelectedRow();
          fixedTable.setRowSelectionInterval(index, index);
        }
        void setScrollableRow() {
          //Highlight the row by calling setRowSelectionInterval with a
          //range of 1
          int index=fixedTable.getSelectedRow();
          scrollTable.setRowSelectionInterval(index, index);
        }
        void adjustColumnWidth(TableColumn c, int size) {
          c.setPreferredWidth(size);
          c.setMaxWidth(size);
          c.setMinWidth(size);
        }

        private void browseItems() throws IOException {
          JPanel findPanel;
          JButton findButton;
          Vector newItems=new Vector();
          Vector closedItems=new Vector();
          Bidder bid=null;
          Enumeration enum;
            String[] treelabels = { "All Auctions", "Closed Auction",
                                    "New Auctions"};
            try {
              BidderHome bhome=(BidderHome) ctx.lookup("bidder");
```

```
      bid=bhome.create();
      enum=(Enumeration)bid.getNewItemList();
      while((enum !=null) && (enum.hasMoreElements())) {
        while(enum.hasMoreElements()) {
          AuctionItem auctionItem=(AuctionItem)enum.nextElement();
          newItems.addElement(new Integer(auctionItem.getId()));
        }
      }
      enum=(Enumeration)bid.getClosedItemList();
      while((enum !=null) && (enum.hasMoreElements())) {
        while(enum.hasMoreElements()) {
          AuctionItem auctionItem=(AuctionItem)enum.nextElement();
          closedItems.addElement(new Integer(auctionItem.getId()));
        }
      }
} catch (Exception e) {
  System.out.println("AuctionServlet <list>:"+e);
}
//Create an array of nodes based on the size of the labels and
//open and closed items
nodes = new DefaultMutableTreeNode[treelabels.length];
DefaultMutableTreeNode[] closednodes = new
                              DefaultMutableTreeNode[closedItems.size()];
DefaultMutableTreeNode[] newnodes = new
                              DefaultMutableTreeNode[newItems.size()];

for(int i=0; i<treelabels.length; i++) {
  nodes[i] = new DefaultMutableTreeNode(treelabels[i]);
}
//Arrange the tree so that from the top level, all
//closed and open auctions are children from that top level
nodes[0].add(nodes[1]);
nodes[0].add(nodes[2]);
for(int i=0; i<closedItems.size(); i++) {
   closednodes[i] = new DefaultMutableTreeNode(closedItems.elementAt(i));
   nodes[1].add(closednodes[i]);
}
for(int i=0; i<newItems.size(); i++) {
   newnodes[i] = new DefaultMutableTreeNode(newItems.elementAt(i));
   nodes[2].add(newnodes[i]);
}
DefaultTreeModel model=new DefaultTreeModel(nodes[0]);
tree = new JTree(model);
JScrollPane scroll = new JScrollPane(tree);
browsePanel.add(scroll, BorderLayout.CENTER);
findPanel= new JPanel();
findField= new JTextField(10);
findButton= new JButton("find");
findButton.addActionListener (new ActionListener() {
  public void actionPerformed (ActionEvent e) {
    String field=findField.getText();
    if(field != null) {
      findNode(findField.getText());
    } else {
      return;
```

```
        }
      }
    });
    findPanel.add(findField);
    findPanel.add(findButton);
    browsePanel.add(findPanel, BorderLayout.SOUTH);
    frame.setSize(300,350);
  }
  private void findNode(String field) {
    //Get an enumeration list of all the nodes.
    //The ordering is generated by starting from the root
    //to the end of each branch, and to the end of
    //the next branch including any nodes not visited before

    Enumeration e = nodes[0].depthFirstEnumeration();
    Object currNode;
    while(e.hasMoreElements()) {
      currNode = e.nextElement();
      if(currNode.toString().equals(field)) {
        TreePath path = new TreePath(((
                        DefaultMutableTreeNode)currNode).getPath());
        tree.makeVisible(path);
        tree.setSelectionRow(tree.getRowForPath(path));
        return;
      }
    }
  }
  public static void main(String args[]) {
    AuctionClient ac= new AuctionClient();
  }
}
class CustomRenderer extends DefaultTableCellRenderer {
  public Component getTableCellRendererComponent(JTable table,
                         Object value, boolean isSelected,
                         boolean hasFocus, int row, int column) {
    Component comp = super.getTableCellRendererComponent(table, value,
                         isSelected, hasFocus, row,column);
    JLabel label = (JLabel)comp;
    //Does the auction item have 30 or more bids? If so, display
    //a hot item image
      if(((Integer)value).intValue() >= 30) {
        label.setIcon(new ImageIcon("Hot.gif"));
      } else {
        label.setIcon(new ImageIcon("Normal.gif"));
      }
      return (JLabel)label;
  }
}
class CustomButtonEditor extends DefaultCellEditor {
    final JButton mybutton;
    JFrame frame;
    CustomButtonEditor(JFrame frame) {
      super(new JCheckBox());
      mybutton = new JButton();
      this.editorComponent = mybutton;
```

```
      //To activate this button requires to mouse clicks (double click)
      this.clickCountToStart = 2;
      this.frame=frame;
      mybutton.setOpaque(true);
      mybutton.addActionListener(new ActionListener() {
        public void actionPerformed(ActionEvent e) {
          fireEditingStopped();
        }
    });
  }
  protected void fireEditingStopped() {
    super.fireEditingStopped();
  }
  public Object getCellEditorValue() {
    JDialog jd= new JDialog(frame, "Time left");
    Calendar today=Calendar.getInstance();
    Calendar end=Calendar.getInstance();
    SimpleDateFormat in=new SimpleDateFormat("yyyy-MM-dd");
    try {
      //Get the button text from the table row. This value is the end date
      //of the auction and was previously initialised when the table
      //was populated with data.
      end.setTime(in.parse(mybutton.getText()));
    } catch (Exception e){
      System.out.println("Error in date"+mybutton.getText()+e);
    }
    int days = 0;
    //To work out if the date in the button is later or earlier than
    //today, roll the date forward a day at a time until it is later
    //than today
    while(today.before(end)) {
      today.roll(Calendar.DATE,true);
      days++;
    }
    jd.setSize(200,100);
    //If the end date was originally after today, mark the auction as
    //completed. Otherwise, display the number of days remaining.
    if(today.after(end)) {
      jd.getContentPane().add(new JLabel("Auction completed"));
    } else {
      jd.getContentPane().add(new JLabel("Days left="+days));
    }
    jd.setVisible(true);
    return new String(mybutton.getText());
  }
  public Component getTableCellEditorComponent(JTable table, Object value,
                        boolean isSelected, int row, int column) {
    ((JButton) editorComponent).setText(((JButton)value).getText());
    if(isSelected) {
        ((JButton)
          editorComponent).setForeground(table.getSelectionForeground());
        ((JButton)
          editorComponent).setBackground(table.getSelectionBackground());
    } else {
      ((JButton) editorComponent).setForeground(table.getForeground());
```

```
        ((JButton) editorComponent).setBackground(table.getBackground());
      }
      return editorComponent;
    }
  }
  class CustomButtonRenderer extends JButton implements TableCellRenderer {
    public CustomButtonRenderer() {
      setOpaque(true);
    }
    public Component getTableCellRendererComponent(JTable table,
      Object value, boolean isSelected, boolean hasFocus,
      int row, int column) {
      if(isSelected) {
        ((JButton)value).setForeground(table.getSelectionForeground());
        ((JButton)value).setBackground(table.getSelectionBackground());
      } else {
        ((JButton)value).setForeground(table.getForeground());
        ((JButton)value).setBackground(table.getBackground());
      }
      return (JButton)value;
    }
  }
```

Report

```
    import javax.swing.*;
    import javax.swing.table.*;
    import java.awt.print.*;
    import java.util.*;
    import java.awt.*;
    import java.awt.event.*;
    import java.awt.geom.*;
    import java.awt.Dimension;

    public class Report implements Printable{
      JFrame frame;
      JTable tableView;
      public Report() {
        frame = new JFrame("Sales Report");
        frame.addWindowListener(new WindowAdapter() {
        public void windowClosing(WindowEvent e) {System.exit(0);}});
        final String[] headers = {"Description", "open price",
                           "latest price", "End Date", "Quantity"};
        final Object[][] data = {
          {"Box of Biros", "1.00", "4.99", new Date(), new Integer(2)},
          {"Blue Biro", "0.10", "0.14", new Date(), new Integer(1)},
          {"legal pad", "1.00", "2.49", new Date(), new Integer(1)},
          {"tape", "1.00", "1.49", new Date(), new Integer(1)},
          {"stapler", "4.00", "4.49", new Date(), new Integer(1)},
          {"legal pad", "1.00", "2.29", new Date(), new Integer(5)}};
        TableModel dataModel = new AbstractTableModel() {
          public int getColumnCount() {
            return headers.length;
          }
```

```java
    public int getRowCount() {
      return data.length;
    }
    public Object getValueAt(int row, int col) {
      return data[row][col];
    }
    public String getColumnName(int column) {
      return headers[column];
    }
    public Class getColumnClass(int col) {
      return getValueAt(0,col).getClass();
    }
    public boolean isCellEditable(int row, int col) {
      return (col==1);
    }
    public void setValueAt(Object aValue, int row, int column) {
      data[row][column] = aValue;
    }};
  tableView = new JTable(dataModel);
  JScrollPane scrollpane = new JScrollPane(tableView);
  scrollpane.setPreferredSize(new Dimension(500, 80));
  frame.getContentPane().setLayout(new BorderLayout());
  frame.getContentPane().add(BorderLayout.CENTER,scrollpane);
  frame.pack();
  JButton printButton= new JButton();
  printButton.setText("print me!");
  frame.getContentPane().add(BorderLayout.SOUTH,printButton);
  //for faster printing turn double buffering off
  RepaintManager.currentManager(frame).setDoubleBufferingEnabled(false);
  printButton.addActionListener(new ActionListener(){
    public void actionPerformed(ActionEvent evt) {
      PrinterJob pj=PrinterJob.getPrinterJob();
      pj.setPrintable(Report.this);
      pj.printDialog();
      try {
        pj.print();
      } catch (Exception PrintException) {}
    }});
    frame.setVisible(true);
}
public int print(Graphics g, PageFormat pageFormat, int pageIndex)
                  throws PrinterException {
  Graphics2D  g2 = (Graphics2D) g;
  g2.setColor(Color.black);
  int fontHeight=g2.getFontMetrics().getHeight();
  int fontDesent=g2.getFontMetrics().getDescent();
//Leave room for page number
  double pageHeight = pageFormat.getImageableHeight()-fontHeight;
  double pageWidth = pageFormat.getImageableWidth();
  double tableWidth = (double)
                tableView.getColumnModel().getTotalColumnWidth();
  double scale = 1;
  if(tableWidth >= pageWidth) {
    scale =  pageWidth / tableWidth;
  }
```

```java
      double headerHeightOnPage=tableView.getTableHeader().getHeight()*scale;
      double tableWidthOnPage=tableWidth*scale;
      double oneRowHeight=(tableView.getRowHeight() +
                                     tableView.getRowMargin())*scale;
      int numRowsOnAPage =
                  (int)((pageHeight-headerHeightOnPage)/oneRowHeight);
      double pageHeightForTable=oneRowHeight*numRowsOnAPage;
      int totalNumPages= (int)Math.ceil((
                  (double)tableView.getRowCount())/numRowsOnAPage);
      if(pageIndex>=totalNumPages) {
        return NO_SUCH_PAGE;
      }
      g2.translate(pageFormat.getImageableX(), pageFormat.getImageableY());
      g2.drawString("Page: "+(pageIndex+1),(int)pageWidth/2-35,
                  (int)(pageHeight+fontHeight-fontDesent));//bottom center
      g2.translate(0f,headerHeightOnPage);
      g2.translate(0f,-pageIndex*pageHeightForTable);
      //If this piece of the table is smaller than the size available,
      //clip to the appropriate bounds.
      if(pageIndex + 1 == totalNumPages) {
        int lastRowPrinted = numRowsOnAPage * pageIndex;
        int numRowsLeft = tableView.getRowCount() - lastRowPrinted;
        g2.setClip(0, (int)(pageHeightForTable * pageIndex),
        (int) Math.ceil(tableWidthOnPage),
        (int) Math.ceil(oneRowHeight * numRowsLeft));
      } else { //else clip to the entire area available.
        g2.setClip(0, (int)(pageHeightForTable*pageIndex),
        (int) Math.ceil(tableWidthOnPage),
        (int) Math.ceil(pageHeightForTable));
      }
      g2.scale(scale,scale);
      tableView.paint(g2);
      g2.scale(1/scale,1/scale);
      g2.translate(0f,pageIndex*pageHeightForTable);
      g2.translate(0f, -headerHeightOnPage);
      g2.setClip(0, 0,(int) Math.ceil(tableWidthOnPage),
                        (int)Math.ceil(headerHeightOnPage));
      g2.scale(scale,scale);
      tableView.getTableHeader().paint(g2);//paint header at top
      return Printable.PAGE_EXISTS;
    }
    public static void main(String[] args) {
      new Report();
    }
  }
```

SalesReport

```java
    import javax.swing.*;
    import javax.swing.table.*;
    import java.awt.print.*;
    import java.util.*;
    import java.awt.*;
    import java.awt.event.*;
```

```java
import java.awt.geom.*;
import java.awt.Dimension;

public class SalesReport extends JApplet implements Printable {
  JTable ppTable;
  JTableHeader tableHeader;
  int [] subTableSplit = null;
  boolean pageinfoCalculated=false;
  int totalNumPages=0;
  int prevPageIndex = 0;
  int subPageIndex = 0;
  int subTableSplitSize = 0;
  double tableHeightOnFullPage, headerHeight;
  double pageWidth, pageHeight;
  int fontHeight, fontDesent;
  double tableHeight, rowHeight;

  public void init() {
    final String[] headers = {
        "Description", "open price", "latest price", "End Date", "Quantity",
        "a","b" "c","d","e","f","g","h","i","j","k","l","m ","n"};
    //Make the data array larger if you want to see the table split
    //over more than one page
    final Object[][] data = { {
        "Box of Biros", "1.00", "4.99", new Date(), new Integer(2),
        "a","b","c","d","e","f","g" "h" "i" "j" "k","l","m","n"},
        {"Blue Biro", "0.10", "0.14", new Date(), new Integer(1),
        "a","b", "c", "d", "e", "f", "g", "h", "i","j","k","l","m","n"},
        {"legal pad", "1.00", "2.49", new Date(),new Integer(1),
        "a","b", "c", "d", "e", "f", "g", "h", "i","j","k","l","m","n"},
        {"legal pad", "1.00", "2.49", new Date(), new Integer(1),
        "a","b", "c", "d", "e", "f", "g", "h", "i","j","k","l","m","n"},
        {"legal pad", "1.00", "2.49", new Date(), new Integer(1),
        "a","b", "c", "d", "e", "f", "g", "h", "i","j","k","l","m","n"},
        {"legal pad", "1.00", "2.49", new Date(), new Integer(1),
        "a","b", "c", "d", "e", "f", "g", "h", "i","j","k","l","m","n"},
        {"tape", "1.00", "1.49", new Date(), new Integer(1),
        "a","b", "c", "d", "e", "f", "g", "h", "i","j","k","l","m","n"},
        {"stapler", "4.00", "4.49", new Date(), new Integer(1),
        "a","b", "c", "d", "e", "f", "g", "h", "i","j","k","l","m","n"},
        {"stapler", "4.00", "4.49", new Date(), new Integer(1),
        "a","b", "c", "d", "e", "f", "g", "h", "i","j","k","l","m","n"},
        {"legal pad", "1.00", "2.29", new Date(), new Integer(5),
        "a","b", "c", "d", "e", "f", "g", "h", "i","j","k","l","m","n"}
    };
    TableModel dataModel = new AbstractTableModel() {
      public int getColumnCount() {
        return headers.length;
      }
      public int getRowCount() {
        return data.length;
      }
      public Object getValueAt(int row, int col) {
        return data[row][col]
      }
```

```
      public String getColumnName(int column) {
         return headers[column];
      }
      public Class getColumnClass(int col) {
         return getValueAt(0,col).getClass();
      }
      public boolean isCellEditable(int row, int col) {
         return (col==1);
      }
      public void setValueAt(Object aValue, int row, int column) {
         data[row][column] = aValue;
      }};
   ppTable = new JTable(dataModel);
   JScrollPane scrollpane = new JScrollPane(ppTable);
   scrollpane.setPreferredSize(new Dimension(500, 80));
   getContentPane().setLayout(new BorderLayout());
   getContentPane().add(BorderLayout.CENTER,scrollpane);
   JButton printButton= new JButton();
   printButton.setText("print me!");
   getContentPane().add(BorderLayout.SOUTH,printButton);

//For faster printing turn double buffering off
   RepaintManager.currentManager(this).setDoubleBufferingEnabled(false);
   printButton.addActionListener( new ActionListener(){
   public void actionPerformed(ActionEvent evt) {
   PrinterJob pj=PrinterJob.getPrinterJob();
   pj.setPrintable(SalesReport.this);
   pj.printDialog();
   try {
     pj.print();
   } catch (Exception PrintException) {}
 }});
 setVisible(true);
}
public int print(Graphics g, PageFormat pageFormat, int pageIndex)
                        throws PrinterException {
  Graphics2D g2=(Graphics2D)g;
  if(!pageinfoCalculated) {
    getPageInfo(g, pageFormat);
  }
  g2.setColor(Color.black);
  if(pageIndex>=totalNumPages) {
    return NO_SUCH_PAGE;
  }
  if(prevPageIndex != pageIndex) {
    subPageIndex++;
    if ( subPageIndex == subTableSplitSize -1) {
     subPageIndex=0;
    }
  }
  g2.translate(pageFormat.getImageableX(), pageFormat.getImageableY());
  int rowIndex = pageIndex/ (subTableSplitSize - 1);
  printTablePart(g2, pageFormat, rowIndex, subPageIndex);
  prevPageIndex= pageIndex;
  return Printable.PAGE_EXISTS;
```

```
      }

      public void getPageInfo(Graphics g, PageFormat pageFormat) {
        subTableSplit = null;
        subTableSplitSize = 0;
        subPageIndex = 0;
        prevPageIndex = 0;
//API Ref: FontMetrics getFontMetrics()
        fontHeight=g.getFontMetrics().getHeight();
        fontDesent=g.getFontMetrics().getDescent();
        tableHeader = ppTable.getTableHeader();
        double headerWidth = tableHeader.getWidth();
        headerHeight = tableHeader.getHeight() + ppTable.getRowMargin();
        pageHeight = pageFormat.getImageableHeight();
        pageWidth =  pageFormat.getImageableWidth();
        double tableWidth = ppTable.getColumnModel().getTotalColumnWidth();
        tableHeight = ppTable.getHeight();
//API Ref: int getRowHeight()
//API Ref: int getRowMargin()
        rowHeight = ppTable.getRowHeight() + ppTable.getRowMargin();
        tableHeightOnFullPage = (int)(pageHeight - headerHeight - fontHeight*2);
        tableHeightOnFullPage = tableHeightOnFullPage/rowHeight * rowHeight;
        TableColumnModel tableColumnModel = tableHeader.getColumnModel();
//API Ref: int getColumnCount()
        int columns = tableColumnModel.getColumnCount();
//API Ref: int getColumnMargin()
        int columnMargin = tableColumnModel.getColumnMargin();
        int [] temp = new int[columns];
        int columnIndex = 0;
        temp[0] = 0;
        int columnWidth;
        int length = 0;
        subTableSplitSize = 0;
        while( columnIndex < columns ) {
          columnWidth = tableColumnModel.getColumn(columnIndex).getWidth();
          if(length + columnWidth + columnMargin > pageWidth ) {
            temp[subTableSplitSize+1] = temp[subTableSplitSize] + length;
            length = columnWidth;
            subTableSplitSize++;
          } else {
            length += columnWidth + columnMargin;
          }
            columnIndex++;
        } //while
        if(length > 0 )  {  //if are more columns left, part page
          temp[subTableSplitSize+1] = temp[subTableSplitSize] + length;
          subTableSplitSize++;
        }
        subTableSplitSize++;
        subTableSplit = new int[subTableSplitSize];
        for(int i=0; i < subTableSplitSize; i++ ) {
          subTableSplit[i]= temp[i];
        }
        totalNumPages = (int)(tableHeight/tableHeightOnFullPage);
        //at least 1 more row left
```

```
      if(tableHeight%tableHeightOnFullPage >= rowHeight ) {
        totalNumPages++;
      }
      totalNumPages *= (subTableSplitSize-1);
      pageinfoCalculated = true;
  }
  public void printTablePart(Graphics2D g2, PageFormat pageFormat,
                             int rowIndex,int columnIndex) {
      String pageNumber = "Page: "+(rowIndex+1);
      if(subTableSplitSize > 1 ) {
        pageNumber += "-" + (columnIndex+1);
      }
      int pageLeft = subTableSplit[columnIndex];
      int pageRight = subTableSplit[columnIndex + 1];
      int pageWidth =  pageRight-pageLeft;
      //page number message
       g2.drawString(pageNumber, pageWidth/2-35, (int)(pageHeight -
                                                  fontHeight));
      double clipHeight = Math.min(tableHeightOnFullPage,
                           tableHeight - rowIndex*tableHeightOnFullPage);
      g2.translate(-subTableSplit[columnIndex], 0);
      g2.setClip(pageLeft ,0, pageWidth, (int)headerHeight);
      tableHeader.paint(g2);    //draw the header on every page
      g2.translate(0, headerHeight);
      g2.translate(0,  -tableHeightOnFullPage*rowIndex);
      //cut table image and draw on the page
      g2.setClip(pageLeft, (int)tableHeightOnFullPage*rowIndex, pageWidth,
                      (int)clipHeight);
      ppTable.paint(g2);
      double pageTop =  tableHeightOnFullPage*rowIndex - headerHeight;
      double pageBottom = pageTop +  clipHeight + headerHeight;
      g2.drawRect(pageLeft, (int)pageTop, pageWidth,
                      (int)(clipHeight+ headerHeight));
  }
}
```

7

Debugging Applets, Applications, and Servlets

An unwritten law of programming states you will spend 10 percent of your time on the first 90 percent of a project, and the other 90 percent of your time on the remaining 10 percent. If this sounds like any of your projects, you are probably spending 90 percent of your time on debugging and integration. While there are plenty of books and people to help you start a project, there are far fewer resources available to help you finish it.

The good news is that this chapter focuses completely on debugging and fixing to get your project out on time. This chapter and Chapter 8, Performance Techniques, depart from the auction application and use simple examples to walk you through the steps to debugging, fixing, and tuning your programs.

By the time you finish this chapter, you should be an expert at troubleshooting programs written in the Java programming language—applets, applications, and servlets—of all shapes and sizes.

Covered in this Chapter

In a Rush?

If you have a pressing problem you need an answer to right now, this table might help. It tells you where to find answers for common problems so that you can go directly to the information.

Problem	Section
Program hangs or crashes	Analyzing Stack Traces (page 231)
Problem in a running program	Getting Behind the Seat with `jdb` (page 216)
Java Web Server problems	Servlet Debugging (page 226) and Analyzing Stack Traces (page 231)

Collecting Evidence

The first step in trying to solve any problem is to gather as much evidence and information as possible. If you can picture a crime scene, you know that everything is checked, cataloged, and analyzed before any conclusions are reached. When debugging a program, you do not have weapons, hair samples, or fingerprints, but there is plenty of evidence you can gather that might contain or ultimately lead to the solution. This section explains how to gather that evidence.

Installation and Environment

The Java platform is a fast-moving and changing technology. You might have more than one release installed on your system, and those releases might have been installed as part of another product installation. In an environment with mixed releases, a program can experience problems due to changes to the platform in a new version or release.

For example, if classes, libraries, or Windows registry entries from previous installations remain on your system after an upgrade, there is a chance the new software mix is causing your problems and needs to be investigated and ruled out. Opportunities for problems related to mixed software releases have increased with the use of different release tools to deliver the Java platform software.

The section on Version Issues at the end of this chapter provides a complete list of major Java platform release and version information to help you rule out software release issues. This next section highlights the most common problems you are likely to encounter.

CLASSPATH

In the Java 2 platform, the CLASSPATH environment variable is needed to specify the application's own classes only, and not the Java platform classes as was required in earlier releases. So it is possible your CLASSPATH environment variable is pointing at Java platform classes from earlier releases and causing problems. To examine the CLASSPATH, type the following at the command line for your operating system.

Windows 95/98/NT:
echo %CLASSPATH%

Unix systems:
echo $CLASSPATH

Java classes are loaded on a first-come, first-served basis from the CLASSPATH list. If the CLASSPATH variable contains a reference to a lib/classes.zip file, which in turn points to a different Java platform installation, this can cause incompatible classes to be loaded.

NOTE   In the Java 2 Platform, the system classes are chosen before any class on the CLASSPATH list, to minimize the possibility of any old broken Java classes being loaded instead of a Java 2 class of the same name.

The CLASSPATH variable can get its settings from the command line or from configuration settings such as those specified in the User Environment on Windows NT, an autoexec.bat file, or a shell startup file like .cshrc on Unix.

You can control the classes the Java virtual machine uses by compiling your program with a special command-line option that lets you supply the CLASSPATH you want. The Java 2 platform option and parameter is -Xboot-classpath classpath, and earlier releases use -classpath classpath and -sysclasspath classpath. Regardless of which release you are running, the classpath parameter specifies the system and user classpath, and zip or Java Archive (JAR) files to be used in the compilation.

As an example, to compile and run the Myapp program with a system CLASS-PATH supplied on the command line, use the Windows or UNIX instructions that follow depending on your platform.

Windows 95/98/NT:

In this example, the Java platform is installed in the C:\java directory. Type everything on one line. The -J option lets you pass extra conditions to the compiler.

```
javac -J -Xbootclasspath:c\java\ib\tools.jar;
   c:\java\jre\ib\rt.jar;c:\java\jre\ib\i18n.jar;.Myapp.java
```

You do not need the -J run-time flag to run the compiled Myapp program; just type the following on one line:

```
java -Xbootclasspath:c:\java\jre\ib\rt.jar;
   c:\java\jre\ib\i18n.jar;. Myapp
```

Unix systems:

In this example, the Java platform is installed in the /usr/local/java directory. Type everything on one line:

```
javac -J-Xbootclasspath:/usr/local/java/lib/tools.jar:/usr/local/java/jre/
lib/rt.jar:/usr/local/java/jre/lib/i18n.jar:. Myapp.java
```

You do not need the -J run-time flag to run the compiled Myapp program; just type the following on one line:

```
java -Xbootclasspath:/usr/local/java/jre/lib/rt.jar:/usr/local/java/jre/lib/
i18n.jar:. Myapp
```

Class Loading

Another way to analyze CLASSPATH problems is to locate where your application is loading its classes. The verbose option to the java interpreter command shows which .zip or .jar file a class comes from when it is loaded. This way, you will be able to tell if it came from the Java platform zip file or from some other application's JAR file.

For example, an application might be using the Password class you wrote for it or it might be loading a Password class from an installed integrated development environment (IDE) tool. You should see each JAR and zip file named as in the example below:

```
$ java -verbose SalesReport
[Opened /usr/local/java/jdk1.2/solaris/jre/lib/rt.jar in 498 ms]
[Opened /usr/local/java/jdk1.2/solaris/jre/lib/i18n.jar in 60 ms]
[Loaded java.lang.NoClassDefFoundError from /usr/local/java/jdk1.2/solaris/
      jre/lib/rt.jar]
[Loaded java.lang.Class from /usr/local/java/jdk1.2/solaris/jre/lib/rt.jar]
[Loaded java.lang.Object from /usr/local/java/jdk1.2/solaris/jre/lib/rt.jar]
```

Including Debug Code

A common way to add diagnostic code to an application is to use System.out.println statements at strategic locations in the application. This technique is fine during development, providing you remember to remove them all when you release your product.

However, there are other approaches that are just as simple, do not affect the performance of your application, and do not display messages that you do not want your customers to see. The following are two techniques that overcome the problems with System.out.println statements.

Turning Debug Information on at Run Time

The first technique is to turn debugging information on at run time. One advantage to this is that you do not need to recompile any code if problems appear at the testing stage or on a customer site. Another advantage is that sometimes software problems can be attributed to race conditions where the same segment of code behaves unpredictably due to timing between other program interactions.

If you control your debug code from the command line instead of adding println debug statements, you can rule out sequence problems caused by race conditions coming from the println code. This technique also saves you from adding and removing println debug statements and having to recompile your code.

To use this technique, you have to set the debug flag to true and include application code to test that system property value. So, for example, you can set the debug flag to true and specify the TestRuntime program as follows:

```
java -Ddebug=true TestRuntime
```

The source code for the TestRuntime class needs to examine this property and set the debug boolean flag as follows:

```
public class TestRuntime {
  boolean debugmode; //global flag that we test
  public TestRuntime () {
    String dprop=System.getProperty("debug");
    if((dprop !=null) && (dprop.equals("yes"))){
      debugmode=true;
    }
    if(debugmode) {
      System.err.println("debug mode!");
    }
  }
}
```

Creating Debug and Production Releases at Run Time

As mentioned earlier, one problem with adding System.out.println debug statements to your code is finding and removing them before you release the product. Apart from adding unnecessary code, println debug statements can contain information you do not want your customers to see.

One way to remove System.out.println debug statements from your code is to use the following compiler optimization to remove predetermined branches from your code at compile time and achieve something similar to a debug pre-processor.

This example uses a static dmode boolean flag that when set to false results in the debug code and the debug test statement being removed. When the dmode value is set to true, the code is included in the compiled class file and is available to the application for debugging purposes.

```
class Debug {
  //set dmode to false to compile out debug code
  public static final boolean dmode=true;
}

public class TestCompiletime {
  if (Debug.dmode) {                        //These
    System.err.println("Debug message");    //are
    }                                       //removed
}
```

Using Diagnostic Methods

You can use diagnostic methods to request debug information from the Java virtual machine. The following two methods from the Runtime class trace the method calls and Java virtual machine byte codes that your application uses. Because both these methods produce a lot of output, it is best to trace very small amounts of code, even as little as one line at a time.

To enable trace calls so you will see the output, you have to start the Java virtual machine with the java_g or java -Xdebug interpreter commands. To list every method as it is invoked at run time, add the following line before the code you wish to start tracing and add a matching traceMethodCalls line with the argument set to false to turn the tracing off. The tracing information is displayed on the standard output.

```
//set boolean argument to false to disable
  Runtime.getRuntime().traceMethodCalls(true);
  callMyCode();
  Runtime.getRuntime().traceMethodCalls(false);
```

You can also add the following line to your application to dump your own stack trace. You can find out how to read a stack trace in Analyzing Stack Traces (page XXX), but for now you can think of a stack trace as a snapshot of the current thread running in the Java virtual machine.

```
Thread.currentThread().dumpStack();
```

Adding Debug Information

Local variable information is not included in the core Java platform system classes. So, if you use a debug tool to list local variables for system classes where you place stop commands, you will get the following output, even when you compile with the -g flag as suggested by the output. This output is from a jdb session. The jdb command-line debugging tool is part of your JDK installation.

```
main[1] locals
No local variables: try compiling with -g
```

To get access to the local variable information, you have to obtain the source (src.zip or src.jar) and recompile it with a debug flag. You can get the source for most java.* classes with the binary downloads from java.sun.com (http://java.sun.com).

Once you download the src.zip or src.jar file, extract only the files you need. For example, to extract the String class, type the following at the command line:

```
unzip /tmp/src.zip src/java/lang/String.java
```

or

```
jar -xf /tmp/src.jar src/java/lang/String.java
```

Recompile the extracted class or classes with the -g option. You could also add your own additional diagnostics to the source file at this point.

```
javac -g src/java/lang/String.java
```

> **NOTE** The Java 2 javac compiler gives you more options than just the original -g option for debug code, and you can reduce the size of your classes by using -g:none, which gives you on average about a 10 percent reduction in size.

To run the application with the newly compiled debug class or classes, you need to use the boot classpath option so that these new classes are picked up first. Type the following on one line with a space before myapp.

Win95/NT Java 2 platform:

This example assumes the Java platform is installed in `c:\java` and the source files are in `c:\java\src`:

```
jdb -Xbootclasspath:c:\java\src;c:\java\jre1ibt.jar;c: \java\jre\i18n.jar;.
myapp
```

Unix systems:

This example assumes the Java platform is installed in `c:\java` and the source files are in `c:\java\src`.

```
jdb -Xbootclasspath:/usr/java/src;/usr/java/jre/lib/rt.jar;/usr/java/jre/
i18n.jar;. myapp
```

Running Tests and Analyzing

If you are still having problems even after you have ruled out installation and environment problems and included debugging code, it is time to use tools to test and analyze your program.

Getting Behind the Seat with jdb

Although there are some very good Integrated Development Environment (IDE) tools on the market, the Java debugger tool, jdb and its successors, have an important role to play in testing and debugging programs. Some advantages of jdb over IDE tools are it is free, it is platform independent (some IDE tools are not), and it runs as a separate process to the program being debugged. The benefit to jdb running as a separate process is that you can attach a debug session to a running program.

The downsides to using jdb are it has only a command-line interface, and it relies on the same code you are trying to debug. This means if there is a bug in the Java virtual machine, jdb could break attempting to diagnose that same bug!

The new JBug architecture was created to solve these problems in jdb. JBug, among other things, provides a debugger helper API in the Java virtual machine called the Java Virtual Machine Debug Interface (JVMDI). This helper communicates with the debugging front end using the Java Debug Wire Protocol (JDWP). The debugging front end uses the remote Java Debug Interface (JDI) to send and receive commands over the Java Debug Wire Protocol. JBug is available for Java 2 platforms and has a jdb-style front end that you will learn more about below.

Simple jdb Test Drive

Back to the classic jdb tool. Here are some simple steps to analyze a program using jdb. This first example debugs a program from application startup. The

Remote Debugging example (page 222) explains how to connect to a running program.

Start the Session.   To begin the debug session, compile the `SimpleJdbTest` program below with full debugging information using `javac` and the `-g` debug flag. In this example, the `SimpleJdbTest.java` program is an application, but it could just as well be an applet. The procedures for debugging applications with `jdb` are the same for debugging applets once the debug session has started.

SimpleJdbTest program:

```
import java.awt.*;
import java.awt.event.*;

public class SimpleJdbTest extends Frame{
  Panel p;
  Button b[]=new Button[2];
  int counter=0;

  SimpleJdbTest() {
    setSize(100,200);
    setup();
  }
  void setup (){
    p=new Panel();
    b[0]= new Button("press");
    p.add(b[0]);
    add(p);
    b[0].addActionListener( new ActionListener() {
      public void actionPerformed(ActionEvent e) {
      counter++;
    }
  });}
  public static void main(String args[]) {
    SimpleJdbTest sjb=new SimpleJdbTest();
    sjb.setVisible(true);
  }
}
```

Compile SimpleJdbTest:

```
javac -g SimpleJdbTest.java
```

Start the jdb tool:

Next, start the `jdb` tool with the program class name as a parameter:

```
jdb SimpleJdbTest
Initializing jdb...
0xad:class(SimpleJdbTest)
```

To debug an applet in appletviewer use the `-debug` parameter as in this example:

```
$ appletviewer -debug MyApplet.html
```

```
Initializing jdb...
0xee2f9808:class(sun.applet.AppletViewer)
>
```

Setting a Breakpoint and Listing Methods.   At this point, the Simple-
JdbTest class has only been loaded; the class constructor has not been called.
To make jdb stop when the program is first instantiated, put a stop, or breakpoint, at the constructor using the stop in command. When the breakpoints
have been set, instruct jdb to run your program using the run command as follows:

```
> stop in SimpleJdbTest.<init>
Breakpoint set in SimpleJdbTest.<init>
run
run SimpleJdbTest
running ...
main[1]
Breakpoint hit: SimpleJdbTest.<init> (SimpleJdbTest:10)
```

The jdb tool stops at the first line in the constructor. To list the methods that
were called to get to this breakpoint, enter the where command:

```
main[1] where
[1] SimpleJdbTest.<init> (SimpleJdbTest:10)
[2] SimpleJdbTest.main (SimpleJdbTest:29)
```

The numbered method in the list is the last stack frame that the Java virtual
machine has reached. In this case the last stack frame is the SimpleJdbTest
constructor that was called from SimpleJdbTest main.

Whenever a new method is called, it is placed on this stack list. Java Hotspot
technology achieves some of its speed gains by eliminating a new stack frame
when a new method is called.

To get a general appreciation of where the code has stopped, enter the list
command.

```
main[1] list
6       Panel p;
7       Button b;
8       int counter=0;
9
10      SimpleJdbTest() {
11          setSize(100,200);
12          setup();
13      }
14      void setup (){
```

Locating the Source.   If the source to the class file stopped in is not available
on the current path, you can tell jdb to find the source with the use command
by giving it the source directory as a parameter. In the following example, the
source is in a subdirectory or folder called book.

```
main[1] list
Unable to find SimpleJdbTest.java
main[1] use book
main[1] list
6   Panel p;
7   Button b[];
8   int counter=0;
9
10  => SimpleJdbTest() {
```

Looking at a Method.   To see what happens in the `setup` method for `SimpleJdbText`, use the `step` command to step through the four lines to get to it.

```
main[1] step
main[1]
Breakpoint hit: java.awt.Frame.<init> (Frame:222)
```

This is now the `Frame` class constructor! If you keep stepping you follow the `Frame` constructor and not the `SimpleJdbText` class. Because `SimpleJdbTest` extends the `Frame` class, the parent constructor, which in this case is `Frame`, is called on your behalf.

The `step up` Command.   You could continue stepping and eventually you will return to the `SimpleJdbTest` constructor, but to return immediately, you can use the `step up` command to go back to the `SimpleJdbTest` constructor.

```
main[1] step up
main[1]
Breakpoint hit: SimpleJdbTest.<init> (SimpleJdbTest:8)
```

The `next` Command.   You can also use the `next` command to get to the `setup` method. In this next example, the `jdb` tool has approximated that the source line is outside the constructor when it processed the last `step up` command. To return to the constructor, use another `step` command, and to get to the `setup` method, use a `next` command. To debug the `setup` method, you can step through the `setup` method.

```
main[1] step
Breakpoint hit: SimpleJdbTest.<init>
                    (SimpleJdbTest:11)
main[1] list
7   Button b[]=new Button[2];
8   int counter=0;
9
10  SimpleJdbTest() {
11  setSize(100,200);<
12  setup();
13  }
14  void setup (){
15  p=new Panel();
16  }
```

```
main[1] next
Breakpoint hit: SimpleJdbTest.<init>
                    (SimpleJdbTest:12)
main[1] step
Breakpoint hit: SimpleJdbTest.setup (SimpleJdbTest:15)
```

The list and print Commands.   Another way to get to the setup method
is to use the stop in SimpleJdbTest.setup command. Before using stop
in, list the source to check where you are:

```
main[1] list
11        setSize(100,200);
12        setup();
13  }
14  void setup (){
15  =>    p=new Panel();
16        b[0]= new Button("press");
17        p.add(b[0]);
18        add(p);
19
```

The first thing the setup method does is create a Panel p. If you try to display
the value of p with the print p command, you will find that the value is null.

```
main[1] print p
p = null
```

This occurred because the line has not been executed and so field p has not
been assigned a value. You need to step over that assignment operation with the
next command and then use the print p command again.

```
main[1] next
Breakpoint hit: SimpleJdbTest.setup (SimpleJdbTest:16)
main[1] print p
p = java.awt.Panel[panel0,0,0,0x0,invalid, layout=java.awt.FlowLayout]
```

Using the stop in Command to Set Breakpoints on Overloaded Methods.
Although stepping through small classes is fast, as a general rule on larger
applications, it is often a lot faster to set breakpoints. This is partly because jdb
has a very simple command set and no shortcuts, so each command has to be
pasted or typed in full.

To set a breakpoint in the Button class, use stop in java.awt.Button.<init>:

```
main[1] stop in java.awt.Button.<init>
java.awt.Button.<init> is overloaded,use one of the following:
void <init>
void <init>(java.lang.String)
```

The message explains why jdb cannot stop in this method without more information, but the message is slightly misleading because you do not need to specify the return type for overloaded methods, you just need to be explicit about

exactly which one of the overloaded methods you want to `stop` in. To `stop` in the constructor that creates this `Button`, use `stop in java.awt.Button.<init>(java.lang.String)`.

Later releases of `jdb` let you choose the desired method as a numbered option.

The cont Command.   To continue the `jdb` session, use the `cont` command. The next time the program creates a `Button` with a `String` as the constructor, `jdb` stops so that you can examine the output.

```
main[1] cont
main[1]
Breakpoint hit: java.awt.Button.<init> (Button:130)
```

If the `Button` class had not been recompiled with debug information as described earlier, you would not see the internal fields from the `print` command.

Clearing Breakpoints.   To clear this breakpoint and not stop every time a `Button` is created, use the `clear` command. This example uses the `clear` command with no arguments to display the list of current breakpoints and the `clear` command with the `java.awt.Button:130` argument to clear the `java.awt.Button:130` breakpoint.

```
main[1] clear
Current breakpoints set:
SimpleJdbTest:10
java.awt.Button:130
main[1] clear java.awt.Button:130
Breakpoint cleared at java.awt.Button: 130
```

Displaying Object Details.   To display details about an object, use the `print` command to call the object's `toString` method, or use the `dump` command to display the object's fields and values.

This example puts a breakpoint at line 17 and uses the `print` and `dump` commands to print and dump the first `Button` object in the array of `Button` objects. The dump command output has been abbreviated.

```
main[1] stop at SimpleJdbTest:17
Breakpoint set at SimpleJdbTest:17
main[1] cont
main[1]
Breakpoint hit: SimpleJdbTest.setup (SimpleJdbTest:17)

main[1] print b[0]
b[0] = java.awt.Button[button1,0,0,0x0,invalid,label=press]
main[1] dump b[0]
b[0] = (java.awt.Button)0x163 {
private int componentSerializedDataVersion = 2
```

```
boolean isPacked = false
private java.beans.PropertyChangeSupport changeSupport = null
long eventMask = 4096
transient java.awt.event.InputMethodListener
          inputMethodListener = null
....
java.lang.String actionCommand = null
java.lang.String label = press
}
```

Ending the Session.   That finishes the simple jdb examples. To terminate the jdb session, use the quit command:

```
0xee2f9820:class(SimpleJdbTest)
> quit
```

Remote Debugging

The jdb tool is an external process debugger, which means it debugs the program by sending messages to and from a helper inside the Java virtual machine. This makes it easy to debug a running program and helps you debug a program that interacts with the end user. A remote debug session from the command line does not interfere with the normal operation of the application.

Starting the Session.   Before the Java 2 release, the only thing required to enable remote debugging was to start the program with the -debug flag as the first argument, and if the application uses native libraries, make the library name end in _g. For example, you would need to copy nativelib.dll to nativelib_g.dll to debug with that library.

In Java 2, choices are a little more complicated. You need to tell the Java virtual machine where the tools.jar file is with the CLASSPATH variable. The tools.jar file contains noncore class files to support tools and utilities in the SDK. It is normally found in the lib directory of the Java platform installation.

You also need to disable the Just In Time (JIT) compiler if one exists. The JIT compiler is disabled by setting the java.compiler property to NONE or to an empty string. Finally, as the -classpath option overrides any previously set user classpath, you also need to add the CLASSPATH needed by your application.

Putting all of this together, here is the command line needed to start a program in remote debug mode. Put this all on one line and include all the classes you need on the command line.

Windows:
```
$ java -debug -classpath C:\java\lib\tools.jar;.
-Djava.compiler=NONE SimpleJdbTest Agent password=4gk5hm
```

Unix:
```
$ java -debug -classpath /usr/java/lib/tools.jar:.
-Djava.compiler=NONE SimpleJdbTest Agent password=5ufhic
```

The output is the agent password (in this case, 4gk5hm) if the program was successfully started. The agent password is supplied when starting jdb so jdb can find the corresponding application started in debug mode on that machine.

To start jdb in remote debug mode, supply a host name, which can be either the machine where the remote program was started or localhost if you are debugging on the same machine as the remote program, and the agent password.

```
jdb -host localhost -password 4gk5hm
```

Listing Threads.   Once inside the jdb session, you can list the currently active threads with the threads command and use the thread *<threadnumber>* command (for example, thread 7) to select the thread to analyze. Once the thread is selected, use the where command to see which methods have been called for this thread.

```
$ jdb -host arsenal -password 5ufhic
Initializing jdb...
> threads
Group system:
1. (java.lang.Thread)0x9          Signal dispatcher
                                  cond. waiting
2. (java.lang.ref.Reference       0xb Reference Handler
       $ReferenceHandler)         cond. waiting
3. (java.lang.ref.                Finalizer
       Finalizer                  cond. waiting
       $FinalizerThread)0xd

4. (java.lang.Thread)0xe          Debugger agent
                                  running
5. (sun.tools.agent.              Breakpoint handler
       Handler)0x10               cond. waiting
6. (sun.tools.agent.              Step handler
       StepHandler)0x12           cond. waiting
Group main:
7. (java.awt.                     AWT-EventQueue-0
       EventDispatchThread)       cond. waiting
       0x19
8. (sun.awt.                      PostEventQueue-0
       PostEventQueue)0x1b        cond. waiting
9. (java.lang.Thread)0x1c         AWT-Motif
                                  running
10. (java.lang.Thread)0x1d        TimerQueue
                                  cond. waiting
11. (sun.awt.                     Screen Updater
       ScreenUpdater)0x1f         cond. waiting
```

```
12. (java.lang.Thread)0x20        Thread-0
                                  cond. waiting
> thread 7
AWT-EventQueue-0[1] where
    [1] java.lang.Object.wait (native method)
    [2] java.lang.Object.wait (Object:424)
    [3] java.awt.EventQueue.getNextEvent (EventQueue:179)
    [4] java.awt.EventDispatchThread.run (EventDispatchThread:67)
```

Listing Source.   To list the source, the thread needs to be suspended using the suspend command. To let this thread continue, use the `resume` command. The example uses `resume 7`.

```
AWT-EventQueue-0[1] suspend 7
AWT-EventQueue-0[1] list
Current method is native
AWT-EventQueue-0[1] where
    [1] java.lang.Object.wait (native method)
    [2] java.lang.Object.wait (Object:424)
    [3] java.awt.EventQueue.getNextEvent    (EventQueue:179)
    [4] java.awt.EventDispatchThread.run (EventDispatchThread:67)
AWT-EventQueue-0[1] resume 7
```

Ending the Session.   When you finish debugging this program remotely, clear any remaining breakpoints before quitting the debug session. To get a list of remaining breakpoints use the `clear` command, and to remove them, enter `clear class:linenumber` as follows:

```
main[1] clear
Current breakpoints set:
SimpleJdbTest:10

main[1] clear SimpleJdbTest:10
main[1] quit
```

Using Auto-Pilot

One little-known trick with jdb is the jdb startup file. In this file, jdb automatically looks for a file called jdb.ini in the user.home directory. If you have multiple projects, it is a good idea to set a different user.home property for each project when you start jdb. To start jdb with a jdb.ini file in the current directory, type the following:

```
jdb -J-Duser.home=.
```

The jdb.ini file lets you set up jdb configuration commands, such as use, without having to enter the details each time a jdb runs. In the following example, jdb.ini file starts a jdb session for the FacTest class. It includes the Java platform sources on the source path list and passes the parameter 6 to the program. It then runs and stops at line 13, displays the free memory, and waits for further input.

```
load FacTest
stop at FacTest:13
use /home/calvin/java:/home/calvin/jdk/src/
run FacTest 6
memory
```

Here is the output from the jdb.ini file execution:

```
$ jdb -J-Duser.home=/home/calvin/java
Initializing jdb...
0xad:class(FacTest)
Breakpoint set at FacTest:13
running ...
Free: 662384, total: 1048568
main[1]
Breakpoint hit: FacTest.compute (FacTest:13)
main[1]
```

You might wonder if jdb.ini files can be used to control an entire jdb session. Unfortunately, commands in a jdb.ini startup file are executed synchronously, and jdb does not wait until a breakpoint is reached before executing the next command. This makes printing variables awkward. You can add artificial delays with repeated help commands, but there is still no guarantee the thread will be suspended when you need it to be.

Creating a Session Log

You can use a little-known jdb feature to obtain a record of your debug session. The output is similar to what you see when you run jdb -dbgtrace. To enable jdb logging, create a file called .agentLog in the directory where you are running jdb or java -debug. In the .agentLog file, put the filename that you want the session information to be written to on the first line. For example, an .agentLog file would have these contents:

```
jdblog
```

When you next run jdb or java -debug, you will see jdb session information as shown below. You can use this information to retrieve the breakpoint hits and the commands entered if you need to reproduce this debug session.

```
---- debug agent message log ----
[debug agent: adding Debugger agent to system thread list]
[debug agent: adding Breakpoint handler to system thread list]
[debug agent: adding Step handler to system thread list]
[debug agent: adding Finalizer to system thread list]
[debug agent: adding Reference Handler to system thread list]
[debug agent: adding Signal dispatcher to system thread list]
[debug agent: Awaiting new step request]
```

```
[debug agent: cmd socket: Socket[addr=localhost/127.0.0.1,
port=38986,localport=3 8985]]
[debug agent: connection accepted]
[debug agent: dumpClasses()]
[debug agent: no such class: HelloWorldApp.main]
[debug agent: Adding breakpoint bkpt:main(0)]
[debug agent: no last suspended to resume]
[debug agent: Getting threads for HelloWorldApp.main]
```

Servlet Debugging

You can debug servlets with the same jdb commands you use to debug an applet or an application. The JavaServer™ Web Development Kit (JSWDK) provides a standalone program called servletrunner that lets you run a servlet without a Web browser. On most systems, this program simply runs the java sun.servlet.http.HttpServer command. You can, therefore, start a jdb session with the HttpServer class.

A key point to remember when debugging servlets is that Java Web Server and servletrunner achieve servlet loading and unloading by not including the servlets directory on the CLASSPATH. This means the servlets are loaded using a custom classloader and not the default system classloader.

Running servletrunner in Debug Mode

In this example, the servlets examples directory is included on the CLASSPATH. You can configure the CLASSPATH for debug mode as follows:

Unix:
```
ksh> export CLASSPATH=./lib/jsdk.jar:./examples:$CLASSPATH
```

Windows:
```
$ set CLASSPATH=lib\jsdk.jar;examples;%classpath%
```

To start the servletrunner program to debug SnoopServlet, either run the supplied startup script called servletrunner or just supply the servletrunner classes as a parameter to jdb. This example uses the parameter to servletrunner.

```
$ jdb sun.servlet.http.HttpServer
Initializing jdb...
0xee2fa2f8:class(sun.servlet.http.HttpServer)
> stop in SnoopServlet.doGet
Breakpoint set in SnoopServlet.doGet
> run
run sun.servlet.http.HttpServer
running ...
main[1] servletrunner starting with settings:
port = 8080
backlog = 50
```

```
max handlers = 100
timeout = 5000
servlet dir = ./examples
document dir = ./examples
servlet propfile = ./examples/servlet.properties
```

To run `SnoopServlet` in debug mode, enter the following URL in a browser where your machine is the machine at which you started `servletrunner` and 8080 is the port number displayed in the settings output.

```
http://yourmachine:8080/servlet/SnoopServlet
```

In this example, `jdb` stops at the first line of the servlet's `doGet` method. The browser will wait for a response from your servlet until a timeout is reached.

```
main[1] SnoopServlet: init

Breakpoint hit: SnoopServlet.doGet (SnoopServlet:45)
Thread-105[1]
```

We can use the `list` command to work out where `jdb` has stopped in the source.

```
Thread-105[1] list
41        throws ServletException, IOException
42        {
43      PrintWriter     out;
44
45 =>    res.setContentType("text/html");
46      out = res.getWriter ();
47
48      out.println("<html>");
49      out.println("<head>
                    <title>Snoop Servlet
                    </title></head>");
Thread-105[1]
```

The servlet can continue using the `cont` command.

```
Thread-105[1] cont
```

Running Java Web Server in Debug Mode

The JWSDK release does not contain classes available in the Java Web Server and it also has its own special servlet configuration. If you cannot run your servlet from `servletrunner`, the other option is to run the Java Web Server in debug mode.

To do this add the -debug flag for the first parameter after the java program. For example in the script `bin/js` change the JAVA line to look like the following. In releases prior to the Java 2 platform release, you will also need to change the program pointed to by the variable $JAVA to `java_g` instead of java.

Before:

```
exec $JAVA $THREADS $JITCOMPILER $COMPILER $MS $MX \
```

After:

```
exec $JAVA -debug $THREADS $JITCOMPILER $COMPILER $MS $MX \
```

Here is how to remotely connect to Java Web Server. The agent password is generated on the standard output from the Java Web Server so that it can be redirected into a file somewhere. You can find out where by checking the Java Web Server startup scripts.

```
jdb -host localhost -password <the agent password>
```

The servlets are loaded by a separate classloader if they are contained in the servlets directory, which is not on the CLASSPATH used when starting Java Web Server. Unfortunately, when debugging remotely with jdb, you cannot control the custom classloader and request it to load the servlet, so you have to either include the servlets directory on the CLASSPATH for debugging or load the servlet by requesting it through a Web browser and placing a breakpoint once the servlet has run.

In this next example, the jdc.WebServer.PasswordServlet is included on the CLASSPATH when Java Web Server starts. The example sets a breakpoint to stop in the service method of this servlet, which is the main processing method of this servlet. The Java Web Server standard output produces this message, which lets you proceed with the remote jdb session:

```
Agent password=3yg23k

$ jdb -host localhost -password 3yg23k
Initializing jdb...
> stop in jdc.WebServer.PasswordServlet:service
Breakpoint set in jdc.WebServer.PasswordServlet.service
> stop
Current breakpoints set:
        jdc.WebServer.PasswordServlet:111
```

The second stop lists the current breakpoints in this session and shows the line number where the breakpoint is set. You can now call the servlet through your HTML page. In this example, the servlet is run as a POST operation

```
<FORM METHOD="post" action="/servlet/PasswordServlet">
<INPUT TYPE=TEXT SIZE=15 Name="user" Value="">
<INPUT TYPE=SUBMIT Name="Submit" Value="Submit">
</FORM>
```

You get control of the Java Web Server thread when the breakpoint is reached, and you can continue debugging using the same techniques as used in Remote Debugging (page 222).

```
Breakpoint hit: jdc.WebServer.PasswordServlet.service
(PasswordServlet:111) webpageservice Handler[1] where
  [1] jdc.WebServer.PasswordServlet.service (PasswordServlet:111)
  [2] javax.servlet.http.HttpServlet.service (HttpServlet:588)
  [3] com.sun.server.ServletState.callService (ServletState:204)
  [4] com.sun.server.ServletManager.callServletService (ServletManager:940)
  [5] com.sun.server.http.InvokerServlet.service (InvokerServlet:101)
```

A common problem when using the Java Web Server and other servlet environments is that Exceptions are thrown but are caught and handled outside the scope of your servlet. The catch command allows you to trap all these exceptions.

```
webpageservice Handler[1] catch java.io.IOException
webpageservice Handler[1]
Exception: java.io.FileNotFoundException
 at com.sun.server.http.FileServlet.sendResponse(FileServlet.java:153)
 at com.sun.server.http.FileServlet.service(FileServlet.java:114)
 at com.sun.server.webserver.FileServlet.service(FileServlet.java:202)
 at javax.servlet.http.HttpServlet.service(HttpServlet.java:588)
 at com.sun.server.ServletManager.callServletService(ServletManager.java:936)
 at com.sun.server.webserver.HttpServiceHandler.handleRequest(
                                        HttpServiceHandler.java:416)
 at com.sun.server.webserver.HttpServiceHandler.handleRequest(
                                        HttpServiceHandler.java:246)
 at com.sun.server.HandlerThread.run(HandlerThread.java:154)
```

This simple example generated the following output when the file was not found, and you can use this technique to troubleshoot problems with posted data. Remember to use cont to allow the Web server to proceed. To clear this trap use the ignore command.

```
webpageservice Handler[1] ignore java.io.IOException
webpageservice Handler[1] cont
webpageservice Handler[1]
```

Abstract Window Toolkit Debugging

Before the new Abstract Window Toolkit (AWT) event mechanism introduced in JDK 1.1, events were received by a component such as a TextField, and propagated upward to its parent components. This meant you could simply add some diagnostic code to the component's handleEvent or action method to monitor the events as they arrived.

With the introduction of JDK 1.1 and the new system event queue, events are delivered to an event queue instead of the component itself. The events are then dispatched from the System Event queue to event listeners that register to be notified when an event has been dispatched for that object.

Using AWTEventListener

You can use an `AWTEventListener` to monitor the AWT events from a system event queue. This listener takes an event mask built from an `OR` operation of the `AWTEvents` you want to monitor.

NOTE Do not use `AWTEventListener` in a shipping product because it will degrade system performance.

```
//EventTest.java
import java.awt.*;
import javax.swing.*;
import java.awt.event.*;

public class EventTest extends JFrame {
    public EventTest() {
        JButton jb1=new JButton("hello");
        getContentPane().add(jb1);
//API Ref:  void addAWTEventListener(AWTEventListener 1, long eventmask)
        getToolkit().addAWTEventListener(new AWTEventListener() {
            public void eventDispatched(AWTEvent e) {
                System.out.println(e + "\n");
            }
        }, AWTEvent.MOUSE_EVENT_MASK | AWTEvent.FOCUS_EVENT_MASK
        );
    }
    public static void main (String args[]) {
        EventTest et=new EventTest();
        et.setSize(300,300);
        et.pack();
        et.show();
    }
}
```

At run time, the `EventTest` program tracks and outputs mouse and focus events. For example, when you click the button, you get this output:

```
java.awt.event.MouseEvent[MOUSE_CLICKED,(58,14),mods=16,clickCount=1] on
javax.swing.JButton[,0,0,96x27,layout=javax.swing.OverlayLayout,alignmentX=0.0,
alignmentY=0.5,border=javax.swing.plaf.BorderUIResource$CompoundBorderUIResource
@e466ea9c,flags=48,maximumSize=,minimumSize=,preferredSize=,defaultIcon=,
disabledIcon=,disabledSelectedIcon=,margin=javax.swing.plaf.InsetsUIResource
[top=2,left=14,bottom=2,right=14],paintBorder=true,paintFocus=true,pressedIcon=,
rolloverEnabled=false,rolloverIcon=,rolloverSelectedIcon=,selectedIcon=,text=hello,
defaultCapable=true]
```

To obtain a simple list of the `AWTEvent` events, use the `javap  -public java.awt.AWTEvent` command.

```
Compiled from AWTEvent.java
public abstract class java.awt.AWTEvent extends java.util.EventObject {
```

```
    public static final long COMPONENT_EVENT_MASK;
    public static final long CONTAINER_EVENT_MASK;
    public static final long FOCUS_EVENT_MASK;
    public static final long KEY_EVENT_MASK;
    public static final long MOUSE_EVENT_MASK;
    public static final long MOUSE_MOTION_EVENT_MASK;
    public static final long WINDOW_EVENT_MASK;
    public static final long ACTION_EVENT_MASK;
    public static final long ADJUSTMENT_EVENT_MASK;
    public static final long ITEM_EVENT_MASK;
    public static final long TEXT_EVENT_MASK;
    public static final long INPUT_METHOD_EVENT_MASK;
    public static final int RESERVED_ID_MAX;
    public java.awt.AWTEvent(java.awt.Event);
    public java.awt.AWTEvent(java.lang.Object,int);
    public int getID();
    public java.lang.String paramString();
    public java.lang.String toString();
}
```

Analyzing Stack Traces

Stack traces have often been considered a mystery to developers. There is little or no documentation available, and when you get one or need to generate one, time is always at a premium. The next sections uncover the secrets to debugging stack traces, and by the end, you might consider a stack trace to be a helpful tool for analyzing other programs—not just broken ones!

A stack trace produced by the Java platform is a user-friendly snapshot of the threads and monitors in a Java virtual machine. Depending on how complex your application or applet is, a stack trace can range from fifty lines to thousands of lines of diagnostics. Regardless of the size of the stack trace, there are a few key things that anyone can find to help diagnose most software problems, whether you are an expert or very new to the Java platform.

There are three popular ways to generate a stack trace: sending a signal to the Java virtual machine; the Java virtual machine generates a stack trace for you; or using debugging tools or API calls.

Sending a Signal to the Java VM

On Unix platforms you can send a signal to a program with the kill command. This is the quit signal, which is handled by the Java virtual machine.

Unix systems:
For example, on the Solaris™ and other Unix platforms, you can use the `kill -QUIT` `process_id` command, where `process_id` is the process number of your program. Alternately, you can enter the key sequence <ctrl>\ in the window where the program started. Sending this signal instructs a signal

handler in the Java virtual machine to recursively print out all the information on the threads and monitors inside the Java virtual machine.

Windows 95/NT:

To generate a stack trace on the Windows 95 or Windows NT platforms, enter the key sequence `<ctrl><break>` in the window where the program is running.

The Java VM Generates a Stack Trace

If the Java virtual machine experienced an internal error such as a segmentation violation or an illegal page fault, it calls its own signal handler to print out the threads and monitor information.

Core Files

If the Java virtual machine generated the stack trace because of an internal error, then some native code in your own application or the Java virtual machine is probably to blame. If you are using Unix, and you find a core file, run the following command to find out which JDK software it came from:

```
strings core | grep JAVA_HOME
```

Using Debugging Tools or API Calls

You can generate a partial stack trace (which in this case is only the threads information) by using the `Thread.dumpStack` method, or the `printStack-Trace` method of the `Throwable` class. You can also obtain similar information by entering `where` inside the Java debugger.

If you are successful at generating a stack trace, you should see something similar to Stack Trace 1 (page XXX).

In the Java 2 software release, threads that called methods resulting in a call to native code are indicated in the stack trace.

Which Release Generated the Stack Trace?

In the Java 2 release the stack trace contains the Java virtual machine version string, the same information you see when using the `-version` parameter.

However, if there is no version string, you can still take a pretty good guess at which release this stack trace came from. Obviously, if you generated the stack trace yourself, this should not be much of an issue, but you may see a stack trace posted on a newsgroup or in an e-mail.

First identify where the Registered Monitor Dump section is in the stack trace:

- If you see a `utf8` hash table lock in the Registered Monitor Dump, this is a Java 2 platform stack trace. The final release of the Java 2 platform also contains a version string, so if a version string is missing, this stack trace may be from a Java 2 beta release.

- If you see a JNI pinning lock and no `utf8` hash lock, this is a JDK 1.1+ release.

If neither of these appears in the Registered Monitor Dump, it is probably a JDK 1.0.2 release.

Which Platform Generated the Stack Trace?

You can also find out if the stack trace came from a Windows 95, an NT, or Unix machine by looking for any waiting threads. On a Unix machine, the waiting threads are named explicitly. On a Windows 95 or NT machine, only a count of the waiting threads is displayed:

- Windows 95/NT: `Finalize me queue lock: <unowned> Writer: 1`
- Unix: `Finalize me queue lock: <unowned> waiting to be notified "Finalizer Thread"`

Which Thread Package Was Used?

Windows 95, Windows NT, and Solaris Java virtual machines use native threads by default. There also exists a pseudo thread implementation called green threads. To make your Java virtual machine use either green or native threads, specify the `-green` or `-native` parameter. For example, `java -native MyClass`.

By verifying the existence of an Alarm monitor in the stack trace output, you can identify that this stack trace came from a green threads Java virtual machine.

What Are the Thread States?

You will see many different threads in many different states in a snapshot from a Java virtual machine stack trace. This table describes the various keys and their meanings.

Key	Meaning
R	Running or runnable thread
S	Suspended thread
CW	Condition wait. Thread waiting on a condition variable.
MW	Monitor wait. Thread waiting on a monitor lock. Could indicate a deadlock.
MS	Thread suspended waiting on a monitor lock.

Normally, only threads in R, S, CW, or MW should appear in the stack trace. If you see a thread in state MS, report it to Sun Microsystems through the Java Developer Connection (JDC) Bug Parade feature, because there is a good chance it is a bug. The reason is that most of the time a thread in MW state will appear in the S state when it is suspended.

Monitors let you manage access to code that should only be run by one thread at a time. See Examining Monitors (below) for more information on monitors.

The other two common thread states you may see are R, runnable threads, and CW, threads in a condition wait state. Runnable threads by definition are threads that could be running or are running at that instance of time. On a multiprocessor machine running a true multiprocessing operating system, it is possible for all the runnable threads to be running at one time. However, it is more likely for the other runnable threads to be waiting on the thread scheduler to have their turn to run.

Threads in a condition wait state can be thought of as waiting for an event to occur. Often a thread will appear in state CW if it is in a Thread.sleep or in a synchronized wait. In our earlier stack trace, our main method was waiting for a thread to complete and to be notified of its completion. In the stack trace this appears as

```
"main" (TID:0xebc981e0, sys_thread_t:0x26bb0, state:CW) prio=5
 at java.lang.Object.wait(Native Method)
 at java.lang.Object.wait(Object.java:424)
 at HangingProgram.main(HangingProgram.java:33)
```

The code that created this stack trace is as follows:

```
synchronized(t1) {
  try {
    t1.wait();      //line 33
  }catch (InterruptedException e){}
}
```

In the Java 2 release, monitor operations, including our wait here, are handled by the Java virtual machine through a JNI call to sysMonitor. The condition wait thread is kept on a special monitor wait queue on the object it is waiting on. This explains why, even though you are only waiting on an object, the code still needs to be synchronized on that object because it is, in fact, using the monitor for that object.

Examining Monitors

This brings us to the other part of the stack trace: the monitor dump. If you consider that the threads section of a stack trace identifies the multithreaded part of your application, then the monitors section represents the parts of your application that are single-threaded.

It may be easier to imagine a monitor as a car wash. In most car washes, only one car can be in the wash at a time. In your Java code only one thread at a time can have the lock to a synchronized piece of code. All the other threads queue up to enter the synchronized code just as cars queue up to enter the car wash.

A monitor can be thought of as a lock on an object, and every object has a monitor. When you generate a stack trace, monitors are either listed as being registered or not. In the majority of cases these registered monitors, or system monitors, should not be the cause of your software problems, but it helps to be able to understand and recognize them. The following table describes the common registered monitors:

Monitor	Description
utf8 hash table	Locks the hash table of defined i18N Strings that were loaded from the class constant pool.
JNI pinning lock	Protects block copies of arrays to native method code.
JNI global reference lock	Locks the global reference table that holds values that need to be explicitly freed, because they will outlive the lifetime of the native method call.
BinClass lock	Locks access to the loaded and resolved classes list. The global table list of classes.
Class linking lock	Protects a class's data when loading native libraries to resolve symbolic references.
System classloader lock	Ensures that only one thread is loading a system class at a time.
Code rewrite lock	Protects code when an optimization is attempted.
Heap lock	Protects the Java heap during heap memory management.
Monitor cache lock	Only one thread can have access to the monitor cache at a time; this lock ensures the integrity of the monitor cache.
Dynamic loading lock	Protects Unix green threads Java virtual machines from loading the shared library stub libdl.so more than one at a time.

(continues)

Monitor	Description
Monitor IO lock	Protects physical I/O, for example, open and read.
User signal monitor	Controls access to the signal handler in the green threads Java virtual machine.
Child death monitor	Controls access to the process wait information when using the run-time system calls to run local commands in a green threads Java virtual machine.
I/O monitor	Controls access to the threads file descriptors for poll/select events.
Alarm monitor	Controls access to a clock handler used in a green threads Java virtual machine to handle timeouts.
Thread queue lock	Protects the queue of active threads.
Monitor registry	Only one thread can have access to the monitor registry at a time; this lock ensures the integrity of that registry.
Has finalization queue lock *	Protects the list of queue lock objects that have been garbage-collected and deemed to need finalization. They are copied to the Finalize me queue.
Finalize me queue lock *	Protects a list of objects that can be finalized at leisure.
Name and type hash table lock *	Protects the Java virtual machine hash tables of constants and their types.
String intern lock *	Locks the hash table of defined strings that were loaded from the class constant pool.
Class loading lock *	Ensures only one thread loads a class at a time.
Java stack lock *	Protects the free stack segments list.

NOTE   * Lock appeared only in pre-Java 2 stack traces.

The monitor registry itself is protected by a monitor. This means the thread that owns the lock is the last thread to use a monitor. It is very likely this thread is also the current thread. Because only one thread can enter a synchronized block at a time, other threads queue up at the start of the synchronized code and appear as thread state MW. In the monitor cache dump, they are denoted as "waiting to enter" threads. In user code, a monitor is called into action wherever a synchronized block or method is used.

Any code waiting on an object or event (a `wait` method) also has to be inside a synchronized block. However, once the `wait` method is called, the lock on the synchronized object is given up.

When the thread in the wait state is notified of an event to the object, it has to compete for exclusive access to that object, and it has to obtain the monitor. Even when a thread has sent a "notify event" to the waiting threads, none of the waiting threads can actually gain control of the monitor lock until the notifying thread has left its synchronized code block. You will see "Waiting to be notified" for threads at the `wait` method.

Putting the Steps into Practice

Example 1. Consider a real-life problem such as Bug ID 4098756, for example. You can find details on this bug in JDC Bug Parade. This bug documents a problem that occurs when using a Choice Component on Windows 95.

When the user selects one of the choices from the Choice Component using the mouse, everything is fine. However, when the user tries to use an Arrow key to move up or down the list of choices, the application freezes.

Fortunately, this problem is reproducible and produces a stack trace to help track down the problem. The full stack trace is in the bug report page, but you only need to focus on the following two key threads:

```
"AWT-Windows" (TID:0xf54b70, sys_thread_t:0x875a80,Win32ID:0x67,
"AWT-Windows" (TID:0xf54b70, sys_thread_t:0x875a80,Win32ID:0x67,
            state:MW) prio=5
 java.awt.Choice.select(Choice.java:293)
 sun.awt.windows.WChoicePeer.handleAction(WChoicePeer.java:86)
 "AWT-EventQueue-0" (TID:0xf54a98,sys_thread_t:0x875c20,
 Win32ID:0x8f, state:R) prio=5
 java.awt.Choice.remove(Choice.java:228)
 java.awt.Choice.removeAll(Choice.java:246)
```

The `AWT-EventQueue-0` thread is in a runnable state inside the `remove` method. Notice that `remove` is synchronized, which explains why the AWT-Windows thread cannot enter the `select` method. The `AWT-Windows` thread is in `MW` state; however, if you keep taking stack traces, this situation does not change and the graphical user interface appears to have frozen.

This indicates that the `remove` call never returned. By following the code path to the `ChoicePeer` class, you can see this is making a native `MFC` call that does not return. That is where the real problem lies and is a bug in the Java core classes. The user's code was okay.

Example 2. In this second example you will investigate a bug that on initial outset appears to be a fault in Project Swing, but as you will discover, it is due to the fact that Project Swing is not thread-safe. Again, the bug report is available to view on the JDC site; the bug number this time is 4098525.

Here is a cut-down sample of the code used to reproduce this problem. The modal dialog is being created from within the JPanel paint method.

```java
import java.awt.event.*;
import java.awt.*;
import java.util.*;
import javax.swing.*;

class MyDialog extends Dialog implements ActionListener {
  MyDialog(Frame parent) {
    super(parent, "My Dialog", true);
    Button okButton = new Button("OK");
    okButton.addActionListener(this);
    add(okButton);
    pack();
  }
  public void actionPerformed(ActionEvent event) {
    dispose();
  }
}
public class Tester extends JPanel {
  MyDialog myDialog;
  boolean firstTime = true;
  public Tester (JFrame frame) throws Exception {
    super();
    myDialog = new MyDialog(frame);
  }
  void showDialogs() {
    myDialog.show();
  }
  public void paint(Graphics g) {
    super.paint(g);
    if (firstTime) {
      firstTime = false;
      showDialogs();
    }
  }
  public static void main(String args[]) throws Exception {
    JFrame frame = new JFrame ("Test");
    Tester gui = new Tester(frame);
    frame.getContentPane().add(gui);
    frame.setSize(800, 600);
    frame.pack();
    frame.setVisible(true);
  }
}
```

When you run this program, you find it deadlocks straightaway. By taking a stack trace you see the key threads shown in Stack Trace 2 (page 242). This stack trace is slightly different from the stack trace that appears in the bug report, but is caused by the same problem.

Stack Trace 2 is produced by the Java 2 Platform release using the -Djava.com-piler=NONE option to the java interpreter command so that you can see the source line numbers. The thread to look for is the thread in monitor wait, which in this case is thread AWT-EventQueue-1.

```
"AWT-EventQueue-1" (TID:0xebca8c20, sys_thread_t:0x376660, state:MW) prio=6
at java.awt.Component.invalidate(Component.java:1664)
at java.awt.Container.invalidate(Container.java:507)
at java.awt.Window.dispatchEventImpl(Window.java:696)
at java.awt.Component.dispatchEvent(Component.java:2289)
at java.awt.EventQueue.dispatchEvent(EventQueue.java:258)
at java.awt.EventDispatchThread.run(EventDispatchThread.java:68)
```

If you look for that line in file java/awt/Component.java, which is contained in the src.jar archive, you see the following:

```
public void invalidate() {
  synchronized (getTreeLock()) { //line 1664
```

This is where the application is stuck. It is waiting for the getTreeLock monitor lock to become free. The next task is to find out which thread has this getTreeLock monitor lock held. To see who is holding this monitor lock, you look at the Monitor Cache Dump, and in this example you can see the following:

```
Monitor Cache Dump:
java.awt.Component$AWTTreeLock@EBC9C228/EBCF2408:
                    owner "AWT-EventQueue-0" (0x263850) 3 entries
Waiting to enter: "AWT-EventQueue-1" (0x376660)
```

The method getTreeLock monitor is actually a lock on a specially created inner class object of AWTTreeLock. This is the code used to create that lock in file Component.java.

```
static final Object LOCK = new AWTTreeLock();
static class AWTTreeLock {}
```

The current owner is AWT-EventQueue-0. This thread called the paint method to create the modal Dialog with a call to the paintComponent method. The paintComponent method was called from an update call of JFrame.

So where was the lock set? Well, there is no simple way to find out which stack frame actually held the lock, but on a simple search of javax.swing.JComponent, you see that getTreeLock is called inside the method paintChildren, which you left at line 388.

```
at Tester.paint(Tester.java:39)
at javax.swing.JComponent.paintChildren(JComponent.java:388)
```

The rest of the puzzle is pieced together by analyzing the MDialogPeer show method. The Dialog code creates a new ModalThread, which is why you see an `AWT-Modal` thread in the stack trace output; this thread is used to post the `Dialog`. It is when this event is dispatched using `AWT-EventQueue-1`, which used to be the AWT Dispatch proxy, that `getTreeLock` monitor access is required, and so you have a deadlock.

Unfortunately, Project Swing code is not designed to be thread-safe, and so the workaround in this example is to not create modal dialogs inside Project Swing `paint` methods. Since Swing has to do a lot of locking and calculations as to which parts of a lightweight component need to be painted, it is strongly recommended to not include synchronized code or code that will result in a synchronized call such as in a modal dialog, or inside a `paint` method.

You should now know what to look for the next time you see a stack trace. To save time, you should make full use of the JDC bug search to see if the problem you are having has already been reported by someone else.

Expert's Checklist

To summarize, these are the steps to take the next time you come across a problem in a Java program:

- **Hanging, deadlocked, or frozen programs:** If you think your program is hanging, generate a stack trace. Examine the threads in states `MW` or `CW`. If the program is deadlocked, some of the system threads will probably show up as the current thread because there is nothing else for the Java virtual machine to do.
- **Crashed or aborted programs:** On Unix look for a core file. You can analyze this file in a native debugging tool such as `gdb` or `dbx`. Look for threads that have called native methods. Because Java technology uses a safe memory model, any corruption probably occurred in the native code. Remember that the Java virtual machine also uses native code, so it might not be a bug in your application.
- **Busy programs:** The best course of action you can take for busy programs is to generate frequent stack traces. This will narrow down the code path that is causing the errors, and you can start your investigation from there.

Stack Trace Examples

- Stack Trace 1 (below)
- Stack Trace 2 (page 242)

Stack Trace 1

```
$ java -Djava.compiler=NONE HangingProgram
^\SIGQUIT
```

```
Full thread dump Classic VM (JDK-1.2-V, green threads):
 "Thread-1" (TID:0xebc9c0f0, sys_thread_t:0x130180, state:MW) prio=5
    at mythread.stopper(HangingProgram.java:9)
    at mythread.run(HangingProgram.java:19)
 "Thread-0" (TID:0xebc9c150, sys_thread_t:0x12f960, state:CW) prio=5
    at java.lang.Thread.sleep(Native Method)
    at mythread.stopper(HangingProgram.java:12)
    at mythread.run(HangingProgram.java:19)
 "Finalizer" (TID:0xebc98320, sys_thread_t:0x69418, state:CW) prio=8
    at java.lang.Object.wait(Native Method)
    at java.lang.ref.ReferenceQueue.remove(ReferenceQueue.java:112)
    at java.lang.ref.ReferenceQueue.remove(ReferenceQueue.java:127)
    at java.lang.ref.Finalizer$FinalizerThread.run(Finalizer.java:174)
 "Reference Handler" (TID:0xebc983b0, sys_thread_t:0x64f68,
                      state:CW) prio=10
    at java.lang.Object.wait(Native Method)
    at java.lang.Object.wait(Object.java:424)
    at java.lang.ref.Reference$ReferenceHandler.run(Reference.java:114)
 "Signal dispatcher" (TID:0xebc983e0, sys_thread_t:0x5e1e8, state:R) prio=5
 "main" (TID:0xebc981e0, sys_thread_t:0x26bb0, state:CW) prio=5
    at java.lang.Object.wait(Native Method)
    at java.lang.Object.wait(Object.java:424)
    at HangingProgram.main(HangingProgram.java:33)
Monitor Cache Dump:
  java.lang.Class@EBC9BEB8/EBCFC538: owner "Thread-0" (0x12f960) 1 entry
     Waiting to enter:
          "Thread-1" (0x130180)
  java.lang.ref.ReferenceQueue$Lock@EBC98338/EBCCE028: <unowned>
     Waiting to be notified:
          "Finalizer" (0x69418)
  mythread@EBC9C150/EBCFC608: <unowned>
     Waiting to be notified:
          "main" (0x26bb0)
  java.lang.ref.Reference$Lock@EBC983C0/EBCCDB20: <unowned>
     Waiting to be notified:
          "Reference Handler" (0x64f68)
Registered Monitor Dump:
  utf8 hash table: <unowned>
  JNI pinning lock: <unowned>
  JNI global reference lock: <unowned>
  BinClass lock: <unowned>
  Class linking lock: <unowned>
  System class loader lock: <unowned>
  Code rewrite lock: <unowned>
  Heap lock: <unowned>
  Monitor cache lock: owner "Signal dispatcher" (0x5e1e8) 1 entry
  Dynamic loading lock: <unowned>
  Monitor IO lock: <unowned>
  User signal monitor: <unowned>
  Child death monitor: <unowned>
  I/O monitor: <unowned>
  Alarm monitor: <unowned>
     Waiting to be notified:
        <unknown thread> (0x2beb8)
  Thread queue lock: owner "Signal dispatcher" (0x5e1e8) 1 entry
  Monitor registry: owner "Signal dispatcher" (0x5e1e8) 1 entry
```

Stack Trace 2

```
Full thread dump Classic VM (JDK-1.2-V, green threads):
    "AWT-Modal" (TID:0xebca8a40, sys_thread_t:0x376d50, state:CW) prio=6
        at java.lang.Object.wait(Native Method)
        at sun.awt.motif.MDialogPeer.pShow(Native Method)
        at sun.awt.motif.ModalThread.run(MDialogPeer.java:247)
    "AWT-EventQueue-1" (TID:0xebca8c20, sys_thread_t:0x376660,
                        state:MW) prio=6
        at java.awt.Component.invalidate(Component.java:1664)
        at java.awt.Container.invalidate(Container.java:507)
        at java.awt.Window.dispatchEventImpl(Window.java:696)
        at java.awt.Component.dispatchEvent(Component.java:2289)
        at java.awt.EventQueue.dispatchEvent(EventQueue.java:258)
        at java.awt.EventDispatchThread.run(EventDispatchThread.java:68)
    "Screen Updater" (TID:0xebca9a08, sys_thread_t:0x3707c8, state:CW) prio=4
        at java.lang.Object.wait(Native Method)
        at java.lang.Object.wait(Object.java:424)
        at sun.awt.ScreenUpdater.nextEntry(ScreenUpdater.java:79)
        at sun.awt.ScreenUpdater.run(ScreenUpdater.java:99)
    "AWT-Motif" (TID:0xebcafa30, sys_thread_t:0x285370, state:CW) prio=5
        at sun.awt.motif.MToolkit.run(Native Method)
        at java.lang.Thread.run(Thread.java:479)
    "SunToolkit.PostEventQueue-0" (TID:0xebcafc58, sys_thread_t:0x263988,
state:CW) prio=5
        at java.lang.Object.wait(Native Method)
        at java.lang.Object.wait(Object.java:424)
        at sun.awt.PostEventQueue.run(SunToolkit.java:363)
    "AWT-EventQueue-0" (TID:0xebcafc28, sys_thread_t:0x263850,
                        state:CW) prio=6
        at java.lang.Object.wait(Native Method)
        at java.lang.Object.wait(Object.java:424)
        at sun.awt.motif.MDialogPeer.show(MDialogPeer.java:181)
        at java.awt.Dialog.show(Dialog.java:368)
        at Tester.showDialogs(Tester.java:32)
        at Tester.paint(Tester.java:39)
        at javax.swing.JComponent.paintChildren(JComponent.java:388)
        at javax.swing.JComponent.paint(JComponent.java:550)
        at javax.swing.JComponent.paintChildren(JComponent.java:388)
        at javax.swing.JComponent.paint(JComponent.java:550)
        at javax.swing.JLayeredPane.paint(JLayeredPane.java:547)
        at javax.swing.JComponent.paintChildren(JComponent.java:388)
        at javax.swing.JComponent.paint(JComponent.java:535)
        at java.awt.Container.paint(Container.java:770)
        at javax.swing.JFrame.update(JFrame.java:255)
        at sun.awt.motif.MComponentPeer.handleEvent(MComponentPeer.java:248)
        at java.awt.Component.dispatchEventImpl(Component.java:2429)
        at java.awt.Container.dispatchEventImpl(Container.java:1032)
        at java.awt.Window.dispatchEventImpl(Window.java:714)
        at java.awt.Component.dispatchEvent(Component.java:2289)
        ... (more frames not shown)
    "Finalizer" (TID:0xebc98320, sys_thread_t:0x69418, state:CW) prio=8
        at java.lang.Object.wait(Native Method)
        at java.lang.ref.ReferenceQueue.remove(ReferenceQueue.java:112)
        at java.lang.ref.ReferenceQueue.remove(ReferenceQueue.java:127)
        at java.lang.ref.Finalizer$FinalizerThread.run(Finalizer.java:174)
```

```
     "Reference Handler" (TID:0xebc983b0, sys_thread_t:0x64f68,
                    state:CW) prio=10
         at java.lang.Object.wait(Native Method)
         at java.lang.Object.wait(Object.java:424)
         at java.lang.ref.Reference$ReferenceHandler.run(Reference.java:114)
     "Signal dispatcher" (TID:0xebc983e0, sys_thread_t:0x5e1e8,
                    state:R) prio=5
     "Thread-0" (TID:0xebcaa000, sys_thread_t:0x26bb0, state:CW) prio=5
Monitor Cache Dump:
    java.awt.Component$AWTTreeLock@EBC9C228/EBCF2408: owner "AWT-EventQueue-0"
            (0x263850) 3 entries
         Waiting to enter:
            "AWT-EventQueue-1" (0x376660)
    java.lang.Class@EBCA5148/EBD11A48: <unowned>
         Waiting to be notified:
            "AWT-Modal" (0x376d50)
    sun.awt.motif.ModalThread@EBCA8A40/EBD67998: owner "AWT-Modal" (0x376d50) 1
entry
         Waiting to be notified:
            "AWT-EventQueue-0" (0x263850)
    java.lang.ref.ReferenceQueue$Lock@EBC98338/EBCCDCD8: <unowned>
         Waiting to be notified:
            "Finalizer" (0x69418)
    sun.awt.PostEventQueue@EBCAFC58/EBD405B0: <unowned>
         Waiting to be notified:
            "SunToolkit.PostEventQueue-0" (0x263988)
    sun.awt.ScreenUpdater@EBCA9A08/EBD633F8: <unowned>
         Waiting to be notified:
            "Screen Updater" (0x3707c8)
    java.lang.ref.Reference$Lock@EBC983C0/EBCCD8A8: <unowned>
         Waiting to be notified:
            "Reference Handler" (0x64f68)
Registered Monitor Dump:
    utf8 hash table: <unowned>
    JNI pinning lock: <unowned>
    JNI global reference lock: <unowned>
    BinClass lock: <unowned>
    Class linking lock: <unowned>
    System class loader lock: <unowned>
    Code rewrite lock: <unowned>
    Heap lock: <unowned>
    Monitor cache lock: owner "Signal dispatcher" (0x5e1e8) 1 entry
    Dynamic loading lock: <unowned>
    Monitor IO lock: <unowned>
    User signal monitor: <unowned>
    Child death monitor: <unowned>
    I/O monitor: <unowned>
         Waiting to be notified:
            "AWT-Motif" (0x285370)
    Alarm monitor: <unowned>
         Waiting to be notified:
            <unknown thread> (0x2beb8)
    Thread queue lock: owner "Signal dispatcher" (0x5e1e8) 1 entry
         Waiting to be notified:
            "Thread-0" (0x26bb0)
    Monitor registry: owner "Signal dispatcher" (0x5e1e8) 1 entry
```

Version Issues

This section summarizes problems and solutions related to having different versions of the Java platform installed on your system.

JDK 1.0.2 Deployment

Uses CLASSPATH to find and load the core system classes.

On Windows 95:
CLASSPATH=c:\java\lib\classes.zip:.

On Unix:
CLASSPATH=/usr/java/lib/classes.zip:.

Unix dynamic libraries, .dll files, shared objects, and .so files are located by the PATH variable.

JDK 1.0.2 Side Effects.   The Win95 Autoexec.bat file contains an outdated CLASSPATH variable set by a user or the installation of other applications.

The WinNT User Environment contains an old CLASSPATH variable.

The Unix .cshrc, .profile, or .login script contains wrong CLASSPATH.

The JAVA_HOME environment variable is also used by programs, so check that this is not set. You can clear this field in the Bourne shell (sh) as follows: unset JAVA_HOME.

JDK 1.0.2 Diagnostics.   Use the -classpath option to force the Java virtual machine to use the command-line CLASSPATH only:

```
java -classpath c:\java\lib\classes.zip;. myapp.
```

JDK 1.1 Deployment

Uses relative paths to find the classes.zip file from the Java platform installation. The CLASSPATH environment variable is used to load application classes.

JDK 1.1 Side Effects.   Other Java releases found on the application path might be picked up if the new JDK bin directory is not explicitly set at the front of the PATH environment variable.

JDK 1.1 Diagnostics.   Use the -sysclasspath option to force the Java virtual machine to use the CLASSPATH supplied on the command line only:

```
java -sysclasspath c:\java\lib\classes.zip;. myapp.
```

Java 2 Platform Deployment

The platform is split into a Java Runtime Environment (JRE) and Java compiler. The JRE is included as a subdirectory in the release, and the traditional java and javac programs in the bin directory invoke the real program in the jre/bin directory. The separate JRE launcher is no longer provided, and the java program is solely used instead.

The Java Archive (JAR) files containing the core Java platform system classes, rt.jar and i18.jar, are located in the jre/lib directory with a relative search path.

Java 2 Platform Side Effects. If applications have previously used the classes.zip file to load the core Java platform systems, they might still try to load an additional set of classes in error.

Java 2 Platform Diagnostics. Use the -Xbootclasspath option to force the Java virtual machine to use the CLASSPATH supplied on the command line only:

```
java -Xbootclasspath:c:\java\jre\lib\rt.jar;c:\java\jre\lib\i18n.jar;. myapp
```

You might need to supply this as a run-time option as follows:

```
javac -J-Xbootclasspath:c\java\lib\tools.jar;c:\java\jre\lib\rt.jar;
c:\java\jre\lib\i18n.jar;. myapp.java
```

Java Plug-In Deployment. On Windows 95 and Windows NT, deployment uses the registry to find installed plug-in Java platform releases.

Java Plug-In Side Effects. Registry can become corrupted, or plug-in can be removed physically, but not from the registry.

Java Plug-In Diagnostics. Display the java.version and java.class.path property in your code and display it on the Java Plug-In Console:

```
System.out.println("version="+System.getProperty("java.version"));
System.out.println("class path="+System.getProperty("java.class.path");
```

If there is a conflict, check the registry with the regedit command, search for the word VM and if it exists, delete it, and reinstall the plug-in.

Netscape Deployment

Uses .jar files such as java40.jar in the Netscape directory.

Netscape Side Effects. Not all Netscape releases are fully JDK 1.1-compliant. You can get upgrade patches at http://www.netscape.com.

Netscape Diagnostics.   Start the browser on the command line with the `-classes` option.

Internet Explorer Deployment

Uses `.cab` files to contain system classes. Also uses system registry on Windows 95/NT.

Internet Explorer Side Effects.   Use the `regedit` command to search for the word VM. There is a CLASSPATH entry to which you can add your own classes.

Internet Explorer Diagnostics.   The registry can become corrupted. Search for CLASSPATH using the `regedit` program, and edit the value that CLASSPATH points to.

8

Performance Techniques

One of the biggest challenges in developing large applications for the Java platform is to make the application meet its performance criteria. This chapter departs from the auction application and uses simple, targeted examples to show you how to track down performance bottlenecks to improve application performance.

Covered in this Chapter

- Improving Applet Download Speed (page 247)
- Thread Pooling (page 250)
- Connection Pooling (page 252)
- Performance Features and Tools (page 263)
- Performance Analysis (page 269)
- Caching Client/Server Applications (page 277)

Improving Applet Download Speed

Applet download performance refers to the time it takes for the browser to download all the files and resources it needs to start the applet. An important factor affecting any applet's download performance is the number of times it has to request data from the server. You can reduce the number of requests by packaging the applet images into one class file, or using Java Archive (JAR) files.

Packaging Images into One Class

Normally, if an applet has, for example, six image buttons, that translates to six additional requests sent back to the Web server to load those image files. Six additional requests might not seem like much on an internal network, but given connections of lesser speed and reliability, those additional requests can have a significant negative impact on performance. So, your ultimate goal should be to load the applet as quickly as possible.

One way to store images in a class file is to use an ASCII encoding scheme such as X-PixMap (XPM) (`http://www.inria.fr/koala/lehors/xpm.html`). This way, rather than maintaining the images as GIF files on the server, the files are encoded as `Strings` and stored in a single class file.

This code sample uses packages from the JavaCup winner at JavaOne 1996, which contains the `XImageSource` and `XpmParser` classes. These classes provide all you need to read a standard XPM file. You can see these files at SunSite (`http://sunsite.utk.edu/winners_circle/developer_tools/DESVS7NU/applet.html`).

For the initial encoding process, there are a number of graphics tools you can use to create XPM files. On Solaris you can use `ImageTool` or a variety of other GNU image packages (`http://www.gnu.ai.mit.edu/software/software.html`). Go to the `Download.com` Web site (`http://download.cnet.com`) to get the encoding software for Windows platforms.

The following code excerpted from the `MyApplet` sample class loads the images shown in Figure 8.1. You can see the coded String form for the images in the XPM `Definition` of the images.

Figure 8.1 Images

The `Toolkit` class creates an `Image` object for each image from the XPM `Image Source` object. The parameters to `XImageSource` represent a coded `String` form from the XPM `Definition`.

```
Toolkit kit = Toolkit.getDefaultToolkit();
Image image;
mage = kit.createImage (new XImageSource (_reply));
image = kit.createImage (new XImageSource (_post));
image = kit.createImage (new XImageSource (_reload));
```

```
image = kit.createImage (new XImageSource (_catchup));
image = kit.createImage (new XImageSource (_back10));
image = kit.createImage (new XImageSource (_reset));
image = kit.createImage (new XImageSource (_faq));
```

The alternative technique below uses GIF files. It requires a request back to the Web server for each image loaded.

```
Image image;
image = getImage (reply.gif);
image = getImage (post.gif);
image = getImage (reload.gif);
image = getImage (catchup.gif);
image = getImage (back10.gif);
image = getImage (reset.gif);
image = getImage (faq.gif);
```

This technique reduces network traffic because all images are available in a single class file.

- Using XPM encoded images makes the class size larger but the number of network requests fewer.
- Making the XPM image definitions part of your applet class file makes the image loading process part of the regular loading of the applet class file with no extra classes.

Once loaded, you can use the images to create buttons or other user interface components. This next code segment shows how to use the images with the javax.swing.JButton class.

```
ImageIcon icon = new ImageIcon(kit.createImage(new XImageSource(_reply)));
JButton button = new JButton (icon, Reply);
```

Using JAR Files

When an applet consists of more than one file, you can improve download performance with JAR files. A JAR file contains all of an applet's related files in one single file for a faster download. Much of the time saved comes from reducing the number of HTTP connections the browser must make. Chapter 9, Deploying the Auction Application, has information on creating and signing JAR files.

The HTML code below uses the CODE tag to specify the executable for the MyApplet applet, and the ARCHIVE tag to specify the JAR file that contains all of MyApplet's related files. The executable specified by the CODE tag is sometimes called the code base.

For security reasons the JAR files listed by the archive parameter must be in the same directory or a subdirectory as the applet's code base. If no codebase parameter is supplied, the directory from where the applet was loaded is used as the code base. The following example specifies `jarfile` as the JAR file that contains the related files for the `MyApplet.class` executable.

```
<APPLET CODE=MyApplet.class ARCHIVE=jarfile WIDTH=100 HEIGHT=200> </APPLET>
```

The applet downloads the entire JAR file, regardless of whether or not the JAR file includes infrequently used files.

```
<APPLET CODE=MyApplet.class ARCHIVE=jarfile1, jarfile2 WIDTH=100 HEIGHT=200>
</APPLET>
```

To improve performance when an applet has infrequently used files, put the frequently used files into the JAR file and the infrequently used files into the applet class directory. Infrequently used files are then located and downloaded by the browser only when needed.

Thread Pooling

Bandwidth restrictions imposed on networks around the world make network-based operations potential bottlenecks that can have a significant impact on an application's performance. Many network-based applications are designed to use connection pools so they can reuse existing network connections and save on the time and overhead invested in opening and closing network connections.

The Java Developer Connection (JDC) applet servers and the Java Web Server make extensive use of thread pooling to improve performance. Thread pooling is creating a ready supply of sleeping threads at the beginning of execution. Thread creation and their startup process is expensive, so run time performance is improved with thread pooling because threads are not created during run time; they are simply reused.

This code sample taken from the `Pool` class (page 282) shows one way to implement thread pooling. In the pool's constructor (shown below), the `WorkerThreads` are initialized and started. The call to the `start` method executes the `run` method of the `WorkerThread`, and the call to `wait` in the `run` method suspends the `Thread` while the `Thread` waits for work to arrive. The last line of the constructor pushes the sleeping `Thread` onto the stack.

```
public Pool (int max, Class workerClass)    throws Exception {
  _max = max;
  _waiting = new Stack();
  _workerClass = workerClass;
  Worker worker;
  WorkerThread w;
  for ( int i = 0; i < _max; i++ ) {
    worker = (Worker)_workerClass.newInstance();
    w = new WorkerThread (Worker#+i, worker);
    w.start();
```

```
    _waiting.push(w);
  }
}
```

Besides the run method, the WorkerThread class has a wake method. When
work comes in, the wake method is called, which assigns the data and notifies
the sleeping WorkerThread (the one initialized by the Pool) to resume running.
The wake method's call to notify causes the blocked WorkerThread to fall out
of its wait state, and the run method of the HttpServerWorker class (page
285) is executed. Once the work is done, the WorkerThread is either put back
onto the Stack (assuming the thread pool is not full) or terminates.

```
synchronized void wake (Object data) {
  _data = data;
  notify();
}
synchronized public void run(){
  boolean stop = false;
  while (!stop){
    if ( _data == null ){
    try {
      wait();
    } catch (InterruptedException e){
      e.printStackTrace(); continue;
    }
    if( _data != null ){
      _worker.run(_data);
    }
    _data = null;
    stop = !(_waiting.push(this));
  }
}
```

At its highest level, incoming work is handled by the performWork method in
the Pool class (shown below). As work comes in, an existing WorkerThread is
popped off of the Stack (or a new one is created if the Pool is empty). The
sleeping WorkerThread is then activated by a call to its wake method.

```
public void performWork (Object data)     throws InstantiationException{
  WorkerThread w = null;
  synchronized (_waiting){
    if( _waiting.empty() ){
      try {
        w = new WorkerThread (additional worker,
                              (Worker)_workerClass.newInstance());
        w.start();
      } catch (Exception e){
        throw new InstantiationException(
              Problem creating instance of Worker.class: + e.getMessage());
      } else{
        w = (WorkerThread)_waiting.pop();
      }
```

```
   }
   w.wake (data);
 }
```

The HttpServer class (page 286) constructor creates a new Pool instance to service HttpServerWorker instances. HttpServerWorker instances are created and stored as part of the WorkerThread data. When a WorkerThread is activated by a call to its wake method, the HttpServerWorker instance is invoked by way of its run method.

```
try{
  _pool = new Pool (poolSize, HttpServerWorker.class);
} catch (Exception e){
  e.printStackTrace();
  throw new InternalError (e.getMessage());
}
```

This next code is in the run method of the HttpServer class (page 286). Every time a request comes in, the data is initialized and the Thread starts work.

> **NOTE**   If creating a new Hashtable for each WorkerThread presents too much overhead, just modify the code so it does not use the Worker abstraction.

```
try {
   Socket s = _serverSocket.accept();
  Hashtable data = new Hashtable();
   data.put (Socket, s);
   data.put (HttpServer, this);
   _pool.performWork (data);
} catch (Exception e){
  e.printStackTrace();
}
```

Thread pooling is an effective performance-tuning technique that puts the expensive thread startup process at the startup of an application. This way, the negative impact on performance occurs once at program startup where it is least likely to be noticed.

Connection Pooling

If you have used SQL or another similar tool to connect to a database and act on the data, you probably know that getting the connection and logging in is the part that takes the most time. An application can easily spend several seconds every time it needs to establish a connection.

In releases prior to JDBC 2.0 every database session required a new connection and login even if the previous connection and login used the same table and user account. If you are using a JDBC release prior to 2.0 and want to improve performance, you can cache JDBC connections instead of creating a new connection and login.

Cached connections are kept in a run-time object pool and can be used and reused as needed by the application. One way to implement the object pool is to make a simple hashtable of connection objects. However, a more flexible way to do it is to write a wrapper JDBC Driver that is an intermediary between the client application and database.

The wrapper approach works particularly well in an enterprise bean that uses bean-managed persistence for two reasons: (1) Only one Driver class is loaded per bean and (2) specific connection details are handled outside the bean. This section explains how to write a wrapper JDBC Driver class.

Wrapper Classes

The wrapper JDBC Driver created for this example consists of the following three classes:

- JDCConnectionDriver
- JDCConnectionPool
- JDCConnection

Connection Driver. The JDCConnectionDriver class implements the java.sql.Driver interface, which provides methods to load drivers and create new database connections. A JDCConnectionDriver object is created by the application seeking a database connection. The application provides the database URL for the database, login user ID, and login password.

The JDCConnectionDriver constructor does the following:

- Registers the JDCConnectionDriver object with the DriverManager
- Loads the Driver class passed to the constructor by the calling program
- Initializes a JDCConnectionPool object for the connections with the database URL, login user ID, and login password passed to the constructor by the calling program

When the calling program needs a database connection, it calls the JDCConnectionDriver.connect method, which in turn, calls the JDCConnectionPool.getConnection method.

```
package pool;

import java.sql.*;
import java.util.*;

public class JDCConnectionDriver implements Driver {
  public static final String URL_PREFIX = "jdbc:jdc:";
  private static final int MAJOR_VERSION = 1;
  private static final int MINOR_VERSION = 0;
  private JDCConnectionPool pool;
  public JDCConnectionDriver(String driver, String url,
                             String user, String password)
                             throws ClassNotFoundException,
                             InstantiationException, IllegalAccessException,
                             SQLException {
  DriverManager.registerDriver(this);
  Class.forName(driver).newInstance();
  pool = new JDCConnectionPool(url, user, password);
}
  public Connection connect(String url, Properties props) throws SQLException
{
    if(!url.startsWith(URL_PREFIX) {
      return null;
    }
    return pool.getConnection();
  }
  public boolean acceptsURL(String url) {
    return url.startsWith(URL_PREFIX);
  }
  public int getMajorVersion() {
    return MAJOR_VERSION;
  }
  public int getMinorVersion() {
    return MINOR_VERSION;
  }
  public DriverPropertyInfo[] getPropertyInfo(String str, Properties props) {
    return new DriverPropertyInfo[0];
  }
  public boolean jdbcCompliant() {
    return false;
  }
}
```

Connection Pool.   The JDCConnectionPool class makes connections available to a calling program in its getConnection method. This method searches for an available connection in the connection pool. If no connection is available from the pool, a new connection is created. If a connection is available from the pool, the getConnection method leases the connection and returns it to the calling program.

```
package pool;

import java.sql.*;
```

```
      import java.util.*;
      import java.io.*;

      class ConnectionReaper extends Thread {
        private JDCConnectionPool pool;
        private final long delay=300000;
        ConnectionReaper(JDCConnectionPool pool) {
          this.pool=pool;
        }
        public void run() {
          while(true) {
            try {
              sleep(delay);
            } catch( InterruptedException e) { }
            pool.reapConnections();
          }
        }
      }
      public class JDCConnectionPool {
        private Vector connections;
        private String url, user, password;
        final private long timeout=60000;
        private ConnectionReaper reaper;
        final private int poolsize=10;

        public JDCConnectionPool(String url, String user, String password) {
          this.url = url;
          this.user = user;
          this.password = password;
          connections = new Vector(poolsize);
          reaper = new ConnectionReaper(this);
          reaper.start();
        }
        public synchronized void reapConnections() {
          long stale = System.currentTimeMillis() - timeout;
          Enumeration connlist = connections.elements();
//API Ref: boolean hasMoreElements()
          while((connlist != null) && (connlist.hasMoreElements())) {
//API Ref: Object nextElement()
            JDCConnection conn = (JDCConnection)connlist.nextElement();
              if((conn.inUse()) && (stale >conn.getLastUse()) && (!conn.vali-
    date())) {
                removeConnection(conn);
              }
            }
          }

        public synchronized void closeConnections() {
          Enumeration connlist = connections.elements();
          while((connlist != null) && (connlist.hasMoreElements())) {
            JDCConnection conn = (JDCConnection)connlist.nextElement();
            removeConnection(conn);
          }
        }
        private synchronized void removeConnection(JDCConnection conn) {
```

```
        connections.removeElement(conn);
    }
    public synchronized Connection getConnection() throws SQLException {
        JDCConnection c;
        for(int i = 0; i < connections.size(); i++) {
            c = (JDCConnection)connections.elementAt(i);
            if(c.lease()) {
                return c;
            }
        }
        Connection conn = DriverManager.getConnection(url, user, password);
        c = new JDCConnection(conn, this);
        c.lease();
        connections.addElement(c);
        return c;
    }

    public synchronized void returnConnection(JDCConnection conn) {
        conn.expireLease();
    }
}
```

The JDCConnection class represents a JDBC connection in the connection
pool, and is essentially a wrapper around a real JDBC connection. The JDCConnection object maintains a state flag to indicate if the connection is in use and
the time the connection was taken from the pool. This time is used by the ConnectionReaper class to identify hanging connections.

```
package pool;

import java.sql.*;
import java.util.*;
import java.io.*;

public class JDCConnection implements Connection {
    private JDCConnectionPool pool;
    private Connection conn;
    private boolean inuse;
    private long timestamp;

    public JDCConnection(Connection conn, JDCConnectionPool pool) {
        this.conn=conn;
        this.pool=pool;
        this.inuse=false;
        this.timestamp=0;
    }
    public synchronized boolean lease() {
        if(inuse)  {
            return false;
        } else {
            inuse=true;
            timestamp=System.currentTimeMillis();
```

```
      return true;
    }
  }
  public boolean validate() {
    try {
      conn.getMetaData();
    } catch (Exception e) {
      return false;
    }
    return true;
  }
  public boolean inUse() {
    return inuse;
  }
  public long getLastUse() {
    return timestamp;
  }
  public void close() throws SQLException {
    pool.returnConnection(this);
  }
  protected void expireLease() {
    inuse=false;
  }
  protected Connection getConnection() {
    return conn;
  }
  public PreparedStatement prepareStatement(String sql) throws SQLException
{
    return conn.prepareStatement(sql);
  }
  public CallableStatement prepareCall(String sql) throws SQLException {
    return conn.prepareCall(sql);
  }
  public Statement createStatement() throws SQLException {
    return conn.createStatement();
  }
  public String nativeSQL(String sql) throws SQLException {
    return conn.nativeSQL(sql);
  }
  public void setAutoCommit(boolean autoCommit) throws SQLException {
    conn.setAutoCommit(autoCommit);
  }
  public boolean getAutoCommit() throws SQLException {
    return conn.getAutoCommit();
  }
  public void commit() throws SQLException {
    conn.commit();
  }
  public void rollback() throws SQLException {
    conn.rollback();
  }
  public boolean isClosed() throws SQLException {
    return conn.isClosed();
  }
  public DatabaseMetaData getMetaData() throws SQLException {
```

```
    return conn.getMetaData();
  }
  public void setReadOnly(boolean readOnly) throws SQLException {
    conn.setReadOnly(readOnly);
  }
  public boolean isReadOnly() throws SQLException {
    return conn.isReadOnly();
  }
  public void setCatalog(String catalog) throws SQLException {
    conn.setCatalog(catalog);
  }
  public String getCatalog() throws SQLException {
    return conn.getCatalog();
  }
  public void setTransactionIsolation(int level) throws SQLException {
    conn.setTransactionIsolation(level);
  }
  public int getTransactionIsolation() throws SQLException {
    return conn.getTransactionIsolation();
  }
  public SQLWarning getWarnings() throws SQLException {
    return conn.getWarnings();
  }
  public void clearWarnings() throws SQLException {
    conn.clearWarnings();
  }
}
```

Deadlocks and Hangs

While many client and server databases have graceful ways to handle deadlocks and hangs so you do not have to write code to handle these situations, many of the newer, lightweight distributed databases are not so well equipped. The connection pool class provides a dead connection reaper to handle these situations.

The ConnectionReaper class in the JDCConnectionPool class file decides a connection is dead if the following conditions are met.

- The connection is flagged as being in use.
- The connection is older than a preset connection time out.
- The connection fails a validation check.

The validation check runs a simple SQL query over the connection to see if it throws an exception. In this example, the validation method requests the high-level description of the database tables. If a connection fails the validation test, it is closed, a new connection is initiated to the database, and added to the connection pool.

```
public boolean validate() {
  try {
    conn.getMetaData();
```

```
  }catch (Exception e) {
     return false;
  }
  return true;
}
```

Closing Connections

The connection is returned to the connection pool when the calling program calls the JDCConnection.close method in its finally clause.

```
public void close() throws SQLException {
  pool.returnConnection(this);
}
```

Example Application

You use a connection pool in an application in a similar way to how you would use any other JDBC driver. The RegistrationBean code for this chapter illustrates this point, and is adapted from the auction house Enterprise JavaBeans example described in Chapters 1–3.

When the first RegistrationBean object is created, it creates one static instance of the JDCConnectionDriver class. This static driver object registers itself with the DriverManager in the JDCConnectionDriver constructor making it available for connection requests to all RegistrationBean objects created by the client application.

Passing the URL as jdbc:jdc:jdcpool in the getConnection method lets the DriverManager match the getConnection request to the registered driver. The DriverManager uses simple String matching to find an available driver that can handle URLs in that format.

```
package registration;

import java.rmi.RemoteException;
import javax.ejb.*;
import java.util.*;
import java.text.NumberFormat;
import java.sql.*;

//uses our connection pool
public class RegistrationBean implements EntityBean {
  protected transient EntityContext ctx;
  public String theuser, password, creditcard, emailaddress;
  public double balance;
  static {
    try {
      new pool.JDCConnectionDriver("COM.cloudscape.core.JDBCDriver",
                                   "jdbc:cloudscape:ejbdemo","none", "none");
    } catch(Exception e){}
```

```
  }
  public Connection getConnection() throws SQLException {
    return DriverManager.getConnection("jdbc:jdc:jdcpool");
  }
  public boolean verifyPassword(String password) throws RemoteException {
    if(this.password.equals(password)) {
      return true;
    } else {
      return false;
    }
  }
  public String getEmailAddress() throws RemoteException {
    return emailaddress;
  }
  public String getUser() throws RemoteException {
    return theuser;
  }
  public int adjustAccount(double amount) throws RemoteException {
    balance=balance+amount;
    return(0);
  }
  public double getBalance() throws RemoteException {
    return balance;
  }
  public RegistrationPK ejbCreate(String theuser, String password,
                                  String emailaddress, String creditcard)
                                  throws CreateException, RemoteException {
    System.out.println("registration create");
    this.theuser=theuser;
    this.password=password;
    this.emailaddress=emailaddress;
    this.creditcard=creditcard;
    this.balance=0;
    Connection con = null;
    PreparedStatement ps = null;;
    try {
      con=getConnection();
      ps=con.prepareStatement("insert into registration (theuser,
      password, emailaddress, creditcard, balance) values (?, ?, ?, ?, ?)");
      ps.setString(1, theuser);
      ps.setString(2, password);
      ps.setString(3, emailaddress);
      ps.setString(4, creditcard);
      ps.setDouble(5, balance);
      if(ps.executeUpdate() != 1) {
        System.out.println("registration create failed");
        throw new CreateException ("JDBC did not create any row");
      }
      RegistrationPK primaryKey = new RegistrationPK();
      primaryKey.theuser = theuser;
      return primaryKey;
    } catch (CreateException ce) {
      throw ce;
    } catch (SQLException sqe) {
      throw new CreateException (sqe.getMessage());
```

```
  } finally {
   try {
     ps.close();
     con.close();
   } catch (Exception ignore) {}
 }
}
public void ejbPostCreate(String theuser, String password,
  String emailaddress, String creditcard)
  throws CreateException, RemoteException {
}
public void setEntityContext(javax.ejb.EntityContext ctx)
                             throws RemoteException {
  this.ctx = ctx;
}
public void unsetEntityContext() throws RemoteException {
  ctx = null;
}
public void ejbRemove() throws RemoteException, RemoveException { }
public void ejbActivate() throws RemoteException { }
public void ejbPassivate() throws RemoteException { }
public void ejbLoad() throws RemoteException {
  System.out.println("registration load");
  try {
    refresh((RegistrationPK) ctx.getPrimaryKey());
  } catch (FinderException fe) {
    throw new RemoteException (fe.getMessage());
  }
}
public void ejbStore() throws RemoteException {
  System.out.println("registration store");
  Connection con = null;
  PreparedStatement ps = null;
  try {
    con = getConnection();
    ps = con.prepareStatement("update registration set password = ?,
      emailaddress = ?, creditcard = ?, balance = ? where theuser = ?");
    ps.setString(1, password);
    ps.setString(2, emailaddress);
    ps.setString(3, creditcard);
    ps.setDouble(4, balance);
    ps.setString(5, theuser);
    int i = ps.executeUpdate();
    if(i == 0) {
      throw new RemoteException ("ejbStore: Registration (" + theuser
                                 + ") not updated");
    }
  } catch (RemoteException re) {
    throw re;
  } catch (SQLException sqe) {
    throw new RemoteException (sqe.getMessage());
  } finally {
    try {
      ps.close();
    con.close();
```

```java
        } catch (Exception ignore) {}
      }
    }
    public RegistrationPK ejbFindByPrimaryKey(RegistrationPK pk)
                                   throws FinderException, RemoteException {
      if((pk == null) || (pk.theuser == null)) {
        throw new FinderException ("primary key cannot be null");
      }
      refresh(pk);
      return pk;
    }
    private void refresh(RegistrationPK pk)
                         throws FinderException, RemoteException {
      if(pk == null) {
        throw new RemoteException ("primary key cannot be null");
      }
      Connection con = null;
      PreparedStatement ps = null;
      try {
        con=getConnection();
        ps=con.prepareStatement("select password, emailaddress, creditcard,
                        balance from registration where theuser = ?");
        ps.setString(1, pk.theuser);
        ps.executeQuery();
        ResultSet rs = ps.getResultSet();
        if(rs.next()) {
          theuser = pk.theuser;
          password = rs.getString(1);
          emailaddress = rs.getString(2);
          creditcard = rs.getString(3);
          balance = rs.getDouble(4);
        } else {
          throw new FinderException ("Refresh: Registration ("
                                  + pk.theuser + ") not found");
        }
      } catch (SQLException sqe) {
        throw new RemoteException (sqe.getMessage());
      } finally {
        try {
          ps.close();
          con.close();
        } catch (Exception ignore) {}
      }
    }
  }
  static {
      try {
        new pool.JDCConnectionDriver("COM.cloudscape.core.JDBCDriver",
                                  "none", "none");
      } catch(Exception e){}
  }
  public Connection getConnection() throws SQLException{
    return DriverManager.getConnection(jdbc:jdc:jdcpool");
  }
}
```

Performance Features and Tools

The new Java virtual machines have features to increase performance, and you can use a number of tools to increase application performance or reduce the size of generated class files. Such features and tools improve the performance of your application with little or no change required to your application.

Java Virtual Machine Features

The Java 2 Platform release has introduced many performance improvements over previous releases, including faster memory allocation, reduction of class sizes, improved garbage collection, streamlined monitors and a built-in Just-In-Time compiler (JIT) as standard.

When using the new Java 2 virtual machine straight out of the box, you will see an improvement; however, by understanding how the speed-ups work, you can tune your application to squeeze out every last bit of performance.

Method Inlining.   The Java 2 release of the Java virtual machine automatically inlines simple methods at run time. In an unoptimized Java virtual machine, every time a new method is called, a new stack frame is created. The creation of a new stack frame requires additional resources as well as some remapping of the stack. The end result is that creating new stack frames incurs a small overhead.

Method inlining increases performance by reducing the number of method calls your program makes. The Java virtual machine inlining code inlines methods that return constants or only access internal fields. To take advantage of method inlining you can do one of two things: You can either make a method look attractive to the virtual machine to inline, or manually inline a method if it does not break your object model. Manual inlining in this context means moving the code from a method into the method that is calling it. Automatic virtual machine inlining is illustrated in this next example:

```
public class InlineMe {
  int counter=0;

  public void method1() {
    for(int i=0;i<1000;i++) {
      addCount();
      System.out.println("counter="+counter);
  }

  public int addCount() {
    counter=counter+1;
    return counter;
  }

  public static void main(String args[]) {
```

```
      InlineMe im=new InlineMe();
      im.method1();
   }
}
```

In its current state the addCount method does not look very attractive to the
inline detector in the virtual machine because the addCount method returns a
value. To find out if this method is inlined, run the compiled example with profiling enabled:

```
java -Xrunhprof:cpu=times InlineMe
```

This generates a java.hprof.txt output file. The top ten methods will look
similar to this:

```
CPU TIME (ms) BEGIN (total = 510)   Thu Jan 28 16:56:15 1999
rank self accum  count trace method
   1 5.88%  5.88%     1  25 java/lang/Character. <clinit>
   2 3.92%  9.80% 5808  13 java/lang/String.charAt
   3 3.92% 13.73%     1  33 sun/misc/Launcher$AppClassLoader.getPermissions
   4 3.92% 17.65%     3  31 sun/misc/URLClassPath.getLoader
   5 1.96% 19.61%     1  39 java/net/URLClassLoader.access$1
   6 1.96% 21.57% 1000  46 InlineMe.addCount
   7 1.96% 23.53%     1  21 sun/io/Converters.newConverter
   8 1.96% 25.49%     1  17 sun/misc/Launcher$ExtClassLoader.getExtDirs
   9 1.96% 27.45%     1  49 java/util/Stack.peek
  10 1.96% 29.41%     1  24 sun/misc/Launcher.<init>
```

If you change the addCount method to no longer return a value, the virtual
machine will inline it for you at run time. To make the code friendly to inlining,
replace the addCount method with the following code:

```
public void addCount() {
  counter=counter+1;
}
```

And run the profiler again:

```
java -Xrunhprof:cpu=times InlineMe
```

This time the java.hprof.txt output should look different. The addCount
method is gone because it has been inlined!

```
CPU TIME (ms) BEGIN (total = 560)   Thu Jan 28 16:57:02 1999
rank self  accum  count trace method
   1 5.36%  5.36%     1  27 java/lang/Character.<clinit>
   2 3.57%  8.93%     1  23 java/lang/System.initializeSystemClass
   3 3.57% 12.50%     2  47 java/io/PrintStream.<init>
   4 3.57% 16.07% 5808  15 java/lang/String.charAt
   5 3.57% 19.64%     1  42 sun/net/www/protocol/file/Handler.openConnection
   6 1.79% 21.43%     2  21 java/io/InputStreamReader.fill
   7 1.79% 23.21%     1  54 java/lang/Thread.<init>
   8 1.79% 25.00%     1  39 java/io/PrintStream.write
   9 1.79% 26.79%     1  40 java/util/jar/JarFile.getJarEntry
  10 1.79% 28.57%     1  38 java/lang/Class.forName0
```

Streamlined Synchronization.   Up until Java 2, synchronized methods and objects have always incurred an additional performance hit. This is because the mechanism used to implement the locking used a global monitor registry, which was only single-threaded in some areas, such as when searching for existing monitors.

In the Java 2 release, each thread has a monitor registry and so many of the existing bottlenecks have been removed. If you have previously used other locking mechanisms because of the performance hit with synchronized methods, it is now worthwhile to revisit this code and incorporate the new Java 2 streamlined locks.

This next example creates monitors for the synchronized block and achieves a 40 percent increase in speed. Time was 14 ms using JDK 1.1.7 and only 10 ms with Java 2 on a Sun Ultra 1.

```java
class MyLock {
  static Integer count=new Integer(5);
  int test=0;

  public void letslock() {
    synchronized(count) {
      test++;
    }
  }
}

public class LockTest {
  public static void main(String args[]) {
    MyLock ml=new MyLock();
    long time = System.currentTimeMillis();
    for(int i=0;i<5000;i++ ) {
      ml.letslock();
    }
    System.out.println("Time taken=" + (System.currentTimeMillis()-time));
  }
}
```

Java Hotspot Technology.   The Java HotSpot technology is Sun Microsystem's next-generation virtual machine implementation. HotSpot adheres to the same specification as the Java 2 virtual machine and runs the same byte codes, but it has been re-engineered to leverage new technologies like adaptive optimization and improved garbage collection models to dramatically improve the speed of the Java virtual machine.

Adaptive Optimization.   HotSpot does not include a plug-in JIT compiler, but instead compiles and inlines methods it determines to be the most used in the application. This means that on the first pass through, Java Bytecodes are interpreted as if you did not have a JIT compiler present. If the code then appears to be a hot spot in your application, the HotSpot compiler compiles the Bytecodes into native code that is stored in a cache and inlines methods at the same time. See Method Inlining (page 263) for details on the advantages to inlining code.

One advantage to selective compilation over a JIT compiler is that the byte compiler can spend more time generating highly optimized code for the areas that would benefit most from the optimization. The compiler can also avoid compiling code that may best run in interpreted mode.

Earlier versions of HotSpot did not optimize code not currently in use. The downside to this is if the application is in a big, busy loop, the optimizer is unable to compile the code for that area until the loop finishes. Later HotSpot releases use on-stack replacement, meaning that code can be compiled into native code even if it is in use by the interpreter.

Improved Garbage Collection.   The garbage collector used in HotSpot introduces several improvements over existing garbage collectors. The first is that the garbage collector is a fully accurate collector. What this means is the garbage collector knows exactly what is an object reference and what is just data. HotSpot uses direct references to objects on the heap instead of object handles. This design means memory fragmentation can be reduced, resulting in a more compact memory footprint.

The second improvement is in the use of generational copying. The Java platform creates a large number of objects on the heap, and often those objects are short lived. By placing newly created objects in a memory bucket, waiting for the bucket to fill up, and copying only the remaining live objects to a new area, the block of memory that bucket used can be freed in one block. This means the virtual machine does not have to search for a hole to fit each new object in the heap, and smaller sections of memory must be manipulated at one time.

For older objects the garbage collector sweeps through the heap and compacts holes from dead objects directly; this approach removes the need for a free list, which was used in earlier garbage collection algorithms.

The third area of improvement is the removal of the perception of garbage collection pauses by staggering the compaction of large, free object spaces into smaller groups and compacting them incrementally.

Fast Thread Synchronization.   HotSpot also improves existing synchronized code. Synchronized methods and code blocks have always had a performance overhead when run in a Java virtual machine. HotSpot implements the monitor entry and exit synchronization points itself and does not depend on the local operating system to provide this synchronization. This results in a large speed improvement, especially to often heavily synchronized GUI applications.

Just-In-Time Compilers

The simplest tool used to increase the performance of your application is the Just-In-Time (JIT) compiler. A JIT compiler is a code generator that converts Java Bytecodes into native machine code. Java programs invoked with a JIT generally run much faster than if the bytecode is executed by the interpreter. HotSpot removes the need for a JIT compiler in most cases; however, you might still find the JIT compiler being used in earlier releases.

The JIT compiler was first made available as a performance update in the JDK 1.1.6 software release and is now a standard tool invoked whenever you use the java interpreter command in the Java 2 Platform release. You can disable the JIT compiler with the `-Djava.compiler=NONE` option to the Java virtual machine. This is covered in more detail at the end of the JIT section.

How Do JIT Compilers Work?   JIT compilers are supplied as standalone platform-dependent native libraries. If the JIT `Compiler` library exists, the Java virtual machine initializes JNI native code hooks to call JIT functions available in that library instead of the equivalent function in the interpreter.

The `java.lang.Compiler` class loads the native library and starts the initialization inside the JIT compiler. When the Java virtual machine invokes a Java method, it uses an invoker method as specified in the method block of the loaded class object. The Java virtual machine has several invoker methods; for example, a different invoker is used if the method is synchronized or if it is a native method.

The JIT compiler uses its own invoker. Sun production releases check the method access bit for value `ACC_MACHINE_COMPILED` to notify the interpreter that the code for this method has already been compiled and stored in the loaded class.

When Does the Code Become JIT Compiled Code?   When a method is called the first time, the JIT compiler compiles the method block into native code for this method and stores it in the code block for the method. Once the code is compiled, the `ACC_MACHINE_COMPILED` bit, which is used on the Sun platform, is set.

How Can I See What the JIT Compiler Is Doing?   The _JIT_ARGS environment variable allows simple control of the Sun Solaris JIT compiler. Two useful values are `trace` and `exclude(list)`. To exclude the methods from the `InlineMe` example and show a trace, set `_JIT_ARGS` as follows:

Unix:

```
export _JIT_ARGS="trace exclude(InlineMe.addCount  InlineMe.method1)"
$ java InlineMe
Initializing the JIT library ...
DYNAMICALLY COMPILING java/lang/System.getProperty mb=0x63e74
DYNAMICALLY COMPILING java/util/Properties.getProperty mb=0x6de74
DYNAMICALLY COMPILING java/util/Hashtable.getProperty mb=0x714ec
DYNAMICALLY COMPILING java/lang/String.hashCode mb=0x44aec
DYNAMICALLY COMPILING java/lang/String.equals mb=0x447f8
DYNAMICALLY COMPILING java/lang/String.valueOf mb=0x454c4
DYNAMICALLY COMPILING java/lang/String.toString mb=0x451d0
DYNAMICALLY COMPILING java/lang/StringBuffer.<init> mb=0x7d690
<<<< Inlined java/lang/String.length (4)
```

Notice that inlined methods such as `String.length` are exempt. The `String.length` is also a special method because it is normally compiled into an internal shortcut bytecode by the Java interpreter. When using the JIT compiler, these optimizations provided by the Java Interpreter are disabled to enable the JIT compiler to understand which method is being called.

How to Use the JIT to Your Advantage.   The first thing to remember is that the JIT compiler achieves most of its speed improvements the second time it calls a method. The JIT compiler compiles the entire method instead of interpreting it line by line; this method can also be a performance gain when running an application with the JIT enabled. This means that if code is only called once, you will not see a significant performance gain. The JIT compiler also ignores class constructors, so if possible, keep constructor code to a minimum.

The JIT compiler also achieves a minor performance gain by not prechecking certain boundary conditions in the Java programming language such as null pointer or array out-of-bounds exceptions. The only way the JIT compiler knows it has a null pointer exception is by a signal raised by the operating system. Because the signal comes from the operating system and not the Java virtual machine, your program takes a performance hit. To ensure the best performance when running an application with the JIT, make sure your code is very clean, with no errors like null pointer or array out of bounds exceptions.

You might want to disable the JIT compiler if you are running the Java virtual machine in remote debug mode or if you want to see source line numbers instead of the label (Compiled Code) in your Java stack traces. To disable the JIT compiler, supply a blank or invalid name for the name of the JIT compiler when you invoke the interpreter command. The following examples show the javac command to compile the source code into bytecodes, and two forms of the java interpreter command to invoke the interpreter without the JIT compiler.

```
javac MyClass.java
java -Djava.compiler=NONE MyClass
```

or

```
javac MyClass.java
java -Djava.compiler="" MyClass
```

Third-Party Tools

Some of the other tools available include those that reduce the size of the generated Java class files. A Java class file contains an area called a constant pool. The constant pool keeps a list of strings and other information for the class file in one place for reference. One of the pieces of information available in the constant pool are the method and field name.

The class file refers to a field in the class as a reference to an entry in the constant pool. This means that as long as the references stay the same, it makes no difference what the values stored in the constant pool are. This knowledge is exploited by several tools that rewrite the names of the field and methods in the constant pool into shortened names. This technique can reduce the class file by a significant percentage with the benefit that a smaller class file means a shorter network download.

Performance Analysis

Another way to improve performance is with performance analysis. *Performance analysis* is looking at program execution to pinpoint where bottlenecks or other performance problems such as memory leaks might occur. Once you know where potential trouble spots are, you can change your code to remove or reduce their impact.

Profiling

Java virtual machines have been able to provide simple profile reports since the introduction of JDK 1.0.2. However, the information provided is limited to a sorted list of methods called by a program.

The Java 2 platform software provides much better profiling capabilities than previously available, and analysis of this generated data is made easier by the Heap Analysis Tool (HAT). The heap analysis tool, as its name implies, lets you analyze heap profile reports. The heap is a block of memory the Java virtual machine uses at run time. You can locate the Heap Analysis Tool using the search engine on the http://java.sun.com Web site.

The heap analysis tool lets you generate reports on objects that were used to run your application. Not only can you get a listing of the most frequently called methods and the memory used in calling those methods, but you can also track down memory leaks. Memory leaks can have a significant impact on performance.

Analyze a Program

This section shows you how to analyze the `TableExample3` program included in the `demo/jfc/Table` directory in the Java 2 Platform download. To do this, you need to generate a profile report. The simplest report to generate is a text profile.

To generate a text profile, run the application with the `-Xhprof` parameter. In the final release of the Java 2 platform software, this option was renamed `-Xrunhprof`. To see a list of the currently available options, run the `java` interpreter command as follows:

```
java -Xrunhprof:help Hprof usage: -Xrunhprof[:help]|[<option>=<value>, ...]
Option Name and Value    Description              Default
---------------------    -----------              -------
heap=dump|sites|all      heap profiling           all
cpu=samples|times|old    CPU usage                off
monitor=y|n              monitor contention       n
format=a|b               ascii or binary output   a
file=<file>              write data to file       java.hprof(.txt for ascii)
net=<host>:<port>        send data over a socket  write to file
depth=<size>             stack trace depth        4
cutoff=<value>           output cutoff poin       0.0001
lineno=y|n               line number in traces    y
thread=y|n               thread in traces?        n
doe=y|n                  dump on exit?            y
Example: java -Xrunhprof:cpu=samples,file=log.txt, depth=3 FooClass
```

The following invocation creates a text output file that you can view without the `java.hprof.txt` heap analysis tool, which is called when the program generates a stack trace or exits. A different invocation is used to create a binary file to use with the heap analysis tool.

```
java -Xrunhprof TableExample3
```

```
d:\jdk12\demo\jfc\Table> java -Xrunhprof TableExample3
Dumping Java heap ... allocation sites ... done.
```

The profile option literally logs every object created on the heap, so even just starting and stopping the small `TableExample3` program results in a four Mb report file. Although the heap analysis tool uses a binary version of this file and provides a summary, there are some quick and easy things you can learn from the text file without using the heap analysis tool.

View the Text File. Choose an editor that can handle large files and go to the end of this file. There could be hundreds of thousands of lines, so use a shortcut instead of scrolling, or search for the words SITES BEGIN. You should see a list of lines that start with an increasing rank number followed by two percentage numbers. The first entry in this list, should look similar to the example below:

```
SITES BEGIN (ordered by live bytes)  Sun Dec 20 16:33:28 1998
        percent               live          alloc'ed      stack    class
rank   self   accum    bytes  objs    bytes   objs      trace    name
1     55.86% 55.86%   826516   5     826516    5        3981     [S
```

The [S notation at the end of the last line above indicates the first entry is an array of short, which is a primitive type. This notation is expected with Project Swing or Abstract Window Toolkit (AWT) applications.

The 5 count under the objs header means there are currently five of these arrays, there have only been five in the lifetime of this application, and they take up 826,516 bytes.

The reference key to this object is the value listed under stack trace. To find where this object was created in this example, search for TRACE 3981. You will see the following:

```
TRACE 3981:
java/awt/image/DataBufferUShort.<init>(DataBufferUShort.java:50)
java/awt/image/Raster.createPackedRaster(Raster.java:400)
java/awt/image/DirectColorModel.createCompatibleWritableRaster(
                              DirectColorModel.java:641)
sun/awt/windows/WComponentPeer.createImage(WComponentPeer.java:186)
```

The TableExample3 code sets a scrollpane that is 700 by 300. When you look at the source of Raster.java, which is in the src.jar file, you find these statements at line 400:

```
case DataBuffer.TYPE_USHORT:d = new DataBufferUShort(w*h);
break;
```

The values w and h above are the width and height from the createImage call at the start of TRACE 3981. The DataBufferUShort constructor creates and array of shorts as follows:

```
data = new short[size];
```

where size is w*h. So, in theory there should be an entry for an array of 210,000 elements. You look for each instantiation of this class by searching for trace=3981. One of the five entries will look like this:

```
OBJ 5ca1fc0 (sz=28, trace=3979,class=java/awt/image/DataBufferUSh-
ort@9a2570)
data 5ca1670
bankdata 5ca1f90
offsets 5ca1340
```

```
ARR 5ca1340 (sz=4, trace=3980, nelems=1, elem type=int)
ARR 5ca1670 (sz=420004, trace=3981, nelems=210000,elem type=short)
ARR 5ca1f90 (sz=12, trace=3982, nelems=1, elem type=[S@9a2d90)
[0] 5ca1670
```

You can see that the data value of this raster image references an array
5ca1670, which in turns lists 210,000 elements of a short of size 2. This
means 420,004 bytes of memory are used in this array.

From this data you can conclude that the TableExample3 program uses nearly
0.5 Mb to map each table. If the example application is running on a small
memory machine, you should make sure you do not keep unnecessary references to large tables or images that are built by the createImage method.

The Heap Analysis Tool.   The Heap Analysis Tool can analyze the same data
for you, but it requires a binary report file as input. You can generate a binary
report file as follows:

```
java -Xrunhprof:file=TableExample3.hprof,format=b TableExample3
```

To generate the binary report, close the TableExample3 window. The binary
report file TableExample3.hprof is created when the program exits. The Heap
Analysis Tool starts an HTTP server that analyzes the binary profile file and
displays the results in HTML that you can view with a browser.

You can get a copy of the Heap Analysis Tool from the java.sun.com Web
site. Once you install it, you can run shell and batch scripts in the installed bin
directory to start the Heap Analysis Tool server as follows:

```
>hat TableExample3.hprof
Started HCODEP server on port 7000
Reading from /tmp/TableExample3.hprof...
Dump file created Tue Jan 05 13:28:59 PST 1999
Snapshot read, resolving...
Resolving 17854 objects...
Chasing references, expect 35 dots.....................
Eliminating duplicate references........................
Snapshot resolved.
Server is ready.
```

The above output tells you an HTTP server is started on port 7000 by default.
To view this report, enter the URL http://localhost:7000 or http://
your_machine_name:7000 in your Web browser. If you have problems starting
the server using the scripts, you can alternately run the application by including
the hat.zip classes file on your CLASSPATH and executing the following command:

```
java hat.Main TableExample3.hprof
```

The default report view contains a list of all the classes. At the bottom of this
initial page are the following two key report options:

```
Show all members of the rootset
Show instance counts for all classes
```

If you select the Show all members of the rootset link, you see a list of the
following references because these references are likely targets for potential
memory leaks.

```
Java Static References
Busy Monitor References
JNI Global References
JNI Local References
System Class References
```

What you look for here are instances in the application that have references to
objects that have a risk of not being garbage collected. This can sometimes
occur in the case of JNI if memory is allocated for an object, the memory is left
to the garbage collector to free up, and the garbage collector does not have the
information it needs to do it. In this list of references, you are mainly interested
in a large number of references to objects or objects of a large size.

The other key report is the Show instance counts for all classes. This lists the
number of calls to a particular method. The String and Character array
objects, [S and [C, are always going to be high on this list, but some objects are
a bit more intriguing. Why are there 323 instances of java.util.SimpleTime-
Zone, for example?

```
5109 instances of class java.lang.String
5095 instances of class [C
2210 instances of class java.util.Hashtable$Entry
968 instances of class java.lang.Class
407 instances of class [Ljava.lang.String;
323 instances of class java.util.SimpleTimeZone
305 instances of class sun.java2d.loops.GraphicsPrimitiveProxy
304 instances of class java.util.HashMap$Entry
269 instances of class [I
182 instances of class [Ljava.util.Hashtable$Entry;
170 instances of class java.util.Hashtable
138 instances of class java.util.jar.Attributes$Name
131 instances of class java.util.HashMap
131 instances of class [Ljava.util.HashMap$Entry;
130 instances of class [Ljava.lang.Object;
105 instances of class java.util.jar.Attributes
```

To get more information on the SimpleTimeZone instances, click on the link
(the line beginning with 323). This will list all 323 references and calculate how
much memory has been used. In this example, 21,964 bytes have been used.

```
Instances of java.util.SimpleTimeZone

class java.util.SimpleTimeZone

java.util.SimpleTimeZone@0x004f48c0 (68 bytes)
```

```
java.util.SimpleTimeZone@0x003d5ad8 (68 bytes)
java.util.SimpleTimeZone@0x004fae88 (68 bytes)
.....
Total of 323 instances occupying 21964 bytes.
```

If you click on one of these SimpleTimeZone instances, you see where this object was allocated.

```
Object allocated from:
```

```
java.util.TimeZoneData.<clinit>(()V) : TimeZone.java line 1222
java.util.TimeZone.getTimeZone((Ljava/lang/String;)
          Ljava/util/TimeZone;) : TimeZone.java line (compiled method)
java.util.TimeZone.getDefault(()Ljava/util/TimeZone;) :
                    TimeZone.java line (compiled method)
java.text.SimpleDateFormat.initialize((Ljava/util/Locale;)V) :
          SimpleDateFormat.java line (compiled method)
```

In this example the object was allocated from TimeZone.java. The source to this file is in the standard src.jar file, and on examining this file, you can see that indeed there are nearly 300 of these objects in memory.

```
static SimpleTimeZone zones[] = {
// Total Unix zones: 343
// Total Java zones: 289
// Not all Unix zones become Java zones due to
// duplication and overlap.
//-------------------------------------------
new SimpleTimeZone(-11*ONE_HOUR,  "Pacific/Niue" /*NUT*/),
```

Unfortunately, you have no control over the memory used in this example because it is allocated when the program first requests a default time zone. However, this same technique can be applied to analyzing your own application to see where you may be able to make some improvements.

Where the Application Spends Its Time.   Again, you can use the -Xrun-hprof parameter to get information about the time the application spent processing a particular method.

You can use one of two CPU profiling options to get this information. The first option is cpu=samples. This option reports the result of a sampling of the running threads of the Java virtual machine to which a statistical count of the frequency of the occurrence of a particular method is used to find busy sections of the applications. The second option is cpu=times, which measures the time taken by individual methods and generates a sorted list ranked as a total percentage of the CPU time taken by the application. By using the cpu=times option, you should see something similar to this at the end of the output file:

```
CPU TIME (ms) BEGIN (total = 11080) Fri Jan  8 16:40:59 1999
rank self  accum count trace    method
1  13.81% 13.81% 1    437  sun/awt/X11GraphicsEnvironment.initDisplay
```

```
2   2.35%   16.16%   4   456   java/lang/ClassLoader$NativeLibrary.load
3   0.99%   17.15%   46  401   java/lang/ClassLoader.findBootstrapClass
```

If you contrast this with the `cpu=samples` output, you see the difference between how often a method appears during the run time of the application in the `samples` output compared to how long that method took in the times output.

```
CPU SAMPLES BEGIN (total = 14520) Sat Jan 09 17:14:47 1999
rank self  accum count trace  method
1   2.93%  2.93%  425 2532 sun/awt/windows/WGraphics.W32LockViewResources
2   1.63%  4.56%  237  763 sun/awt/windows/WToolkit.eventLoop
3   1.35%  5.91%   96 1347 java/text/DecimalFormat.<init>
```

The `W32LockView` method, which calls a native windows lock routine, is called 425 times. So when it is sampled, it appears in the active runnings threads because 425 calls take time to complete. However, although the `initDisplay` method is called only once, it takes the longest time to complete in real time.

Operating System Performance Tools

Sometimes the performance bottleneck occurs at the system or operating system level. This is because the Java virtual machine depends on many operating system libraries for functionality such as disk access or networking. However, what occurs in these libraries after the Java virtual machine calls them is beyond the reach of most profiling tools for the Java platform.

The next sections describe tools you can use to analyze performance problems on some common operating systems.

Solaris platform tools:

- `sar`
- `truss`

The System Accounting Reports (`sar`) tool reports the activity of the system in terms of disk IO, user program activity, and system level activity. If your application is using excessive amounts of memory, it might require disk swap space, which shows up as high percentage values in the `wio` column. User programs that get stuck in a busy loop show a high percentage in the user (`usr`) column:

```
developer$ sar 1 10

SunOS developer 5.6 Generic_105181-09 sun4u  02/05/99

11:20:29    %usr    %sys    %wio    %idle
11:20:30      30       6       9      55
11:20:31      27       0       3      70
11:20:32      25       1       1      73
11:20:33      25       1       0      74
11:20:34      27       0       1      72
```

The `truss` command traces and records the details of every system call called by the Java virtual machine to the Solaris kernel. A common way to run `truss` is:

```
truss -f -o /tmp/output -p <process id>
```

The `-f` parameter follows any child processes that are created, the `-o` parameter writes the output to the named file, and the `-p` parameter traces an already running program from its process ID. Alternately, you can replace `-p <process id>` with the Java virtual machine, for example:

```
truss -f -o /tmp/output java MyDaemon
```

The `/tmp/output` is used to store the `truss` output, which should look similar to the following:

```
15573:  execve("/usr/local/java/jdk1.2/solaris/bin/java", 0xEFFFF2DC,
        0xEFFFF2E8)  argc  = 4
15573:  open("/dev/zero", O_RDONLY) = 3
15573:  mmap(0x00000000, 8192, PROT_READ|PROT_WRITE|PROT_EXEC,
        MAP_PRIVATE, 3, 0) = 0xEF7C0000
15573:  open("/home/calvin/java/native4/libsocket.so.1",  O_RDONLY)
        Err#2 ENOENT
15573:  open("/usr/lib/libsocket.so.1", O_RDONLY) = 4
15573:  fstat(4, 0xEFFFEF6C)                    = 0
15573: mmap(0x00000000, 8192, PROT_READ|PROT_EXEC,
        MAP_SHARED, 4, 0) = 0xEF7B00 00
15573: mmap(0x00000000, 122880, PROT_READ|PROT_EXEC,
        MAP_PRIVATE, 4, 0) = 0xEF7 80000
15573: munmap(0xEF78E000, 57344) = 0
15573: mmap(0xEF79C000, 5393, PROT_READ|PROT_WRITE|PROT_EXEC,
        MAP_PRIVATE|MAP_FIXED, 4, 49152) = 0xEF79C000
15573: close(4) = 0
```

In the `truss` output, look for files that fail when opened due to access problems, such as error ENOPERM, or a missing file error ENOENT. You can also track data read or written with the `truss` parameters `-rall`, to log all data read, or `-wall`, to log all data written by the program. With these parameters, it is possible to analyze data sent over a network or to a local disk.

Linux platform:

Linux has a trace command called `strace`. It traces system calls to the underlying Linux kernel. This example traces the `SpreadSheet` example in the JDK demo directory.

```
$ strace -f -o /tmp/output java sun.applet.AppletViewer example1.html
$ cat /tmp/output

639    execve("/root/java/jdk117_v1at/java/jdk117_v1a/bin/java"
       , ["java","sun.applet.AppletViewer ", "example1.html"], [/* 21 vars */
])  = 0
639    brk(0) = 0x809355c
```

```
639    open("/etc/ld.so.preload", O_RDONLY)  = -1 ENOENT
       (No such file or directory)
639    open("/etc/ld.so.cache", O_RDONLY) = 4
639    fstat(4, {st_mode=0, st_size=0, ...}) = 0
639    mmap(0, 14773, PROT_READ, MAP_PRIVATE, 4, 0) = 0x4000b000
639    close(4)                                 = 0
639    open("/lib/libtermcap.so.2", O_RDONLY)   = 4
639    mmap(0, 4096, PROT_READ, MAP_PRIVATE, 4, 0) = 0x4000f000
```

To obtain system information similar to the Solaris `sar` command, read the contents of the file /proc/stat. The format of this file is described in the `proc` man page. Look at the `cpu` line to get the user and system time.

```
cpu   4827 4 1636 168329
```

In the above example, the `cpu` line indicates 48.27 seconds in user space, 0.04 at nice priority, 16.36 seconds processing system calls, and 168 seconds idle. This is a running total; individual entries for each process are available in /proc/<process_id>/stat.

Windows95/98/NT platforms:

There are no standard performance analysis tools included on this platform, but the following tools are available by way of freeware or shareware resources such as http://www.download.com.

- Run time memory analysis: Memory meter
- Network Analysis:traceplus

Caching Client/Server Applications

Caching is one of the first techniques used to improve the performance of Web browsers and Web servers. The browser cache makes network lookup operations unnecessary because a recent copy of the file is kept in the local cache and the Web server cache reduces the cost of loading the file from disk for each request. This section explains how you can use caching in a similar way to improve performance in many client/server applications written in the Java programming language.

The Collections API available in the Java 2 SDK software makes implementing a cache simple. This API provides the `HashMap` class, which works well for caching one object, and the `LinkedList` class, which works well in combination with the `HashMap` class for caching many objects.

Caching One Object

A `HashMap` object stores data in key and value pairs. When you put a data value in the `HashMap`, you assign it a key and later use that key to retrieve the data.

A HashMap object is very similar to a Hashtable and can be used to keep a temporary copy of previously generated results. Objects kept in the HashMap cache could, for example, be a list of completed auction results.

In this case, the results of a JDBC query might be requested hundreds of times a second by persons wanting to know who was the highest bidder, but the completed results lists only actual changes once a minute as each auction completes. You can write your program to retrieve unchanged objects from the results cache instead of querying the database every time so that you can gain a significant performance improvement.

This code example runs a database query once a minute and returns cached copies for requests that come between the queries.

```java
//File DBCache.java
import java.util.*;
import java.io.*;

class DBCacheRecord {
  Object data;
  long time;

  public DBCacheRecord(Object results, long when) {
    time=when;
    data=results;
  }
  public Object getResults() {
    return data;
  }
  public long getLastModified() {
          return time;
  }
}

public class DBCache {
  Map cache;

  public DBCache() {
    cache = new HashMap();
  }

  public Object getDBData(String dbcommand) {
    if(!cache.containsKey(dbcommand)) {
      synchronized(cache) {
        cache.put(dbcommand, readDBData(dbcommand));
      }
    } else {
      if((new Date().getTime() ) -((DBCacheRecord)cache.get(
                    dbcommand)).getLastModified()>=1000){
        synchronized(cache) {
          cache.put(dbcommand, readDBData(dbcommand));
        }
      }
```

```
    }
    return ((DBCacheRecord)cache.get(dbcommand)).getResults();
  }

  public Object readDBData(String dbcommand) {
  /*Insert your JDBC code here For Example:
    ResultSet results=stmt.executeQuery(dbcommand);
  */
    String results="example results";
    return(new DBCacheRecord(results,new Date().getTime()));
  }
  public static void main(String args[]) {
    DBCache d1=new DBCache();
    for(int i=1;i<=20;i++) {
            d1.getDBData("select count(*) from results where TO_DATE(
              results.completed) <=SYSDATE");
    }
  }
}
```

Caching Many Objects

Sometimes you will want to cache more than one object. For example, you might want to keep the most recently accessed files on a Web server in a cache. If you use a HashMap object for this, it will continue to grow and use a lot of memory.

If your machine has large amounts of memory and only a small number of objects to cache, a growing HashMap may not be a problem. However, if you intend to cache a lot of objects, you might find that keeping only the most recent objects in the cache provides the best use of the machine's memory. You can combine a HashMap object with a LinkedList to create what is called a Most Recently Used (MRU) cache.

NOTE   There are other techniques to constrain cache size besides MRU. MRU is one of the simpler algorithms.

With an MRU cache, you can place a constraint on which objects remain in cache, and thereby, control the size of the cache. There are three main operations that the MRU cache has to perform:

- If the cache is not full, new objects not already in the cache are inserted at the head of the list.
- If the cache is not full and the object to be inserted already exists in the cache, it is moved to the head of the list.
- If the cache is full and a new object is to be inserted, the last object in the cache is removed and the new object is inserted at the head of the list.

Figure 8.2 shows how the LinkedList and HashMap work together to implement the operations described above. A discussion of the diagram follows.

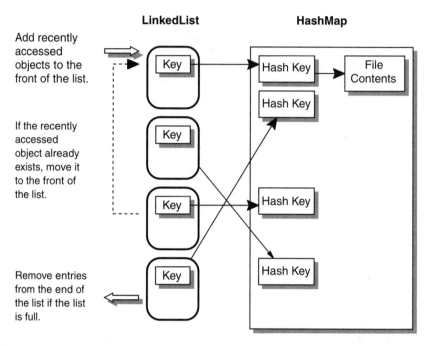

Figure 8.2 MRU cache with LinkedList (left) and HashMap (right)

The LinkedList provides the queue mechanism, and the entries in the LinkedList contain the key to the data in the HashMap. To add a new entry to the front of the list, the addFirst method is called.

- If the list is already full, the removeLast method is called and the data entry is also removed from the HashMap.

- If an entry is already in the list, it is removed with a call to the remove method and inserted at the front of the list with a call to the addFirst method.

The Collections API does not implement locking, so if you remove entries from or add entries to LinkedList or HashMap objects, you need to lock access to these objects. You can also use a Vector or ArrayList to get the same results as shown in the code below with the LinkedList.

This code example uses an MRU cache to keep a cache of files loaded from disk. When a file is requested, the program checks to see if the file is in the cache. If the file is not in the cache, the program reads the file from disk and places the cache copy at the beginning of the list.

- If the file is in cache, the program compares the modification times of the file and cache entry.
- If the cache entry time is older, the program reads the file from disk, removes the cache copy, and places a new copy in the cache at the front of the LinkedList.
- If the file time is older, the program gets the file from the cache and moves the cache copy to the front of the list.

```
//File MRUCache.java
import java.util.*;
import java.io.*;

class myFile {
  long lastmodified;
  String contents;

  public myFile(long last, String data) {
    lastmodified=last;
    contents=data;
  }
  public long getLastModified() {
    return lastmodified;
  }
  public String getContents() {
    return contents;
  }
}

public class MRUCache {

  Map cache;
  LinkedList mrulist;
  int cachesize;

  public MRUCache(int max) {
    cache = new HashMap();
    mrulist= new LinkedList();
    cachesize=max;
  }

  public String getFile(String fname) {
//API Ref: boolean containsKey(Object key
    synchronized (cache) {
        if(!cache.containsKey(fname)) {
          if(mrulist.size() >=cachesize) {
//API Ref: Object remove(Object key)
                        cache.remove(mrulist.getLast());
//API Ref: Object removeLast()
                    mrulist.removeLast();
          }
//API Ref: Object put(Object key, Object value)
          cache.put(fname, readFile(fname));
//API Ref: void addFirst(Object value)
```

```
                mrulist.addFirst(fname);
            } else {
              if((new File(fname).lastModified())>
//API Ref: Object get(Object key)
                ((myFile)cache.get(fname)).getLastModified()) {
                            cache.put(fname, readFile(fname));
              }
            boolean remove(Object value)
              mrulist.remove(fname);
                        mrulist.addFirst(fname);
            }
            return ((myFile)cache.get(fname)).getContents();
        }
        public myFile readFile(String name) {
          File f = new File(name);
          StringBuffer filecontents= new StringBuffer();

          try {
            BufferedReader br=new BufferedReader(new FileReader(f));
            String line;
            while((line =br.readLine()) != null) {
                        filecontents.append(line);
            }
          } catch (FileNotFoundException fnfe){
            return (null);
          } catch ( IOException ioe) {
                    return (null);
          }
            return (new myFile(f.lastModified(),
                    filecontents.toString()));
        }

        public void printList() {
          for(int i=0;i<mrulist.size();i++) {
            System.out.println("item "+i+"="+mrulist.get(i));
          }
        }

        public static void main(String args[]) {
          // Number of entries in MRU cache is set to 10
          MRUCache h1=new MRUCache(10);
          for(int i=1;i<=20;i++) {
            // files are stored in a subdirectory called data
            h1.getFile("data"+File.separatorChar+i);
          }
            h1.printList();
        }
    }
```

Pool

```
    import java.util.*;

    //Implements Thread Pooling. Thread Pool simply keeps a
```

```java
//bunch of suspended threads around to do some work.
public class Pool {
//Handler class to perform work requested by the Pool.
  class WorkerThread extends Thread {
    private Worker _worker;
    private Object _data;
    //Create a new WorkerThread @param id Thread ID
    //@param worker Worker instance associated with the WorkerThread
    WorkerThread(String id, Worker worker) {
      super(id);
      _worker = worker;
      _data = null;
    }
  //Wake the thread and does some work @param data Data to send
  //to the Worker. @return void
  synchronized void wake (Object data) {
    _data = data;
    notify();
  }
  //WorkerThread's thread routine
  synchronized public void run() {
    boolean stop = false;
      while (!stop) {
        if( _data == null ) {
          try {
            wait();
          } catch (InterruptedException e) {
            e.printStackTrace();
            continue;
          }
        }
        if( _data != null ) {
          _worker.run(_data);
        }
        _data = null;
        stop = !(_waiting.push (this));
      }
    }
};

  private Stack _waiting;
  private int _max;
  private Class _workerClass;

  //Creates a new Pool instance
  //@param max Max number of handler threads
  //@param workerClass Name of Worker implementation
  //@throws Exception
  public Pool (int max, Class workerClass) throws Exception {
    _max = max;
    _waiting = new Stack();
    _workerClass = workerClass;
    Worker worker;
    WorkerThread w;
    for( int i = 0; i < _max; i++ ) {
```

```
      worker = (Worker)_workerClass.newInstance();
      w = new WorkerThread ("Worker#"+i, worker);
      w.start();
      _waiting.push(w);
    }
  }

  //Request the Pool to perform some work.
  //@param data Data to give to the Worker
  //@return void
  //@throws InstantiationException Thrown if additional worker can't be created
  public void performWork (Object data) throws InstantiationException {
    WorkerThread w = null;
    synchronized (_waiting) {
      if( _waiting.empty()) {
        try {
          w = new WorkerThread("additional worker",
                               (Worker)_workerClass.newInstance());
          w.start();
        } catch (Exception e) {
          throw new InstantiationException(
                    "Problem creating instance of Worker.class: " +
                    e.getMessage());
        }
      } else {
        w = (WorkerThread)_waiting.pop();
      }
    }
    w.wake (data);
  }

  //Convience method used by WorkerThread to put Thread back on the stack
  //@param w WorkerThread to push
  //@return boolean True if pushed, false otherwise
    private boolean _push (WorkerThread w) {
      boolean stayAround = false;
      synchronized (_waiting) {
        if( _waiting.size() < _max ) {
          stayAround = true;
          _waiting.push(w);
        }
      }
      return stayAround;
    }
}
```

Worker

```
  public interface Worker {
  //Method invoked to request worker to perform task
    public void run(Object data);
  }
```

HttpServerWorker

```java
import java.io.*;
import java.net.*;
import java.util.*;

//Implements the Worker interface for the HttpServer
public class HttpServerWorker implements Worker {
//Invoked by the Pool when a job comes in for the Worker
//@param data Worker data
//@return void
public void run(Object data) {
  Socket socket = (Socket)((Hashtable)data).get ("Socket");
  HttpServer server = (HttpServer)((Hashtable)data).get ("HttpServer");
  try {
    DataInputStream input = new DataInputStream(
                      new BufferedInputStream(socket.getInputStream()));
    String line = input.readLine();
    if(line.toUpperCase().startsWith ("POST") ) {
      for( ; (line=input.readLine()).length() > 0; );
      int type = input.readInt();
      switch (type) {
        case HttpClient.DATA : {
          int length = input.readInt();
          byte buffer[] = new byte[length];
          input.readFully (buffer);
          ByteArrayOutputStream dataOut = new ByteArrayOutputStream();
          server.notifyListener(new ByteArrayInputStream (buffer), dataOut);
          DataOutputStream output = new DataOutputStream(
                    new BufferedOutputStream(socket.getOutputStream()));
          server.writeResponse (output);
```
//API Ref: void writeInt(int value)
```java
          output.writeInt (HttpClient.DATA);
```
//API Ref: byte[] toByteArray()
```java
          output.writeInt (dataOut.toByteArray().length);
          output.write (dataOut.toByteArray());
          output.flush();
          input.close();
          output.close();
          socket.close();
          break;
        } case HttpClient.PENDING : {
        //DON'T CLOSE THE SOCKET!
          server.addClient (socket);
          break;
        } default : {
        System.err.println ("Invalid type: " + type);
        }
      }
    } else {
      System.err.println ("Invalid HTTP request: " + line);
    }
```

```
  } catch (IOException e) {
    e.printStackTrace();
  }
 }
}
```

HttpServer

```
import java.io.*;
import java.net.*;
import java.util.*;

//Implementation of a basic HTTP server for Firewall tunneling.
//The server supports both Client->Server and Server->Client communication.
public class HttpServer implements Runnable {
//Accept socket
  private ServerSocket _serverSocket;
//Server Listener
  private HttpServerListener _listener;
//Thread accepting connections
  private Thread _acceptTID;
//Handler threads
  private Pool _pool;
//Client sockets
  private Vector _clients;
//Default HTTP Response
  private String _httpResponse;
//Create a new HttpServer instance
//@param port Port to listen on
//@param poolSize Number of handler threads
//@throw IOException Thrown if the accept socket cannot be opended
  public HttpServer (int port, int poolSize) throws IOException {
    _serverSocket = new ServerSocket (port);
    _httpResponse = "HTTP/1.0 200 MyServer \nCache-Control:
                no-cache\nPragma: no-cache \r\n\r\n";
    try {
      _pool = new Pool (poolSize, HttpServerWorker.class);
    } catch (Exception e) {
      e.printStackTrace();
      throw new InternalError (e.getMessage());
    }
    _clients = new Vector();
    _acceptTID = new Thread(this);
    _acceptTID.start();
  }

//Adds a new client
//@param s Socket
  synchronized void addClient (Socket s) {
    _clients.addElement(s);
  }

//Adds a new HttpServerListener. Only one listener can be added
//@param l HttpServerListener
```

```
//@throws TooManyListenersException Thrown if more then one listener is
added
  public void addHttpServerListener (HttpServerListener l)
                                     throws TooManyListenersException {
    if( _listener == null ) {
      _listener = l;
    } else {
      throw new TooManyListenersException();
    }
  }
//Removes a new HttpServerListener.
//@param l HttpServerListener
public void removeHttpServerListener (HttpServerListener l){
  _listener = null;
}
//Notifies the listener when a message arrives
//@param data Message data
//@param out Stream to write results too
  synchronized void notifyListener (InputStream data, OutputStream out){
    if( _listener != null ) {
      _listener.service (data, out);
    }
  }
//Simple implementation that sends data to all clients
//@param data Array of bytes containing data to send
  synchronized public void send (byte data[]) {
    Enumeration elements = _clients.elements();
    while( elements.hasMoreElements() ) {
      Socket s = (Socket)elements.nextElement();
      try {
        DataOutputStream output = new DataOutputStream(
                          new BufferedOutputStream (s.getOutputStream()));
        int length;
        writeResponse (output);
        output.writeInt (data.length);
        output.write (data);
        output.flush();
        output.close();
      } catch (IOException e) {
        e.printStackTrace();
      } finally {
        try {
          s.close();
        } catch (IOException e) {
        }
      }
    }
  }
  _clients.removeAllElements();
}
//Thread to accept connections
  public void run() {
    while(true) {
      try {
        Socket s = _serverSocket.accept();
        Hashtable data = new Hashtable();
```

```
            data.put ("Socket", s);
            data.put ("HttpServer", this);
            _pool.performWork (data);
        } catch (Exception e) {
            e.printStackTrace();
        }
    }
}
}
//Convience method to write the HTTP Response header
  * @param out Stream to write the response too
  * @throws IOException Thrown if response can't be written
  void writeResponse (DataOutputStream out) throws IOException {
    out.writeBytes (_httpResponse);
  }
}
```

9

Deploying the
Auction Application

With the auction application tested, debugged, and tuned, you are ready to deploy it. In this chapter, `Administration` applet replaces the `AuctionClient` application so you can see how to deploy an applet; this process is a little more involved than deploying an application.

To deploy the complete application, you bundle the application files, move the application files to their production locations, install Java Plug-In so auction administrators can run the `Administration` applet from their browsers, and install the `Administration` applet policy file. Java Plug-In is needed because the `Administration` applet is written with JDK 1.2 APIs, but the administrators' browsers will likely run an earlier version of the Java Runtime Environment™ (JRE) software.

This chapter explains how to use the JAR file format to bundle and deploy the application files, and how to install Java Plug-In and a security policy file for the Solaris and Win32 platforms to run the `Administration` applet.

Covered in this Chapter

JAR File Format

Java Archive file format is a compression and file packaging format and tool for bundling executable files with other related application files so they can be deployed as a single unit. The auction application has the following three sets of files to deploy to three different locations:

1. The HTML files that make up the auction application user interface deploy to a publicly accessible location under the Web server.
2. The enterprise beans deploy to an internal location accessible to your production installation of the Enterprise JavaBeans server.
3. The Administration applet deploys to an internal location accessible to auction administrators where it is run from their browsers.

Bundle and Deploy the HTML Files

Here is the list of HTML files that make up the auction application user interface:

- all.html
- close.html
- details.html
- index.html
- juggler.med.gif
- new.html
- registration.html
- search.html
- sell.html

And here is the jar command to bundle them. Everything goes on one line. This command is executed in the same directory with the files. If you execute the command from a directory other than where the files are found, specify the full or relative pathname as appropriate.

```
jar cvf HTML.jar all.html close.html details.html index.html
juggler.med.gif new.html registration.html search.html sell.html
```

jar is the Java Archive command. If you type jar with no options, you get the following help screen. You can see from the help screen that the cf options to the jar command mean create a new JAR file named HTML.jar and put the list of files that follows into it. The new JAR file is placed in the current directory.

```
kq6py% jar
Usage: jar {ctxu}[vfm0M][jar-file][manifest-file][-C dir] files ...
Options:
  -c  create new archive
```

```
-t  list table of contents for archive
-x  extract named (or all) files from archive
-u  update existing archive
-v  generate verbose output on standard output
-f  specify archive file name
-m  include manifest information from specified  manifest file
-0  store only; use no ZIP compression
-M  Do not create a manifest file for the entries
-C  change to the specified directory and include the following file
```
If any file is a directory then it is processed recursively. The manifest
file name and the archive file name needs to be specified in the same order
the 'm' and 'f' flags are specified.

Example 1: to archive two class files into an archive called classes.jar: jar
cvf classes.jar Foo.class Bar.class
Example 2: use an existing manifest file 'mymanifest' and archive all the
files in the foo/ director into 'classes.jar': jar cvfm classes.jar mymanifest -C foo/ .

To deploy the HTML files, all you have to do is move the HTML.jar file to a
publicly accessible directory under the Web server and decompress the JAR
file:

`jar xvf HTML.jar`

NOTE If you included a full or relative pathname when you
added the files to the JAR file, the files are placed in the same directory structure when they are unpacked.

The JAR file contains a manifest file, META-INF/MANIFEST.MF that the jar tool
automatically placed there. A manifest file contains information about the files
packaged in the JAR file. You can tailor this information to enable JAR file
functionality such as electronic signing, version control, package sealing, and
more.

Bundle and Deploy the Enterprise Beans

Some Enterprise JavaBeans servers create the JAR file for you. However, if
yours does not or if you just wonder how it's done, this section describes the
steps.

These are the server-side files you need to deploy the enterprise beans. This
list is taken from the original auction application described in Chapter 2,
Auction House Application, before any modifications were made. Note the
inclusion of the deployment descriptor, and the container-generated stub and
skel classes.

NOTE   Because there are so many files, these steps bundle the example code into four JAR files, one each for the `auction`, `registration`, `bidder`, and `seller` packages. You could also bundle all the packages into one JAR file and deploy that instead.

`auction` Package.   These are the application files in the auction package that make up the `AuctionServlet` servlet and `AuctionItemBean` enterprise bean. Because they are all to be installed in an auction directory accessible to the production Enterprise JavaBeans server, bundle them together so they can be unpacked in one step in the destination directory and placed in the auction subdirectory.

- `auction.AuctionServlet.class`
- `auction.AuctionItem.class`
- `auction.AuctionItemBean.class`
- `auction.AuctionItemHome.class`
- `auction.AuctionItemPK.class`
- `auction.DeploymentDescriptor.txt`
- `AuctionItemBeanHomeImpl_ServiceStub.class`
- `WLStub1h1153e3h2r4x3t5w6e82e6jd412c.class`
- `WLStub364c363d622h2j1j422a4oo2gm5o.class`
- `WLSkel1h1153e3h2r4x3t5w6e82e6jd412c.class`
- `WLSkel364c363d622h2j1j422a4oo2gm5o.class`

Here is how to bundle them. Everything goes on one line, and the command is executed one directory above the place where the class files are located.

Unix:
```
jar cvf auction.jar  auction/*.class auction/*.txt
```

Win32:
```
jar cvf auction.jar  auction\*.class auction\*.txt
```

Once the JAR file is copied to the destination directory for the enterprise beans, unpack it as follows. The extraction creates an `auction` directory with the class files in it.

```
jar xvf auction.jar
```

`Registration` Package.   Here are the application files in the registration package that make up the `Registration` enterprise bean.

- `registration.Registration.class`
- `registration.RegistrationBean.class`

- `registration.RegistrationHome.class`
- `registration.RegistrationPK.class`
- `registration.DeploymentDescriptor.txt`
- `RegistrationBeanHomeImpl_ServiceStub.class`
- `WLStub183w4u1f4e70p6j1r4k6z1x3f6yc21.class`
- `WLStub4z67s6n4k3sx131y4fi6w4x616p28.class`
- `WLSkel183w4u1f4e70p6j1r4k6z1x3f6yc21.class`
- `WLSkel4z67s6n4k3sx131y4fi6w4x616p28.class`

Here is how to bundle them. Everything goes on one line, and the command is executed one directory above the place where the class files are located.

Unix:
```
jar cvf registration.jar  registration/*.class registration/*.txt
```

Win32:
```
jar cvf registration.jar  registration\*.class registration\*.txt
```

Once the JAR file is copied to the destination directory for the enterprise beans, unpack it as follows. The extraction creates a `registration` directory with the class files in it.

```
jar xvf registration.jar
```

bidder Package.   Here are the application files in the bidder package that make up the `Bidder` enterprise bean.

- `bidder.Bidder.class`
- `bidder.BidderHome.class`
- `bidder.BidderBean.class`
- `bidder.DeploymentDescriptor.txt`
- `BidderBeanEOImpl_ServiceStub.class`
- `BidderBeanHomeImpl_ServiceStub.class`
- `WLStub1z35502726376oa1m4m395m4w5j1j5t.class`
- `WLStub5g4v1dm3m271tr4i5s4b4k6p376d5x.class`
- `WLSkel1z35502726376oa1m4m395m4w5j1j5t.class`
- `WLSkel5g4v1dm3m271tr4i5s4b4k6p376d5x.class`

Here is how to bundle them. Everything goes on one line, and the command is executed one directory above the place where the class files are located.

Unix:
```
jar cvf bidder.jar  bidder/*.class bidder/*.txt
```

Win32:
```
jar cvf bidder.jar  bidder\*.class bidder\*.txt
```

Once the JAR file is copied to the destination directory for the enterprise beans, unpack it as follows. The extraction creates a `bidder` directory with the class files in it.

```
jar xvf bidder.jar
```

Seller Package.   Here are the application files in the seller package that make up the `Seller` enterprise bean.

- `seller.Seller.class`
- `seller.SellerHome.class`
- `seller.SellerBean.class`
- `seller.DeploymentDescriptor.txt`
- `SellerBeanEOImpl_ServiceStub.class`
- `SellerBeanHomeImpl_ServiceStub.class`
- `WLStub3xr4e731e6d2x3b3w5b693833v304q.class`
- `WLStub86w3x4p2x6m4b696q4kjp4p4p3b33.class`
- `WLSkel3xr4e731e6d2x3b3w5b693833v304q.class`
- `WLSkel86w3x4p2x6m4b696q4kjp4p4p3b33.class`

Here is how to bundle them. Everything goes on one line, and the command is executed one directory above the place where the class files are located.

Unix:
```
jar cvf seller.jar  seller/*.class seller/*.txt
```

Win32:
```
jar cvf seller.jar  seller\*.class seller\*.txt
```

Once the JAR file is copied to the destination directory for the enterprise beans, unpack it as follows. The extraction creates a `seller` directory with the class files in it.

```
jar xvf seller.jar
```

Bundle and Deploy the `Applet` Program

For this chapter, the `Administration` applet family of files consists of two source files: `AdminApplet.java` and `java.policy`. For reference, Figure 9.1 shows the `Admin` applet.

```
grant {
  permission java.lang.RuntimePermission "queuePrintJob";
};
```

Here is the `jar` command to bundle them. Everything goes on one line, and the command is executed where the policy file is located, which is one directory above the place where the class files are located.

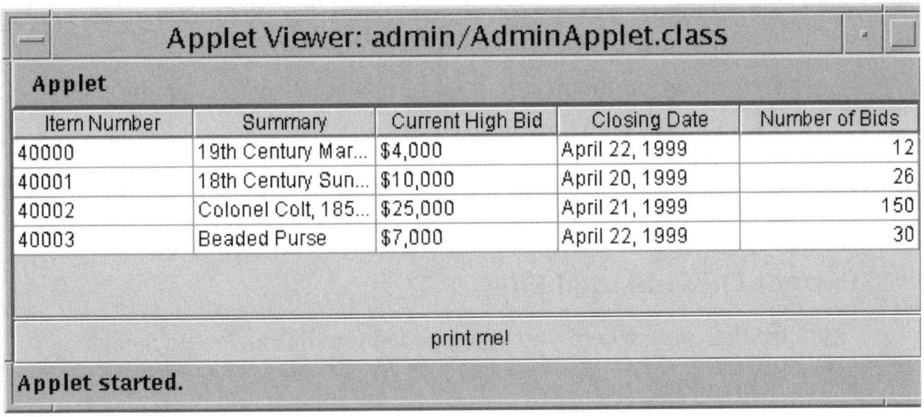

```
Applet Viewer: admin/AdminApplet.class
```

Item Number	Summary	Current High Bid	Closing Date	Number of Bids
40000	19th Century Mar...	$4,000	April 22, 1999	12
40001	18th Century Sun...	$10,000	April 20, 1999	26
40002	Colonel Colt, 185...	$25,000	April 21, 1999	150
40003	Beaded Purse	$7,000	April 22, 1999	30

print me!

Applet started.

Figure 9.1 Administration applet

Unix:
```
jar cvf applet.jar admin/*.class java.policy
```

Win32:
```
jar cvf applet.jar admin\*.class java.policy
```

To deploy the applet, copy the `applet.jar` file to the destination applet directory and extract it as follows. The extraction creates an `admin` directory with the `Administration` applet class files in it.

```
jar xvf applet.jar
```

Deploy to Solaris Operating System

Java Plug-in software lets you direct applets or JavaBeans components on intranet Web pages to run using the JRE instead of the Web browser's default virtual machine. The Java Plug-In works with Netscape Communicator and Microsoft Internet Explorer. Free downloads of all the software you need to install and use Java Plug-In are available from the download page (`http://java.sun.com/products/plugin/1.2/download/all.html`).

This section explains how to install Java Plug-In with Netscape Communicator on the Solaris operating system.

Get Downloads

To install and use Java Plug-In on Solaris 2.6 or Solaris 7, you need the following downloads. Put the downloads in a directory anywhere you want.

- Java Plug-In for Solaris operating systems. It is available for either Intel or Sparc platforms.

- Java Plug-In patches for either Solaris 2.6 or Solaris 7, depending on which one you have.
- Netscape Communicator 4.5.1 or newer (Webstart version).
- Java Plug-In HTML Converter

These instructions were tested on a Sun Microsystems Ultra 2 running Solaris 2.6 with Netscape Communicator 4.5.1.

Extract Downloaded Files

Go to the directory where you downloaded the files and extract each one.

Extract Java Plug-In files:
```
zcat plugin-12-webstart-sparc.tar.Z | tar -xf -
```

Extract patch files for Solaris 2.6:
```
zcat JPI1.2-Patches-Solaris2.6-sparc.tar.Z | tar -xf -
```

Extract Netscape Navigator 4.5.1:
```
zcat NSCPcom_webstart_sparc.tar.Z | tar -xf -
```

Install Java Plug-In

The Java Plug-In download includes a user guide that you can view in your browser from the following directory:

```
plugin-12-webstart-sparc/Java_Plug-in_1.2.2/common/Docs/en/
Users_Guide_Java_Plug-in.html
```

The user guide explains how to install Java Plug-In. There are several easy ways to do it, and the command sequence below is one quick way that installs Java Plug-In in the default /opt/NSCPcom directory using the pkgadd command:

```
su
<root password>
cd ~/plugin-12-webstart-sparc
pkgadd -d ./Java_Plug-in_1.2.2/sparc/Product
```

Install Java Plug-In Patches

Before you can run Java Plug-In, you have to install the patches. You install the patches one at a time as root. The following command sequence goes to the patch directory, lists the files, and issues the command to install the first patch:

```
cd ~/JPI1.2-Patches-Solaris2.6-sparC
su
<password>
kq6py#ls
105210-19   105490-07   105568-13
kq6py#./105210-19/installpatch 105210-19
```

You will see this output when the patch is successfully installed:

```
Patch number 105210-19 has beenZ successfully installed.
See /var/sadm/patch/105210-19/log for details

Patch packages installed:
  SUNWarc
  SUNWcsu
```

Continue installing the patches one-by-one until all patches have successfully installed. The user's guide provides a list of required and suggested patches and links to where you can download additional suggested patches if you want to install them.

Install Netscape Communicator

The extracted Netscape Communicator 4.5.1 files provide a user's guide in the ~/NETSCAPE/Netscape_Communicator_4.51/common/Docs/en directory that explains the installation. The following command sequence is one easy way to do it with the pkgadd command. By default, the installation puts Netscape Communicator in the /opt/NSCPcom directory where your Java Plug-In and patches are also installed.

When you extracted the NSCPcom_webstart_sparc.tar.Z download, it placed the files in a NETSCAPE directory. From the NETSCAPE directory, execute the following command sequence:

```
cd ~/NETSCAPE/Netscape_Communicator_4.51/sparc/Product
su
<password>
pkgadd -d .
```

Check the Installation

There are two ways to check your Java Plug-In, patch, and Netscape Communicator installation.

1. Open the Netscape Help menu and select About Plug_Ins. You will see a list of Mime types. Check this list against the list presented in the user's guide. If your mime types are correct, the installation is correct and complete.

2. Start the control panel applet by loading the /opt/NSCPcom/j2pi/ControlPanel.html file, which contains the Control Panel applet. If the Control Panel applet starts, the installation is correct and complete. The control panel applet lets you change the default settings used by Java Plug-In at startup. All applets running inside Java Plug-In use these settings.

You can also run the `Control Panel` as an application like this:

```
cd /opt/NSCPcom/j2pi
ControlPanel &
```

Install the HTML Converter

Your browser will not automatically use the Java Plug-In when you load an HTML file with an applet. You have to download and run the Java Plug-In HTML Converter on the HTML page that invokes the applet to direct the applet to run using the plug-in instead of the browser's default run time.

Unzip the Java Plug-In HTML Converter download:

```
unzip htmlconv12.zip
```

Add the `HTMLConverter.java` program or its directory to your `CLASSPATH`.

Security Policy File

In the Java 2 Platform, applets are restricted to a sandbox-like environment and need permission to access system resources outside their restricted environment. Applets are restricted to access operations within their local directory. All other access operations require permission.

Types of Policy Files.   You need a policy file to grant access permissions to the `Administration` applet. If the applet runs on a disk other than the disk where the browser is running, the applet will also need to be signed. See Signed Applets (Chapter 10) for information on signing and deploying applets.

There are three kinds of policy files: system, user, and program. The system policy file is located in `jdk1.2/jre/lib/security/java.policy` or `jre1.2/lib/security/java.policy` and contains permissions for everyone on the system.

The user policy file is located in the user's home directory. The user policy file provides a way to give certain users additional permissions over those granted to everyone on the system. The permissions in the system file are combined with the permissions in the user file.

A program policy file can be located anywhere. It is specifically named when an application is invoked with the `java` interpreter command or when an applet is invoked with applet viewer. When an application or applet is invoked with a specific policy file, the permissions in that policy file take the place of (are not combined with) permissions specified in the system or user policy file. Program policy files are used for program testing or intranet deployment of applets and applications.

Install the Policy File.   Place the security policy file in your home directory and name it .java.policy. When the applet tries to perform an action that requires a policy file with a permission, the policy file is loaded from this directory and remains in effect until you exit and restart the browser. If an applet tries to perform an access operation without the right permission, it quietly quits without raising either an applet or browser error.

Change the Name or Location.   You can change the name and/or location of the default system or user policy file. Edit the jdk1.2/jre/lib/security/ java.security or jre1.2/lib/security/java.security file and add a third entry specifying the name and location of an alternative policy file.

```
policy.url.1=file:${java.home}/lib/security/java.policy
policy.url.2=file:${user.home}/.java.policy
policy.url.3=file:/<mypolicyfile path and name>
```

Run the Administration Applet

Copy the JAR file with the Administration applet and policy file to its final location. In this example, that location is the /home/zelda/public_html directory. Next, extract the applet class file and policy file from the JAR file:

```
cp admin.jar /home/zelda/public_html/
jar xvf applet.jar
```

The extraction places the policy file under the public_html directory and creates an admin directory under the public_html directory with the applet class file in it. Make sure the policy file in the public_html directory is named .java.policy and copy it to your home directory.

In the public_html directory, create an HTML file that invokes the Administration applet class. Be sure to include the admin directory when you specify the applet class to the CODE option. Note that when using Java Plug-In, you cannot have the browser load the class file from the JAR file.

```
<HTML>
<BODY>
<APPLET CODE=admin/AdminApplet.class
  WIDTH=550
  HEIGHT=150>
</APPLET>
</BODY>
</HTML>
```

Start the HTML Converter.
```
java HTMLConverter
```

In the HTML Converter graphical user interface shown in Figure 9.2, select
One File, specify the path to the admin.html file, and click the Convert button. After the conversion completes, load the admin.html file in your browser.

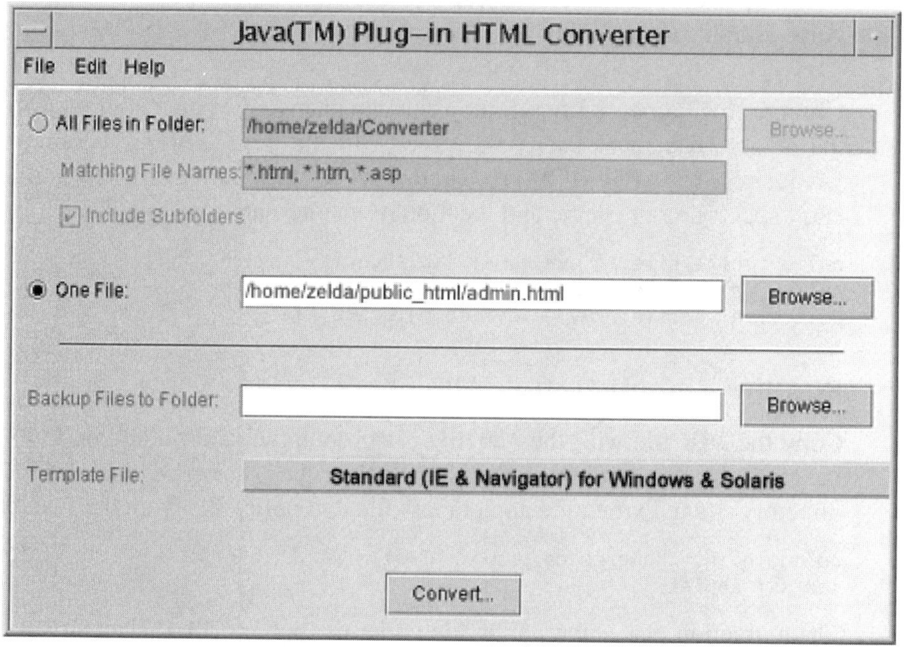

Figure 9.2 HTML Converter user interface

Deploy to Win32 Platform

On Win32 platforms, Java Plug-In software is bundled with the Java 2 Runtime
Environment. Java Plug-In lets Web browsers use the Java 2 Runtime Environment to run 1.2-based applets and JavaBeans components instead of the Web
browser's default virtual machine. The Java Plug-In works with Netscape Communicator and Microsoft Internet Explorer.

This section explains how to install Java Plug-In with Netscape Communicator
on the Win32 operating system.

Get Downloads

To install and use the Java Runtime Environment with Java Plug-In, you need
the following downloads. Put the downloads in a temporary directory.

- Java Runtime Environment with Java Plug-In for Win32 Platforms.
- Java Plug-In HTML Converter

Install JRE with Java Plug-In

An optionally installable version of the Java 2 Runtime Environment with Java Plug-In is included with the Java 2 SDK download. You can also download and install Java 2 Runtime Environment with Java Plug-In separately (`http://java.sun.com/products/jdk/1.2/jre/download-windows.html`).

Either way, install the Java 2 Runtime Environment with Java Plug-In by double-clicking its icon and following the installation instructions. When the installation completes, you will see the Java Plug-In control panel on your Windows `Start` menu under `Programs`.

Install the HTML Converter

Your browser will not automatically use the Java Plug-In when you load an HTML file with an applet. You have to download and run the Java Plug-In HTML Converter on the HTML page that invokes the applet to direct the applet ro run using the plug-in instead of the browser's default run time.

Unzip the Java Plug-In HTML Converter download:

```
unzip htmlconv12.zip
```

Add the `HTMLConverter.java` program or its directory to your `CLASSPATH`.

Security Policy File

In the Java 2 platform, applets are restricted to a sandbox-like environment and need permission to access system resources outside their restricted environment. Applets are restricted to resource access operations within their local directory. All other access operations require permission.

Types of Policy Files.   You need a policy file to grant access permissions to the `Administration` applet. If the applet runs on a disk other than the disk where the browser is running, the applet will also need to be signed. See Signed Applets (page 305) for information on signing and deploying applets.

There are three kinds of policy files: system, user, and program. The system policy file is located in `jdk1.2\jre\lib\security\java.policy` or `jre1.2\lib\security\java.policy` and contains permissions for everyone on the system.

The user policy file is located in the user's home directory. The user policy file provides a way to give certain users additional permissions over those granted to everyone on the system. The permissions in the system file are combined with the permissions in the user file.

A program policy file can be located anywhere. It is specifically named when an application is invoked with the `java` command or when an applet is invoked with applet viewer.

When an application or applet is invoked with a specific policy file, the permissions in that policy file take the place of (are not combined with) permissions specified in the system or user policy file. Program policy files are used for program testing or intranet deployment of applets and applications.

Install the Security Policy File.   Place the security policy file in your home directory and make sure it is named `java.policy`. When the applet tries to perform an action that requires a policy file with a permission, the policy file is loaded from this directory and remains in effect until you exit and restart the browser. If an applet tries to perform an access operation without the right permission, it quietly quits without raising either an applet or browser error.

Change the Name or Location.   You can change the name and/or location of the default system or user policy file. Edit the `jdk1.2\jre\lib\security\java.security` or `jre1.2\lib\security\java.security` file and add a third entry specifying the name and location of an alternative policy file.

```
policy.url.1=file:${java.home}\lib\security\java.policy
policy.url.2=file:${user.home}\java.policy
policy.url.3=file:\<mypolicyfile path and name>
```

NOTE   On Windows/NT machines, you might place the policy file in the `C:\Winnt\Profiles\<userid>\java.policy` directory.

Run the Administration Applet

Copy the JAR file with the `Administration` applet and policy file to its final location. In this example, that location is the `\home\zelda\public_html` directory. Next, extract the applet class file and policy file from the JAR file:

```
copy admin.jar \home\zelda\public_html jar xf applet.jar
```

The extraction places the policy file under `public_html` and creates an `admin` directory under the `public_html` directory with the applet class file in it. Rename the policy file in the `public_html` directory to `java.policy` and copy it to your home directory.

In the `public_html` directory, create an HTML file that invokes the `Administration` applet class. Be sure to include the `admin` directory when you specify the applet class to the CODE option. Note that when using Java Plug-In, you cannot have the browser load the class file from the JAR file.

```
<HTML>
<BODY>
<APPLET CODE=admin/AdminApplet.class
  WIDTH=550
  HEIGHT=150>
</APPLET>
</BODY>
</HTML>
```

Start the HTML Converter.

```
java HTMLConverter
```

In the HTML Converter graphical user interface shown in Figure 9.3, select `One File`, specify the path to the `admin.html` file, and click the `Convert` button. After the conversion completes, load the `admin.html` file in your browser.

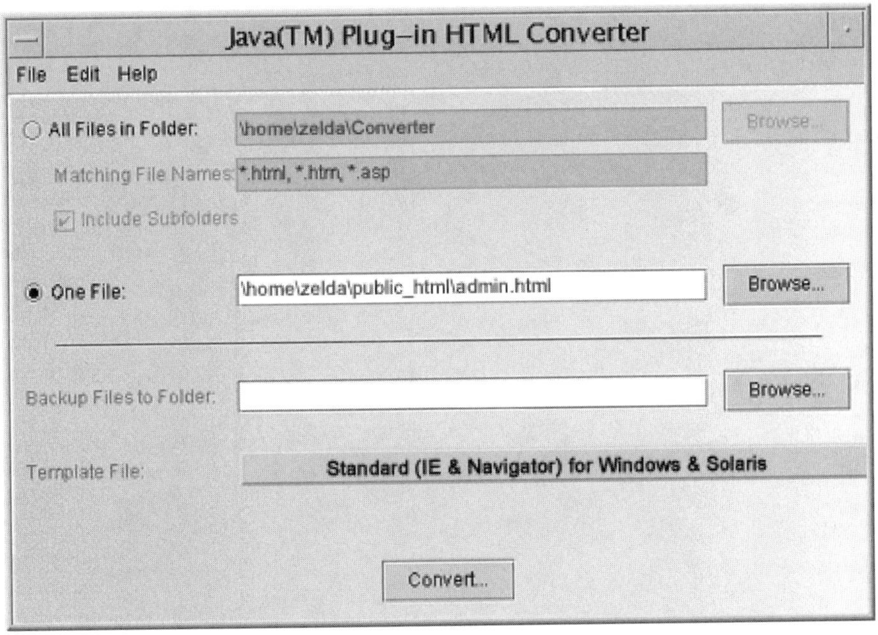

Figure 9.3 HTML Converter user interface

How Does It Work?

On Windows machines, the Java Plug-In finds the JRE by running the OLE custom control file `beans.ocx` installed by default in the `\Program Files\JavaSoft\1.2\bin` Web browser directory. The OLE control examines the Windows registry to find the Java Plug-In key and uses the value associated with that key to find the installed JRE.

If you find that the wrong JRE is being loaded, use `regedit` to check the Java Plug-In registry values for the current user. If no JRE is installed, the control checks the Java Plug-in values for `HKEY_LOCAL_MACHINE`. You should see a value for Java Runtime Environment under `Software\JavaSoft`.

10

Signed Applets and Security Managers

This chapter concludes the book with security topics you should find useful—signing applets and writing a security manager. The examples do not relate directly to the auction house, but are simple and targeted to illustrate these concepts.

Covered in this Chapter

Signed Applets

A policy file can be defined to require a signature on all applets or applications that attempt to run with the policy file. The signature is a way to verify that the applet or application is from a reliable source and can be trusted to run with the permissions granted in the policy file.

If a policy file requires a signature, an applet or application can get the access granted by the policy file only if it has the correct signature. If the applet or application has the wrong signature or no signature, it will not get access to the file.

This section walks through an example of signing an applet, verifying the signature, and running the applet with a policy file.

Signed Applet Example

The policy file granting access can be set up to require or not require a signature. If a signature is required, the applet has to be bundled into a JAR file before it can be signed. This example shows you how to sign and grant permission to an applet so it can create demo.ini in the user's home directory when it executes in Applet Viewer (Figure 10.1).

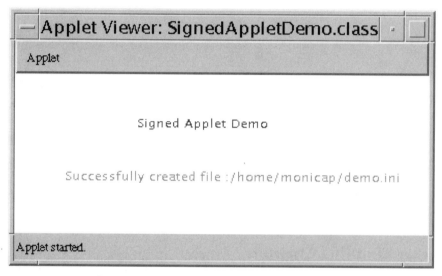

Figure 10.1 Signed applet

The following files are used in the example. You can copy them to or create them in your working directory.

SignedAppletDemo.   The SignedAppletDemo.java source file contains the applet code.

```
//File: @(#)SignedAppletDemo.java
//(#)author:  Satya Dodda
import java.applet.Applet;
import java.awt.Graphics;
import java.io.*;
import java.awt.Color;
public class SignedAppletDemo extends Applet {
    public String test() {
      setBackground(Color.white);
       String fileName = System.getProperty("user.home") +
```

```
            System.getProperty("file.separator") + "demo.ini";
        String msg  = "This message was written by a signed applet!!!\n";
        String s ;
        try {
          FileWriter fos = new FileWriter(fileName);
          fos.write(msg, 0, msg.length());
          fos.close();
          s = new String("Successfully created file :" + fileName);
        } catch (Exception e) {
          System.out.println("Exception e = " + e);
          e.printStackTrace();
          s = new String("Unable to create file :  " + fileName);
        }
      return s;
   }
    public void paint(Graphics g) {
        g.setColor(Color.blue);
        g.drawString("Signed Applet Demo", 120, 50);
        g.setColor(Color.magenta);
        g.drawString(test(), 50, 100);
    }
}
```

Policy File.   The `Write.jp` policy file grants access to the user's home directory.

```
/* AUTOMATICALLY GENERATED ON Mon Sep 14 09:55:03 PDT 1998*/
/* DO NOT EDIT */

keystore "raystore";

grant signedBy "susan" {
  permission java.util.PropertyPermission "user.home", "read";
  permission java.io.FilePermission "${user.home}/newfile", "write";
};
```

HTML file.   The `SignedApplet.html` file has the applet tag that loads the SignedAppletDemo applet.

How It Works.   Usually an applet is bundled and signed by an intranet developer and handed off to the end user who verifies the signature and runs the applet. In this example, the intranet developer performs Steps 1 through 5 and Ray, the end user, performs Steps 6 through 8. But, to keep things simple for this example, all steps occur in the same working directory.

1. Compile the applet

2. Create a JAR file

3. Generate keys

4. Sign the JAR file

5. Export the public key certificate

6. Import the certificate as a Trusted Certificate

7. Create the policy file

8. Run the applet

Intranet Developer

Susan, the intranet developer, bundles the applet executable in a JAR file, signs the JAR file, and exports the public key certificate.

1: Compile the Applet.   In her working directory, Susan uses the `javac` command to compile the `SignedAppletDemo` class. The output from the `javac` command is the `SignedAppletDemo.class`.

```
javac SignedAppletDemo.java
```

2: Make a JAR File.   Susan then stores the compiled `SignedApplet-Demo.class` file into a JAR file. The `cvf` option to the `jar` command creates a new archive (c), using verbose mode (v), and specifies the archive file name (f). The archive file name is `SignedApplet.jar`.

```
jar cvf SignedApplet.jar SignedAppletDemo.class
```

3: Generate Keys.   A JAR file is signed with the private key of the creator of the JAR file and the signature is verified by the recipient of the JAR file with the public key in the pair. The certificate is a statement from the owner of the private key that the public key in the pair has a particular value so the person using the public key can be assured the public key is authentic. Public and private keys must already exist in the keystore database before `jarsigner` can be used to sign or verify the signature on a JAR file.

Susan creates a keystore database named `compstore` that has an entry for a newly generated public and private key pair with the public key in a certificate, by using the `keytool` command. In her working directory, Susan creates a keystore database and generates the keys. Everything goes on one line.

```
keytool -genkey -alias signFiles -keystore compstore
        -keypass kpi135 -dname "cn=jones" -storepass ab987c
```

The above `keytool -genkey` command invocation generates a key pair that is identified by the alias `signFiles`. Subsequent `keytool` command invocations use this alias and the key password (`-keypass kpi135`) to access the private key in the generated pair.

The generated key pair is stored in a keystore database called `compstore` (`-keystore compstore`) in the current directory and accessed with the `compstore` password (`-storepass ab987c`).

The `-dname "cn=jones"` option specifies an X.500 Distinguished Name with a `commonName` (cn) value. X.500 Distinguished Names identify entities for X.509 certificates. In this example, Susan uses her last name, Jones, for the common name. She could use any common name that suits her purposes. You can view all `keytool` options and parameters by typing:

```
keytool -help
```

4: Sign the JAR File. JAR `Signer` is a command-line tool for signing and verifying the signature on JAR files. In her working directory, Susan uses `jarsigner` to make a signed copy of the `SignedApplet.jar` file.

```
jarsigner -keystore compstore -storepass ab987c -keypass kpi135
          -signedjar SSignedApplet.jar SignedApplet.jar signFiles
```

The `-storepass ab987c` and `-keystore compstore` options specify the keystore database and password where the private key for signing the JAR file is stored. The `-keypass kpi135` option is the password to the private key, `SSignedApplet.jar` is the name of the signed JAR file, and `signFiles` is the alias to the private key. The `jarsigner` command extracts the certificate from the keystore whose entry is `signFiles` and attaches it to the generated signature of the signed JAR file.

5: Export the Public Key Certificate. The public key certificate is sent with the JAR file to the end user who will be using the applet. That person uses the certificate to authenticate the signature on the JAR file. A certificate is sent by exporting it from the `compstore` database.

In her working directory, Susan uses `keytool` to copy the certificate from `compstore` to a file named `CompanyCer.cer` as follows:

```
keytool -export -keystore compstore -storepass ab987c -alias signFiles -
file CompanyCer.cer
```

As the last step, Susan posts the JAR and certificate files to a distribution directory on a Web page.

End User

Ray, the end user, downloads the JAR file from the distribution directory, imports the certificate, creates a policy file granting the applet access, and runs the applet.

6: Import the Certificate as a Trusted Certificate.   Ray downloads `SSignedApplet.jar` and `CompanyCer.cer` to his home directory. Ray must now create a keystore database (`raystore`) and import the certificate into it using the alias company. Ray uses `keytool` in his home directory to do this:

```
keytool -import -alias company -file CompanyCer.cer
                    -keystore raystore -storepass abcdefgh
```

7: Create the Policy File.   The policy file grants the `SSignedApplet.jar` file signed by the `alias` company permission to create `demo.ini` (and no other file) in the user's home directory.

Ray creates the policy file in his home directory using either `policytool` or an ASCII editor.

```
keystore "/home/ray/raystore";
//A sample policy file that lets a program
//create demo.ini in user's home directory
//Satya N Dodda
grant SignedBy "company"
{
   permission java.util.PropertyPermission "user.home", "read";
   permission java.io.FilePermission "${user.home}/demo.ini", "write";
};
```

8: Run the Applet in `Applet Viewer`.   The `Applet Viewer` tool connects to the HTML documents and resources specified in the call to the `appletviewer` command and displays the applet in its own window. To run the example, Ray copies the signed JAR file and HTML file to `/home/aURL/public_html` and invokes the `Applet Viewer` tool from his home directory as follows:

```
appletviewer -J-Djava.security.policy=Write.jp
  http://aURL.com/SignedApplet.html
```

NOTE   Type everything on one line and put a space after `Write.jp`.

The `-J-Djava.security.policy=Write.jp` option tells the `Applet Viewer` tool to run the applet referenced in the `SignedApplet.html` file with the `Write.jp` policy file.

NOTE   The policy file can be stored on a server and specified in the appletviewer invocation as an URL.

Running an Application with a Policy File

This application invocation restricts `MyProgram` to a sandbox-like environment the same way applets are restricted, but allows access as specified in the `pol-file` policy file.

```
java -Djava.security.manager -Djava.security.policy=polfile MyProgram
```

Signed Applets in JDK 1.1

JDK 1.1 signed applets can access local system resources if the local system is properly set up to allow it. See the JDK 1.1 Signed Applet Example page (`http://java.sun.com/security/signExample/index.html`) for details.

Writing a Security Manager

A security manager is a Java virtual machine object that implements a security policy. By default, the Java 2 Platform software provides a security manager that disallows all access to local system resources apart from the directory and its subdirectories where the program is invoked.

You can extend the default security manager to implement customized verifications and approvals for applets and applications, but the implementation must include the appropriate access verification code for every `check<type>` method you override. If you do not include this code, no access verification check happens, and your code breaches system security policy.

This section uses an example application to explain how to write a custom security manager that prompts the end user for password identification before reading from and writing to specific files. The implementation includes access verification code so once the end user makes it through the password check, he or she still needs the file read and write permissions in his or her policy file.

The example consists of the `FileIO` application, and the `PasswordSecurity-Manager` program that provides the custom security manager implementation.

The `FileIO` Program

The FileIO program displays a simple user interface and asks the end user to enter some text. When the end user clicks the `Click Me` button (see Figure 10.2), the text is saved to a file in the end user's home directory, and a second file is opened and read. The text read from the second file is displayed to the end user.

The custom security manager for this program prompts the end user to enter a password before it allows `FileIO` to write text to or read text from a file. The

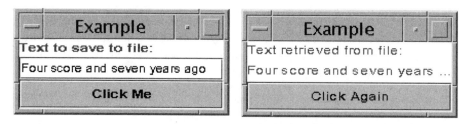

Figure 10.2 FileIO program before the button click (left) and after the button click (right)

main method of FileIO creates a custom security manager called PasswordSecurityManager.

```
import java.awt.Color;
import java.awt.BorderLayout;
import java.awt.event.*;
import javax.swing.*;
import java.io.*;

class FileIO extends JFrame implements ActionListener {
  JLabel text;
  JButton button;
  JPanel panel;
  JTextField textField;
  private boolean _clickMeMode = true;

  FileIO() { //Begin Constructor
    text = new JLabel("Text to save to file:");
    button = new JButton("Click Me");
    button.addActionListener(this);
    textField = new JTextField(20);
    panel = new JPanel();
    panel.setLayout(new BorderLayout());
    panel.setBackground(Color.white);
    getContentPane().add(panel);
    panel.add(BorderLayout.NORTH, text);
    panel.add(BorderLayout.CENTER, textField);
    panel.add(BorderLayout.SOUTH, button);
  } //End Constructor

  public void actionPerformed(ActionEvent event){
    Object source = event.getSource();
//The equals operator (==) is one of the few operators
//allowed on an object in the Java programming language
    if(source == button) {
      String s = null;
      //Write to file
      if (_clickMeMode){
        FileInputStream in=null
        FileOutputStream out=null;
        try {
```

```
          String text = textField.getText();
          byte b[] = text.getBytes();
          String outputFileName = System.getProperty("user.home",
                            File.separatorChar + "home" +
                            File.separatorChar + "zelda") +
                            File.separatorChar + "text.txt";
        out = new FileOutputStream(outputFileName);
        out.write(b);
      } catch(java.io.IOException e) {
        System.out.println("Cannot write to text.txt");
      }
    //Read from file
      try {
        String inputFileName = System.getProperty("user.home",
                          File.separatorChar + "home" +
                          File.separatorChar + "zelda") +
                          File.separatorChar + "text.txt";
        File inputFile = new File(inputFileName);
        in = new FileInputStream(inputFile);
        byte bt[] = new byte[(int)inputFileName.length()];
        in.read(bt);
        s = new String(bt);
      } catch(java.io.IOException e) {
        System.out.println("Cannot read from text.txt");
      } finally {
        try {
          in.close;
          out.close();
        } catch(Java.io.IOException e) {
          System.out.println("Cannot close");
        }
      }

    //Clear text field
      textField.setText("");
    //Display text read from file
      text.setText("Text retrieved from file:");
      button.setText("Click Again");
      _clickMeMode = false;
    } else {
//Save text to file
      text.setText("Text to save to file:");
      textField.setText("");
      button.setText("Click Me");
      _clickMeMode = true;
    }
   }
  }
  public static void main(String[] args){
    FileIO frame = new FileIO();
    frame.setTitle("Example");
    WindowListener l = new WindowAdapter() {
      public void windowClosing(WindowEvent e) {
        System.exit(0);
```

```
      }
    };
    frame.addWindowListener(l);
    frame.pack();
    frame.setVisible(true);
  }
}
```

The PasswordSecurityManager Class

The PasswordSecurityManager class declares two private instance variables, which are initialized by the constructor when the custom security manager is installed. The password instance variable contains the actual password, and the buffy instance variable is an input buffer that stores the end user's password input.

```
import java.io.*;
import java.security.AccessController;

public class PasswordSecurityManager extends SecurityManager {
  private String password;
  private BufferedReader buffy;
  public PasswordSecurityManager(String p, BufferedReader b) {
    super();
    this.password = p;
    this.buffy = b;
  }
  private boolean accessOK() {
    int c;
    String response;
    System.out.println("What's the secret password?");
    try {
      response = buffy.readLine();
      if(response.equals(password)) {
        return true;
      } else {
        return false;
      }
    } catch (IOException e) {
      return false;
    }
  }
  public void checkRead(String filename) {
//Mention file by name so don't get prompted for password
//for everything the application loads to create itself
    if((filename.equals(File.separatorChar +
        "home" + File.separatorChar + "monicap" + File.separatorChar +
                                        "text2.txt"))){
      if(!accessOK()){
        super.checkRead(filename);
        throw new SecurityException("No Way!");
      } else {
        FilePermission perm = new FilePermission(File.separatorChar +
                        "home" + File.separatorChar +
```

```
                              "monicap" + File.separatorChar +
                              "text2.txt", "read");
            checkPermission(perm);
        }
      }
    }
    public void checkWrite(String filename) {
  //Mention file by name so don't get prompted for password
  //for everything the application loads to create itself
      if((filename.equals(File.separatorChar + "home" +
                         File.separatorChar + "monicap"
                         + File.separatorChar + "text.txt"))){
        if(!accessOK()){
          super.checkWrite(filename);
          throw new SecurityException("No Way!");
        } else {
          FilePermission perm = new FilePermission(File.separatorChar +
                              "home" + File.separatorChar + "monicap" +
                              File.separatorChar + "text.txt" , "write");
          checkPermission(perm);
        }
      }
    }
  }
```

The accessOK method prompts the end user for a password, verifies the password, and returns true if the password is correct and false if it is not.

```
private boolean accessOK() {
  int c;
  String response;

  System.out.println("Password, please:");
  try {
    response = buffy.readLine();
    if (response.equals(password))
      return true;
    else
      return false;
  } catch (IOException e) {
    return false;
  }
}
```

Verify Access.   The SecurityManager parent class provides methods to verify file system read and write access. The checkRead and checkWrite methods each have a version that accepts a String and another version that accepts a file descriptor. This example overrides only the String versions to keep the example simple and because the FileIO program accesses directories and files as Strings.

```
//API Ref: void checkRead(String filename)
    public void checkRead(String filename) {
```

```
      if((filename.equals(File.separatorChar + "home" +
                       File.separatorChar + "monicap" +
                       File.separatorChar + "text2.txt"))){
    if(!accessOK()){
      super.checkRead(filename);
      throw new SecurityException("No Way!");
    } else {
      FilePermission perm = new FilePermission(
                       File.separatorChar + "home" +
                       File.separatorChar + "monicap" +
                       File.separatorChar + "text2.txt", "read");
                       checkPermission(perm);
      }
    }
  }
//API Ref: void checkWrite(String filename)
    public void checkWrite(String filename) {
      if((filename.equals(File.separatorChar + "home" +
                       File.separatorChar + "monicap" +
                       File.separatorChar + "text.txt"))){
      if(!accessOK()){
        super.checkWrite(filename);
        throw new SecurityException("No Way!");
      } else {
        FilePermission perm = new FilePermission(
                       File.separatorChar + "home" +
                       File.separatorChar + "monicap" +
                       File.separatorChar + "text.txt" , "write");
//API Ref: void checkPermission(Permission perm)
      checkPermission(perm);
      }
    }
  }
}
```

The checkWrite method is called before the end user input is written to the output file. This is because the FileOutputStream class calls SecurityManager.checkWrite first.

The custom implementation for SecurityManager.checkWrite tests for the pathname /home/monicap/text.txt, and, if true, prompts the end user for the password. If the password is correct, the checkWrite method performs the access check by creating an instance of the required permission and passing it to the SecurityManager.checkPermission method. This check will succeed if the security manager finds a system, user, or program policy file with the specified permission. Once the write operation completes, the end user is prompted for the password two more times. The first time is to read the /home/monicap directory, and the second time is to read the text2.txt file. An access check is performed before the read operation takes place.

Policy File. Here is the policy file the `FileIO` program needs for its read and write operations. It also grants permission to the custom security manager to access the event queue on behalf of the application and show the application window without the warning banner.

```
grant {
  permission java.io.FilePermission "${user.home}/text.txt", "write";
  permission java.util.PropertyPermission "user.home", "read";
  permission java.io.FilePermission "${user.home}/text2.txt", "read";
  permission java.awt.AWTPermission "accessEventQueue";
  permission java.awt.AWTPermission "showWindowWithoutWarningBanner";
};
```

Run the `FileIO` Program. Here is how to run the `FileIO` program with the policy file:

```
java -Djava.security.policy=polfile FileIO
```

Reference Information

Appendix A, Security and Permissions, describes the available permissions and explains the consequences of granting permissions. One way to use this information is to help you limit what permissions a given applet or application might need to successfully execute. Another way to use this information is to educate yourself on the ways in which a particular permission can be exploited by malicious code.

Appendix B, Classes, Methods, and Permissions, provides lists of Java 2 platform software methods that are implemented to perform security access checks, the permission each requires, and the `java.security.SecurityManager` method called to perform the access check. You can use this reference to write your own security manager implementations or when you implement abstract methods that perform security-related tasks.

Appendix C, Security Manager Methods, lists the permissions checked for by the `SecurityManager` methods.

A
Security and Permissions

All applets and any applications invoked with a security manager must be granted explicit permission to access local system resources apart from accessing the directory where the program is invoked and its subdirectories. The Java platform provides permissions to allow various levels of access to different types of local information. Because permissions let an applet or application override the default security policy, you should be very careful when you assign permissions to not create an opening for malicious code to attack your system.

This appendix describes the available permissions and explains how each permission can create an opening for malicious attacks. One way to use this information is to help you limit what permissions a given applet or application might need to successfully execute. Another way to use this information is to educate yourself on the ways in which a particular permission can be exploited by malicious code so you can take steps against that.

As a safeguard, never trust an unknown applet or application. Always check the code carefully against the information in this appendix to be sure you are not giving malicious code permission to cause serious problems on the local system.

Covered in this Appendix

Overview

Permissions are granted to a program with a policy file. A policy file contains permissions for specific access. A permission consists of the permission name, a target, and in some cases, a comma-separated list of actions.

For example, the following policy file entry specifies a `java.io.FilePermission` permission that grants `read` access (the action) to the `${user.home}/text2.txt` target.

```
grant {
  permission java.io.FilePermission "${user.home}/text2.txt", "read";
};
```

There is one policy file for the Java platform installation (system) and an optional policy file for each user. The system policy file is in `{java.home}/lib/security/java.policy`, and the user policy file is in each user's home directory. The system and user policy files are combined. So, for example, there could be a system policy file with very few permissions granted to all users on the system, and individual policy files granting additional permissions to certain users.

To run an application with the security manager and a policy file named `polfile` in the user's home directory, type:

```
java -Djava.security.main  -DJava.security.policy=polfile  FileIO
```

To run an applet in `appletviewer` with a policy file named `polfile` in the user's home directory, type:

```
appletviewer -J-Djava.security.policy=polfile fileIO.html
```

When running an applet in a browser, the browser looks for the user and system policy files to find the permissions the applet needs to access local system resources on behalf of the user who downloaded the applet.

Knowing Which Permissions

When you run an applet or invoke an application with a security manager that needs permissions, you will get a stack trace if you did not provide a policy file with all the needed permissions. The stack trace contains the information you need to add the permission to the policy file. If the program needs additional permissions, you will keep getting stack traces until all required permissions are added to the policy file. The only drawback to this approach is you have to try every possible code path in your application.

Another way to determine which permission your program needs is to browse Appendix B (Classes, Methods, and Permissions). This appendix tells you which Java 2 Platform software methods are prevented from executing without the listed permission. The information is also useful for developers who want to write their own security manager to customize the verifications and approvals needed in a program.

Here is a short example to show how to translate the first couple of lines in a stack trace to a policy file entry. The first line tells you access is denied. This means this stack trace was generated because the program tried to access a system resource without the proper permission. The second line means you need a java.net.SocketPermission that gives the program permission to connect to and resolve the host name for Internet Protocol (IP) address 129.144.176.176, port 1521.

```
java.security.AccessControlException: access denied
    (java.net.SocketPermission 129.144.176.176:1521 connect,resolve)
```

To turn this into a policy file entry, list the permission name, a target, and an action list as follows, where java.net.SocketPermission is the permission name, 129.144.176.176:1521 is the target, and connect,resolve is the action list.

```
grant {
permission java.net.SocketPermission  "129.144.176.176:1521", "connect,resolve";
};
```

AllPermission

java.security.AllPermission specifies all permissions in the system for all possible targets and actions. This permission should be used only during

testing because it grants permission to run with all security restrictions disabled
as if there were no security manager.

```
grant {
  permission java.security.AllPermission;
};
```

AWTPermission

`java.awt.AWTPermission` grants access to the following Abstract Window
Toolkit (AWT) targets. The possible targets are listed by name with no action
list.

```
grant {
  permission java.awt.AWTPermission "accessClipboard";
  permission java.awt.AWTPermission "accessEventQueue";
  permission java.awt.AWTPermission "showWindowWithoutWarningBanner";
};
```

accessClipboard: This target grants permission to post information to and
retrieve information from the AWT clipboard. Granting this permission could
allow malicious code to share potentially sensitive or confidential information.

accessEventQueue: This target grants permission to access the AWT event
queue. Granting this permission could allow malicious code to peek at and
remove existing events from the system, or post bogus events that could cause
the application or applet to perform malicious actions.

listenToAllAWTEvents: This target grants permission to listen to all AWT
events throughout the system. Granting this permission could allow malicious
code to read and exploit confidential user input such as passwords.

Each AWT event listener is called from within the context of that event queue's
`EventDispatchThread`, so if the `accessEventQueue` permission is also
enabled, malicious code could modify the contents of AWT event queues
throughout the system, which can cause the application or applet to perform
unintended and malicious actions.

readDisplayPixels: This target grants permission to read pixels back from
the display screen. Granting this permission could allow interfaces such as
`java.awt.Composite` that allow arbitrary code to examine pixels on the display to include malicious code that snoops on user activities.

showWindowWithoutWarningBanner: This target grants permission to display a window without also displaying a banner warning that the window was
created by an applet. Without this warning, an applet might pop up windows
without the user knowing they belong to an applet. This could be a problem in
environments in which users make security-sensitive decisions based on

whether the window belongs to an applet or an application. For example, disabling the banner warning might trick the end user into entering sensitive user name and password information.

FilePermission

`java.io.FilePermission` grants access to a file or directory. The targets consist of the target pathname and a comma-separated list of actions. This policy file grants `read`, `write`, `delete`, and `execute` permission to all files.

```
grant {
  permission java.io.FilePermission
        "<<ALL FILES>>", "read, write, delete, execute";
};
```

This policy file grants `read` and `write` permission to `text.txt` in the user's home directory.

```
grant {
  permission java.io.FilePermission
               "${user.home}/text.txt", "read, write";
};
```

You can use the following wild cards to specify the target pathname.

- A pathname that ends in /*, where /* is the file separator character and indicates a directory and all the files contained in that directory.
- A pathname that ends with /- indicates a directory, and recursively, all files and subdirectories contained in that directory.
- A pathname consisting of a single asterisk (*) indicates all files in the current directory.
- A pathname consisting of a single dash (-) indicates all files in the current directory, and recursively, all files and subdirectories contained in the current directory.

The actions are specified in a list of comma-separated keywords and have the following meanings:

- `read`: Permission to read a file or directory
- `write`: Permission to write to and create a file or directory
- `execute`: Permission to execute a file or search a directory
- `delete`: Permission to delete a file or directory

When granting file permissions, always think about the implications of granting read and especially write access to various files and directories. The <<ALL FILES>> permission with write action is especially dangerous because it grants permission to write to the entire file system. This means the system binary can be replaced, which includes the Java1 virtual machine run-time environment.

NetPermission

`java.net.NetPermission` grants access to various network targets. The possible targets are listed by name with no action list.

```
grant {   permission java.net.NetPermission "setDefaultAuthenticator";
   permission java.net.NetPermission "requestPasswordAuthentication"; };
```

setDefaultAuthenticator: This target grants permission to set the way authentication information is retrieved when a proxy or HTTP server asks for authentication. Granting this permission could mean malicious code can set an authenticator that monitors and steals user authentication input as it retrieves the input from the user.

requestPasswordAuthentication: This target grants permission to ask the authenticator registered with the system for a password. Granting this permission could mean malicious code might steal the password.

specifyStreamHandler: This target grants permission to specify a stream handler when constructing a URL. Granting this permission could mean malicious code might create a URL with resources to which it would not normally have access, or specify a stream handler that gets the actual bytes from somewhere to which it does have access. This means the malicious code could trick the system into creating a `ProtectionDomain/CodeSource` for a class even though the class really did not come from that location.

PropertyPermission

`java.util.PropertyPermission` grants access to system properties. The `java.util.Properties` class represents persistent settings such as the location of the installation directory, the user name, or the user's home directory.

```
grant {   permission java.util.PropertyPermission "java.home", "read";
   permission java.util.PropertyPermission "os.name", "write";  ·
   permission java.util.PropertyPermission "user.name", "read, write"; };
```

The target list contains the name of the property, for example, `java.home` or `os.name`. The naming convention for the properties follows the hierarchical property naming convention, and includes wild cards. An asterisk at the end of the property name, after a dot (.), or alone signifies a wild card match. For example, `java.*` or `*` are valid, but `*java` or `a*b` are invalid.

The actions are specified in a list of comma-separated keywords, and have the following meanings:

- `read`: Permission to read (`get`) a property
- `write`: Permission to write (`set`) a property

Granting property permissions can leave your system open to intrusion. For example, granting permission to access the `java.home` property makes the installation directory vulnerable to attack, and granting permission to access the `user.name` and `user.home` properties might reveal the user's account name and home directory to code that might misuse the information.

ReflectPermission

`java.lang.reflect.ReflectPermission` grants permission for various reflective operations. The possible targets are listed by name with no action list.

```
grant {
 permission java.lang.reflect.ReflectPermission "suppressAccessChecks";
};
```

suppressAccessChecks: This target grants permission to access fields and invoke methods in a class. This includes public, protected, and private fields and methods. Granting this permission could reveal confidential information and make normally unavailable methods accessible to malicious code.

RuntimePermission

`java.lang.RuntimePermission` grants access to various run-time targets such as the classloader, Java virtual machine, and thread. The possible targets are listed by name with no action list.

```
grant {
  permission java.lang.RuntimePermission "createClassLoader";
  permission java.lang.RuntimePermission "getClassLoader";
  permission java.lang.RuntimePermission "exitVM";
  permission java.lang.RuntimePermission "setFactory";
  permission java.lang.RuntimePermission "setIO";
  permission java.lang.RuntimePermission "modifyThread";
  permission java.lang.RuntimePermission "modifyThreadGroup";
  permission java.lang.RuntimePermission "getProtectionDomain";
  permission java.lang.RuntimePermission "setProtectionDomain";
  permission java.lang.RuntimePermission "readFileDescriptor";
  permission java.lang.RuntimePermission "writeFileDescriptor";
  permission java.lang.RuntimePermission "loadLibrary.<library name>";
  permission java.lang.RuntimePermission "accessClassInPackage.<package name>";
  permission java.lang.RuntimePermission "defineClassInPackage.<package name>";
```

```
    permission java.lang.RuntimePermission "accessDeclaredMembers.<class name>";
    permission java.lang.RuntimePermission "queuePrintJob";
};
```

The naming convention for target information where a library, package, or class name is added follows the hierarchical property naming convention, and includes wild cards. An asterisk at the end of the target name, after a dot (.), or alone signifies a wild card match. For example, loadLibrary.* or * are valid, but *loadLibrary or a*b are not.

createClassLoader: This target grants permission to create a classloader. Granting this permission might allow a malicious application to instantiate its own classloader and load harmful classes into the system. Once loaded, the class loader could place these classes into any protection domain and give them full permissions for that domain.

getClassLoader: This target grants permission to retrieve the classloader for the calling class. Granting this permission could enable malicious code to get the class loader for a particular class and load additional classes.

setContextClassLoader: This target grants permission to set the context classloader used by a thread. System code and extensions use the context class loader to look up resources that might not exist in the system classloader. Granting this permission allows code to change the context class loader that is used for a particular thread, including system threads. This can cause problems if the context class loader has malicious code.

setSecurityManager: This target grants permission to set or replace the security manager. The security manager is a class that allows applications to implement a security policy. Granting this permission could enable malicious code to install a less restrictive manager, and thereby bypass checks that would have been enforced by the original security manager.

createSecurityManager: This target grants permission to create a new security manager. Granting this permission could give malicious code access to protected and sensitive methods that might disclose information about other classes or the execution stack. It could also allow the introduction of a weakened security manager.

exitVM: This target grants permission to halt the Java virtual machine. Granting this permission could allow malicious code to mount a denial-of-service attack by automatically forcing the virtual machine to stop.

setFactory: This target grants permission to set the socket factory used by the ServerSocket or Socket class, or the stream handler factory used by the URL class. Granting this permission allows code to set the actual implementation for the socket, server socket, stream handler, or RMI socket factory. An attacker might set a faulty implementation that mangles the data stream.

setIO: This target grants permission to change the value of the `System.out`, `System.in`, and `System.err` standard system streams. Granting this permission could allow an attacker to change `System.in` to steal user input, or set `System.err` to a null output stream, which would hide any error messages sent to `System.err`.

modifyThread: This target grants permission to modify threads by calls to the `stop`, `suspend`, `resume`, `setPriority`, and `setName` methods in the `Thread` class. Granting this permission could allow an attacker to start or suspend any thread in the system.

stopThread: This target grants permission to stop threads. Granting this permission allows code to stop any thread in the system provided the code already has permission to access that thread. Malicious code could corrupt the system by killing existing threads.

modifyThreadGroup: This target grants permission to modify threads by calls to the `destroy`, `resume`, `setDaemon`, `setmaxPriority`, `stop`, and suspend methods of the `ThreadGroup` class. Granting this permission could allow an attacker to create thread groups and set their run priority.

getProtectionDomain: This target grants permission to retrieve the `ProtectionDomain` instance for a class. Granting this permission allows code to obtain policy information for that code source. Although obtaining policy information does not compromise the security of the system, it does give attackers additional information, such as local file names for example, to better aim an attack.

readFileDescriptor: This target grants permission to read file descriptors. Granting this permission allows code to read the particular file associated with the file descriptor; this ability is dangerous if the file contains confidential data.

writeFileDescriptor: This target grants permission to write file descriptors. Granting this permission allows code to write to the file associated with the descriptor, which is dangerous if the file descriptor points to a local file.

loadLibrary.{library name}: This target grants permission to dynamically link the specified library. Granting this permission could be dangerous because the security architecture is not designed to and does not extend to native code loaded by way of the `java.lang.System.loadLibrary` method.

accessClassInPackage.{package name}: This target grants permission to access the specified package by way of a classloader's `loadClass` method when that class loader calls the `SecurityManager.checkPack-`

ageAcesss method. Granting this permission gives code access to classes in packages to which it normally does not have access. Malicious code may use these classes to help in its attempt to compromise security in the system.

defineClassInPackage.{package name}: This target grants permission to define classes in the specified package by way of a classloader's defineClass method when that class loader calls the SecurityManager.checkPackageDefinition method. Granting this permission allows code to define a class in a particular package; this action can be dangerous because malicious code with this permission might define rogue classes in trusted packages like java.security or java.lang, for example.

accessDeclaredMembers: This target grants permission to access the declared members of a class. Granting this permission allows code to query a class for its public, protected, default (package), and private fields and methods. Although the code would have access to the private and protected field and method names, it would not have access to the private and protected field data and would not be able to invoke any private methods. Nevertheless, malicious code may use this information to better aim an attack. Additionally, malicious code might invoke any public methods or access public fields in the class; this action could be dangerous if the code would normally not be able to invoke those methods or access the fields because it cannot cast the object to the class or interface with those methods and fields.

queuePrintJob: This target grants permission to initiate a print job request. Granting this permission could allow code to print sensitive information to a printer or maliciously waste paper.

SecurityPermission

java.security.SecurityPermission grants access to various security configuration parameters. The possible targets are listed by name with no action list. Security permissions currently apply to methods called on the following objects:

- java.security.Policy, which represents the system security policy for applications.
- java.security.Security, which centralizes all security properties and common security methods. It manages providers.
- java.security.Provider, which represents an implementation of such things as security algorithms (DSA, RSA, MD5, or SHA-1) and key generation.
- java.security.Signer, which manages private keys. Even though Signer is deprecated, the related permissions are available for backward compatibility.

- `java.security.Identity`, which manages real-world objects such as people, companies, or organizations whose identities can be authenticated using their public keys.

```
grant {
  permission java.security.SecurityPermission "getPolicy";
  permission java.security.SecurityPermission "setPolicy";
  permission java.security.SecurityPermission "getProperty.os.name";
  permission java.security.SecurityPermission "setProperty.os.name";
  permission java.security.SecurityPermission "insertProvider.SUN";
  permission java.security.SecurityPermission "removeProvider.SUN";
  permission java.security.SecurityPermission "setSystemScope";
  permission java.security.SecurityPermission "setIdentityPublicKey";
  permission java.security.SecurityPermission "setIdentityInfo";
  permission java.security.SecurityPermission "addIdentityCertificate";
  permission java.security.SecurityPermission "removeIdentityCertificate";
  permission java.security.SecurityPermission "clearProviderProperties.SUN";
  permission java.security.SecurityPermission
                        "putProviderProperty.<provider name>";
  permission java.security.SecurityPermission "removeProviderProperty.SUN";
  permission java.security.SecurityPermission "getSignerPrivateKey";
  permission java.security.SecurityPermission "setSignerKeyPair";
};
```

getPolicy: This target grants permission to retrieve the system-wide security policy. Granting this permission discloses which permissions would be granted to a given application or applet. Although revealing the policy does not compromise the security of the system, it does provide malicious code with additional information that it could use to better aim an attack.

setPolicy: This target grants permission to set the system-wide security policy. Granting this permission could allow malicious code to grant itself all the necessary permissions to successfully mount an attack on the system.

getProperty.{key}: This target grants permission to retrieve the security property specified by {key}. Depending on the particular key for which access has been granted, the code may have access to the list of security providers and the location of the system-wide and user security policies. Although revealing this information does not compromise the security of the system, it does provide malicious code with additional information that it may use to better aim an attack.

setProperty.{key}: This target grants permission to set the security property specified by {key}. This could include setting a security provider or defining the location of the system-wide security policy. Malicious code that has permission to set a new security provider may set a rogue provider that steals confidential information such as cryptographic private keys. In addition, malicious code with permission to set the location of the system-wide security policy may point it to a security policy that grants the attacker all the necessary permissions it requires to successfully mount an attack on the system.

insertProvider.{provider name}: This target grants permission to add the new security provider specified by {provider name}. Granting this permission allows the introduction of a possibly malicious provider that could do such things as disclose the private keys passed to it. This is possible because the Security object, which manages the installed providers, does not currently check the integrity or authenticity of a provider before attaching it.

removeProvider.{provider name}: This target grants permission to remove the provider specified by {provider name}. Granting this permission could change the behavior or disable execution of other parts of the program. If a provider requested by the program has been removed, execution might fail.

setSystemScope: This target grants permission to set the system identity scope. Granting this permission could allow an attacker to configure the system identity scope with certificates that should not be trusted. This could grant code signed with those certificates privileges that would be denied by the original identity scope.

setIdentityPublicKey: This target grants permission to set the public key for an Identity object. If the identity is marked trusted, this allows an attacker to introduce its own public key that is not trusted by the system's identity scope. This could grant code signed with that same public key privileges that would be otherwise denied.

SetIdentityInfo: This target grants permission to set a general information string for an Identity object. Granting this permission allows attackers to set the general description for an identity. Doing so could trick applications into using a different identity than intended or prevent applications from finding a particular identity.

addIdentityCertificate: This target grants permission to add a certificate for an Identity object. Granting this permission allows attackers to set a certificate for an identity's public key making the public key trusted to a wider audience than originally intended.

removeIdentityCertificate: This target grants permission to remove a certificate for an Identity object. Granting this permission allows attackers to remove a certificate for an identity's public key. This could be dangerous because the public key suddenly becomes considered less trustworthy than it otherwise would be.

printIdentity: This target grants permission to print out the name of a principal, the scope in which the principal is used, and whether the principal is considered trusted in that scope. The printed scope could be a file name, in which case it might convey local system information. For example, here is a sample printout of an identity named `carol`, who is marked not trusted in the user's identity database:

`carol[/home/luehe/identitydb.obj][not trusted].`

`clearProviderProperties.{provider name}`: This target grants permission to clear a `Provider` object so that it no longer contains the properties used to look up services implemented by the provider. Granting this permission disables the lookup of services implemented by the provider. This could change the behavior or disable execution of other parts of the program that would normally utilize the `Provider`, as described under the `removeProvider.{provider name}` permission above.

`putProviderProperty.{provider name}`: This target grants permission to set properties for the specified provider. The provider properties each specify the name and location of a particular service implemented by the provider. Granting this permission allows code to replace the service specification with another one with a different implementation and could be dangerous if the new implementation has malicious code.

`removeProviderProperty.{provider name}`: This target grants permission to remove properties from the specified provider. Granting this permission disables the lookup of services implemented by the provider, making them inaccessible. Granting this permission to malicious code could allow the malicious code to change the behavior or disable execution of other parts of the program that would normally utilize the `Provider` object, as described under the `removeProvider.{provider name}` permission above.

`getSignerPrivateKey`: This target grants permission to retrieve the private key of a `Signer` object. Private keys should always be kept secret. Granting this permission could allow malicious code to use the private key to sign files and claim the signature came from the `Signer` object.

`setSignerKeyPair`: This target grants permission to set the public and private key pair for a `Signer` object. Granting this permission could allow an attacker to replace the target's key pair with a possibly weaker (smaller) key pair. This would also allow an attacker to listen in on encrypted communication between the target and its peers. The target's peers might wrap an encryption session key under the target's new public key, which would allow the attacker (who possesses the corresponding private key) to unwrap the session key and decipher the communication data encrypted under that session key.

SerializablePermission

`java.io.SerializablePermission` grants access to serialization operations. The possible targets are listed by name with no action list.

```
grant {
  permission java.io.SerializablePermission "enableSubclassImplementation";
  permission java.io.SerializablePermission "enableSubstitution";
};
```

enableSubclassImplementation: This target grants permission to implement a subclass of `ObjectOutputStream` or `ObjectInputStream` to override the default serialization or deserialization of objects. Granting this permission could allow code to use this to serialize or deserialize classes in a malicious way. For example, during serialization, malicious code could store confidential private field data in a way easily accessible to attackers; or, during deserialization malicious code could deserialize a class with all its private fields zeroed out.

enableSubstitution: This target grants permission to substitute one object for another during serialization or deserialization. Granting this permission could allow malicious code to replace the actual object with one that has incorrect or malignant data.

SocketPermission

The `java.net.SocketPermission` permission grants access to a network by way of sockets. The target is a host name and port address, and the action list specifies ways to connect to that host. Possible connections are `accept`, `connect`, `listen`, and `resolve`.

This policy file entry allows a connection to and accepts connections on port 7777 on the host `puffin.eng.sun.com`.

```
grant {
  permission java.net.SocketPermission
                "puffin.eng.sun.com:7777","connect, accept";
};
```

This policy file entry allows connections to, accepts connections on, and listens on any port between 1024 and 65535 on the local host.

```
grant {
  permission java.net.SocketPermission
                "localhost:1024-","accept, connect, listen";
};
```

The host is expressed with the following syntax as a DNS name, as a numerical IP address, or as `localhost` (for the local machine). The asterisk (*) wild card

can be included once in a DNS name host specification. If included, it must be
in the leftmost position, as in `*.sun.com`.

```
host = (hostname | IPaddress)[:portrange]
portrange = portnumber | -portnumber | portnumber-[portnumber]
```

The port or port range is optional. A port specification of the form N-, where N
is a port number, means all ports numbered N and above, while a specification
of the form -N indicates all ports numbered N and below.

The `listen` action is only meaningful when used with localhost, and the
`resolve` (`resolve host/ip` name service lookups) action is implied when
any of the other actions are present.

Granting code permission to accept or make connections to remote hosts may
be dangerous because malevolent code can more easily transfer and share
confidential data among parties that might not otherwise have access to the
data.

NOTE   On Unix platforms, only root is normally allowed access
to ports lower than 1024.

B

Classes, Methods, and Permissions

A number of Java 2 Platform methods are implemented to verify access permissions. This means that before they execute, they verify that the system, user, or program has a policy file with the required permissions for execution to continue. If no such permission is found, execution stops with an error condition.

The access verification code passes the required permissions to the security manager, and the security manager checks that permission against the policy file permissions to determine whether to allow access. This means that Java 2 Platform API methods are associated with specific permissions, and specific permissions are associated with specific `java.security.SecurityManager` methods.

This appendix lists the Java 2 Platform methods, the permission associated with each method, and the `java.security.SecurityManager` method called to verify the existence of that permission. You need this information when you implement certain abstract methods or create your own security manager so you can include access verification code to keep your implementations in line with Java 2 Platform security policy. If you do not include access verification code, your implementations will bypass the built-in Java 2 Platform security checks.

Covered in this Appendix

java.awt.Graphics2D

```
public abstract void setComposite(Composite comp)
java.Security.SecurityManager.checkPermission
java.awt.AWTPermission "readDisplayPixels"
```

The access verification code for setComposite should call java.Security.SecurityManager.checkPermission and pass it java.awt.AWTPermission "readDisplayPixels" when a Graphics2D context draws to a Component on the display screen and the Composite is a custom object rather than an AlphaComposite object.

java.awt.Toolkit

```
public void addAWTEventListener(AWTEventListener listener, long eventMask)
public void removeAWTEventListener(AWTEventListener listener)
checkPermission
java.awt.AWTPermission "listenToAllAWTEvents"
public abstract PrintJob getPrintJob(Frame frame, String jobtitle,
                                      Properties props)
checkPrintJobAccess
java.lang.RuntimePermission "queuePrintJob"
public abstract Clipboard getSystemClipboard()
checkSystemClipboardAccess
java.awt.AWTPermission "accessClipboard"
public final EventQueue getSystemEventQueue()
checkAwtEventQueueAccess
java.awt.AWTPermission "accessEventQueue"
```

java.awt.Window

```
Window()
checkTopLevelWindow
java.awt.AWTPermission "showWindowWithoutWarningBanner"
```

java.beans.Beans

```
public static void setDesignTime(boolean isDesignTime)
public static void setGuiAvailable(boolean isGuiAvailable)
checkPropertiesAccess
java.util.PropertyPermissions "*", "read,write"
```

java.beans.Introspector

```
public static synchronized void setBeanInfoSearchPath(String path[])
checkPropertiesAccess
java.util.PropertyPermissions "*", "read,write"
```

java.beans.PropertyEditorManager

```
public static void registerEditor(Class targetType, Class editorClass)
public static synchronized void setEditorSearchPath(String path[])
checkPropertiesAccess
java.util.PropertyPermissions "*", "read,write"
```

java.io.File

```
public boolean delete()
public void deleteOnExit()
checkDelete(String)
java.io.FilePermission "{name}", "delete"
public boolean exists()
public boolean canRead()
public boolean isFile()
public boolean isDirectory()
public boolean isHidden()
public long lastModified()
public long length()
public String[] list()
public String[] list(FilenameFilter filter)
public File[] listFiles()
public File[] listFiles(FilenameFilter filter)
public File[] listFiles(FileFilter filter)
checkRead(String)
java.io.FilePermission "{name}", "read"
public boolean canWrite()
public boolean createNewFile()
public static File createTempFile(String prefix, String suffix)
public static File createTempFile(String prefix, String suffix,File directory)
public boolean mkdir()
public boolean mkdirs()
public boolean renameTo(File dest)
public boolean setLastModified(long time)
public boolean setReadOnly()
checkWrite(String)
java.io.FilePermission "{name}", "write"
```

java.io.FileInputStream

```
FileInputStream(FileDescriptor fdObj)
checkRead(FileDescriptor)
java.lang.RuntimePermission "readFileDescriptor"
FileInputStream(String name)
FileInputStream(File file)
checkRead(String)
java.io.FilePermission "{name}", "read"
```

java.io.FileOutputStream

```
FileOutputStream(FileDescriptor fdObj)
checkWrite(FileDescriptor)
java.lang.RuntimePermission "writeFileDescriptor"
FileOutputStream(File file)
FileOutputStream(String name)
FileOutputStream(String name, boolean append)
checkWrite(String)
java.io.FilePermission "{name}", "write"
```

java.io.ObjectInputStream

```
protected final boolean enableResolveObject(boolean enable);
checkPermission
java.io.SerializablePermission "enableSubstitution"
protected ObjectInputStream()
protected ObjectOutputStream()
checkPermission
java.io.SerializablePermission "enableSubclassImplementation"
```

java.io.ObjectOutputStream

```
protected final boolean enableReplaceObject(boolean enable)
checkPermission
java.io.SerializablePermission "enableSubstitution"
```

java.io.RandomAccessFile

```
RandomAccessFile(String name, String mode)
RandomAccessFile(File file, String mode)
checkRead(String)
java.io.FilePermission "{name}", "read"
```

In both these constructors the mode is read.

```
RandomAccessFile(String name, String mode)
checkRead(String) and checkWrite(String)
java.io.FilePermission "{name}", "read,write"
```

In this constructor the mode is read-write.

java.lang.Class

```
public static Class forName(String name, boolean initialize, ClassLoader loader)
checkPermission
java.lang.RuntimePermission("getClassLoader")
```

The access verification code for this method calls checkPermission and passes it `java.lang.RuntimePermission("getClassLoader")` when loader is null and the caller's classloader is not null.

```
public Class[] getClasses()
checkMemberAccess(this, Member.DECLARED)
java.lang.RuntimePermission "accessDeclaredMembers"
java.lang.RuntimePermission "accessClassInPackage.{pkgName}
```

The access verification code for this class and each of its superclasses calls `checkMemberAccess(this, Member.DECLARED)`. If the class is in a package, `checkPackageAccess({pkgName})` is also called. By default, `checkMemberAccess` does not require permission if this class's classloader is the same as that of the caller. Otherwise, it requires `java.lang.RuntimePermission "accessDeclaredMembers"`. If the class is in a package, `java.lang.RuntimePermission "accessClassInPackage.{pkgName}"` is also required.

```
public ClassLoader getClassLoader()
checkPermission
java.lang.RuntimePermission "getClassLoader"
```

If the caller's class loader is null, or is the same as or an ancestor of the classloader for the class whose classloader is being requested, no permission is needed. Otherwise, `java.lang.RuntimePermission "getClassLoader"` is required.

```
public Class[] getDeclaredClasses()
public Field[] getDeclaredFields()
public Method[] getDeclaredMethods()
public Constructor[] getDeclaredConstructors()
public Field getDeclaredField(String name)
public Method getDeclaredMethod(...)
public Constructor getDeclaredConstructor(...)
checkMemberAccess(this, Member.DECLARED)
checkPackageAccess({pkgName})
java.lang.RuntimePermission "accessDeclaredMembers"
java.lang.RuntimePermission "accessClassInPackage.{pkgName}"
```

If Class is in a package, the access verification code should call `checkPackageAccess({pkgName})` and pass it `java.lang.RuntimePermission "accessClassInPackage.{pkgName}"`.

If Class is not in a package, the access verification code for these methods should call `checkMemberAccess(this, Member.DECLARED)` and pass it `java.lang.RuntimePermission "accessClassInPackage.{pkgName}"`.

```
public Field[] getFields()
public Method[] getMethods()
public Constructor[] getConstructors()
public Field getField(String name)
public Method getMethod(...)
public Constructor getConstructor(...)
checkMemberAccess(this, Member.PUBLIC)
checkPackageAccess({pkgName})
java.lang.RuntimePermission "accessClassInPackage.{pkgName}"
```

If Class is not in a package, the access verification code for these methods calls checkMemberAccess(this, Member.PUBLIC), but no permission is passed.

If Class is in a package, the access verification code for these methods should call checkPackageAccess({pkgName}) and pass it checkPackageAccess({pkgName}).

```
public ProtectionDomain getProtectionDomain()
checkPermission
java.lang.RuntimePermission "getProtectionDomain"
```

java.lang.ClassLoader

```
ClassLoader()
ClassLoader(ClassLoader parent)
checkCreateClassLoader
java.lang.RuntimePermission "createClassLoader"
public static ClassLoader getSystemClassLoader()
public ClassLoader getParent()
checkPermission
java.lang.RuntimePermission "getClassLoader"
```

If the caller's class loader is null or is the same as or an ancestor of the class loader for the class whose classloader is being requested, no permission is needed. Otherwise, java.lang.RuntimePermission "getClassLoader" is required.

java.lang.Runtime

```
public Process exec(String command)
public Process exec(String command, String envp[])
public Process exec(String cmdarray[])
public Process exec(String cmdarray[], String envp[])
checkExec
java.io.FilePermission "{command}", "execute"
public void exit(int status)
public static void runFinalizersOnExit(boolean value)
checkExit(status) where status is 0 for runFinalizersOnExit
java.lang.RuntimePermission "exitVM"
public void load(String lib)
public void loadLibrary(String lib)
```

```
checkLink({libName})
java.lang.RuntimePermission "loadLibrary.{libName}"
```

In these methods {libName} is the lib, filename or libname argument.

java.lang.SecurityManager

```
<all methods>
checkPermission
See Security Manager Methods (page 351).
```

java.lang.System

```
public static void exit(int status)
public static void runFinalizersOnExit(boolean value)
checkExit(status) where status is 0 for runFinalizersOnExit
java.lang.RuntimePermission "exitVM"
public static void load(String filename)
public static void loadLibrary(String libname)
checkLink({libName})
java.lang.RuntimePermission "loadLibrary.{libName}"
```

In these methods {libName} is the lib, filename, or libname argument.

```
public static Properties getProperties()
public static void setProperties(Properties props)
checkPropertiesAccess
java.util.PropertyPermission "*", "read,write"
public static String getProperty(String key)
public static String getProperty(String key, String def)
checkPropertyAccess
java.util.PropertyPermission "{key}", "read"
public static void setIn(InputStream in)
public static void setOut(PrintStream out)
public static void setErr(PrintStream err)
checkPermission
java.lang.RuntimePermission "setIO"
public static String setProperty(String key, String value)
checkPermission
java.util.PropertyPermission "{key}", "write"
public static synchronized void setSecurityManager(SecurityManager s)
checkPermission
java.lang.RuntimePermission "setSecurityManager"
```

java.lang.Thread

```
public ClassLoader getContextClassLoader()
checkPermission
java.lang.RuntimePermission "getClassLoader"
```

If the caller's class loader is null or is the same as or an ancestor of the context class loader for the thread whose context class loader is being requested, no permission is needed. Otherwise, java.lang.RuntimePermission "get-ClassLoader" is required.

```
public void setContextClassLoader(ClassLoader cl)
checkPermission
java.lang.RuntimePermission "setContextClassLoader"
public final void checkAccess()
public void interrupt()
public final void suspend()
public final void resume()
public final void setPriority(int newPriority)
public final void setName(String name)
public final void setDaemon(boolean on)
checkAccess(this)
java.lang.RuntimePermission "modifyThread"
public static int enumerate(Thread tarray[])
checkAccess({threadGroup})
java.lang.RuntimePermission "modifyThreadGroup"
public final void stop()
checkAccess(this).
checkPermission
java.lang.RuntimePermission "modifyThread"
java.lang.RuntimePermission "stopThread"
```

The access verification code should call checkAccess and pass it java.lang.RuntimePermission "modifyThread", unless the current thread is trying to stop a thread other than itself. In this case, the access verification code should call checkPermission and pass it java.lang.RuntimePermission "stopThread".

```
public final synchronized void stop(Throwable obj)
checkAccess(this).
checkPermission
java.lang.RuntimePermission "modifyThread"
java.lang.RuntimePermission "stopThread"
```

The access verification code should call checkAccess and pass it java.lang.RuntimePermission "modifyThread" unless the current thread is trying to stop a thread other than itself or obj is not an instance of Thread-Death. In this case, the access verification code should call checkPermission and pass it java.lang.RuntimePermission "stopThread".

```
Thread()
Thread(Runnable target)
Thread(String name)
Thread(Runnable target, String name)
checkAccess({parentThreadGroup})
java.lang.RuntimePermission "modifyThreadGroup"
Thread(ThreadGroup group, ...)
checkAccess(this) for ThreadGroup methods, or
checkAccess(group) for Thread methods
java.lang.RuntimePermission "modifyThreadGroup"
```

java.lang.ThreadGroup

```
public final void checkAccess()
public int enumerate(Thread list[])
public int enumerate(Thread list[],boolean recurse)
public int enumerate(ThreadGroup list[])
public int enumerate(ThreadGroup list[],boolean recurse)
public final ThreadGroup getParent()
public final void setDaemon(boolean daemon)
public final void setMaxPriority(int pri)
public final void suspend()
public final void resume()
public final void destroy()
checkAccess(this) for ThreadGroup methods, or
checkAccess(group) for Thread methods
java.lang.RuntimePermission "modifyThreadGroup"
ThreadGroup(String name)
ThreadGroup(ThreadGroup parent,
String name)
checkAccess({parentThreadGroup})
java.lang.RuntimePermission "modifyThreadGroup"
public final void interrupt()
checkAccess(this)
java.lang.RuntimePermission "modifyThreadGroup"
java.lang.RuntimePermission "modifyThread"
```

The access verification code for this method also requires java.lang.Runtime-Permission "modifyThread" because the java.lang.Thread interrupt() method is called for each thread in the thread group and in all of its subgroups.

```
public final void stop()
checkAccess(this)
java.lang.RuntimePermission "modifyThreadGroup"
java.lang.RuntimePermission "modifyThread"
java.lang.RuntimePermission "stopThread"
```

The access verification code for this method also requires java.lang.Runt-imePermission "modifyThread" and possibly java.lang.RuntimePermis-sion "stopThread" because the java.lang.Thread stop() method is called for each thread in the thread group and in all of its subgroups.

java.lang.reflect.AccessibleObject

```
public static void setAccessible(...)
public void setAccessible(...)
checkPermission
java.lang.reflect.ReflectPermission "suppressAccessChecks"
```

java.net.Authenticator

```
public static PasswordAuthentication
requestPasswordAuthentication(InetAddress addr,int port,
        String protocol, String prompt, String scheme)
checkPermission
```

```
java.net.NetPermission "requestPasswordAuthentication"
public static void setDefault(Authenticator a)
checkPermission
java.net.NetPermission "setDefaultAuthenticator"
```

java.net.DatagramSocket

```
public void send(DatagramPacket p)
checkMulticast(p.getAddress())
checkConnect(p.getAddress().getHostAddress(), p.getPort())
java.net.SocketPermission((p.getAddress()).getHostAddress(), "accept,connect")
java.net.SocketPermission "{host}","resolve"
```

The access verification code for send calls checkMulticast in the following case:

```
if(p.getAddress().isMulticastAddress()) {
  java.net.SocketPermission((p.getAddress()).getHostAddress(),"accept,connect")
}
```

The access verification code for send calls checkConnect in the following case:

```
else {
  port = p.getPort();
  host = p.getAddress().getHostAddress();
  if (port == -1) {
    java.net.SocketPermission
            "{host}","resolve";
} else {
  java.net.SocketPermission
  "{host}:{port}","connect"
}
public InetAddress getLocalAddress()
checkConnect({host}, -1)
java.net.SocketPermission "{host}", "resolve"
DatagramSocket(...)
checkListen({port})
```

The access verification code for this method calls checkListen and passes in socket permissions as follows:

```
if (port == 0){
  java.net.SocketPermission "localhost:1024-", "listen";
} else {
  java.net.SocketPermission "localhost:{port}", "listen";
}
public synchronized void receive(DatagramPacket p)
checkAccept({host}, {port})
java.net.SocketPermission "{host}:{port}", "accept"
```

java.net.HttpURLConnection

```
public static void setFollowRedirects(boolean set)
checkSetFactory
java.lang.RuntimePermission "setFactory"
```

java.net.InetAddress

```
public String getHostName()
public static InetAddress[] getAllByName(String host)
public static InetAddress getLocalHost()
checkConnect({host}, -1)
java.net.SocketPermission "{host}", "resolve"
```

java.net.MulticastSocket

```
public void joinGroup(InetAddress mcastaddr)
public void leaveGroup(InetAddress mcastaddr)
checkMulticast(InetAddress)
java.net.SocketPermission(mcastaddr.getHostAddress(),"accept,connect")
public synchronized void send(DatagramPacket p, byte ttl)
checkMulticast(p.getAddress(), ttl)
checkConnect(p.getAddress().getHostAddress(), p.getPort())
java.net.SocketPermission((p.getAddress()).getHostAddress(),"accept,connect")
java.net.SocketPermission "{host}","resolve"
```

The access verification code for send calls checkMulticast in the following case:

```
if(p.getAddress().isMulticastAddress()) {
  java.net.SocketPermission((p.getAddress()).getHostAddress(), "accept,connect")
}
```

The access verification code for this method calls checkConnect in the following case:

```
} else {
  port = p.getPort();
  host = p.getAddress().getHostAddress();
  if (port == -1) {
     java.net.SocketPermission "{host}","resolve"
  } else {
     java.net.SocketPermission "{host}:{port}","connect"
}
MulticastSocket(...)
checkListen({port})
```

The access verification code for this method calls checkListen in the following case:

```
if (port == 0) {
  java.net.SocketPermission "localhost:1024-", "listen";
} else {
  java.net.SocketPermission "localhost:{port}","listen";
}
```

java.net.ServerSocket

```
ServerSocket(...)
checkListen({port})
```

The access verification code for this method calls `checkListen` in the following case:

```
if (port == 0) {
  java.net.SocketPermission "localhost:1024-","listen";
} else {
  java.net.SocketPermission "localhost:{port}","listen";
}
public Socket accept()
protected final void implAccept(Socket s)
checkAccept({host}, {port})
java.net.SocketPermission "{host}:{port}", "accept"
public static synchronized void setSocketFactory(...)
checkSetFactory
java.lang.RuntimePermission "setFactory"
```

java.net.Socket

```
public static synchronized void setSocketImplFactory(...)
checkSetFactory
java.lang.RuntimePermission "setFactory"
Socket(...)
checkConnect({host}, {port})
java.net.SocketPermission "{host}:{port}", "connect"
```

java.net.URL

```
public static synchronized void setURLStreamHandlerFactory(...)
checkSetFactory
java.lang.RuntimePermission "setFactory"
URL(...)
checkPermission
java.net.NetPermission "specifyStreamHandler"
```

java.net.URLConnection

```
public static synchronized void setContentHandlerFactory(...)
public static void setFileNameMap(FileNameMap map)
checkSetFactory
java.lang.RuntimePermission "setFactory"
```

java.net.URLClassLoader

```
URLClassLoader(...)
checkCreateClassLoader
java.lang.RuntimePermission "createClassLoader"
```

java.rmi.activation.ActivationGroup

```
public static synchronized ActivationGroup createGroup(...)
public static synchronized void setSystem(ActivationSystem system)
checkSetFactory
java.lang.RuntimePermission "setFactory"
```

java.rmi.server.RMISocketFactory

```
public synchronized static void setSocketFactory(...)
checkSetFactory
java.lang.RuntimePermission "setFactory"
```

java.security.Identity

```
public void addCertificate(...)
checkSecurityAccess("addIdentityCertificate")
java.security.SecurityPermission "addIdentityCertificate"
public void removeCertificate(...)
checkSecurityAccess("removeIdentityCertificate")
java.security.SecurityPermission "removeIdentityCertificate"
public void setInfo(String info)
checkSecurityAccess("setIdentityInfo")
java.security.SecurityPermission "setIdentityInfo"
public void setPublicKey(PublicKey key)
checkSecurityAccess("setIdentityPublicKey")
java.security.SecurityPermission "setIdentityPublicKey"
public String toString(...)
checkSecurityAccess("printIdentity")
java.security.SecurityPermission "printIdentity"
```

java.security.IdentityScope

```
protected static void setSystemScope()
checkSecurityAccess("setSystemScope")
java.security.SecurityPermission "setSystemScope"
```

java.security.Permission

```
public void checkGuard(Object object)
checkPermission(this)
```

This Permission object is the permission checked.

java.security.Policy

```
public static Policy getPolicy()
checkPermission
java.security.SecurityPermission "getPolicy"
public static void setPolicy(Policy policy);
checkPermission
java.security.SecurityPermission "setPolicy"
```

java.security.Provider

In the following methods, the parameter name represents the provider name.

```
public synchronized void clear()
checkSecurityAccess("clearProviderProperties."+{name})
```

```
java.security.SecurityPermission "clearProviderProperties.{name}"
public synchronized Object put(Object key, Object value)
checkSecurityAccess("putProviderProperty."+{name})
java.security.SecurityPermission "putProviderProperty.{name}"
public synchronized Object remove(Object key)
checkSecurityAccess("removeProviderProperty."+{name})
java.security.SecurityPermission "removeProviderProperty.{name}"
```

java.security.SecureClassLoader

```
SecureClassLoader(...)
checkCreateClassLoader
java.lang.RuntimePermission "createClassLoader"
```

java.security.Security

```
public static void getProperty(String key)
checkPermission
java.security.SecurityPermission "getProperty.{key}"
public static int addProvider(Provider provider)
public static int insertProviderAt(Provider provider, int position);
checkSecurityAccess("insertProvider." + provider.getName())
java.security.SecurityPermission "insertProvider.{name}"
public static void removeProvider(String name)
checkSecurityAccess("removeProvider."+name)
java.security.SecurityPermission "removeProvider.{name}"
public static void setProperty( String key, String datum)
checkSecurityAccess("setProperty."+key)
java.security.SecurityPermission "setProperty.{key}"
```

java.security.Signer

```
public PrivateKey getPrivateKey()
checkSecurityAccess("getSignerPrivateKey")
java.security.SecurityPermission "getSignerPrivateKey"
public final void setKeyPair(KeyPair pair)
checkSecurityAccess("setSignerKeypair")
java.security.SecurityPermission "setSignerKeypair"
```

java.util.Locale

```
public static synchronized void setDefault(Locale newLocale)
checkPermission
java.util.PropertyPermission "user.language","write"
```

java.util.zip.ZipFile

```
ZipFile(String name)
checkRead
java.io.FilePermission "{name}","read"
```

C

Security Manager Methods

This appendix lists the `java.lang.SecurityManager` methods and the permissions their default implementations check for. Each check<*type*> method calls the `SecurityManager.checkPermission` method with the indicated permission, except the checkConnect and checkRead methods, which take a context argument instead. The checkConnect and checkRead methods expect the context to be an `AccessControlContext` and call the context's checkPermission method with the specified permission.

```
public void checkAccept(String host, int port);
java.net.SocketPermission "{host}:{port}", "accept";
public void checkAccess(Thread g);
java.lang.RuntimePermission "modifyThread");
public void checkAccess(ThreadGroup g);
java.lang.RuntimePermission "modifyThreadGroup");
public void checkAwtEventQueueAccess();
java.awt.AWTPermission "accessEventQueue";
public void checkConnect(String host, int port);
  if(port == -1) {
    java.net.SocketPermission "{host}","resolve";
  } else
    java.net.SocketPermission "{host}:{port}","connect";
  }
public void checkConnect(String host, int port, Object context);
  if(port == -1){
    java.net.SocketPermission "{host}","resolve";
```

```
  } else {
    java.net.SocketPermission "{host}:{port}","connect";
  }
public void checkCreateClassLoader();
java.lang.RuntimePermission "createClassLoader";
public void checkDelete(String file);
java.io.FilePermission "{file}", "delete";
public void checkExec(String cmd);
  if(cmd is an absolute path) {
    java.io.FilePermission "{cmd}", "execute";
  } else {
    java.io.FilePermission "-", "execute";
  }
public void checkExit(int status);
java.lang.RuntimePermission "exitVM");
public void checkLink(String lib);
java.lang.RuntimePermission "loadLibrary.{lib}";
public void checkListen(int port);
  if(port == 0) {
    java.net.SocketPermission "localhost:1024-","listen";
  } else {
    java.net.SocketPermission "localhost:{port}","listen";
  }
public void checkMemberAccess(Class clazz, int which);
  if(which != Member.PUBLIC) {
    if(currentClassLoader() != clazz.getClassLoader()) {
     checkPermission(
     new java.lang.RuntimePermission("accessDeclaredMembers"));
    }
  }
public void checkMulticast(InetAddress maddr);
java.net.SocketPermission(maddr.getHostAddress(),"accept,connect");
public void checkMulticast(InetAddress maddr, byte ttl);
java.net.SocketPermission(maddr.getHostAddress(),"accept,connect");
public void checkPackageAccess(String pkg);
java.lang.RuntimePermission "accessClassInPackage.{pkg}";
public void checkPackageDefinition(String pkg);
java.lang.RuntimePermission "defineClassInPackage.{pkg}";
public void checkPrintJobAccess();
java.lang.RuntimePermission "queuePrintJob";
public void checkPropertiesAccess();
java.util.PropertyPermission "*", "read,write";
public void checkPropertyAccess(String key);
java.util.PropertyPermission "{key}", "read,write";
public void checkRead(FileDescriptor fd);
java.lang.RuntimePermission "readFileDescriptor";
public void checkRead(String file);
java.io.FilePermission "{file}", "read";
public void checkRead(String file, Object context);
java.io.FilePermission "{file}", "read";
public void checkSecurityAccess(String action);
```

```
java.security.SecurityPermission "{action}";
public void checkSetFactory();
java.lang.RuntimePermission "setFactory";
public void checkSystemClipboardAccess();
java.awt.AWTPermission "accessClipboard";
public boolean checkTopLevelWindow(Object window);
java.awt.AWTPermission "showWindowWithoutWarningBanner";
public void checkWrite(FileDescriptor fd);
java.lang.RuntimePermission "writeFileDescriptor";
public void checkWrite(String file);
java.io.FilePermission "{file}", "write";
public SecurityManager();
java.lang.RuntimePermission "createSecurityManager";
```

D
API Reference

This appendix lists Java class and interface methods used in the examples for this book. The methods are grouped by the class or interface to which they belong. Each method listing provides a page number where the method is used. You can find information on the method in the surrounding text or earlier in the chapter. You can also use the Index to locate these same methods using the method names or the fully qualified class or interface names to which the methods belong.

ActionListener Interface

```
Interface java.awt.event.ActionListener

void actionPerformed(ActionEvent e) (page 175)
```

WindowListener Interface

```
Interface java.awt.event.WindowListener

void windowClosing(WindowEvent e) (page 176)
```

Graphics Class

Class java.awt.Graphics

void drawRect(int x, int y, int width, int height) (page 183)

FontMetrics getFontMetrics() (page 207)

void setClip(int x, int y, int width, int height) (page 181)

Graphics2D Class

Class java.awt.Graphics2D

void translate(double x, double y) (page 189)

void scale(double sx, double sy) (page 189)

Book Class

Class java.awt.print.Book

void append(Printable painter, PageFormat page) (page 187)

void append(Printable painter, PageFormat page, int numPages) (page 187)

PageFormat Class

Class java.awt.print.PageFormat

double getImageableX() (page 183)

double getImageableY() (page 183)

double getImageableWidth() (page 188)

double getImageableHeight() (page 188)

void setOrientation(int orientation) (page 187)

Printable Interface

Interface java.awt.print.Printable

int print(Graphics graphics, PageFormat pageFormat, int pageIndex) (page 183)

PrinterJob Class

Class java.awt.print.PrinterJob

PageFormat defaultPage() (page 186)

static PrinterJob getPrinterJob() (page 186)

PageFormat pageDialog(PageFormat page) (page 186)

void print() (page 186)

boolean printDialog() (page 186)

void setPageable(Pageable document) (page 187)

void setPrintable(Printable painter) (page 186)

Toolkit Class

Class java.awt.Toolkit

void addAWTEventListener(AWTEventListener l, long eventmask) (page 230)

DataOutputStream Class

Class java.io.DataOutputStream

byte[] toByteArray() (page 285)

Double Class

Class java.lang.Double

static Double valueOf(double doublevalue) (page 100)

SecurityManager Class

Class java.lang.SecurityManager

void checkRead(String filename) (page 315)

void checkWrite(String filename) (page 316)

void checkPermission(Permission perm) (page 316)

System Class

Class java.lang.System

static SecurityManager getSecurityManager() (page 79)

static SecurityManager setSecurityManager(SecurityManager s) (page 79)

static void loadLibrary(String libraryname) (pages 137, 145, 146, 149, 151)

Naming Class

Class java.rmi.Naming

static void rebind(String rminame, Remote obj) (pages 62, 79)

static Remote lookup(String rminame) (pages 64, 66)

RMISocketFactory Class

Class java.rmi.server.RMISocketFactory

static void setFailureHandler(RMIFailureHandler fh) (page 79)

CallableStatement Interface

Class java.sql.CallableStatement

void setString(int index, String s) (page 106)

void registerOutParameter(int index, int sqltype) (page 106)

Date getDate(int index) (page 106)

Connection Interface

Class java.sql.Connection

CallableStatement prepareCall(String sql) (page 106)

Statement createStatement() (pages 106, 115)

DatabaseMetaData getMetaData() (pages 109, 117)

PrepareStatement prepareStatement(String sql) (pages 39, 40, 52, 97, 101, 107, 109) void rollback() (page 116)

void setAutoCommit(boolean autoCommit) (page 115)

DatabaseMetaData Interface

Class java.sql.DatabaseMetaData

boolean supportsResultSetConcurrency(int type, int concurrency) (page 109)

DriverManager Class

Class java.sql.DriverManager

static Connection getConnection(String url) (page 105)

static Connection getConnection(String url, String user, String password) (page 105)

static void setLogStream(PrintStream out) (page 105)

PreparedStatement Interface

Class java.sql.PreparedStatement

ResultSet executeQuery() (pages 97, 102, 108)

int executeUpdate() (pages 41, 111)

void setDate(int index, Date datavalue) (page 115)

void setDouble(int index, double doublevalue) (pages 41, 97, 102, 115)

void setInt(int index, int intvalue) (page 111)

void setString(int index, String s) (pages 41, 106)

void setBinaryStream(int index, InputStream stream, int length) (page 111)

ResultSet Interface

Interface java.sql.ResultSet

void close() (page 111)

```
boolean first() (page 110)

byte[] getBytes(String ColumnName) (page 111)

double getDouble(String columnName) (pages 97, 110)

int getInt(String ColumnName) (page 102)

boolean next() (pages 108, 127)

String getString(String columnName) (pages 40, 97, 108)

double updateDouble(String columnName) (page 110)
```

Statement Interface

```
Class java.sql.Statement

void close() (page 111)

int executeQuery(String sql) (page 106)

int executeBatch() (page 110)

int executeUpdate(String sql) (pages 106, 116)

ResultSet getResultSet() (pages 40, 115, 116)
```

ArrayList Class

```
Class java.util.ArrayList

boolean add(Object object) (page 97)

Object[] toArray(Object[] objarray) (page 98)
```

Calendar Class

```
Class java.util.Calendar

void add(int partofdate, int dateamount) (page 115)

boolean before(Object when) (page 179)

static Calendar getInstance() (page 115)

void roll(int datefield, boolean up) (page 179)

void setTime(Date date) (page 179)
```

Date Class

Class java.util.Date

long getTime() (page 115)

Enumeration Interface

Interface java.util.Enumeration

boolean hasMoreElements() (page 255)

Object nextElement() (page 255)

HashMap Class

Class java.util.HashMap

boolean containsKey(Object key (page 281)

Object get(Object key) (page 282)

Object put(Object key, Object value) (page 281)

Object remove(Object key) (page 281)

Iterator Interface

Class java.util.Iterator

boolean hasNext() (page 96)

LinkedList Class

Class java.util.LinkedList

void addFirst(Object value) (page 281)

Object get(Object key) (page 282)

remove(Object value) (page 281)

Object removeLast() (page 281)

List Class

Class java.util.List

Interator iterator() (page 96)

EntityBean Interface

Interface javax.ejb.EntityBean

void ejbRemove() (page 33)

void ejbActivate() (page 33)

void ejbPassivate() (page 33)

void ejbLoad() (page 26)

void ejbStore() (page 26)

void setEntityContext(EntityContext ectx) (page 25)

void unsetEntityContext(EntityContext ectx) (page 25)

UserTransaction Interface

Interface javax.jts.UserTransaction

void begin() (page 49)

void commit() (page 49)

void rollback() (page 49)

PortableRemoteObject Class

Class javax.rmi.PortableRemoteObject

static object narrow(Object narrowFrom, Class narrowTo (page 66)

Cookie Class

Class javax.servlet.http.Cookie

void setPath(String path) (page 123)

void setMaxAge(int expire) (page 123)

void setDomain(String domainstring) (page 123)

Cookie(String name, String value) (page 123)

HttpServlet Class

Class javax.servlet.http.HttpServlet

void service(HttpServletRequest request, HttpServletResponse response) (page 121)

HttpServletRequest Interface

Class javax.servlet.http.HttpServletRequest

Cookie[] getCookies() (page 124)

HttpServletResponse Interface

Class javax.servlet.http.HttpServletResponse

void addCookie(Cookie cookie) (page 123)

void sendRedirect(String urlstring) (page 126)

void setDateHeader(String name, long datevalue) (page 125)

void setHeader(String name, String value) (page 125)

ServletConfig Interface

Interface javax.servlet.ServletConfig

String getInitParameter(String parametername) (page 126)

ServletContext getServletContext() (page 126)

ServletRequest Interface

Interface javax.servlet.ServletRequest

String getProtocol() (page 125)

ServletResponse Interface

Interface javax.servlet.ServletResponse

PrintWriter getWriter() (page 128)

void setContentType(String type) (page 128)

Box Class

Class javax.swing.Box

Component createRigidArea(Dimension d) (page 169)

DefaultCellEditor Class

Class javax.swing.DefaultCellEditor

void fireEditingStopped() (page 179)

```
Object getCellEditorValue() (page 179)

Component getTableCellEditorComponent(JTable table, Object
value, boolean isSelected, int row, int column) (page 180)
```

JButton Class

```
Class javax.swing.JButton

void addActionListener(ActionListener l) (page 175)
```

JComponent Class

```
Class javax.swing.JComponent

void setAlignmentY() (page 197)
```

JFrame Class

```
Class javax.swing.JFrame

void addWindowListener(WindowListener l) (page 176)
```

JLabel Class

```
Class javax.swing.JLabel

void setIcon(Icon icon) (page 177)
```

JScrollPane Class

```
Class javax.swing.JScrollPane

JScrollBar getHorizontalScrollBar() (page 169)

void setColumnHeaderView(Component view) (page 170)

void setViewport(JViewport viewport) (page 170)
```

JTable Class

```
Class javax.swing.JTable

int getRowHeight() (page 207)

int getRowMargin() (page 207)

ListSelectionMode getSelectionModel() (page 169)

JTableHeader getTableHeader() (page 169)
```

boolean isCellEditable(int row, int column) (page 166)

void setAutoResizeMode(int mode) (page 165)

void setDefaultRenderer(Class columnClass, TableCellRenderer renderer) (page 178)

JTree Class

Class javax.swing.JTree

void makeVisible(TreePath path) (page 176)

void setSelectionRow(int row) (page 176)

JViewPort Class

Class javax.swing.JViewport

Point getViewPosition() (page 170)

void setView(Component view) (page 170)

ListSelectionModel Interface

Interface javax.swing.ListSelectionModel

void addListSelectionListener(ListSelectionListener l) (page 196)

SwingUtilities Class

Class javax.swing.SwingUtilities

static void invokeLater(Runnable run) (page 180)

DefaultTableCellRenderer Class

Class javax.swing.table.DefaultTableCellRenderer

Component getTableCellRendererComponent(JTable table, Object value, boolean isSelected, boolean hasFocus, int row, int column) (pages 177, 178)

DefaultTableModel Class

Class javax.swing.table.DefaultTableModel

void fireTableStructureChanged() (page 167)

TableColumn Class

Class javax.swing.table.TableColumn

void setCellRenderer(TableCellRenderer renderer) (pages 169, 178)

TableColumnModel Interface

Interface javax.swing.table.TableColumnModel

TableColumn getColumn(int index) (page 161)

int getColumnCount() (page 207)

int getColumnMargin() (page 207)

DefaultMutableTreeNode Class

Class javax.swing.tree.DefaultMutableTreeNode

DefaultMutableTreeNode(Object node) (page 175)

Enumeration depthFirstEnumeration() (page 176)

TreePath Class

Class javax.swing.tree.TreePath

TreePath(Object singlePath) (page 176)

Any Class

Class org.omg.CORBA.Any

void insert_double(double doublevalue) (page 100)

void insert_string(String stringvalue) (page 100)

IntHolder Class

Class org.omg.CORBA.IntHolder

IntHolder() (page 95)

ORB Class

Class org.omg.CORBA.ORB

status ORB init(String[] args, Properties props) (pages 61, 92)

Any create_any() (page 100)

void connect(Object object) (pages 61, 92)

void disconnect(Object object) (page 92)

String object_to_String(Object object) (page 64)

Object resolve_initial_references(String servicename) (page 62)

Object string_to_object(String stringvalue) (page 64)

NameComponent Class

Class org.omg.CosNaming.NameComponent

NameComponent(String nameid, String kind) (pages 61, 93, 94, 96, 100)

NamingContext Interface

Interface org.omg.CosNaming.NamingContext

NamingContext bind_new_context(NameComponent[] nc) (page 61)

Object resolve_initial_references(String servicename) (page 62)

JNI C Methods

CallVoidMethod(JNIEnv *env, jobject object, jmethodId methodid, object arg1) (page 147)

void DeleteLocalRef(JNIEnv *env, jobject localref) (page 155)

void ExceptionClear(JNIEnv *env) (page 147)

void ExceptionDescribe(JNIEnv *env) (page 148)

jthrowable ExceptionOccurred(JNIEnv *env) (page 148)

jclass FindClass(JNIenv *env, const char *name) (page 144)

jfieldID GetFieldID(JNIEnv *env, jclass class, const char *fieldname, const char *fieldsig) (page 148)

jint* GetIntArrayElements(JNIEnv *env, jintArray array, jboolean *iscopy) (page 147)

jobject GetObjectArrayElement(JNIEnv *env, jobjectArray array, jsize index) (page 147)

jclass GetObjectClass(JNIEnv *env, jobject obj) (page 147)

jmethodID GetMethodId(JNIEnv *env, jclass class, const char *methodname, const char *methodsig) (page 147)

const char* GetStringUTFChars(JNIEnv *env, jstring string, jboolean *iscopy) (page 138)

const jchar *GetStringChars(JNIEnv *env, jstring string, jboolean *iscopy) (page 141)

jint JNI_CreateJavaVM(JavaVM **pvm, void **penv, void *args) (page 157)

jint MonitorEnter(JNIEnv *env, jobject object) (page 147)

jint MonitorExit(JNIEnv *env, jobject object) (page 147)

jbyteArray NewByteArray(JNIEnv *env, jsize length) (pages 139, 143)

jobject NewGlobalRef(JNIEnv *env, jobject object) (page 155)

jintArray NewIntArray(JNIEnv *env, jsize length) (page 147)

jarray NewObjectArray(JNIEnv *env, jsize length, jclass element-Class, jobject initialElement) (page 152)

jstring NewStringUTF(JNIEnv *env, const char *bytes) (pages 141, 144)

void ReleaseByteArrayElements(JNIEnv *env, jbyteArray array, jbyte *elems, jint mode) (page 143)

void ReleaseStringChars(JNIEnv *env, jstring string, const jchar *chars) (page 141)

SetByteArrayRegion(JNIEnv *env, jbyteArray array, jsize start-element, jsize length, jbyte *buffer) (pages 139, 143)

SetIntArrayRegion(JNIEnv *env, jintArray array, jsize startelement, jsize length, jint *buffer) (page 147)

void SetObjectArrayElement(JNIEnv *env, jobjectArray array, jsize index, jobject value) (page 144)

Index

Java™ Technology from Addison-Wesley

ISBN 0-201-37949-X

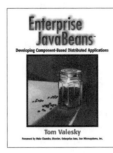

ISBN 0-201-37963-5

ISBN 0-201-60446-9

ISBN 0-201-43329-X

ISBN 0-201-48543-5

ISBN 0-201-61563-0

ISBN 0-201-30972-6

ISBN 0-201-59614-8

ISBN 0-201-18393-5

ISBN 0-201-32582-9

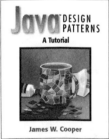

ISBN 0-201-48539-7

ISBN 0-201-65768-6

ISBN 0-201-70720-9

ISBN 0-201-70421-8

ISBN 0-201-67491-2

ISBN 0-201-61585-1

ISBN 0-201-36065-9

ISBN 0-201-65758-9

ISBN 0-201-70429-3

http://www.aw.com/cseng   **⋏⋎ Addison-Wesley**